SOVIET PLANNING IN PE.
1938-1945

SOVIET AND EAST EUROPEAN STUDIES

Editorial Board

JULIAN COOPER, RON HILL,
MICHAEL KASER, PAUL LEWIS, MARTIN McCAULEY,
FRED SINGLETON, STEPHEN WHITE

The National Association for Soviet and East European Studies exists for the purpose of promoting study and research on the social sciences as they relate to the Soviet Union and the countries of Eastern Europe. The Monograph Series is intended to promote the publication of works presenting substantial and original research in the economics, politics, sociology and modern history of the USSR and Eastern Europe.

SOVIET AND EAST EUROPEAN STUDIES

Rudolf Bićanić *Economic Policy in Socialist Yugoslavia*
Galia Golan *Yom Kippur and After: The Soviet Union and the Middle East Crisis*
Maureen Perrie *The Agrarian Policy of the Russian Socialist-Revolutionary Party from its Origins through the Revolution of 1905–1907*
Paul Vyšný *Neo-Slavism and the Czechs 1898–1914*
Gabriel Gorodetsky *The Precarious Truce: Anglo-Soviet Relations 1924–1927*
James Riordan *Sport in Soviet Society: Development of Sport and Physical Education in Russia and the USSR*
Gregory Walker *Soviet Book Publishing Policy*
Felicity Ann O'Dell *Socialisation through Children's Literature: The Soviet Example*
T. H. Rigby *Lenin's Government: Sovnarkom 1917–1922*
Stella Alexander *Church and State in Yugoslavia since 1945*
M. Cave *Computers and Economic Planning: The Soviet Experience*
Jozef M. Van Brabant *Socialist Economic Integration: Aspects of Contemporary Economic Problems in Eastern Europe*
R. F. Leslie ed. *The History of Poland since 1863*
M. R. Myant *Socialism and Democracy in Czechoslovakia 1945–1948*
Blair A. Ruble *Soviet Trade Unions: Their Development in the 1970s*
Angela Stent *From Embargo to Ostpolitik: The Political Economy of West German–Soviet Relations 1955–1980*
William J. Conyngham *The Modernisation of Soviet Industrial Management*
Jean Woodall *The Socialist Corporation and Technocratic Power*
Israel Getzler *Kronstadt 1917–1921: The Fate of a Soviet Democracy*
David A. Dyker *The Process of Investment in the Soviet Union*
S. A. Smith *Red Petrograd: Revolution in the Factories 1917–1918*
Saul Estrin *Self-Management: Economic Theories and Yugoslav Practice*
Ray Taras *Ideology in a Socialist State*
Silvana Malle *The Economic Organization of War Communism 1918–1921*
S. G. Wheatcroft and R. W. Davies *Materials for a Balance of the Soviet National Economy 1928–1930*
Mark Harrison *Soviet Planning in Peace and War 1938–1945*
James McAdams *East Germany and Detente: Building Authority after the Wall*
J. Arch Getty *Origins of the Great Purges: The Soviet Communist Party Reconsidered 1933–1938*
Tadeusz Swietochowski *Russian Azerbaijan 1905–1920: The Shaping of National Identity*
David S. Mason *Public Opinion and Political Change in Poland 1980–1982*
Nigel Swain *Collective Farms Which Work?*
Stephen White *The Origins of Detente: The Genoa Conference and Soviet–Western Relations 1921–1922*

SOVIET PLANNING IN PEACE AND WAR
1938–1945

MARK HARRISON
DEPARTMENT OF ECONOMICS
UNIVERSITY OF WARWICK

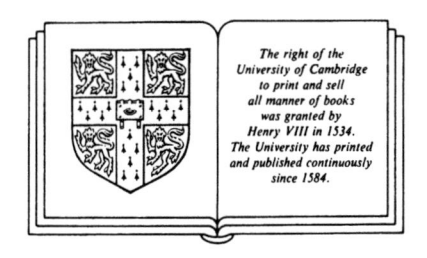

CAMBRIDGE UNIVERSITY PRESS

CAMBRIDGE

LONDON   NEW YORK   NEW ROCHELLE

MELBOURNE   SYDNEY

PUBLISHED BY THE PRESS SYNDICATE OF THE UNIVERSITY OF CAMBRIDGE
The Pitt Building, Trumpington Street, Cambridge, United Kingdom

CAMBRIDGE UNIVERSITY PRESS
The Edinburgh Building, Cambridge CB2 2RU, UK
40 West 20th Street, New York NY 10011–4211, USA
477 Williamstown Road, Port Melbourne, VIC 3207, Australia
Ruiz de Alarcón 13, 28014 Madrid, Spain
Dock House, The Waterfront, Cape Town 8001, South Africa

http://www.cambridge.org

© Cambridge University Press 1985

This book is in copyright. Subject to statutory exception
and to the provisions of relevant collective licensing agreements,
no reproduction of any part may take place without
the written permission of Cambridge University Press.

First published 1985
First paperback edition 2002

A catalogue record for this book is available from the British Library

Library of Congress catalogue card number: 84-23219

ISBN 0 521 30371 0 hardback
ISBN 0 521 52937 9 paperback

Contents

		page
Preface		ix
Acknowledgements		xiii

1 ECONOMIC PLANNING AND THE SEARCH FOR BALANCE
   Introduction 1

   Part One: A planned economy in crisis
   Economic imbalance in the prewar years 5
   The administrative context 11
   The rise of Voznesensky 13

   Part Two: Responses to crisis 1938–41
   Gosplan under the Voznesensky regime 19
   Plans and performance 1938–41 28
   Conclusions 34

2 THE COMING OF WAR: PLANS AND REALITIES IN 1941
   Introduction 42

   Part One: Preparing for war
   The Soviet military–economic potential 45
   Contingency planning for war 53

   Part Two: The German invasion
   The impact of war: the evacuation process 63
   A note on the evacuation of 1942 79

   Part Three: Plans and realities
   The impact of war: mobilisation and conversion 81
   Planning and the regime of emergency measures 93
   Conclusions 100

v

3 THE SOVIET PRODUCTIVE EFFORT
Introduction … 109

Part One: The tide of combat
Battle losses and arms balances … 110
The role of supply … 115

Part Two: Outputs and inputs
The structure of production … 121
Fixed capacity and new investment … 133
The workforce and labour inputs … 137

Part Three: Measures of mobilisation
Mobilisation of the working population … 142
Mobilisation of the national income … 148
Conclusion: phases of economic mobilisation … 154

4 THE SEARCH FOR ECONOMIC BALANCE IN WARTIME
Introduction … 165

Part One: The restoration of economic balance
Arms and the basic industries … 168
Planning and the regime of emergency measures … 175
The centralisation of manpower controls … 185

Part Two: Gosplan under Voznesensky again
Reconstruction and reconversion … 192
Further changes in plan methodology … 198

Part Three: Wartime planning and economic self-regulation
Planning and self-regulation of the enterprise … 204
Planning and the market economy … 209
Conclusions … 213

5 SOVIET LESSONS FROM WORLD WAR II
Introduction … 222

Part One: The political economy of socialism
The law of value 1941–7 … 224
Voznesensky, Stalin and afterwards … 230

Part Two: The lessons of war and the system of government
The reform of Stalinist institutions … 235
Permanent lessons from World War II … 242
Conclusions … 243

Contents vii

APPENDICES
1 Soviet arms production 1930–45   249
2 Soviet heavy industry output 1928–45   253
3 Soviet arms balances 1941–5   256
4 Composition of the USSR Sovnarkom 1938–45   267
5 Abbreviations and technical terms   287

Bibliography   294
Index   305

TO CHRISTINE AND SAMUEL
WITH MY LOVE

Preface

This book is an attempt at a history of the Soviet economic system and planned economy between 1938 and 1945. For the Soviet Union these were the last years of war preparations, followed by the years of 'patriotic war' against the German invader. Disaster was followed by recovery and ultimate victory. In this drama the economic factor was never far from the centre of the stage. Soviet wartime economic experience was so strikingly different from that of the other major powers that the story could hardly fail to be of intrinsic interest in its own right.

It is all the more surprising, therefore, to find that no major study or book-length analysis of the Soviet wartime economy has been published in the West for over thirty years. The last was the official Soviet account by Voznesensky, the wartime planning chief, translated into English and published in London and Washington in 1948. Since then the Soviet wartime economy has featured only in a handful of journal articles, textbook chapters and incidental comments in studies of related topics (among these, easily the most important are the two chapters in Zaleski's monumental study of Soviet economic planning under Stalin). This neglect contrasts oddly with the large volume of materials available from Soviet sources – official histories, personal memoirs and scholarly accounts.

I set out to write this book, therefore, partly because I wanted to work on an inherently interesting subject and at the same time help to remedy what I saw as unjustified neglect. I also had other reasons, which may help the reader to understand the nature of the result.

One ulterior motive was my interest in alternatives to Stalinism within the communist tradition, and in the postwar reform of Stalinist institutions in the Soviet Union. I already knew a little of such prewar opponents of Stalin as Trotsky and Bukharin. I was sympathetic to Stephen Cohen's view that, whatever critics of Stalin might learn from Trotsky, the real pioneer of 'reformed' Bolshevism and of 'socialism with a human face' was Bukharin. But by the Second World War Bukharin and his associates had been exterminated and his tradition had been ruthlessly stamped out. If it had been revived (and, I thought, radically altered) by 1956, then something of great importance had happened within Soviet society in between.

Political historians had already convincingly demonstrated the importance of the Second World War in throwing up a new political generation in Soviet life, new sources of authority and new values within the Soviet regime. One had only to read Khrushchev's speech to the closed session of the Twentieth CPSU Congress in 1956 to see how the experience of Stalinism at war had scarred the feelings towards Stalin of those for whom Khrushchev spoke. But I thought that the economic side of this – the changes in economic institutions arising from the war, the alterations in official models of the socialist economic system and the resulting lessons for postwar economic organisation – had not been sufficiently studied.

The few Western accounts of the Soviet wartime economy seemed to beg more questions than they answered. One received the impression that the Soviet economy at war was little different from the economy in peacetime, only that its harsher organisational features were somewhat accentuated. In this view the Stalinist economic system was already organised, even in peacetime, as a virtual 'war economy', so that the transition to war itself implied no fundamental change. As for the postwar process of economic reform initiated by Khrushchev, its origins were portrayed either as lying exclusively in postwar economic retardation or as stretching back in unbroken continuity to the political struggles of the 1920s. There seemed to be a gap in this picture which could only be filled by a political economy of the Soviet Union at war; the latter would allow us to grasp the links between prewar and postwar pressures for change within Stalinism.

These considerations pointed to research on the Soviet wartime economy as important for understanding the forces shaping the Soviet economic system today. But there was also another reason for my wish to understand more about the Soviet experience of the Second World War. I was becoming increasingly interested in the problem of the East–West arms race and how to put it into reverse through unilateral disarmament initiatives. I wanted to understand more about the Soviet outlook on war and its roots in historical experience. Work on the wartime economy represented a chance to study the real outlines of a past phase of militarisation and demilitarisation of the Soviet economic system. In turn this might throw light on the degree of entrenchment of defence priorities in the economy, and on conflicts between resource mobilisation for economic development and for rearmament.

Soviet wartime economic experience thus seemed to raise a multiplicity of issues. What was the dynamic of change in the prewar economic system? How, and how well, was the economy prepared for war? What was the character of the war which followed, and what costs did it inflict? How did the economy measure up to its requirements, and what changes in economic organisation resulted? What lessons were laid down for future Soviet approaches to both peaceful and warlike tasks?

The book itself is divided into five chapters. Chapter 1 finds that the Soviet system of economic planning before the war was being continually reorganised. Behind revisions in plan methodology, in the degree of centralisation and in the nature of central authority lay the conflicting needs of rapid economic mobilisation versus economic balance. Chapter 2 considers this economic system's capacity for war, its war preparations and war plans, and the impact upon it of surprise attack in 1941. The German invasion plunged the Soviet economy into a desperate crisis which was managed at first by means of emergency measures of harsh mobilisation; these measures bought survival in the short term, but in order to gear the economy as a whole up to the huge resource demands of a protracted war a new economic balance had first to be imposed. This turned out to be a slow process.

Chapter 3 traces the outlines of overall economic mobilisation through the years of war from 1941 to 1945. This chapter may be of greatest interest to the quantitative economist, and the reader with primarily social and institutional interests may omit Parts One and Two. Part Three examines some measures of the extent of Soviet economic mobilisation and concludes that, by Second World War standards, by 1943 the Soviet economy had become mobilised to a high degree.

How was this high degree of economic mobilisation eventually secured? Chapter 4 returns to the development of the institutions of economic management, their changing tasks and consequent changes in the role of economic planning. Emergency mobilisations were still the main method of economic coordination in 1942, but as economic balance was gradually restored the administrative planning system recaptured its central authority. Associated with the restoration of economic balance and the resumption of postwar perspectives were further reorganisations of economic planning and its role in the economy. Chapter 5 summarises the lessons of wartime experience in terms of the political economy of socialism and the reform of the Stalinist government system. It concludes that, while some aspects of the war stimulated conservative and militaristic economic ideas, others served to show the limits of dictatorial rule and to renew the Soviet tradition of reform-mindedness in seeking solutions to immediate economic problems.

The book concludes with five appendices. The first four provide statistical and other source materials for the text. The fifth lists the relatively small number of Soviet acronyms and other technical terms employed in the text. The lay reader is encouraged to refer to this list for preliminary definitions.

Acknowledgements

I am grateful to many for helping me to write this book. My interest in the Soviet Union at war was first stimulated by my friend Jan Šling. Others also encouraged my work. From the start Professor Bob Davies of the Centre for Russian and East European Studies (CREES), University of Birmingham, and later Alastair McAuley of the Department of Economics, University of Essex, kept watch over my progress.

The University of Warwick provided me with generous study leave from my teaching duties – two terms in 1981 and another term in 1982. I used one term to take up a Senior Fellowship at the Russian Institute of Columbia University in New York in the spring of 1981. I should like to thank the Russian Institute for its financial help, and Jonathan Sanders and Johanna Gurland for their practical support. While at Columbia I benefited greatly from discussion of my work with Professors Alexander Erlich of the Russian Institute and John Hazard of the Law Faculty. Professors Stephen Cohen of the Department of Politics, Princeton University, and Lynn Turgeon of the Department of Economics, Hofstra University, also spent long hours with me, and I owe them special thanks for their encouragement and advice.

In 1982 the British Academy and USSR Academy of Sciences made it possible for me to spend a month at the Institute of USSR History in Moscow. My thanks are due to these bodies for an invaluable experience. My work was greatly helped by access to the experience and advice of Professors G. A. Kumanev and A. V. Mitrofanova. Other members of the Institute's sector for study of Soviet history of the period of the Great Patriotic War also gave freely of their precious time and unrivalled expertise. In particular I must thank

Yu. L. D'yakov and Yu. K. Strizhkov. Everywhere my path was smoothed by the Institute's administrative staff N. F. Bugai and E. B. Nichaeva.

The Public Record Office in London kindly provided me with access to Foreign Office files relating to the Soviet Union in the period of my research.

As my work progressed I received important help from a number of British colleagues. These included Dr Julian Cooper of CREES, University of Birmingham, Dr Peter Gatrell of the Department of History, University of Manchester, Dr David Holloway of the Department of Politics, University of Edinburgh, Professor Alan Milward of the Department of European Studies, University of Manchester Institute of Science and Technology, and Professor Alec Nove of the Department of International Economic Studies, University of Glasgow. Peter Law of my own Department and Dr Stephen Wheatcroft of CREES, University of Birmingham, made themselves freely available to discuss my problems and help me solve them as they arose. Also at CREES, Jennifer Brine of the Alexander Baykov Library was especially helpful.

I am grateful to many colleagues for discussion of materials contained in Chapter 1 at the Third Conference of the International Work Group on Soviet Interwar Economic History, sponsored by the SSRC (now ESRC), at Birmingham in 1982; of Chapter 2 at seminars at the Universities of Birmingham, Essex and Warwick at various times; and of some ideas which eventually formed part of Chapter 5 at a European Nuclear Disarmament conference on the Soviet Union and the arms race in Oxford in 1982.

I am also grateful to Margaret Osburn and Yvonne Slater, who between them typed the first two chapters, and to Teresa Forysiak, who typed the index.

At the final stage Julian Cooper and Bob Davies read the whole typescript and provided me with detailed comments. Peter Gatrell did the same for the first two chapters. I am immensely grateful to them for their painstaking trouble, which saved me from many obvious and less obvious mistakes.

However, neither they nor anyone other than myself is responsible for any errors of fact or opinion which this book may still contain.

Department of Economics M.H.
University of Warwick

I

Economic planning and the search for balance

> For us, for Bolsheviks, a Five Year plan is not something finalised and given once and for all. For us a Five Year Plan, like any plan, is only a plan adopted as a first approximation which we must refine, adapt and perfect in the light of local experience, in the light of experience of plan implementation ... Only bureaucrats can suppose that the work of planning *finishes* with compilation of the plan. Plan compilation is only the *beginning* of planning. Real leadership in planning is revealed only after compilation of the plan, after checking up on the ground in the course of plan fulfilment, correction and refinement.
>
> (General Secretary I. V. Stalin in a speech in June 1930)[1]

INTRODUCTION

To find out how Soviet economic planning was changed by the experience of the Second World War, we must first set out the system of economic planning which had been brought into being before the war broke out. But this is no easy matter. The most important difficulty is that Soviet planning before the war was not a fixed system, with unchanging rules and permanent institutions. Built into the system was the tendency of the system to change.

The prewar planning system did have certain permanent features – a basic structure of hierarchy, information and command – which had been laid down in the formative years of the first Five Year Plan (1928–32). However, this basic structure had not been created all at once according to a ready-made, fully formed model of a functioning socialist economy, although such system-building ideas played an indispensable part in the process. In fact the process of creating a planning system involved a period of bitter struggle between different schools of planning philosophy, and no less bitter clashes between the aspirations of economic policy and unpalatable economic realities. By the end of the formative period these clashes had been not so much

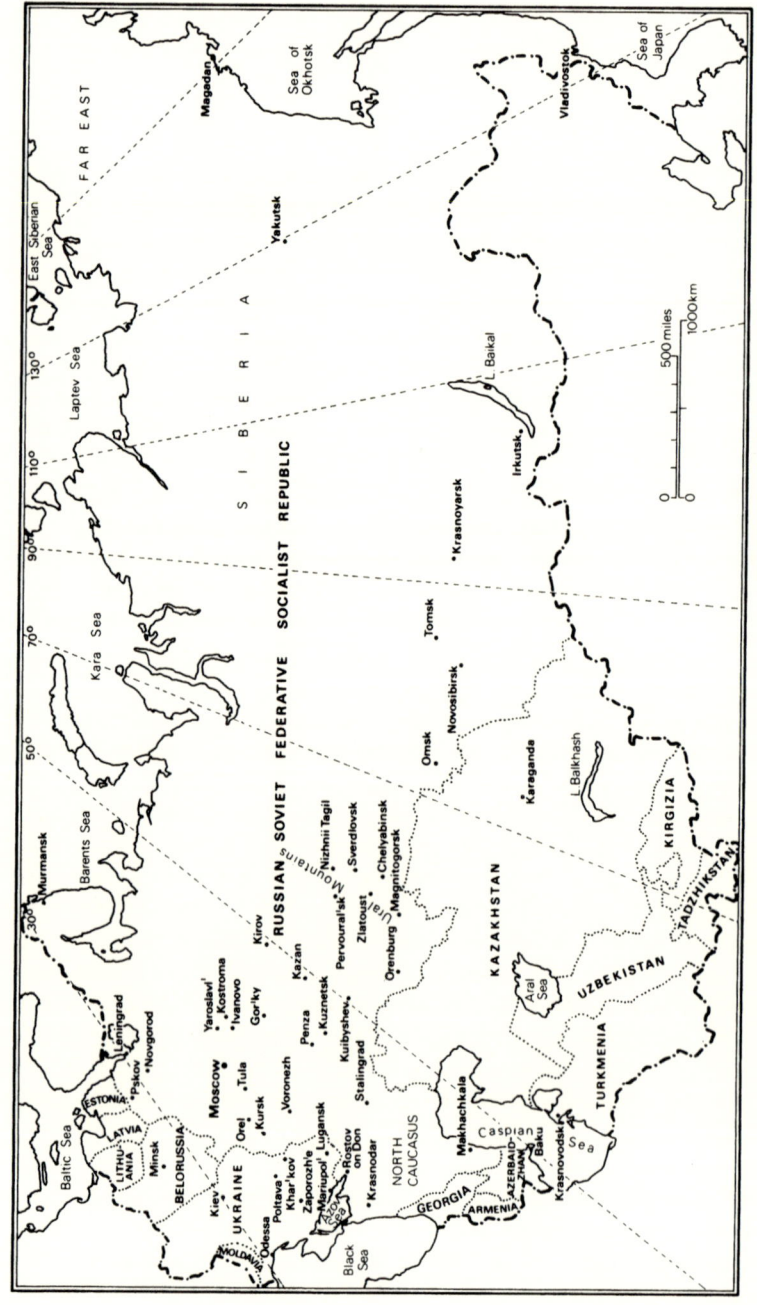

The Republics, major cities and other towns of the USSR 1938–45

finally resolved as suppressed or accommodated for the time being.[2] The planning system which resulted was not a logically coherent, smoothly functioning machine, but a working compromise.

At the heart of the compromise lay an unresolved conflict over the nature of economic planning. We can picture it as a conflict between two currents of planning philosophy and practice. One current saw economic planning as a law-governed process in which the authority of the plan, to be effective, must respect inherent limits. The other current rejected the idea of limits to the exercise of authority; it embraced a voluntaristic outlook and dictatorial methods of getting things done. The two currents also maintained quite opposed ideas about the purpose of planning. They agreed on the need for capital accumulation to bring about rapid economic development, but there the agreement stopped. The first current saw the plan as a means of guaranteeing in advance that the demands of accumulation would not disrupt social and economic equilibrium; capital construction would be limited to the real capacities of the economy, and would be adapted to the needs of household consumption and other determinants of social welfare. In direct conflict with this, the second current saw the plan not as a guarantee of economic and social equilibrium but as an instrument of mobilisation – of pouring resources into capital projects in order to get things done, regardless of the impact upon the economy's equilibrium or of the attendant sacrifices, exertions and wastes.[3]

Associated with the two currents were two alternative views of how the economic plan was related to political decisions. Within the framework of planning as a means of mobilisation, the primary role was to be played out by politicians and industrial bosses. It was their job to designate the key projects and priorities in the field of capital construction. The planners then faced the auxiliary task of working out the implications of these targets, handed down to them from above, for the industries supplying investment goods, for the workforce and for its consumer supplies and demands. Once the plan was under way, the planners' job was to follow its progress in order to safeguard the key sectors against shortfalls and bottlenecks arising elsewhere. But within the framework of planning as a means of securing social and economic equilibrium, the plan itself became the primary decision and the content of economic planning was enlarged. First the planners had to assess society's needs and resources and to establish which of the economy's possible expansion paths would be consistent with principles of balance. Decisions about sectoral priorities could only be taken within this analytical context. Thus economic analysis and political leadership would be to some extent fused into a single process.

The history of the Stalinist economic system suggests that these two different plan concepts tended to alternate in practical importance. They were first clearly worked out in the struggle between the 'genetic' (balance) and 'teleological' (mobilisation) schools of planning in the period from 1926 to 1929.[4] The immediate victor in this struggle was the teleological school, but the concepts developed by the genetic planners were repressed and modified rather than eliminated. The periodic supremacy of the mobilisation principles was facilitated by the Stalinist political system with its tendencies towards personal dictatorship and acts of political will. However, after each period of forced mobilisation we find a temporary adjustment phase, forced upon the political leaders by the need to repair damage caused by the shock waves of the investment mobilisation rippling through the economy. At such times the mobilisation simply exhausted itself and ground to a halt; then it became possible to voice the need for restored balance as a precondition of any further mobilisation.

It would be false to portray the two concepts of planning for balance and mobilisation as exclusively antagonistic. There was a sense in which they needed each other. They coexisted within the same economic system for good reason. Economic mobilisation, to be sustained over many years, had to respect certain rules, and these rules were to be found in the principles of balance. Securing economic balance could not be a completely pragmatic process, because the results of pragmatism and experiment had to be judged and acted on. 'Balance' principles were still being talked about and refined in the most violent years of Stalinist transformation. At the same time, in the context of the Stalinist political system, the 'balance' current was forced to share the same permanent objectives as the system as a whole. A state of harmony in the economy was never regarded as an end in itself, but only as a means towards some greater goal of socialisation or industrial growth. The attainment of harmony would be the signal for resumed mobilisation. Thus the compromise between balance and mobilisation was constantly under review. As a result it was not uncommon to find individual leaders at many levels of the apparatus visibly shifting from one current to another as the compromise altered and their perception of it changed. Of course there were probably just as many who stuck loyally to their principles, although the gap between principles and behaviour might be very great.

The search for economic balance was always associated with institutional change in the planning system. The tendency of the system to change was inbuilt, in the sense that the need for change resulted directly from the functioning of the system itself. Economic planners tried to resolve the problems thrown up by the mobilisation drive by enhancing the position of the planning system in the central process for making political decisions. At the same time they sought to endow the planning system with more effective mechanisms of communication and control. However, the results of change were not predetermined. Just as each phase of Stalinist mobilisation revealed its own specific features (conditions, objectives, methods, duration etc.), the following adjustment phase did not follow a single pattern. On the contrary, in each period the evolution of the crisis and the changes introduced in response to it showed rich variety, building new features into the Soviet economic system and laying down new precedents for the future. Important changes were maturing in Soviet planning in the last prewar phase of crisis and adjustment, which falls within the years 1938–41. They form essential background to study of the response to the much greater crisis caused by the German invasion.

This chapter is divided into two parts. In the first we examine the factors conditioning the economic difficulties of the late 1930s and the state of economic planning. In the second part we look at the measures adopted to rebalance the economy and resume economic mobilisation, and the directions of change in central coordination of the economy.

PART ONE: A PLANNED ECONOMY IN CRISIS

ECONOMIC IMBALANCE IN THE PREWAR YEARS

Soviet industrial growth in the 1930s was rapid and highly uneven. Under the first Five Year Plan, from 1928 to 1932, the national income measured in constant 1928 prices grew by over 60 per cent. Associated with rapid expansion was rapid structural change – nearly all the increased output was accounted for by industry, construction

Table 1. *Soviet heavy industrial production 1928–40*

	1928	1932	1937	1940
Crude steel, mn tons	4.3	5.9	17.7	18.3
Coal, mn tons	35.5	64.4	128.0	165.9
Electricity, bn kWh	5.0	13.5	36.2	48.3
Metal-cutting machine tools, thou.	2.0	19.7	48.5	58.4
Motor vehicles, thou.	0.8	23.9	199.9	145.4

Sources: See Appendix 2.

and transport while agriculture showed a tendency to stagnate or even decline. Moreover, almost all the increased output was reinvested, while consumption lagged far behind.[5] Meanwhile the most dramatic upsurge, illustrated in Table 1, was recorded by heavy industry. But the upsurge broke in 1931–2, the signs of deceleration first appearing in the iron and steel industry and spreading via the metal-using sectors. This was the first crisis of excessive accumulation under Stalinist planning.

The main feature of this crisis was that the demands upon the economy had grown more rapidly than the economy was able to create new capacity to meet them. The drive to create new capacity itself added to the strain. Disruption spread to the point where the economy could no longer protect the supply of producer goods for capital construction; investment projects already begun could not be completed, and industry itself was starved of inputs. The volume of unfinished investment rose sharply, the expansion of new capacity slowed down, and the utilisation of existing capacity fell.

The crisis was resolved in 1933 by means of a thorough rationalisation of the investment balance. Total investment was cut back and investible resources were concentrated on unfinished capacity. For most of the second Five Year Plan period (1933–7), rapid growth was resumed in all sectors of heavy industry. The years 1934–6 saw more huge investments and climbing output levels. The backlog of unfinished investments left over from the first Five Year Plan period was eliminated, yielding rapid returns. Uncompleted construction rose less rapidly than the capital stock as a whole, and investment costs remained stable or fell. In 1937, however, signs of trouble reappeared; there was a sharp increase in the volume of unfinished investment, at the same time as total investment began to fall.[6]

Nineteen thirty-seven saw the beginning of a new crisis of excessive accumulation. Symptoms of control loss began to multiply. Underfulfilment of 1937 construction plans in heavy industry was combined with rising building costs. The building workforce grew faster than planned limits, while most building workers were undershooting their labour norms.[7] In the economy as a whole plans for labour recruitment from the countryside to industry greatly exceeded forthcoming supplies.[8] Lags in project completion once more became a topic of anxious discussion.[9] Defects in investment management were the subject of a Sovnarkom resolution of 26 February 1938 which castigated the excessive ambitiousness of project evaluation staff and toleration of cost overruns by those in charge of subcontracting for construction work.[10]

Industrial stagnation had first emerged in iron and steelmaking in the course of 1936, and the effects had travelled through the economy via the engineering industry and other metal-using branches. Behind the slowdown in iron and steel lay failures both of capital construction and of capacity utilisation. In 1936 a sharp decline in realised investment in the industry set in.[11] By the period of the third Five Year Plan (1938 to the first half of 1941), the rate of completion of new iron and steel capacity was running at less than half the rate of the previous Five Year Plan period – by the standards of 1933–7 the completion of new rolling capacity was down by more than 70 per cent.[12] By May 1940, of 124 planned projects in the industry, work was proceeding only on 41, and only 22 were in operating condition.[13] The failure of construction was matched by failures of utilisation. Between 1938 and 1940 new capacity was added to the industry, but output stagnated while the average productivity of blast furnaces and open hearth smelting capacity declined.[14]

An independent factor in the economy's overcommitment at this time was rearmament. Table 2 shows that by the end of the first Five Year Plan period Soviet industry was producing all types of modern weapons on a large scale, as well as more traditional military goods such as artillery and infantry armament. During the thirties there were two phases of extremely rapid growth of weapons output, 1930–3 and 1936–40, with a plateau in between. In both phases rapid growth in the volume of output was combined with active transformation of the technology of production and of the weapons themselves, especially for aircraft and armoured vehicles (for example a sharp dip in tank production in 1937 compared with 1936 marked a

Table 2. *Soviet arms production 1930–40*

	1930	1933	1936	1940
Aircraft	899	2,952	3,770	10,565
Tanks	170	3,509	4,800	2,794[a]
Artillery pieces	952	4,368	4,324	15,300
Rifles and carbines, thou.	126	241	403	1,461

[a] In 1937 the Soviet tank industry went over from producing largely light tanks to medium and heavy tanks. The figure of 2,794 tanks produced in 1940 represented an 80 per cent increase over 1937.
Sources: See Appendix 1.

switch away from light tanks to much more heavily armed, armoured and powered models). However, the sheer volume of output was still impressive by itself. Just comparing 1937 and 1939, the rates of production of aircraft, tanks, artillery, infantry armament and ammunition all doubled or trebled.

Rapid rearmament in the late thirties is still more impressive when it is remembered that at the same time the supporting basic and heavy industries were stagnating. If one looks at the economy as a whole, by 1940 military equipment narrowly defined took up 7 per cent of national income, and military subsistence another 4 per cent.[15] Military needs more broadly defined increased the total drain on national income to 15 per cent. Military needs accounted for 26 per cent of industrial production, 16 per cent of transport services and 9 per cent of agriculture's produce in 1940.[16] By June 1941 the armed forces had more than 5 million able bodies,[17] while the manufacture of aircraft, armoured vehicles, armament, ammunition and naval construction employed an estimated 3 million workers,[18] compared to a 1940 workforce in manufacturing industry as a whole of 13 million.[19]

Rearmament had a substantial influence on the economy. Its impact on the pattern of industrial growth was primarily through preempting previously existing and newly created engineering capacity and supplies of metals and chemicals. As far as material supplies are concerned, in 1938 the arms industries were already being allocated a third of the available structural iron and steel, nearly a third of iron and steel for fabricating, and 42 per cent of high-grade rolled steel.[20] This allocation had been achieved by converting the steel industry to high-grade products for defence needs and starving civilian industry of ferrous metals.

Rearmament also depended upon the conversion of existing engineering capacity both to full-time arms manufacture and to occasional defence contracts. Conversion of civilian capacity was especially important in so far as the economy's ability to lay down and complete new industrial capacity had fallen below expectations, so that the fixed capacity required for rapid increases in arms production (also largely unanticipated) had to be diverted from other uses.[21] In the prewar years substantial resources were being invested in converting and newly creating arms capacity – the arms industries themselves took over a quarter of all industrial investment between 1938 and the outbreak of war.[22] If investment in heavy and light industry is reckoned at just over 35 per cent of total Soviet investment in the same period,[23] then the arms industries were accounting for about one-tenth of this total, and over 13 per cent in 1940 alone.[24] However, the real increase in fixed capacity available for meeting defence orders was greater than would be implied just by looking at new investment, since civilian industry was being widely involved in a system of subcontracting for components and parts by the big specialised defence producers.[25] The cost to civilian consumption as well as investment must have been considerable – Bergson reckons the decline in household consumption per head between 1937 and 1940 at between 4.4 and 8.2 per cent, depending on the price weights used.[26] However, the cost to both was probably less than would have resulted from a greater insistence on plant specialisation, new capacity and independence of civilian suppliers for the arms industries.[27]

Rearmament has been emphasised by Soviet historians as a decisive factor unbalancing the economy in the prewar years.[28] At the same time rearmament must be placed in context. It would be wrong to blame prewar economic imbalances on the breakdown of international relations while downplaying the independent role of the economic system's responses to new demands. The economic system, faced with a rapidly changing environment, failed to adapt its priorities smoothly in order to safeguard the permanent objectives of economic development. Consequently initial responses to new demands, such as the rearmament bill, were often inappropriate. The list of priorities was expanded indiscriminately so that the whole economy was placed under intolerable strain. As a result priorities were sacrificed inevitably under the pressure of events, by accident rather than by design. Thus investment goods for iron and steel were diverted to weapons production, but the result was to hamper the expansion of the whole complex of metal-producing and -using industries and to intensify the consumption sacrifices arising from rearmament.

The general effect of systemic responses to new demands was demoralising. For example a government commission, set up in the summer of 1939 to look into the causes of stagnation in the iron and steel industry,[29] reported a year later that the industry was pervaded by disorganisation. The latter affected fuel and ore supplies, labour discipline and morale, innovation and rationalisation, and supplying agencies.[30] We should hardly list these as direct costs of rearmament.

In this already complex situation a further independent factor was at work. Failures in investment coordination were condemned as the work of enemies and wreckers, unmasked by 'our famous Soviet intelligence service'.[31] Purges swept through the planning and management apparatus. The devotion of excessive resources to grandiose projects, wishful thinking about investment costs and completion forecasts, shortages of inputs necessary for project completion, the commitment of additional investment resources to increase capacity in sectors constraining the completion of capacity elsewhere, the multiplication of projects far beyond the economy's capacity to supply them and the resulting unstoppable decline in the efficiency of investment — all these formed the substance of 'sabotage' allegations against the planners.[32] The difficulties arising from overcommitment of the economy were thus used by the security organs to frame criminal charges against — and eventually eliminate — broad sections of industrial and economic officialdom. But in the process the difficulties themselves were compounded, and certainly did not disappear.

In summary, by 1937 the Soviet economy had entered a new overinvestment crisis. This crisis was the compound result of three independent processes. The first was the piling up of unfinished investment projects resulting from the investment mobilisation pursued since 1934. During 1936 the second process, rapid rearmament, was resumed. By now the economy was overcommitted and the efficiency of capacity construction and utilisation was falling. Initial responses to the unfolding economic crisis ranged from the uncontrolled multiplication of priorities, although the economy was unable to meet existing targets, to the repression of those held responsible for failure to meet targets which had either been infeasible in the first place or had been rendered infeasible by changing circumstances. Thus the purges and repressions of 1936–8 were the third process contributing to the economic crisis.

THE ADMINISTRATIVE CONTEXT

Connected with the process of purging the economic apparatus was its reorganisation. This proceeded along two main dimensions. One was the break-up of the administrative empires created by the first Stalinist generation of industrial leaders, especially G. K. Ordzhonikidze at the People's Commissariat for Heavy Industry. The other was the upward movement of the next generation into the positions vacated by their predecessors and into the new positions created by an extending apparatus composed of a growing number of little empires.

At the time the fragmentation of the economic apparatus was explained in terms of the growing scale and increased complexity of the economy, and the growing distance between the shop floor and the highest levels of such super-large bureaucracies as the heavy industry commissariat.[33] Undoubtedly these factors had played their part in the developing control loss of the late thirties. However, the subdivision of commissariats and turnover of leading personnel proceeded far more rapidly than an orderly process of bureaucratic response to economic change would suggest. Between December 1936 and June 1941 Ordzhonikidze's old empire was split into no fewer than seventeen separate industrial branches. The first moves in this direction, and the purging of his subordinates, contributed to Ordzhonikidze's suicide in February 1937.[34] The most rapid fragmentation, however, occurred in 1938 and 1939.[35] Other commissariats were also affected by subdivision, and one or two new commissariats were also set up. In January 1938 there had been twenty-one USSR People's Commissars; by the outbreak of the war there were as many as forty-three. At the same time all but three of the original twenty-one had lost their jobs (one of the three had merely been transferred), so virtually all of the full commissars of June 1941 were new to work at this level of the apparatus.[36] Such turnover, far in excess of that required by normal processes of career movement and recruitment to existing and new posts, characterised the apparatus at lower levels as well.

These reorganisations had substantial implications for the functioning of the economic system which will be considered at a later point. Here they are of interest as a symptom of the state of Soviet administration at the time. They suggest that in the late thirties the basic structures of the economic apparatus had been destabilised; formal chains of communication, authority and responsibility had lost what validity and clarity they had previously possessed, and instead showed a tendency to shift and overlap. Corresponding to the lack of authority of stable, bureaucratic relationships was the increased role of competition among personal administrative factions for priority in the allocation system, and the resort by higher-level leaders to informal and extra-legal methods of solving disputes and repressing problems at lower levels.

This style of administration has sometimes been called 'shapeless'.[37] I hesitate to apply it as a defining term to the whole period of Stalinist administration, but it undoubtedly describes a recurring aspect. Moreover it has been suggested that 'shapelessness' in administration often carries important penalties. These have been found to include difficulties in statistical data collection, information processing and decision making where these require inter-agency collaboration and the crossing of departmental boundaries. Those below the system's summit can rarely form a coherent picture of the context within which they must act; loss of morale and initiative are the characteristic effects. The quality of decision making at all levels depends to a high degree upon the qualities of leading individuals.[38]

Fragmentation of the industrial apparatus in the late thirties was recognised to have weakened central coordination of inter-industry supply and increased the range of problems which each commissariat would be unable to solve by itself.[39] Consequently greater importance than before would fall to those central party and government organs with direct responsibility for aggregating information, integrating conflicts of interest and ensuring the coherence of decision making at all levels from the point of view of the balance of the national economy. However, these central organs were subject to the same destabilising processes as the rest of the administrative apparatus and encountered the same penalties listed above. Their functioning too was dominated by the personal qualities of their leaders.

During the late thirties USSR Gosplan and its leadership were thoroughly 'turned over'. During the decade the central staff and lower planning organs had grown rapidly and recruited widely, but employment in planning offered poor conditions and low status, so that there was already a background of high turnover rates.[40] The turnover of staff was greatly accelerated between the spring of 1937 and the end of that year, when the central staff was 'completely renewed',[41] its experienced and technically qualified core being eliminated in the Great Terror.[42]

The need to restore the authority and effectiveness of the central economic organs was now expressed in two preliminary measures.[43] First was the creation on 23 November 1937 of a permanent Sovnarkom subcommittee, the Economic Council, composed of the Sovnarkom chairman and his deputies and the head of the Soviet trade unions. The Economic Council was to take governmental responsibility for inspection and confirmation of the central planning and management process and for supervision of economic performance, and was endowed with a number of delegated powers.[44] Its effectiveness would clearly depend above all upon the proper functioning of the planning organs. The second measure, therefore, was to be the renewal of the Gosplan leadership, staff and charter.

THE RISE OF VOZNESENSKY

It was against this unhappy background that N. A. Voznesensky took over as chief of USSR Gosplan on 19 January 1938. He was only thirty-four years old. His team, like him, was also young and mainly of recent appointment – highly qualified in political and educational terms, but lacking practical experience of the planning and management routine.[45]

Voznesensky was already an outstanding representative of the younger generation of Stalinist cadres. Of provincial Russian origin, he had joined the Bolshevik party as a young manual worker and political activist in 1919. Study of political economy and philosophy at party school in Moscow had been followed by an apprenticeship in local and industrial party work in the coal and steel towns of the Donbass. During the 1920s Voznesensky proved a reliable supporter of the Stalinist general line. But this was not his only asset. He also displayed original intellectual and leadership qualities. His reward was admission to the economics section of the Institute of Red Professors in Moscow in 1928. There he studied and subsequently taught political economy.[46]

In the early and middle thirties Voznesensky made an important contribution to analysis of the results of Stalinist economic policy.

How was the turmoil resulting from the first great investment mobilisation of 1928–32 to be understood and resolved? How could the newly centralised system of authoritarian economic planning be made more effective, more adaptable to reality and more sensitive to its own results? Voznesensky's early writings, published between 1931 and 1936, may give us some insight into his perception of the problems of 1938.

In 1931–2 Voznesensky wavered between the imperatives of mobilisation and adjustment. For example during 1931 he argued for sticking to and attaining inflated plan targets for expansion of the basic industries, when others were already advocating their downward revision. He described the plan as 'an economic law of the Soviet economy, formulated by the proletarian state' and the task of planning as one of struggling to enforce target fulfilment against the disruptive influence of market shortfalls.[47] At the same time Voznesensky distanced himself from those who were seeking to resolve the economic difficulties resulting from investment mobilisation by means of immediate transition to a moneyless economic system ruled exclusively by decrees handed down from above. Thus he identified himself with the spring 1931 return to profit and cost accounting in state enterprises and material incentives for producers based on reductions in production costs. He argued that, while higher-level output targets should be the prime determinant of management objectives, a subordinate but still essential discipline should be the monitoring of production costs and their minimisation, stimulated from below. This would enhance central authority, because it would break the association between ambitious higher-level output targets and lower-level cost inflation. He affirmed this as marking a transition from the initial act of 'nationalisation' of capital to its 'socialisation', i.e. bringing it under true social control.[48]

Voznesensky saw these issues as connected with the role of money and the market in a socialist economy. He was against the immediate abolition of money, but in favour of its gradual elimination as a fully socialist economy was achieved. He thought that in a fully socialist economy there would still be accounting of costs and surpluses, but in non-monetary terms. In this field he thought that the way forward would be found among the various radical experiments of the time in non-monetary cost accounting. For the time being, however, money and trade were necessary evils inherited from the capitalist economic system, to be tolerated and even used as temporary expedients.[49]

At this time, therefore, Voznesensky was among those who saw the Soviet economic system as law-governed. This meant that objective economic laws necessarily constrained the acts of powerful agencies and individuals. At the same time he saw the constraints as loose, since the most important law was the economic plan itself, with its politically determined goals of electrification, industrialisation and agricultural socialisation. Principles of economic balance were recognised rather than discarded, but were to be seen as auxiliary to the plan's targets for key sectors. He described the plan target, not the underlying supply balance, as the 'leading principle'; the balance was 'only a lever of struggle for the plan'.[50]

Thus if the economic system was law-governed, Voznesensky regarded the laws as already known, and to be realised through administrative processes – through economic plans and other deliberate acts of state policy. As a result any objective tendency to economic imbalance was being swiftly eliminated. If imbalances or crises tended to recur, their roots would be found in poor implementation of policy, not in policy's design. Maladministration itself could be analysed as a product of capitalist mentality and practice.[51] The implication was to free Stalin and the political leadership from any responsibility for disruption of the economy by setting excessive expansion targets; the fault lay with the planners and other officials whose job it was to work out the consequences of policy priorities for the rest of the economy, and safeguard the former against the demands of the latter.

In the mid-1930s Voznesensky's views moderated. This was under the impact of several influences. His own practical experience broadened. In 1932 he joined the economic planning and statistics group of the party–state Central Control Commission and Workers' and Peasants' Inspectorate, while continuing to teach and research at the Economics Institute of Red Professors. Distinguishing himself in his new work, he survived the reorganisation of the control apparatus, being elected from the Seventeenth Party Congress in early 1934 to serve on the newly constituted Commission for Soviet Control. At some point he also came to the notice of A. A. Zhdanov, appointed to head the Leningrad party organisation after S. M. Kirov's assassination in December 1934. This led to Voznesensky's posting to Leningrad in early 1935 to take charge of the city's economic planning commission.

Another influence on Voznesensky, no less important, was the changing assessment of the experience of the first – and goals of the second – Five Year Plan among political leaders and economic officials. One aspect was the growing realisation that money and trade, far from being temporary expedients, had remained an integral part of the Soviet economy. The reassessment culminated at the Seventeenth Party Congress in January 1934 when Stalin reinstated money and trade at regulated prices as elements of a fully socialist economy.[52] This had substantial implications for the law-governed character of the economic system and the results of rule by decree.

Voznesensky's last major theoretical article on political economy appeared in early 1935, about the time of his posting to Leningrad. It fully reflected the changing climate. Voznesensky now argued that money, although formerly an instrument of bourgeois economics, had been converted into a tool of socialist accounting and distribution. Part of the need for money arose from monetary exchange between socialist and non-socialist producers (i.e. collective farmers) through a market. But even in a fully socialised economy, money and prices would still play a role because they represented the only means of organising distribution among socialist producers, differentiated by accumulated skills and mechanical power as well as by natural advantages, according to labour contributed to society. The experiments in non-monetary cost accounting which Voznesensky had endorsed in 1931 were now a closed chapter.[53]

Thus money would retain its role until the transition to communism had unravelled all economic contradictions. Meanwhile, Voznesensky recognised, the premature elimination of money would only drive commodity exchange underground, or result in administrative rationing of consumer goods with the attendant abuses seen in the years of the first Five Year Plan. Instead, monetary levers had all kinds of positive roles to play – encouraging the minimisation of enterprise costs, producers' responsiveness to consumers and workers' willingness to work.[54]

The break with Voznesensky's views of 1931–2 need not be exaggerated. His new views did not make him a market socialist. He stood for effective central authority, not for administrative devolution or wholesale replacement of administrative controls by economic ones. The plan remained the 'economic law',[55] and the money economy was defined as an instrument for stimulating fulfilment of higher-level plan targets. But the limits on effective central authority were

Economic planning and the search for balance 17

more clearly stated than before, and for the first time these limits were seen to be permanent features of a socialist economy.

Voznesensky's understanding of the problem of securing effective central authority has meanwhile acquired a practical side. This is best illustrated by his biographer's account of his work in Leningrad, which may be introduced with the following anecdote. At the first meeting with his new team, Voznesensky asked how they saw their job. Having heard their answers, he replied:

> '... plan compilation is only the beginning of our work. Practice has shown that life itself will compel correction of any, even the most complete plan ... And correcting the plan by means of studying the real conditions for its fulfilment on the ground is our job, and no one else's...'
> He paused.
> 'We weren't involved in that before,' someone said.
> 'Let's make a deal,' Voznesensky replied. 'We won't go back over what you haven't done. We'll think about what we must do.'[56]

In these phrases Voznesensky repeated, almost word for word, a famous speech by Stalin which is cited at the head of this chapter. But Stalin had uttered these words in June 1930, to defend his upward 'correction' of the already inflated targets of the first Five Year Plan. From 1930 to 1935 the formula lived on, but its meaning was changing with the economic context. In 1930 'studying the real conditions for plan fulfilment' had meant persuading everyone below the top to participate in the process of output target inflation. But in the next months and years the same phrase acquired another, unwanted significance – the accumulation of evidence of plan failure and the investigation of reasons contributing to it. During Voznesensky's tenure at Leningrad 'correcting the plan' was far more likely to mean a scaling down of excessive demands than upward revision, taking into account the clash between ambitious targets and restricted possibilities revealed in the course of plan implementation and fulfilment checks.

At Leningrad Voznesensky is said to have forced the planning office into a more intimate relationship with reality. He himself was rarely at his desk – more usually he was to be found touring factories, inspecting building sites or checking whether the trams were running on time. He expected his staff likewise to interest themselves in the real conditions pertaining to their spheres of responsibility. A centralised apparatus must take into account not only the opportunities but also the difficulties encountered down below; for this it must possess both good intelligence and a methodology for analysing it. Because Voznesensky knew this, and knew how to put it into practice, he made his agency the central repository of information, expertise and authority on the city's economic life. This not only expanded the role of the planning organs in political decisions, but secured the basis for his own advancement.[57]

At the end of 1937 Voznesensky was called to Moscow. He was made a deputy chairman of USSR Gosplan and in January 1938 himself became Gosplan chief. He was the third person to hold this office in less than a year, and both his predecessors (V. I. Mezhlauk and G. I. Smirnov) had been arrested. The context of mass repressions, administrative instability and economic crisis could hardly have seemed less auspicious.

Yet the results of Voznesensky's promotion were surprisingly fruitful. He was fortunate to belong to the new generation of Soviet leaders which, rising with dizzying rapidity into the posts vacated by the leading victims of the purges, had reached the top just as the wave of terror subsided. The members of this generation would have a unique opportunity to take hold of the means of power, restore their stability and effectiveness, and consolidate their personal regimes. Many of them did this with such success (this was the 'Brezhnev' generation of A. N. Kosygin, M. A. Suslov, D. F. Ustinov and others) that they would dominate Soviet politics for the next forty years and more.

As a young official Voznesensky was committed to the centralised system of authority, the goals of which he shared. He owed allegiance to Stalinism, through which he had been educated and promoted. He had acquiesced in its most violent excesses, and benefited from the destruction of his superiors by stepping into their shoes. But the ways in which he would use his authority could not be predicted from these circumstances alone. Voznesensky did not set out to dismantle the centralised system of authoritarian planning, but neither did he lay stress upon its dictatorial and violent tendencies. The measures which he sponsored in the years from 1938 to 1940 were designed to make central authority more effective and more law-governed, more responsive to reality, less liable to individual voluntarism and arbitrary rule by decree. All the same, this did not become clear straight away.

PART TWO: RESPONSES TO CRISIS 1938-41

GOSPLAN UNDER THE VOZNESENSKY REGIME

What changes did Voznesensky introduce at Gosplan? It is easy to imagine a new broom sweeping the offices clean of obsolete rubbish, vigorously rationalising plan methodology.[58] In reality the appearance of a new regime was not so immediate. The malfunctions in planning in 1937 and 1938 were largely systemic, not the result of individual planners' styles of work, and the renewal of personnel could not immediately have caused planning to operate in a new way. Plan methodology developed significantly under Voznesensky's leadership, but the changes did not follow immediately and were surely not all the result of his personal initiative. Some must have been prepared under Mezhlauk or Smirnov, and Voznesensky was responsible for implementing them. Other changes, more clearly the result of his personal initiative, took months and years to implement.

A starting point was the new USSR Gosplan statute adopted by the government on 2 February 1938, a fortnight after Voznesensky's appointment. 'The chief task of the State Planning Commission', it declared,

is to secure, in the plan of national economy of the USSR, correct proportions in the development of sectors and necessary measures for elimination of disproportions in the national economy.

On the State Planning Commission is laid the task of coordination, in the plan of national economy of the USSR, of the work of adjacent branches of socialist production, of extractive and manufacturing industry, of agriculture and industry, of transport and the national economy; of coordination of the growth of production and the growth of consumption; of the finance of production and its material provision; of realisation of a correct regional disposition of enterprises, proceeding from the necessity of eliminating long-distance and cross hauls, and of bringing enterprises closer to sources of raw materials and to regions of consumption of their output.[59]

These duties were to be carried out by means of compiling, and presenting for approval of the Sovnarkom, perspective, annual and quarterly economy-wide plans, presenting subsequently their results and running fulfilment checks; working on specific problems of socialist economy on the instructions of the Sovnarkom and on Gosplan's own initiative; and developing the methodology of socialist planning which, subject to confirmation by the Sovnarkom, would also be obligatory for planning organs at lower and local levels.[60]

The statute's emphasis on balancing the national economy, on coordinating its sectors and proportions in advance, and on running fulfilment checks was in part a response to alleged defects in the work of Gosplan in the recent past, under conditions of excessive mobilisation and investment crisis. It was said that the planners had compiled exaggerated investment plans which underestimated construction costs and time lags and overestimated the speed of recoupment. It was also said that they had restricted themselves to compiling plans while taking no responsibility for results (in many cases this charge was 'justified' after the event, in that those who compiled the plans had been removed by the time the results began to emerge). In a keynote article to mark his appointment, Voznesensky attacked indifference to results, which, he held, was one of the main causes of imbalances and disproportions in the economy. Arising unnoticed, they could spread unchecked through the system and throw the whole economy off course. 'Planning of the national economy', he repeated, 'only begins with plan compilation.'[61]

The public tone of these remarks was disciplinarian; that is, the indiscipline of plan officials and the failure of their lines of information and command were held responsible for plan failure. Voznesensky did not blame the highest levels of political leadership for placing exaggerated demands on the economy, for putting Gosplan staff under intolerable pressures, or for discouraging initiative and commitment through repeated, murderous purges. He did not criticise existing procedures for fixing targets or advocate a new plan methodology. His main demand was for greater strictness in checking up on plan fulfilment, in order to allow quicker reaction to shortfalls, to avert the worst consequences of unplanned deficits and to hold the economy to its chief priorities. Planners must become the 'combat staff' for defending the plan.[62] This perspective could scarcely be distinguished from Jack Miller's inside observation of 1937 that Gosplan operated not a coherent planning system but a system for defending the state's priorities against the consequences of inevitable plan failure.[63]

Thus the new leadership did not signal a retreat from ambitious planning. As recently as the end of 1937, in branches where output plans had actually been fulfilled, the responsible planners were being charged with sabotage – for deliberately preferring modest but attainable targets to more ambitious targets which would mobilise greater effort, at the cost of plan failure.[64] The aim of the new leadership was rather to make ambitious planning more effective.

In the period 1938–41 the planning system under Voznesensky saw six main changes. The first four involved restoring central communication and control functions lost in the years of administrative fragmentation and purging of personnel, but innovation turned out to be involved as much as restoration. These four meant procedures for checking plan fulfilment, the creation of a network of local agents of the central plan, the planning of labour recruitment to industry and the use of materials and equipment balances. The last two changes were more innovatory in conception and showed most clearly Voznesensky's personal initiative. These involved work on the 'balance of the national economy' and on long-term national economic planning. Each of these is set out in detail as follows.

First, Voznesensky transferred to Moscow the methods of work on which he had insisted in the Leningrad city planning office. He required his new staff to involve themselves in actively checking plan fulfilment at a national level. Through TsUNKhU, the statistical administration, he demanded five-day and ten-day reports on plan fulfilment in the main branches of heavy industry, and placed discussion of the results at the head of regular Gosplan session agendas.[65] Work on strengthening plan fulfilment checks culminated in February 1940 in a formal Gosplan resolution which dealt with central controls over the progress and completion of construction projects, the operation of newly completed industrial plant and the output of rolling stock, fuels and electrical energy. At the same time the revision of industrial branch plan fulfilment indicators used by central planners was also set in motion.[66] Attention was paid to the delicate balance between the increased variety and more complex specification of products on the one hand and the need to restrict the number of indicators on the other to essentials and to avoid excessive regulation of enterprises from above.[67]

Secondly, a new institution was created with wide implications for data collection, plan fulfilment checks, plan compilation and the centralisation of the system. This was the establishment under the statute of 2 February 1938 of a system of Gosplan plenipotentiary agents at regional and subregional levels. Existing local planning offices were subordinate to local government, not to the central planners at USSR Gosplan, and the assessment was that this had come to hinder centralised coordination of regional development and interregional transfers. The plenipotentiaries of USSR Gosplan would act as its local agents, directly responsible to Moscow, independent of the local plan offices but with powers of inspection over them and over the local economy.[68] By the summer of 1940 fourteen plenipotentiaries had been appointed, each with an apparatus of ten to fourteen staff; they included such leading economists of the 1960s and 1970s as G. M. Sorokin and L. Volodarsky.[69]

The substance of work of the plenipotentiaries was intended to be checking on local fulfilment of central plans, uncovering of local reserves of products and capacity to eliminate slack and enable the realistic setting of higher targets, the assessment of efficiency of regional specialisation and interregional shipments, and the supervision of interregional electrical power distribution.[70] They played an important role in such critical questions of the prewar period as the development of new fuel and metallurgical bases, especially in the Eastern USSR, the achievement of fuel and power savings, and the rationalisation of the complex subcontracting network around the engineering industry, to give some examples.[71] Within a short time this innovation brought about changes in the internal structure of USSR Gosplan. In October 1940 nine regional departments were created to develop the spatial dimension of central planning – industrial location, transport, inter-plant subcontracting, regional supply balances and local fulfilment checks. Their organisation was designed to complement the plenipotentiary system.[72]

Resort to a system of plenipotentiaries was already a traditional Soviet administrative response to breakdown of central authority over local bodies, and may be seen as an emergency measure of centralisation. Its emergency character would be reflected in the associated cost of increased 'shapelessness' (the uncertainty and overlap of powers and responsibilities) at lower levels. However, it is accepted that the creation of the plenipotentiary system enhanced the position of USSR Gosplan in terms of central supervision and management of economy-wide coordination.[73]

Thirdly, Gosplan became more involved in the planning of labour recruitment to industry. By the late thirties the existing system of 'organised recruitment' of the rural population to industrial work was in a mess. On the demand side it was overburdened by the needs of capital construction and rearmament, and improved rural conditions had reduced the voluntary supply of labour. The system itself had disintegrated into several different agencies competing with each other to impose arbitrary levies upon the rural population. This situation was the subject of a Sovnarkom decree of 21 July 1938 which ordered, among other things, that the planning of 'organised recruitment' should be placed under the corresponding sections of USSR Gosplan, the major Republican Gosplans and the planning organs in the main localities of outmigration. Operational controls were vested in the Economic Councils of the USSR and major Republican Sovnarkoms and local government.[74] These and other concurrent measures on control of labour mobility did not result in any marked improvement in fulfilment of recruitment plans or in the degree of central control over the labour market as a whole,[75] but represented a significant extension of Gosplan's sphere of influence.

Fourthly, in 1939 and 1940 further changes elevated the role of balances in the planning of supply. At the end of 1937 Gosplan's material balances department had been closed down following the arrest of its chief earlier in the year. The task of balance planning was devolved upon the industrial commissariats, and Gosplan's own industrial departments retained only small 'balance groups' with an advisory role. This division of authority was confirmed in the statute of 2 February 1938.[76] However, in April 1939, among various alterations in Gosplan's internal structure, the material balances department was revived and a new department of equipment balances was formed.[77] At the same time quarterly balances were reintroduced alongside annual balance planning procedures, in order to facilitate checking up on plan fulfilment.[78] From 1939 onwards a new section on balances appeared in economy-wide plan documents.[79]

Two more aspects of change show the influence of Voznesensky at his most reform-minded and innovative. These were, fifthly, the development of the 'balance of the national economy' and, sixthly, initiatives in long-term economic planning.

Behind the 'balance of the national economy' lay the concept of the macroeconomy as an equilibrium system. The term 'equilibrium' is not used here in the sense of a tendency towards a long-run steady-state general equilibrium; all Stalinist economists rejected this notion as associated with the 'genetic' planners of the Bukharin deviation and implying a stagnant economy.[80] A more appropriate sense might be that of a 'temporary' macroeconomic equilibrium secured subject to constraints in the course of expansion. The 'balance of the national economy' meant a unified set of accounts showing the interrelatedness of gross and net production, input stocks and flows, factor incomes, intermediate and final demands and financial flows disaggregated by the industrial branch, the type of economic unit and its social form.[81] Implicit within this framework was definition of the task of economic planning as securing an appropriate balance both within the centrally administered economy and between the latter and the market sphere. This required recognition both of the impact of centrally planned supplies and factor requirements upon the money economy, and the latter's role as an element in the overall macroeconomic equilibrium. Work upon such balances was therefore, in economic planning, the most important practical expression of the socialist economic system's law-governed character.

A plan methodology based on the 'balance of the national economy' could easily clash with the mobilisation system based on setting ambitious targets in key sectors and then defending them regardless of the costs incurred elsewhere. Thus such balances tended to be thrown out of the window when capital construction was the only consideration, then reinstated once the costs of mobilisation had breached social tolerance limits. After the excesses of 1929–30, practical work on the 'balance of the national economy' had played a role in moderating successive drafts of the second Five Year Plan, but was virtually suspended between 1933 and 1936. In fact this retreat became an issue in the 1937 purge of statisticians.[82]

Gosplan produced a new set of balances in 1939, and the accounting scheme used then became the basis for this kind of work for the next thirty years. Systematic work also began on the use of these balances in operational planning.[83] The stated objective was not to increase the number of plan indicators for direction of lower-level units, but to use existing indicators more consistently and efficiently.[84] Thus in 1939 and 1940 practical work concentrated on improving the set of balances for consumption, accumulation and finance of the 'nonproductive' economy; for production and utilisation of manufactured (producer and consumer) goods and farm output; and for household income and expenditure. This work in turn required revision of various conventional classifications and norms. The division of industry into groups 'A' (producer goods) and 'B' (consumer goods) was transferred from an industrial branch basis to a product utilisation basis where this could be established from input–output analysis.[85] The pricing of new industrial products (for constant-price time series) and of agricultural goods traded in different types of market (for current price output, income and expenditure accounts) was also reformed.[86]

Credit for the renewal of practical work on the 'balance of the

Economic planning and the search for balance 25

national economy' within Gosplan in 1938 is due, we are told, to Voznesensky personally.[87] And in an article written for Stalin's sixtieth birthday celebrations at the end of 1939 Voznesensky himself made reinstatement of the 'balance of the national economy' explicit. Once permanent objectives had been identified, he wrote, 'plan compilation must begin from balance'[88] – reversing the subordination of balance to plan targets which he had supported in 1932.

The last field of innovation in planning, where Voznesensky's personal influence was again visible, was that of long-term planning methodology. Central to building 'socialism in a single country' was a concept of scientific and technical revolution and its place in the transformation of society. Where Lenin spoke of communism as 'Soviet power plus electrification of the whole country', Voznesensky used to imagine million-kilowatt power grids carrying current over a thousand kilometres at 400,000 volts.[89] The technological preconditions of a communist society remained his lifelong preoccupation. But taking into account the experience of investment mobilisation, Voznesensky could also see the damage done to the economy's inner balances by unrestrained enthusiasm for large-scale construction projects and new technologies. The scientific and technical revolution of the twentieth century could not be realised all at once. A practical methodology was needed to plan its introduction within the economy's capacity limits, as well as within a finite time horizon.

Voznesensky made his move in a speech to the Eighteenth Party Congress in March 1939. He told the delegates that the task of 'completion of building a communist society and of transition to communism, the task of catching up and overtaking the advanced capitalist countries in economic terms' went beyond the scope of the third Five Year Plan, and he called for a General Plan embracing this task within several five-year periods.[90] According to his biographer these proposals were met with a deafening silence, since they had not been endorsed beforehand by Stalin.[91] After the congress Voznesensky ordered the work to go ahead without waiting for higher approval. Experts were assembled and projections drawn up. A draft Fifteen Year Plan for rapid industrial growth, aiming to close the gap with the main capitalist countries in terms of industrial and agricultural output per head of the population by 1957, began to emerge.[92] A 'balance of the national economy for the period of transition from socialism to communism' was also compiled in 1940.[93] But Voznesensky had to wait until September 1940 for a telephone call from Stalin authorising him just to make his proposal in more detail; permission to proceed with the drafting of the General Plan arrived at Gosplan only on 7 February 1941.[94]

The outcome of these six reorganisations was to enhance the role of Gosplan in the planning and management process. This was reflected in increased centralisation of the economy's administrative structures. In 1938 Gosplan was involved in supply planning for 218 categories of fuel and material inputs and 104 equipment categories. In 1939 and 1940 Gosplan acquired responsibility for a further 69 input categories and 'significantly more' categories of equipment. In 1938 Gosplan carried out supply planning for thirty-four commissariats and central agencies, and by 1941 the number of agencies covered in this way had grown to eighty.[95] Increase in the number of agencies subordinated to Gosplan for supply planning meant only that Gosplan's authority had kept pace with their fragmentation. A stronger index of centralisation was the increase in the number of centrally planned inputs and equipment categories, implying both more detailed planning within existing limits and the extension of these limits to take in more of the economy.

A full account of Gosplan's position in these years must also comment on the changing role of subordinate, parallel and higher bodies in the central planning and management process. As far as subordinate bodies are concerned, Gosplan maintained the authority of planning organs over statistics and accountancy. During the thirties statistics and accountancy had largely been collapsed into each other. The statistical apparatus was headed by a Central Administration of National Economic Accounts (TsUNKhU); the latter was formally subject to (*pri*) USSR Gosplan.[96] TsUNKhU operated a central staff and local bodies which, after 2 February 1938, worked side by side with Gosplan's local plenipotentiaries. When the Gosplan statute was altered on 21 March 1941 TsUNKhU was at last restored its original title TsSU (Central Statistical Administration), but now lost its local apparatus altogether; the local statistical offices were merged into the Gosplan plenipotentiary network, and the latter was now to report both to TsSU and directly to USSR Gosplan.[97] From the point of view of the statisticians this was one step forward, one step back; at the centre they had won more recognition and status, but locally their functions had been more thoroughly submerged into the planning organisations.

In this prewar period, the chief statistical functions were: 'processing and analysis of statistical data showing the course of fulfilment of state plans, proportions in the development of different branches of the national economy, the growth of the socialist national economy and culture and of national welfare, the stock, distribution and utilisation of material resources in the national economy'.[98] Later the subordination of statistics to planning in the thirties would be criticised because it had inhibited the statisticians from fundamental professional tasks – deep analysis of economic problems and critical evaluation of plan projections and their execution.[99]

Accountancy too was seen just as a planning tool, and USSR Gosplan was awarded formal authority over the practice of accountancy by the statutes of 2 February 1938 and 21 March 1941.[100] This too left its mark. If the statisticians resented being seen as just a superior class of accountant, the accountants did not like the view of their profession as the junior partner of statistics, only more elementary and more limited in scope. Soviet accountants were undervalued and underqualified. The failure to develop an autonomous profession hindered the unification of accounting categories, the improvement of accounting coverage and the popularisation of accounting balance techniques.[101]

As far as competition with parallel bodies for influence was concerned, the most important field was that of management functions. USSR Gosplan was clearly the only competent planning organ, but the drift of economic reorganisation in the late thirties was to involve Gosplan more and more in management of the economy. Here one could pick out competition with the industrial branch commissariats over the management of material–technical supply, arising from the changing allocation of responsibility for material balance compilation. Another area of potential conflict was between local agents of USSR Gosplan and local party bodies. Here there was considerable instability. In March 1939 the 'production-branch' departments of leading party committees from the Republican level down to the regional, subregional and municipal level were abolished. Their role had been to coordinate party work in industry and transport, to supervise local enterprises, and to carry out fulfilment checks regarding their plans, problems and performance. Shortly after, however, 'life revealed' that their liquidation had been a mistake, and in November 1939 they were reestablished.[102] Thus in the sensitive field of checks on local fulfilment of central plans and of management response to planning problems, the division of authority continued to shift and lines of responsibility to overlap.

Lastly, the organisation of bodies superior to USSR Gosplan continued to evolve. Changes in the organisation of the Sovnarkom Economic Council in 1940 probably followed upon the party reorganisations of 1939. Following the March 1940 Central Committee plenum the apparatus of the Economic Council was expanded to include six new production-branch councils covering the defence industries, metallurgy and chemicals, engineering, fuels and electricity, mass consumption goods and agriculture.[103] These councils were evidently to exercise in greater detail the functions of plan inspection, confirmation and fulfilment checks which were already the role of the Economic Council in general terms. The changes also implies tighter external supervision of Gosplan's work. The likelihood of conflict was perhaps lessened since Voznesensky, a deputy prime minister since 5 May 1939, was now ex officio a member of the Economic Council. He was also appointed chairman of the Economic Council subcommittee for the defence industries.[104] His star continued to rise.

PLANS AND PERFORMANCE 1938-41

To what extent did planning improve between 1938 and the outbreak of war? The new Gosplan staff and the plan reorganisations did not succeed in rescuing the third Five Year Plan. This plan, covering the years 1938-42, was originally commissioned in 1936. However, a combination of poor economic results in the final stage of the second Five Year Plan period, the growing need for large-scale rearmament, and the discrediting of the staff responsible for early plan drafts meant that the basic tasks of Five Year Plan compilation still confronted Voznesensky's team when it took over Gosplan early in 1938.[105] The new planners had to redraft the plan during the year and then again at the beginning of 1939 to take into account increased defence spending plans and the stagnant performance of basic industries. They had to struggle to cut back inflated demands for investment resources being voiced by the industry commissariats.[106]

The third Five Year Plan, adopted in March 1939, placed much emphasis on raising the efficiency of investment. It aimed at cutting construction lags and the backlog of unfinished investment. Unlike the preceding two perspective plans it indicated that the value of productive capacity to be completed or reconstructed within the plan period should exceed the volume of total investment by a small margin.[107] The investment plan was also to be rationalised in terms of reducing the scale and increasing the dispersal of projects in order to reduce demands on the transport system.[108] Side by side with the final stages of plan compilation the construction industry was being reorganised and centralised with the creation of commissariats for construction materials (January 1939) and for construction itself (May 1939),[109] and with a campaign to speed up construction methods.[110] These were the foundations for an ambitious set of five-year output growth targets. An important source of output growth was to be falling capital–output ratios in iron and steelmaking, construction materials, textiles and other sectors.[111] The plan also depended on gains from lowered metal input utilisation norms, lighter machinery and higher machinery utilisation.[112]

This was a plan for economic mobilisation to be financed by greater discipline in investment and production – an 'austerity' plan, as Zaleski calls it.[113] The plan's expectations, however, were not fulfilled, and in 1939 and 1940 the economy continued to wander off course. Annual plans became unstable, were revised downward below the path implied by Five Year Plan 1942 targets, and were still underfulfilled. In most areas of the economy, meeting the 1941 plan could no longer have led the economy to Five Year Plan fulfilment in 1942.[114]

However, more detailed examination of the record shows nonetheless that economic performance in the basic industries improved sharply in the last year before the war, and that economic mobilisation had been resumed.

Figure 1 shows indices of output of some main branches of the Soviet defence and basic industries from 1937 to the first half of 1941. Stagnation in ferrous metallurgy is clearly marked during 1938–40, while expansion of high-grade rolling capacity for arms production was largely at the expense of civilian metal supplies and metal manufactures. The 1938 annual plan was badly underfulfilled. In its report on 1939 plan fulfilment (on which we lack precise data) Gosplan noted not only the failures of iron and steelmaking but also lags in the development of the fuel and energy sectors.[115] Also in 1939, after a tremendous upsurge, most branches of arms production peaked and began to mark time. And at the end of 1939 the economy

30   *Soviet planning in peace and war*

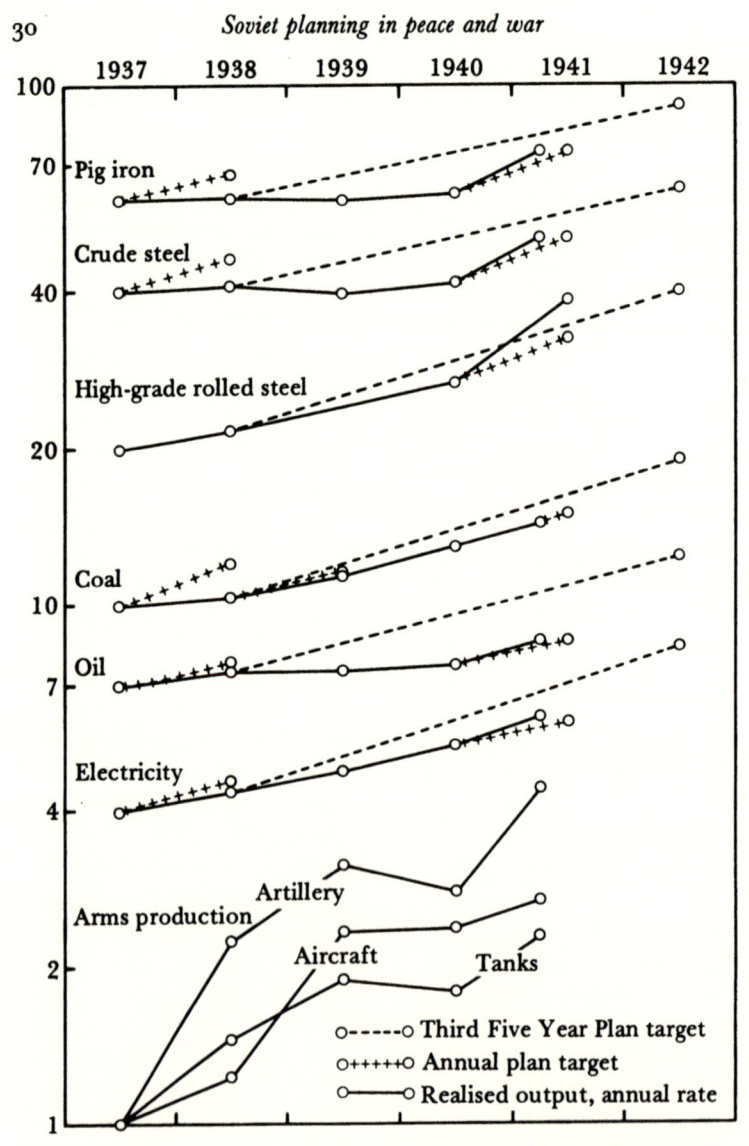

Figure 1. Planned and realised outputs of main branches of the Soviet defence industry and basic industry 1937–41 (1937 = 100)

Notes to Figure 1

The solid graphs in the figure show volume indices of realised annual output based on 1937 and ending in the first half of 1941, for which six months' output is expressed at an annual rate. The one exception is the series for high-grade rolled steel, where 1939 output is not known and has been was disrupted by the 'winter war' with Finland, which threw the railway system into confusion and disrupted material and fuel supplies to the northwestern region,[116] especially to Leningrad's engineering and defence plants.

Nineteen-forty was the year in which economic mobilisation began to revive. In June a crash programme of investment completion and capital reconstruction in iron and steel was initiated. Clear priorities were established for allocating scarce resources, a large number of unfinished or long-delayed projects were brought to completion and new capacity was blown in.[117] Output expanded once more, although the rate of turnaround faltered in the autumn; plan fulfilment figures for the third quarter and for October remained a source of disquiet.[118] Mobilisation of workers in this and other industries must have been eased by the measures of June and October 1940, lengthening the working day and week, criminalising absenteeism and lateness, and establishing a State Labour Reserve of young workers for industrial conscription.[119] Other basic industries now turned upwards,[120] as did arms production. Civilian engineering, however, continued to suffer from conversion to defence needs and from arms industry competition for inputs; machine tool output began to fall, and the number of new machine tool plants in the 1940 investment plan was halved to make room for other projects.[121] In fact, when war broke out the ambitious 1941 annual plan was well on the way to being 'fulfilled and overfulfilled' in the main branches of basic industry. At the same time there were very many sectors with lower priority where this result would not have been obtained.

By 1941 the industrial economy had been rebalanced, and a new mobilisation drive was under way. However, this does not mean that planning had actually become more coherent. Criticism of plan organisation began to surface again in 1940 and 1941. In mid-1940

Notes to Figure 1 (cont.)
interpolated, and where 1941 output is known only taking the year as a whole. Realised output figures are taken from Appendices 1 and 2. The crossed graphs show annual plan targets for 1938–41, where known, and are shown in relation to realised output of the preceding year. Annual plan targets are taken from Zaleski, 1980, pp. 578–9, except high-grade rolled steel for 1941 (Gos. plan, 1941, p. 18). The dashed graphs show 1942 targets from the third Five Year Plan. This plan was revised in early 1939 before being adopted, in order to take into account economic results for 1938, so 1942 targets are shown in relationship to realised 1938 outputs. Targets for 1942 are taken from Resheniya, v. 2, 1967, p. 682.

two young Gosplan staff members charged the Gosplan journal *Planned Economy* with failing to publish analysis of current problems such as the balance of the national economy, regional development and industrial location, the role of accountancy and statistics and the character of new technology.[122] Several new discussions began.

One of the more striking themes emerged at the end of 1940 and in early 1941 with a number of references to the failure to establish a working system of plan indicators and fulfilment checks. In an economics journal in the new year a lone voice explained that, while more concrete and detailed industrial planning was of course a good thing, it could also restrict the autonomy of plant management and tie the director's hands. The enterprise could no longer manoeuvre or adapt efficiently to the situation it alone knew best.[123] This, incidentally, is an aspect of prewar planning which Soviet historians emphasise today – planning and management at the centre were brought closer to the realities encountered at the point of production by means of shorter chains of command and tighter vertical controls on the enterprise; but the possibilities of horizontal manoeuvre and interaction among enterprises were not sufficiently developed.[124] However, at the time the majority of critics of the planning system wanted to develop it still further along existing lines. They wanted to extend the coverage of plan indicators and central fulfilment checks over the enterprise in terms of product types, quality, ranges and mix, production costs and the spatial and temporal distribution of output.[125] The problem seemed to be that any control system, once put into operation, proved to be insufficiently detailed and comprehensive, and this tended to stimulate demands for tighter, more detailed controls.

It would have been surprising had the coherence of planning suddenly improved on account of the changes introduced under Voznesensky. Three factors stood in the way of a favourable outcome. One was the inexperience of the responsible planning staff and the circumstances of their recruitment. Another was the unpredictable strategic environment which kept multiplying its demands on the economy. Finally the reorganisations themselves served to centralise economic authority under USSR Gosplan, but not to improve the logic of the planning process.

Talking to students in 1939, Voznesensky described his aim as steering a course between two evils. 'In planning', he said,

Economic planning and the search for balance 33

one mustn't be bound by overcautious forecasts, but it's dangerous to become caught up in investment mania ... Under cover of 'revolutionary' phrases bureaucrats are enticed from planning into investment mania, which disrupts the national economy. Bureaucratic overenthusiasm in planning is no less harmful than the opportunistic plan which conceals reserves in the national economy and sabotages Bolshevik growth rates of socialist production...[126]

Steering this middle course was, no doubt, an inherently frustrating process. Each new injection of realism into the planning process tended to throw up new problems for evaluation and analysis, new demands for information, new decisions to implement and follow through. There was a circular logic in the rationalisation process in which each addition to the planners' informational, logical and decision-making capacities stimulated new demands which were loaded onto them. In the face of urgent political priorities, the plan which would secure permanent objectives while remaining sensitive to changing reality and the needs of balance would remain an elusive ideal. It would often prove temptingly easy to abandon its pursuit in favour of a return to brutal, insensitive rule by decree.

Economic performance remained unsatisfactory for some time, and had only just started to improve by 1941. However, the odium of stagnation did not rub off on Voznesensky, who moved to the centre of the political stage. He had come to Gosplan in 1937 as Zhdanov's protégé. At the Eighteenth Party Congress in March 1939 he made an important speech and was elected to the Central Committee; in May he became a deputy of V. M. Molotov, the Soviet prime minister. In February 1941 he gave a keynote speech to the Eighteenth Party Conference. His report was dominated by the theme of the European war and its dangers. While critical of many aspects of the economy, it showed no failure of confidence, and Voznesensky was able to point to the quickening tempo in industry.[127] At the same time he became a candidate Politburo member.[128]

Further changes transpired at Gosplan in February and March 1941. On 10 March 1941 Voznesensky was promoted to first deputy prime minister and head of the Sovnarkom Economic Council. At this time he was released from Gosplan, where the leadership was assumed by his deputy M. Z. Saburov.[129] To judge from coincidences in their biographies, Saburov was an old colleague of Voznesensky's in the days of party work in the Donbass, and perhaps Voznesensky was responsible for his transfer to Gosplan in 1938 from his post in the engineering commissariat.[130] Around this change in the Gosplan leadership there took place some quiet codification of procedures and institutions. In February 1941 a conference of Gosplan's plenipotentiaries redefined their functions and their relationship to the regional departments at Gosplan itself.[131] And on 21 March 1941, a few days after Saburov had taken over, a new Gosplan statute redefined Gosplan's own functions and relationship to the government apparatus.[132] These new codes did not release more waves of reforming energy. Rather the impression is given that, in spite of the critics of 1940 and early 1941, the reorganised planning system was being validated and confirmed. Voznesensky's transfer certainly did not signal any major change in the line of command; he retained overall responsibility for economic planning, and apparently kept his office at Gosplan, where for example he was to be found on the day war broke out.[133] Day-to-day responsibility for planning, however, had been handed to his subordinates with the instruction that the system was once more operational, not to be disturbed by further gratuitous alteration.

CONCLUSIONS

The compilation of economic plans is a necessary but not sufficient condition for the establishment of social control over economic development. In Soviet experience a particularly difficult problem has been how to reconcile the mobilisation and balance functions in development planning. Resource mobilisation for economic development is based on plans which exceed the resources available. There is a clash between plans and reality – the operation of the plans brings about a state of overcommitment of resources which at first mobilises, then disrupts, the economy as a whole.

A plan, as Stalin once said, can only be 'a first approximation which we must refine, adapt and perfect in the light of local experience, in the light of experience of plan implementation'. More recently Eugène Zaleski has suggested that 'planning is a continuous process, and a planner's greatest virtue is his ability to adjust plans according to permanent objectives'.[134] According to Michael Ellman, too, the most important problem in central planning is that central agencies are inherently uncertain about the rate and direction of change of their environment. The real object of planning is the continuous adaptation of the economic system and its ostensible targets to changing reality. Adaptation to reality is inevitable in the end but, if not organised smoothly and deliberately, it may be temporarily delayed and suppressed. In the latter case it may become sudden and discontinuous, forced to the point where survival is threatened.[135]

On this basis the most important problem of the Soviet economy in the 1930s was not its failure to fulfil planned targets, since, under the real conditions of operation which planners cannot know in advance, no plan is guaranteed success and the detailed fulfilment of targets is at best an accidental byproduct of the adaptive process. The most important problem was the failure to adapt plans smoothly and continuously to the resources really available and to the real conditions under which they would be supplied. The reason for this failure lay in the authoritarian relationship between the plan and the enterprise. The information concerning real conditions which would permit adaptation of the plan was held (or withheld) in the enterprise, while the power to authorise adaptation of the plan was held (or withheld) in the central organs. The withholding by lower levels of information, and the refusal by higher levels of permission to adapt the plan, became systemic features of the planning process. Consequently, needed adaptations of particular plans and of the entire planning system could not occur smoothly and automatically, but only when absolutely required, and then only when authorised by high-level political decisions. These conditions arose periodically, when the stress and imbalances generated by plans for economic mobilisation passed the limit of tolerance. The result was an alternating pattern of mobilisation and rebalancing phases, the former being separated from the latter by an economic crisis.

Soviet experience has revealed a wide variety of solutions to these periodically recurring crises. In the period from 1938 to 1941 the principal means of solving the crisis in planning was rationalisation of the economy-wide planning system. This method was not used in isolation but was combined with other methods as well.

Rationalisation can be compared with two other kinds of response to crisis, which can be termed repression and reform. Repression is the attempt to repress the symptoms of a mobilisation crisis while continuing with the original programme of objectives. This implies sticking to the capital construction programme or even expanding it in order to build additional capacity to produce scarce investment goods in bottleneck areas. It implies a search for hidden reserves and for tighter central controls on enterprise performance, and it requires harder work and reduced living standards. The basis for sustaining the mobilisation drive is not the restoration of economic and social balance but the whipping up of a 'class' struggle against slackers, wreckers and other so-called enemies.

In contrast rationalisation policies attempt to reverse the crisis by moderating the mobilisation drive, cutting back the investment plan and adapting the plan to reality. There is acceptance that the planning process has become a bureaucratic paper chase divorced from the real situation in the economy's productive units. The authority of the central plan has been weakened. Measures are taken to restore the effectiveness of central economic policy by means of more efficient data collection and evaluation, more comprehensive and realistic balance compilation and more detailed, sensitive hierarchical control systems. Another description appropriate to the rationalisation urge would be 'conservative reform-mindedness' – the sponsorship of limited reforms within the existing system, in order to improve its viability, falling well short of a commitment to reforms for their own sake.

Rationalisation policies can therefore be distinguished from reformism. A commitment to reform implies acceptance that the erosion of central authority, which accompanies the unfolding of the mobilisation crisis, is a necessary process which cannot be reversed, since it reflects the inescapable resistance of enterprises and households to the imposition of production, consumption and leisure choices upon them from above. Reform policies seek to restrain the authority of the higher-level bodies not in order to make the authority more effective, but in order to devolve it upon the economy's basic units. Planning the areas of collective choice means rendering the dynamic of the development process adaptable to the interests and operational decisions of households and enterprises.

Thus both rationalisation and reform currents share a desire for the restoration of economic and social equilibrium as a precondition of resumed economic development. But they have different attitudes to the traditional system of authoritarian planning as a framework for achieving this shared goal. For the systemic framework is not only a means to an end, but possesses certain values in itself which are positive or negative depending on one's conservative or reformist standpoint.

In the period from 1938 to 1941 Soviet planning was rationalised, but in practice there was no sharp dividing line between rationalisation policies and some other options. Voznesensky's leadership at Gosplan was formed in a highly repressive atmosphere, and the initial stress which was then laid upon strengthening discipline through tighter central checks upon plan fulfilment continued the repressive, not the reform-minded tradition. However, closer plan fulfilment checks, once established, tended to result in a greater volume of information flowing to the centre and a greater awareness of real problems being encountered in the economy's basic units. The same ambiguity was present in the formation of the Gosplan plenipotentiary system, which in itself was a measure of centralisation of naked authority – virtually an 'emergency' measure – but which also turned out to be a precondition for more rational planning of interregional and inter-industry transfers and of inter-plant subcontracting. Thus they blended into the rationalising themes of Voznesensky's prewar leadership – the emphasis upon balances in the planning of supply, upon the 'balance of the national economy', and upon long-term planning – which expressed a desire to make plans more realistic, more responsive and adaptable to their environment, more consistent with social and economic equilibrium.

The reorganisations of 1939 and 1940 amounted to a determined rationalisation of the planning system. In modern terminology they could be described as 'reforms', but the motivation behind them was conservative rather than reformist. At this stage in the evolution of the Stalinist economic system reform motives played little part.

NOTES

1 Stalin, v. 12, 1949, p. 347 ('Politicheskii otchet Tsentral'nogo Komiteta XVI s"ezdu VKP(B').
2 Davies, 1977, pp. 21–3.
3 Carr and Davies, 1974, ch. 32 ('Principles of Planning').
4 Ibid., pp. 839–42.
5 Barsov, 1969, pp. 90–2.
6 Davies, 1982, pp. 23–4 and Table 8. The annual average of gross investment valued in current roubles between 1934 and 1936 was almost twice the annual average for 1930–2. But at the same time a growing share of this investment went to increase the back-log of unfinished capacity – according to one estimate, in 1935 −3.4 per cent, in 1936 1.3 per cent, in 1937 6.8 per cent. Another estimate suggests a sharper increase from −2.0 per cent in 1935 to 15.7 and 16.4 per cent in 1936 and 1937 respectively.

7 Lokshin, 1938, pp. 40, 43.
8 Barber, 1979, p. 12.
9 Lokshin, 1938, p. 40.
10 Resheniya, v. 2, 1967, pp. 633–9.
11 Clark, 1956, p. 44.
12 Nar. khoz., 1961, p. 604.
13 Kas'yanenko, 1972, p. 211.
14 Clark, 1956, pp. 49, 312.
15 G. S. Kravchenko, 1970, p. 125.
16 ISE, v. 5, 1978, p. 183.
17 Tupper, 1982, p. 202.
18 Ibid., p. 336.
19 Nar. khoz., 1972, p. 346.
20 Clark, 1956, pp. 315–16.
21 Tupper, 1981, p. 14.
22 ISE, v. 5, 1978, p. 97.
23 See Chapter 3, Table 24.
24 V. Sokolov, 1946, p. 19.
25 Tupper, 1982, p. 222.
26 Bergson, 1961, p. 252.
27 Tupper, 1982, p. 222.
28 ISE, v. 5, 1978, p. 49.
29 IVMV, v. 2, 1974, p. 183. Members were A. I. Mikoyan (deputy prime minister and trade commissar), N. A. Voznesensky (Gosplan chairman), I. F. Tevosyan (shipbuilding commissar) and Academician I. P. Bardin, an expert on iron and steel technology.
30 Lokshin, 1940, p. 26.
31 Lokshin, 1938, p. 43.
32 Zaleski, 1980, p. 251.
33 Lokshin, 1939, p. 45.
34 Tupper, 1982, pp. 69–70.
35 Rubin, 1969, pp. 126–7.
36 See Appendix 4 below.
37 Bialer, 1980, p. 16.
38 Milward, 1977, p. 27.
39 Lokshin, 1939, p. 51; Kats, 1940, p. 137.
40 Zaleski, 1980, pp. 51–6.
41 Zelenovsky, 1941, p. 17.
42 Zaleski, 1980, pp. 169–71.
43 ISE, v. 5, 1978, p. 36.
44 Resheniya, v. 2, 1967, pp. 630–1.
45 Zaleski, 1980, p. 171.
46 The most important source of information about Voznesensky's career is the memoir by Kolotov, 1976. Kolotov was Voznesensky's personal secretary from 1938 to 1949. He gives a very favourable impression, largely without warts. For a more detailed evaluation see Harrison, 1983.
47 Voznesensky, 1931a, p. 43. See also his article in *Pravda*, 8 October 1931,

Economic planning and the search for balance

entitled 'Bor'ba za plan v sovremennyi period', reprinted with deletions in Voznesensky, 1979, pp. 50–8.
48 Voznesensky, 1931a, pp. 29–31, 41–3; 1931b, pp. 37–40, 44, 47–50.
49 Voznesensky, 1931a, pp. 32–8; 1931b, p. 44.
50 Voznesensky, 1931b, pp. 38–42; 1932, pp. 39–42.
51 Voznesensky, 1931b, p. 46; 1933a, p. 49; 1933b, pp. 94–5. See also two articles published in *Pravda* on 21 May 1932 ('Obespechim vypolnenie plana zavershayushchego goda pyatiletki') and 28 March 1934 ('O perezhitkakh kapitalizma v ekonomike i soznanii lyudei'), reprinted in Voznesensky, 1979, pp. 141–4 and 269–70 respectively.
52 Stalin, 1940, pp. 512–13 ('Report to the Seventeenth Congress of the C.P.S.U.(B)').
53 Voznesensky, 1935, pp. 33–8.
54 Voznesensky, 1935, pp. 36–43.
55 Ibid., p. 45.
56 Kolotov, 1976, p. 154.
57 Kolotov, 1976, pp. 153–60.
58 Kolotov, 1976, pp. 167ff conveys this impression.
59 Upravlenie, 1968, p. 215.
60 Ibid., pp. 214–16.
61 Voznesensky, 1938, pp. 14–16.
62 Ibid., p. 16.
63 Miller, 1964, p. 120.
64 Zaleski, 1980, p. 251.
65 Kolotov, 1976, pp. 173, 182, 190.
66 Zalkind and Miroshnichenko, 1980, p. 189.
67 ISE, v. 5, 1978, p. 17.
68 Upravlenie, 1968, pp. 216–17.
69 Volodarsky, 1971, p. 61.
70 Kolotov, 1976, pp. 234–5; Zaleski, 1980, pp. 42–3.
71 Volodarsky, 1971, p. 62.
72 SPRP, 1940, No. 28, art. 674.
73 Rubin, 1969, pp. 130–1.
74 Conquest, ed., 1967, pp. 24–7; Barber, 1979, p. 13.
75 Barber, 1979, pp. 13–14.
76 Zaleski, 1980, pp. 94–5.
77 Ivanov and Pribluda, 1967, p. 37. Also created at this time were a Prices Bureau, a Council of Scientific and Technical Expertise and an Institute of Technical and Economic Information.
78 Zelenovsky, 1941, pp. 18–19.
79 Kolotov, 1976, pp. 129, 192.
80 Pashkov, 1938, p. 109; Kursky, 1940, p. 21.
81 Pashkov, 1938, pp. 121–2; Kursky, 1940, pp. 24–35; Kursky, 1941a, pp. 73–6.
82 See 'The Balance of the National Economy: A Brief History', in Wheatcroft and Davies, eds., forthcoming.
83 Po ed. plan., 1971, pp. 75–6.
84 Pashkov, 1938, p. 119.

85 Zalkind and Miroshnichenko, 1980, pp. 164–71.
86 Ibid., p. 171; ISE, v. 5, 1978, p. 18.
87 Sorokin, 1963, p. 151.
88 Voznesensky, 1940, p. 84.
89 This vision was realised in the Soviet Union at the end of the 1950s; see Kolotov, 1976, p. 113.
90 Voznesensky, 1979, p. 372 ('Iz rechi na XVIII s"ezde VKP(b)').
91 Kolotov, 1963b.
92 Zalkind and Miroshnichenko, 1973, p. 48.
93 Zalkind and Miroshnichenko, 1980, p. 168.
94 Kolotov, 1963b; Kolotov, 1976, pp. 224–33.
95 Zelenovsky, 1941, p. 19.
96 Upravlenie, 1968, p. 215.
97 Starovsky and Ezhov, 1975, p. 4.
98 Tsikulin, 1966, p. 164.
99 Starovsky, 1969, pp. 16–17.
100 Upravlenie, 1968, p. 214; Ivanov and Pribluda, 1967, p. 38.
101 Kiparisov, 1940, pp. 86–8.
102 Ist. KPSS, v. 5(i), 1970, p. 33; see also IVMV, v. 3, 1974, p. 374; IVMV, v. 4, 1975, p. 135.
103 Ist. KPSS, v. 5(i), 1970, p. 33.
104 See Appendix 4.
105 Zaleski, 1980, pp. 162–7.
106 Zalkind and Miroshnichenko, 1980, p. 159.
107 Resheniya, v. 2, 1967, p. 692; Kosyachenko, 1939, pp. 124–5. See also V. Sokolov, 1946, p. 7; Po ed. plan., 1971, p. 69; Kursky, 1974, p. 69.
108 Voznesensky, 1979, p. 368 ('Iz rechi na XVIII s"ezde VKP(B)').
109 See Appendix 4.
110 V. Sokolov, 1946, p. 34.
111 Kursky, 1939, p. 35.
112 ISE, v. 5, 1978, p. 16.
113 Zaleski, 1980, p. 185.
114 Ibid., pp. 198–202.
115 Zalkind and Miroshnichenko, 1980, p. 194.
116 Kumanev, 1976, pp. 41–3.
117 Clark, 1956, p. 49; Morekhina, 1974, p. 23.
118 Lokshin, 1940, p. 30.
119 Resheniya, v. 2, 1967, pp. 757–8, 774–9. P. G. Moskatov was appointed head of the Chief Administration of Labour Reserves; see SPRP, 1940, No. 25, art. 621. By the end of 1940 36 per cent of workers in iron and steel making were aged twenty-five years or less; see Morekhina, 1974, p. 31. This percentage was higher in new plant.
120 Nikitin, 1960, p. 15; Zalkind and Miroshnichenko, 1980, p. 196. During 1940 Soviet frontiers expanded, but this does not account for the increases in production. The new territories in the Baltic and southwestern regions contributed only insignificant amounts to Soviet capacity in heavy industry; see data for 1940 in Nar. khoz., 1972, pp. 595, 608, 620, 682.

121 Kas'yanenko, 1972, p. 198.
122 Gladkov and Zalkind, 1940, pp. 92-4.
123 Birman, 1941, pp. 115-16.
124 ISE, v. 5, 1978, p. 35.
125 Kursky, 1940, p. 31; Zelenovsky, 1941, p. 21; Nosov, 1941, p. 17; Plan. khoz., 1941a, pp. 3-7.
126 Kolotov, 1976, p. 208.
127 Voznesensky, 1941, p. 11.
128 BSE, 3rd edn, v. 5, 1971, p. 268.
129 See Appendix 4.
130 BSE, 2nd edn, v. 37, 1955, p. 563.
131 Volodarsky, 1971, p. 61.
132 Ivanov and Pribluda, 1967, p. 38.
133 Shakhurin, 1975, p. 134.
134 Zaleski, 1971, p. 294.
135 Ellman, 1978, p. 254.

2

The coming of war: plans and realities in 1941

What does planning mean in war? We draw up plans alone, but carry them out, so to say, together with the enemy, taking into account his counteraction.

(Marshal I. S. Konev)[1]

INTRODUCTION

At a very high level of generality there is no difference between peacetime and wartime economic planning. In both cases the central problem remains one of adaptation of plans and goals to the resources really available and the conditions under which they may be supplied. The action of competitors, whether peaceful or warlike, is merely one of the factors conditioning the adaptive process. Both in peacetime and in time of war plans must be adaptable to the counteraction of adversaries, since their counteraction cannot be known in advance of the compilation and initiation of the plans themselves. The counteraction of adversaries can only be guessed at beforehand; forecasting it is an inherently uncertain process, and the forecast may turn out wrong. Once the adversary's counter is embarked upon and actually in progress, its purpose and direction may still remain uncertain to those who must authorise the adaptive response, if they are out of touch with those directly experiencing the adversary's action. Whether this action is peaceful or warlike – for example a trade war or a shooting war – makes no difference. The problem of adaptation to changing realities remains the same.

At a lower level of generality we can look at the character of the adaptive process in Stalinist economic planning. A feature of Stalinist planning was the tension between different views of the purpose of plans as instruments of rapid mobilisation of resources on the one

The coming of war: plans and realities in 1941   43

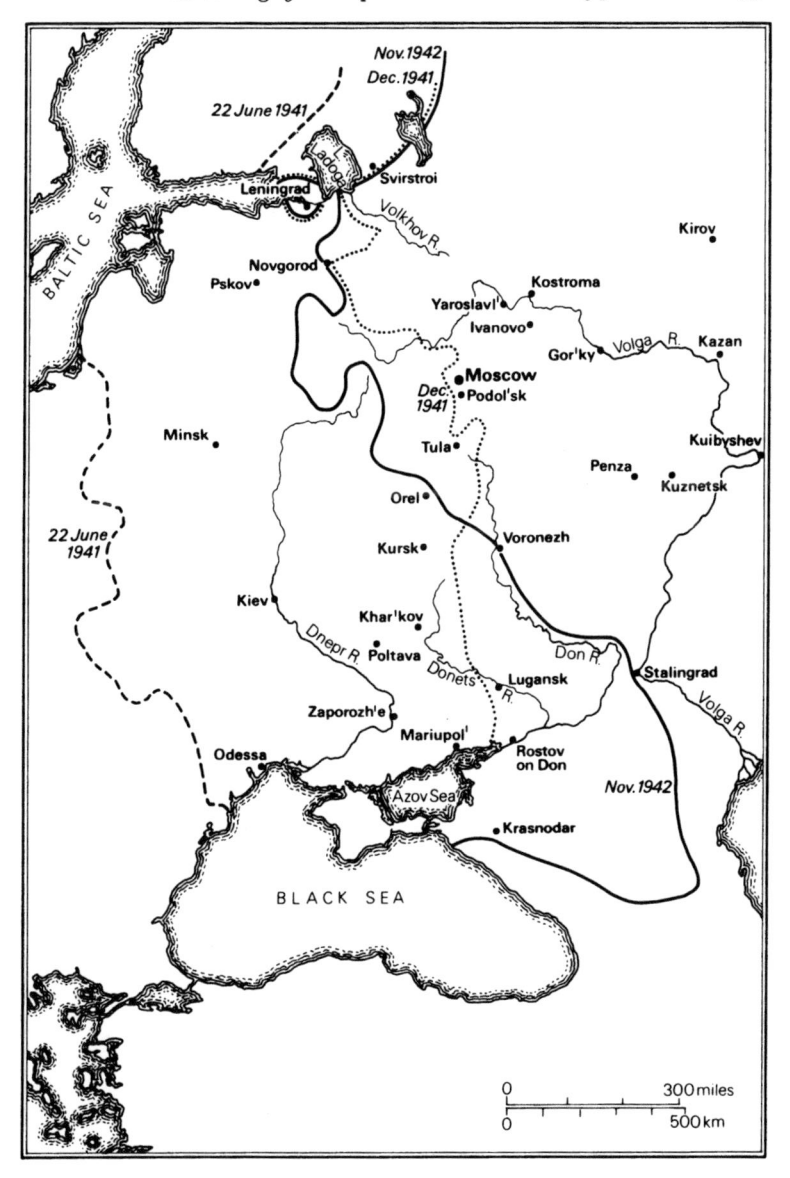

The Soviet–German front 1941-2

hand and as means of ensuring social and economic balance on the other. The priority of the mobilisation functions in planning gave rise to periodic crises and forced adaptation of plans and planning to the requirements of balance. At this lower level of generality, we still find that the transition from peace to war made no difference to the basic dynamic of Stalinist planning. The mobilisation of resources by dictatorial means remained a basic motive force, but even in wartime this basic force was unable to drive indefinitely onward without regard to the needs of social and economic equilibrium. In wartime, too, crises would emerge and require the economy to be rebalanced as a precondition for resuming resource mobilisation.

At a still more basic level we may take into account the specific differences between acts of peace and war. A real war is different from a trade war. The modern weapons available to twentieth-century combatants enable them to proceed without warning from bombardment and blockade to the seizure of territory and the destruction of assets, lines of communication and nerve centres organic to their adversary's economic system. In wartime Soviet planners faced the same problem of adaptation to changing realities, but the rate of change of the environment and the urgency of adaptation had changed qualitatively. At the same time, over and above their destructive power, modern weapons carried the power to disrupt the organisations of the front and rear, inducing powerful 'frictions' of shock, danger, fatigue and breakdown of communications and of morale, and so to slow down or even prevent altogether the adaptation of the economy to war. Consequently the moment of transition from peace to war would be a very big test of the adaptive powers of the Soviet planning system and of the stability of its mobilisation processes.

Even here it could be argued that the coming of war should not alter the substance of the planning process. Peacetime planning must logically take into account the likelihood of war and its likely character, and must include preparation of the economy in peacetime to absorb surprise shocks and emergencies without fatal disruption. Certainly Soviet plans of the prewar period had been operated on the basis of such forecasts. However, an insoluble dilemma tends to inhibit the creation of a full 'war economy' in advance of war itself. This is because whether or not there will be a war is uncertain. Moreover the risk of war depends upon the character of peacetime preparations for it. Peacetime preparations reduce the risk of war by deterring aggression (or resistance), or raise it by provoking a preemptive attack. Either case reduces the desirability of converting the economy to a full war footing in advance of war. In the first case one does no more than enough to avoid war, and in the second case one does less than enough to provoke it. If one foresees hostilities, one aims to keep them short. One does not really expect to have to fight at all. Consequently, when war comes, those who start it believe that it will be over by Christmas, while the rest are taken by surprise with their preparations incomplete.

This chapter is divided into three parts. Part One deals with Soviet military–economic preparations for war. Parts Two and Three examine how these preparations stood up to the impact of the German invasion. Part Two is devoted to the impact of invasion and evacuation of the Soviet territories lost to Germany in 1941, while Part Three deals with the first wartime plans for mobilisation of the economy and its conversion to a war footing.

PART ONE: PREPARING FOR WAR

THE SOVIET MILITARY–ECONOMIC POTENTIAL

The Soviet economy has been regarded by tradition as highly adaptable to war. The source of this tradition has been its ability to build up its military–economic potential.[2] In the modern world the military–economic potential of a country is measured by its stocks of weapons, the capacity of its arms industries to add to them and the ability of its basic and engineering industries to supply and expand arms capacity. The reason for measuring military–economic potential in this way is the growing mechanisation of modern means of destruction and of the means of producing them. The mechanisation of weapon systems, by adding constantly to their range, speed of delivery and destructive power, has meant that only short wars can be fought with the weapons already deployed in advance of hostilities. For more protracted conflicts the capacity to add rapidly to the stock of weapons must also have been laid down in advance. Mechanisation of the means of producing modern weapons has in turn required the creation of specialised, permanently operating defence industries; the ability to sustain and expand them has depended in its turn upon the economy's general level of industrial development and its capacity for diversification, specialisation and structural change.[3]

In the long run the concept of military–economic potential is hardly distinct from the concept of economic potential in general. The longer the time horizon, the less the potential of the economy to meet any objective, civil or military, is constrained by existing assets and reserves, since the latter can always be added to or substitutes found for them. Over a shorter period, however, the idea of military–economic potential becomes more precise, being limited by the existing pattern of stocks and fixed capacities, which cannot be altered at will.

The long-term objectives of Stalinist military–economic policy were formed within the web of insecurities surrounding the attempt to build 'socialism in a single country'. In the 1920s the Soviet Union found herself a backward agrarian state, isolated and contained by unfriendly neighbours with powerful industries, in an age of growing identification of industrial with military power. In recent memory her people had suffered the imperialist warfare of 1914–18, then imperialist intervention in her civil war of 1918–21. These experiences had strongly reinforced her rulers' theory of Marxism–Leninism, which stressed the warmaking tendencies and hostile objectives of the imperialist states.

Through practical absorption of the 'lessons' of 1914–21, an iron link was forged between Soviet security objectives and industrial capacities. With restoration of a peacetime economy, military–economic experts soon began to plan Soviet industry's mobilisation potential.[4] The development of war industries became a major goal of industrialisation policy.[5] Stalin crystallised the association between military and industrial power in a famous speech of February 1931 which captured precisely the urgent atmosphere of the first Five Year Plan:

One feature of the history of Old Russia was the continual beatings she suffered for falling behind, for being backward. She was beaten by the Mongol Khans. She was beaten by the Turkish beys. She was beaten by the Swedish feudal lords. She was beaten by the Polish and Lithuanian gentry. She was beaten by the British and French capitalists. She was beaten by the Japanese barons. All beat her – for her backwardness: for military backwardness, for cultural backwardness, for political backwardness, for industrial backwardness, for agricultural backwardness. She was beaten because to do so was profitable and could be done with impunity ... Such is the law of the exploiters ... You are backward, you are weak ... therefore you are wrong;

hence you can be beaten and enslaved. You are mighty – therefore you are right; hence we must be wary of you.
That is why we must no longer lag behind.
We are fifty or a hundred years behind the advanced countries. We must make good this distance in ten years. Either we do it, or they crush us.[6]

The prophetic accuracy of Stalin's forecast ('We must make good this distance in ten years') was unintentional, since he feared war from other quarters than Germany, where the Nazis had not yet come to power. He feared war in general as much as any specific war, and under him the industrial foundations of military power were laid down as insurance against a range of evil possibilities as much as to secure particular military goals.

The awareness of the military significance of industrial development also resulted in a tendency to militarise civilian institutions. Industrial development was regarded as a military struggle for terrain, involving battles on various fronts with internal and external enemies; the population was seen as an army subject to military discipline and led by the Communist Party as its officer corps.[7] This outlook had practical results to the extent that it reinforced the dictatorial character of the central planning and management process, and was used to persuade the population to tighten belts and show discipline in the face of difficulties.[8] It bolstered repressive responses to economic problems and encouraged economic leaders to continue with ambitious mobilisation plans beyond the point where they might otherwise have been forced to modify the plans and lower their aspirations. Militarisation of civilian values and forms helped to force adaptation to plans by the population, rather than the other way around.

The results of Stalinist military–economic policy were an impressive and wide-ranging rearmament. This rearmament went further than the quantities of weapons produced in each year, which were shown in Table 2. In the German terminology, it was a policy of 'armament in depth',[9] that is, of investment not only in considerable stocks of weapons but also in arms capacity and supporting civilian engineering and basic industries. These would enable replacement of weapons losses, expansion of arms capacity over a period of time and the conversion of the whole economy to a war footing in the event of a protracted war. Much of the investment expenditure associated with armament in depth would come under civilian, not military, headings because it was associated with the economy's war potential but not the immediate production of weapons. Such industries remained within the civilian economy and available for peaceful utilisation, but would be an indispensable element in any future adaptation of the economy to the needs of war.

Considered in this light, the scale of Soviet rearmament was not only impressive in itself, but it also revealed a more thorough and long-term character than the rearmament of any other great power, including Germany. Of course this was not accidental, since Germany's Nazi leaders planned only to fight short, victorious wars on single fronts at times of their own choosing and at small cost in terms of weaponry.

Thus the objectives, methods and results of Stalinist military–economic policy in the thirties all lend support to the tradition that the Soviet economy has proved itself highly adaptable to war. However, this tradition amounts to a crude oversimplification, to the extent that it only considers the ability to build up a military–economic potential, and does not consider the problem of how to realise this potential when war breaks out. This problem arises from the 'insoluble dilemma' discussed above, which tends to inhibit any attempt to realise the economy's full potential for war in advance of war itself. Instead the country must possess the ability to realise its military–economic potential, if necessary, under conditions of active warfare.

Why should the realisation of military–economic potential in wartime be difficult? 'Everything is very simple in War,' writes Clausewitz, 'but the simplest thing is very difficult. These difficulties accumulate and produce a friction which no man can imagine who has not seen War.'[10] Modern weapons place a high premium upon military concepts such as surprise and preemption of the adversary's potential for waging war, not only by destroying it piecemeal but by disrupting it on a systemic scale. The frictions induced by these means may prevent the economy's potential for war from ever being realised. Each combatant has to struggle against such frictions while seeking to induce them in the enemy. How may the frictions of war be overcome? The only 'oil', we find, is 'the habituation of an Army to War' – the creation of systems of habit, conditioning and ingrained responses to the emergencies of war.[11] Here too is an insoluble dilemma. Such systems can only be based on the experience of war itself; but survival in war may depend upon having such systems available for operation at the moment when war breaks out.

In summary, the ability of an economy to adapt to war depends upon two aspects. One is its military–economic potential, and the other is its ability to realise this potential under wartime conditions. The aspects of the Soviet economy of the thirties which are traditionally emphasised to show its adaptability to war are relevant to the Soviet military–economic potential. But there was no policy of aiming to realise fully this potential by a particular peacetime date, and civilian goals and constraints continued to limit the current production of arms. How quickly could the potential be realised under conditions of warfare? Soviet leaders had communicated their objective of a broad military–industrial build-up, but this did not guarantee that the timing of investments and rate of accumulation of weapons would prove justified after the event. A war potential aimed too far into the future might take too long to mobilise if war came soon. Military discipline had been imposed on many areas of civilian life, enabling belt-tightening forms of mobilisation for 'armament in depth', but authoritarian centralisation did not guarantee that those in the economic front line would be able to adapt to war, or that those at the centre would be able to tell them how best to do so. The arms infrastructure of basic and engineering industries had been built up, but Hitler planned to deny the Soviet government the time to bring them to bear upon the balance of forces.

Some aspects of Soviet 'armament in depth' were designed as direct investments in the economy's potential for manoeuvre, to purchase time and space in the event of war. They were directed towards building up the Soviet military–economic potential for the short run. This involved policies for the dispersal of strategic industries, for import self-sufficiency in strategic materials and for the creation of strategic reserves. Here there were both achievements and problems, which can be looked at in some detail.

The importance of dispersing industries with defence significance arose from their concentration in the Western USSR, especially in the border regions most vulnerable to attack from the west and south. While the Eastern USSR was not immune to border threats, vast stretches of the country's interior (especially the Ural region and Western Siberia) represented a secure base for mineral extraction and processing and manufacture. It was recognised that modern war creates the necessity of regional despecialisation and of building semi-autonomous regional complexes of heavy and defence industries with their own fuel and metallurgical bases.[12] During the thirties

Table 3. *The east–west balance of iron and steelmaking 1928–40*

	Share of the Eastern USSR in production levels (%)		Share of the Eastern USSR in the increase in production (%)
	1928 (i)	1940[a] (ii)	1928–40 (iii)
Iron ore	18.0	28.8	31.6
Pig iron	21.4	28.9[b]	31.0
Crude steel	23.6	32.3[b]	34.8
Rolled steel	25.7	28.0[b]	28.8

[a] For other heavy industries, corresponding figures for 1940 shares of the Eastern USSR in production levels were: coal 35.9 per cent, oil 11.6 per cent, electricity 22.1 per cent, metal-cutting machine tools 7.1 per cent.

[b] In a previous estimate Clark, 1956, p. 231 shows each of these shares peaking in the mid-thirties at slightly above their 1940 levels. Clark's data for 1928 and 1939 (his final year) are close to those given in the table except for crude steel, where his 1939 figure is over three points below Kravchenko's 1940 figure.

Sources: (i) and (ii) from G. S. Kravchenko, 1970, p. 59 and IVMV, v. 3, 1974, p. 380; (iii) calculated from (i) and (ii) and from Appendix 2.

much effort went into duplicating the industries of the vulnerable south and west with new coal basins (the Kuzbass and Karaganda fields), new metallurgical and engineering centres (Magnitogorsk and Novo-Tagil),[13] and new oilfields (the 'second Baku' in the east).

These projects proved costly and time-consuming. Table 3 shows the changing balance between the Western and Eastern USSR in iron and steelmaking and other heavy industries. There was some dispersal of ferrous metallurgy towards the east. Much of this dispersal occurred in the early thirties; for each branch of the industry the share of the Eastern regions was probably lower in 1940 than in mid-decade. The 1928 weight of Western iron and steelmaking was very large, the growth of all-Union production between 1928 and 1940 was also very large, and the Western areas accounted for two-thirds or more of the incremental output. Moreover in 1940 the Eastern shares of electricity generated and especially of toolmaking output lagged far behind the creation of new coal and metallurgical bases in the east.

In theory the opportunity to disperse capacity was greatest in the industries where new capacity was being created most rapidly, but in

Table 4. *The regional balance of defence industry plant in mid-1941*

	Per cent of industrial enterprises located in		
	Western USSR, of which		Eastern USSR
	As a whole (i)	Future war zones (ii)	(iii)
Aircraft industry	93	85	7
Tank industry	74	—	26
Armament industry	82	60	18
Ammunition industry	66	—	34[a]

[a] Kravchenko lists this figure along with the others in column (iii) which originate from the first source given; he describes them as percentages of production. But if this figure is comparable with the others, then it too must be a percentage of the number of enterprises in the industry.

Sources: (i) by subtraction from (iii), given in IVOVSS, v. 2, 1961, p. 498 except for the ammunition industry figure given by G. S. Kravchenko, 1970, p. 122; (ii) from Cooper, 1976, pp. 11, 18.

the last prewar years new developments in these industries were concentrated heavily in the Western USSR. This applied most of all to specialised steelmaking and the arms industries. In 1938 two-thirds of the structural steel used for building new ferrous metallurgical capacity, and almost 80 per cent of that used in the arms industries, was invested just in the central, southern and northwestern regions of the European part of the country. In the same year 95 per cent of blast-furnace smelted alloy steel (mainly ferrosilicon and ferromanganese) and the greater part of electrically smelted alloys were being produced in these vulnerable areas.[14] Many unique processes, and 70 to 75 per cent of heavy steel rolling capacity, were to be found in the southern region alone.[15]

Regional imbalance was especially marked in the arms industries. Table 4 shows that aircraft, tank and armament plants were heavily concentrated in the Western USSR and, in the case of aircraft and armament, most were in areas subject to German invasion. Tank-building plants, too, were concentrated in Leningrad, Podol'sk, Khar'kov and other western locations.[16] Tank armour and alloys and much narrow-diameter and virtually all wide-diameter specialised tubing required for both armament and aeroengine manufacture were concentrated in the south and centre of the Western USSR.[17]

Why were the results of policies for industrial dispersal not more impressive? Undoubtedly investment in already industrialised areas would have produced more rapid returns than in undeveloped regions. To this extent, pressure for quick results made any diffusion of industrial capacity into the interior of the country very difficult. Where pressure for quick results prevailed over more long-term objectives of regional development, entrenched bureaucratic interests may have tipped the balance, as a Soviet historian suggests.[18] Certainly such pressure had become very strong by the late thirties, just as the need for protection of the economy against an invasion from the west had become apparent.

Similar unevenness characterised other aspects of investment in economic flexibility, aimed at securing import self-sufficiency in strategic materials and the creation of strategic reserves. Independence of foreign suppliers had never been a problem where fuel supplies and energy sources were concerned. Soviet self-sufficiency in the main categories of high-grade steel had been won by the mid-thirties.[19] In the case of rubber and of nonferrous metals, industrialisation and rearmament meant a constant struggle between investments in programmes to extract or synthesise these materials from domestic sources, and rapidly rising consumption needs.[20] The period from 1938 to 1940 saw a special drive to expand home production and reserves of strategic commodities; something of a climax was reached in 1940 with a rather mixed assessment in January of the nonferrous metals balance,[21] the initiation in March of a number of economy measures,[22] and the initiation in December 1940 and January 1941 of new projects for exploration and mining.[23]

Strategic materials were intensively stockpiled in the eighteen months before the war. In January 1940 the Politburo issued a demand for a big increase in mobilisation stocks and in August approved a plan for reserves of metals, petrochemicals and foodstuffs. During 1939 and 1940 the rate of growth of these reserves was clearly rapid, resulting in at least a doubling of stocks for the main metals categories.[24] The rouble value of all strategic reserves almost doubled just in the eighteen months from January 1940 to the outbreak of war.[25] However, the absolute level of stocks achieved was not very great. As of January 1941 they amounted to four to six months' military wartime consumption of subsistence and fodder; measured against national peacetime utilisation the reserve of petrochemicals would last eighteen days, that of pig iron four days and that of rolled steel six days.[26] After another Central Committee resolution in mid-January 1941 more stockpiling took place, but the 1941 plan for reserve accumulation was adopted only in June.[27] A relevant aspect of policy for strategic reserves was a discussion which took place in 1940 on their location. The proposition of the General Staff was to store them safely behind the Volga. The view of the Red Army general political administration chief, General L. Z. Mekhlis, was that this was military defeatism; the stocks should be held close to the Soviet frontiers. Mekhlis's view, being shared by Stalin, was eventually adopted as the basis of policy.[28]

These measures of investment in the economy's flexibility undoubtedly enhanced its short-run military–economic potential. With all their shortcomings, they helped to increase the time and space available to economic agents at all levels for bringing about full conversion to a war footing, once war had broken out. By themselves, however, these measures did not guarantee that the conversion would actually be brought about and the potential for war realised. Again we return to the question of what Soviet leaders could do to map out in advance a system for ensuring that reserves of capacity and materials would indeed be brought into play at the proper time.

By looking at prewar Soviet contingency plans for economic mobilisation and the operation of mobilisation plans in the first months of the war, we can begin to answer this question. We can also learn a great deal about the adaptability of Stalinist economic planning to war and its resistance or vulnerability to disruptive change.

CONTINGENCY PLANNING FOR WAR

Prewar Soviet contingency plans stemmed from a general belief in the likelihood of a large-scale European conflict, and from particular beliefs about the likelihood of Soviet involvement and the character which this might assume. The general belief was associated with the build-up of a military–economic potential side by side with rapid industrialisation. More detailed contingencies were also envisaged, and were reflected in plans for converting industry to a war footing. These plans were the object of widespread activity in the late thirties against a background of growing concern. There were two immediate sources of anxiety. One was the rising military tension, not only to the west but also in the Far East. The other was the slowdown in Soviet industrial growth, which made it more difficult to create new arms capacity or to expand and modernise existing defence plants. The result was to heighten interest in the conversion possibilities of civilian industry and to focus attention on the adequacy of contingency plans for economic mobilisation.

The most basic area of contingency planning was in the industrial enterprise. Large-scale plants had contingency plans for wartime mobilisation and, in the case of civilian plants, for conversion to arms manufacture. For example tankbuilding was to be the wartime role of tractor building and motor manufacturing enterprises and of shipbuilding and boilermaking operations. The engineering industry as a whole was designated for conversion to armament and ammunition production.[29] Contingency plans evidently paid attention not only to what the enterprise would produce in wartime, but also to the technological, material and skill requirements, implying previous acquaintance of the workforce with unfamiliar tasks, study of the modification requirements of specialised machinery and instruments, and laying in reserves of materials and components. We shall find that in practice the compilation of contingency plans was closely linked to the course of actual prewar mobilisation of industry for defence production and conversion of civilian industry. We shall also find contingency plans being drawn up, or perhaps plant contingency plans coordinated, at higher levels of the economic apparatus – in the industrial branch and sub-branch, and in the municipality. Here too contingency plans ran together with current mobilisation and conversion work; in fact the distinction between them was more blurred than at plant level. For those administering the economy as a whole, the distinction between contingency plans and operational plans disappeared, and economy-wide plans for realising military–economic potential in the event of war did not apparently exist independently of the long-term, perspective and current plans compiled by Gosplan.

Who was responsible for contingency planning? Until 1937 this was the function of the war mobilisation administration of the heavy industry commissariat (and before 1932 of VSNKh). However, the process of breaking up the heavy industry commissariat, which began in December 1936, meant that unified control over contingency plans could no longer be operated from an industry level. On 30 April 1938 a military–industrial commission was set up under the Sovnarkom Defence Committee. This had responsibility for mobilisation readiness of the defence industries and of industry in general, and for prompt fulfilment of defence contracts throughout industry.[30] Shifting responsibility from an industrial administration to a government commission may have opened up something of a gap between those in charge of policy and those charged with implementing it in the industrial enterprise, because it was followed in fifteen months by a change in the opposite direction. On 15 July 1939 a Sovnarkom 'Statute on military representatives of the People's Commissariat of Defence in industry' appointed defence representatives to major plants with responsibility for developing plant mobilisation plans and checking fulfilment of defence contracts.[31] The defence representatives administered special workshops for development of work with defence significance, and had the right 'to reorganise equipment and disrupt normal work in the main shops of the factory'.[32]

Following these reorganisations the pace of contingency planning was accelerated. In September 1939, as war flared in the west, an 'experimental partial mobilisation of industry' was held, revealing 'a number of defects'; 'energetic measures' were taken to eliminate them.[33] Conversion planning was stepped up again in 1940, after the Finnish war. In Moscow, already one of the main centres of arms manufacture, conversion planning at city level was thoroughly reviewed following the Politburo's March discussion of the lessons of the Finnish campaign. The review was carried out through the agencies of the city soviet, the city party committee and the arms industry commissariats. It involved checking current conversion to defence work, including work subcontracted to civilian plants, designating more local enterprises for immediate conversion to arms manufacture, and going over contingency plans for wartime mobilisation.[34]

At the industrial branch level, contingency plans were still being elaborated in the last months of peace. The ammunition industry provides a rare example of the planning process. The military contingency plan for ammunition, indicating likely wartime requirements, was revised by the General Staff in March 1941. The plan was despatched to the Sovnarkom Defence Committee with an accompanying memorandum on the serious shortage of ammunition, and both plan and memorandum were passed on to the defence and ammunition commissariats for comment. According to Marshal G. K. Zhukov, Voznesensky regarded the stated military requirement for 1941 as inflated, and persuaded Stalin that it need be met by only 20 per cent. At first Stalin agreed with Voznesensky, but then he changed his mind after receiving further reports, and he eventually agreed that ammunition production should be stepped up in the second half of 1941 and in 1942.[35] An eighteen-month mobilisation plan resulted.[36] This was both more and less than an industry-level contingency plan. In its final form, approved on 6 June 1941, it was in part an operational plan for accelerated production through conversion of designated civilian engineering enterprises to ammunition manufacture. For the rest it fell short of the requirements of a real industrial contingency plan; it issued instructions to enterprises to draw up plant-level contingency plans for wartime conversion, to work out the technological requirements of a transfer to ammunition production using existing equipment, and on this basis to prepare necessary tools and instruments and stockpile materials and semi-finished products.[37]

Both for the plant and for the industrial branch the process of contingency planning for wartime mobilisation of the military–economic potential was closely bound up with the creation of the potential itself. Contingency plans influenced the character of the industrialisation and rearmament drives through measures to build flexibility into the industrial structure. These measures involved the creation of reserves of specialised capacity in the arms industries, and the widespread subcontracting of defence orders to civilian industry in order to foster its ability to switch specialisations.[38]

Creation of a reserve of specialised arms capacity was successfully pursued in the tankbuilding and armament industries. For example about 1,500 modernised (KV and T-34) tanks were built in the first half of 1941 but the two largest existing tankbuilding plants had the capacity to produce at nearly double this rate.[39] Reserve capacity in a number of sectors was fostered by creating 'shadow' factories in the Urals. Reserves of engineering capacity in general,[40] and of artillery manufacturing capacity in particular,[41] were formed in this way. A contrast is provided by the ammunition industry, however, which was jammed up against capacity limits in the prewar period.[42] Explosives were a special problem. The question of how to relax these constraints received special attention in the prewar years. A 1939 mobilisation plan proposed not only building or rebuilding 56 specialised plants but also subcontracting work to 235 others, half of which had no experience of ammunition technology.[43] Continuing difficulties with the industry's limited capacity culminated in the June 1941 plan to convert and mobilise new plant. By the outbreak of war ammunition production relied on 382 suppliers outside the industry, amounting to about two-thirds of all plants involved.[44] Even so the industry had little in reserve when war broke out.

Subcontracting of defence orders to civilian industry was important not only for ammunition production but also for tankbuilding.[45] Typically components, sub-assemblies and repair facilities would be subcontracted; in tankbuilding even assembly of the finished product took place in civilian plant.[46] Spreading defence orders around civilian industry created a large number of 'part-time' defence plants whose main contribution remained to the civilian economy, but which had acquired a foretaste of what would be involved in a real war from the point of view of production. Aircraft and artillery manufacture alone remained 'relatively free of civilian ties',[47] and in the case of the aircraft industry it was mainly because most potential subcontractors were wholly integrated into the industry in 1940.[48] Outside the specialised business of arms manufacture, dispersal of defence-related orders was also used to stimulate partial conversion. Most Soviet metallurgical centres were obliged to start up production of some kinds of special steels (mainly alloy steels, high-grade tubing and sheet metal for arms manufacture) to prepare them for wartime tasks. Actual conversion, which remained far below the limits achieved in wartime, was most visible in expanded high-grade rolling capacity; increased output of high-grade rolled steel was almost entirely at the expense of steelmaking for civilian purposes between 1938 and 1941.[49]

The practice of dispersing defence orders through civilian industry had a significance far beyond the increases in arms production achieved in this way. In fact from the point of view of immediate satisfaction of the needs of the armed forces, the significance was probably negative, because civilian subcontractors had constant difficulties in matching up to the level and rate of change of military technology. Civilian output was disrupted too. The benefit lay in habituating the workforce of wide sectors of civilian industry to the requirements of wartime conversion, and of stimulating the adaptation of military technology to the limits achievable within civilian mass production, without incurring prematurely the huge costs of full conversion to defence specialisations throughout civilian industry.[50] Thus at limited cost to the volume and quality of current output, civilian industry could acquire the foundations of practical experience to underpin its contingency plans for full conversion in wartime.

Was there contingency planning for wartime conversion of the economy as a whole, taking an economy-wide perspective on the violent changes in balances of inputs and outputs and in industrial and regional structure which might be required? It has been suggested that input–output analysis is ideally suited to mapping out in advance the feasibility and implications of the large, rapid shifts in final demand associated with a war production programme.[51] As is well known, Soviet planning techniques are distinguished from input–output analysis by their lack of completeness, consistency and simultaneity and also, it should be added, by their flexibility. Nonetheless they are close enough in principle for one to look for evidence of macroeconomic contingency planning, in the sense of the modification and updating of hypothetical variants of operational economy-wide plans for the contingency of war.

Evidence on this point is indirect, unrevealing and tainted with hindsight. The fact is that an economy-wide mobilisation plan for the third quarter of 1941 was indeed approved by the Central Committee and the Sovnarkom on 30 June 1941, on the ninth day of the German invasion. Its central features were an increase of a quarter in arms production compared with the peacetime plan for the same period, and a curtailment or abandonment of other plans to make room for this shift (see p. 86 below). Some Soviet historians indicate that this first wartime economic plan was based on preparatory work carried out in peacetime against the contingency of war.[52] Since we cannot compare the texts of the peacetime and wartime plans for the third quarter of 1941, nor the wartime plan with the peacetime preparatory work on which it is said to have been based, we are in no position to judge the character of the peacetime preparations. There are two alternative interpretations. One is that to have compiled a wartime plan in a week implies very considerable detailed preparatory work. The other is that the wartime plan was a hasty, schematic document composed of marginal variations in the peacetime plan (abandoning plans altogether where the changes looked more than marginal), and the peacetime preparatory work involved was correspondingly vacuous. A personal opinion is that the second interpretation is more plausible.

Absence of detailed economy-wide contingency plans for wartime mobilisation could be explained by both strategic and political considerations. The study of strategy suggests that, when war breaks out, preceding attempts to foresee the required responses in a highly

The coming of war: plans and realities in 1941

detailed, comprehensive way may turn out to be useless or even harmful. Their motive may be to overcome the frictions of war, speed up adaptation to wartime conditions and eliminate waste from the adaptive process, but the effects may be the opposite. First, even small changes in the strategic environment may render very detailed plans completely worthless. Secondly, excessive tautness induced in a comprehensive, centralised plan which does not permit independent initiatives at lower levels in response to rapidly changing circumstances may prevent necessary adaptations and actually multiply the frictions at work.[53] There is good reason, therefore, to restrict very detailed contingency planning to lower levels of economic decision making, leaving the higher levels the task of establishing a broad frame-work of strategic expectations within which contingency plans may be drawn up at lower levels, and of ensuring that the economy as a whole possesses the necessary flexibility for its basic units to carry out these plans under conditions not wholly foreseeable in advance. Here, securing the economy's freedom of manoeuvre means building up the aspects of short-run military–economic potential which we considered above (dispersal of strategic industries, self-sufficiency in strategic materials, creation of strategic reserves).

Examining the prewar Soviet context suggests strongly that political, not strategic, considerations prevented the compilation of detailed economy-wide contingency plans for wartime conversion. The strategic argument against such plans is that they did not take friction into account and were likely to multiply it. Soviet military–economic authorities did not recognise friction as an impediment to mobilisation of a planned socialist economy, or they regarded authoritarian planning as a sufficient means of eliminating it. They tended to stress the Soviet capacity for rapid wartime mobilisation based on plans, patriotism and lack of internal class contradictions which might slow down a capitalist war effort.[54] Therefore the fear of compounding wartime frictions was not their reason for avoiding detailed previous consideration of the economic weight of a protracted war. Their real reason was that it was politically out of the question to give serious consideration either to modelling the hypothetical impact of such a war in economy-wide terms, or to formation of a realistic framework of strategic expectations within which lower-level contingency plans would be compiled. Why was this so?

Prewar contingency plans, both military and economic, were powerfully influenced by political frictions and inertias. These had the effect of preventing the normal contemplation of hypothetical worst cases; the most dangerous contingency facing the Soviet Union – a protracted war involving defence in depth – was not allowed to be stated. Real fears were at work. Compiling plans for this worst case meant planning to fall back from Soviet frontiers in the face of the invader, accepting substantial losses of territory, population and assets before the nation's full potential could be brought to bear upon the war. Such plans might make war more likely by encouraging defeatism at home and inviting foreign enemies to regard Soviet border regions as easy meat. Such fears should not have been decisive, but were exploited and given compelling weight by the Red Army purge of 1937. During this purge existing military contingency plans for the event of a German invasion, ordering Soviet forces to fall back from frontier defence in order to execute a defence in depth, were denounced as the work of defeatists and provocateurs in enemy pay.[55] From then on concepts of mass frontier defence and of immediately carrying a counteroffensive onto the enemy's territory governed military planning for war and even the first wartime military orders.[56]

The situation to which this gave rise in the military field can be summed up as follows. Soviet leaders thought that their military posture had a high deterrent value. Their numerically very substantial forces were trained and deployed for offensive operations. However, the real combat value of these forces was much lower than this would suggest. The speed of rearmament and the desire to deploy very large forces as rapidly as possible meant that quality had been sacrificed to quantity. Modern equipment had entered service side by side with obsolete weaponry which had not been retired. Troops were inadequately equipped and trained in the use of modern weapons. The emphasis on offensive operations resulting in rapid victory did not provide a basis for reorganisation and reequipment of Soviet forces under circumstances not envisaged. This emphasis was associated with an underestimate of likely loss rates in combat, and consequently of the likely economic weight of a war effort.[57]

None of this would have mattered had Soviet military preparations been sufficient to avert war altogether. However, had they been sufficient to postpone war until 1942, giving the Soviets more time to complete their existing plans for military reorganisation and deployment, they would still have proved unsuited to the real conditions of war with Germany. German military success in June 1941 was aided greatly by Soviet unreadiness, complacency and concession of strategic surprise to the aggressor. But even without these on their side, the impact of German arms would still have cost the Soviet defenders far more dearly than Soviet prewar plans imagined, as German successes in 1942 and 1943 would continue to demonstrate.[58]

Soviet military miscalculations were mirrored by mistakes in the economic field. Military–economic authorities simultaneously underestimated the likely demands of a defensive war fought out in the depth of the Soviet homeland, and overestimated the capacity of the existing balance of the economy to respond to them. In February 1941 Voznesensky told the Eighteenth Party Conference that 'if you want to be prepared for any "surprises", if you do not want our people to be caught unawares', the thing was to 'keep your powder dry, and do not stint means for the production of aircraft, tanks, armaments, warships and shells'.[59] But in March he was persuading Stalin that military demands for ammunition should not, or could not, be met (see p. 56 above). Meanwhile others were describing to the Soviet people the rebuff which would be speedily delivered to enemy invaders and the unlimited mobilisation potential of the Soviet economic system.[60]

In consequence the central authorities failed to create some necessary conditions for effective economic contingency planning at lower levels. Earlier I defined these necessary conditions to include establishment of a realistic framework of strategic expectations and creation of degrees of flexibility in the economy as a whole within which lower-level units could compile, implement and if necessary adapt industrial branch and plant contingency plans. In fact policies for dispersing industries, for developing alternative resource and energy bases in the interior of the country, and for accumulating strategic reserves were not pursued with consistent vigour. At the same time incorrect beliefs about the strategic environment encouraged high-level complacency about the economy-wide dimensions of the coming conflict, and induced gaps and distortions in contingency plans at lower levels. Industries in potential combat zones which were tied to immovable resources (such as oil) lacked defensive preparations.[61] More mobile industries lacked evacuation plans – a Soviet historian compares this omission unfavourably with detailed German contingency plans for plant evacuation which were drawn up despite the fact that Germany did not expect to suffer invasion herself.[62] The substance of lower-level contingency plans was distorted too. A postwar defector, formerly an official of the steel tubes administration of the commissariat for the iron and steel industry, recalled that

> In the years of work in administrative positions in industry, I was often present and participating when secret mobilization plans were worked out. We took into consideration all sorts of needs – nonferrous metals, oil, coal, machinery, manpower – and the problems of their storage and transport ... But the planning was concerned expressly and solely with offensive operations. They were tied to the assumption, often repeated by Stalin and therefore beyond challenge, that the war would be fought on foreign soil.
> Faced with a defensive war of immense weight, we were helpless. We had to improvise everything from scratch ...[63]

In summary, powerful frictions inhibited the adaptation of Soviet planning to the needs of war before the war broke out. Contingency planning did take place. It was stimulated from above, and took detailed form mainly at the plant, municipal and industrial branch levels. It may be argued that, in conditions of strategic uncertainty, these were the essential levels at which to plan for the surprises and disruptions inherent in the coming war. It was these levels which would demand the critical human response, the motivated reflexes that would keep the economic system operating, warding off shock, paralysis and disintegration. At the same time such lower-level planning does not take place in a vacuum, isolated from the strategic expectations of central agencies. At the highest levels the expectation of war was continually displaced into the future, and the character which it would assume was not understood.

In his memoirs the wartime aircraft industry commissar A. I. Shakhurin describes the atmosphere of a meeting called by Voznesensky at Gosplan on the first morning of the war. Voznesensky, he explains,

> normally a rather serious person, was at that moment especially intense. Indeed we had all been powerfully changed in the course of those few hours of the morning. Knowing that war was inevitable, anticipating it, each [of us] in the depth of his soul had put off the outbreak of war to some future moment of his own choosing ... How much time was still needed by Voznesensky as deputy prime minister and leader of Gosplan is hard for me to say.[64]

In less personal terms an authoritative work states:

> In general, accomplishment of the most important plans of economic mobilisation was reckoned on more distant time horizons than those which the developing situation permitted to the land of the Soviets.[65]

The coming of war: plans and realities in 1941

However, even if more time had been available, the most devastating consequences of war would still not have been averted.

PART TWO: THE GERMAN INVASION

THE IMPACT OF WAR: THE EVACUATION PROCESS

German forces invaded the Soviet Union in the early hours of Sunday, 22 June 1941. They advanced rapidly along a front which stretched from the Baltic to the Black Sea, fanning out through the Polish and Baltic territories into the Ukraine and Russia itself. By the end of September Leningrad was besieged, most of the Ukraine occupied, and Moscow itself directly threatened. Through the autumn and winter battles raged along this front.

Table 5 shows that by November 1941 German forces had occupied Soviet territories accounting for two-fifths of the prewar population and the bulk (in some cases the overwhelming bulk) of capacity in a number of key industrial sectors and farming operations. These impressive figures do not provide an unambiguous estimate of the economic impact of the German invasion. First, they are selective and omit a number of less affected branches, the most important in 1941 being the oil industry. Nor do they include arms industries, for which comparable figures can be obtained from Table 4 (p. 51 above). Secondly, they exaggerate ultimate losses because some of the population and assets involved would be saved through evacuation and relocation in the interior of the country. Thirdly, however, they do not imply that the capacity originally located on territories remaining in Soviet hands was immediately available to fight the Germans – some of it was being evacuated as a precautionary measure or was otherwise deprived of normal conditions of operation, and some had first to be brought to bear upon the tasks of evacuation, relocation and conversion to war production. Only after this was capacity available for the war economy itself.

The sudden need to evacuate millions of people and thousands of economic installations from the west and south of the USSR was the greatest unforeseen emergency of the war. The emergency had two dimensions which inevitably became mixed up with each other – the displacement of the civil population and the threat to the productive forces which were the simultaneous results of invasion.

Table 5. *Per cent shares of Soviet population and productive capacity located in territories lost to German occupation up to November 1941*

Population	40	Rolled steel	57
		Electricity	42
Coke	74	Railway lines	41
Iron ore	71		
Pig iron	68	Sugar	87
Coal	63	Pig herds	60
Aluminium	60	Cattle herds	38
Crude steel	58	Grains	38

Sources: Voznesensky, pp. 36–7; G. S. Kravchenko, 1970, pp. 123–4.

Previous victims of the German blitzkrieg (especially France and Poland) had encountered evacuation primarily in terms of a refugee problem – the need to lend purpose and direction to the flight of the civilian population from bombardment. The need arose from considerations of both military and social policy. A populace suddenly deprived of its customary conditions of existence, faced with the most deadly threat imaginable at the time, finding no leadership or protection from its own government, inevitably bred disaffection. Masses of people on the move, shorn of ties and loyalties, flowing uncontrollably along highways, railway tracks and river banks, clogged the circulation of troops, sapped morale and hindered military operations. This problem faced the Soviet government in the early weeks of the war, although it was alleviated by the very speed of the German advance coupled with the inability and even unwillingness of a certain part of the population to take flight.

However, in Soviet practice and administration the refugee aspect was coupled from the start with the other aspect, the German threat to Soviet industries. The directive of the Sovnarkom and Central Committee of 29 June 1941 ('To party and Soviet organisations of frontline districts'),[66] the terms of which were repeated by Stalin in his radio broadcast of 3 July,[67] addressed this problem in terms of a strategy of denial – the need to deny resources to the enemy through a policy of removal of assets where possible in the face of the invading forces, and destruction of what had to be abandoned. These addresses to the Soviet people were certainly of historic importance, although to see them as containing 'a general programme of conversion of the economy and creation within a short period of a coherent, rapidly

The coming of war: plans and realities in 1941

growing war economy' is perhaps to read into them more than was there.[68] Side by side with the formulation of the strategy of denial, however, first steps had already been taken towards a more ambitious strategy. This broader strategy included the element of denial, but extended to a more positive goal – the relocation of evacuated plant, including assets, workforce and management of the enterprise, in new military–industrial production complexes in the interior of the country. This new goal was first expressed in a GKO resolution of 4 July ordering Voznesensky to compile 'a wartime economic plan of provision for defence of the country, taking into account utilisation of existing resources and enterprises on the Volga, in Western Siberia and the Urals, and also resources and enterprises removed to the indicated regions in the course of evacuation'.[69]

To some extent the solutions to the refugee problem and to the industrial evacuation became complementary. Where workers were to be evacuated with their enterprises, the refugee problem was reduced to one of workers' dependents. Workers would stick together as production collectives more willingly when they knew that their families were being incorporated into an organised refugee flow along known lines to known destinations. In fact in the first weeks of the evacuation both the refugee problem and the industrial evacuation were dealt with from under a single administrative roof, but after three months they were separated into two distinct agencies.

Although these two aspects of the evacuation were so closely linked, it is fair to say that in practice the evacuation and relocation of the productive forces were at the focus of attention and even took priority over the evacuation of refugees. The evacuation of enterprises was given organisational form at an earlier stage, and was led from a higher level in the party–state apparatus. It was set in motion on the third day of the war, 24 June, when (according to a recent account) Stalin put before the Politburo a proposition for evacuation of the southern tank armour rolling mills;[70] on the same day a decision of the Central Committee and Sovnarkom established a Council for Evacuation. This was the first measure of wartime state reorganisation, preceding even the formation of a war cabinet by several days. It was followed on 27 June by the first general policy resolution of the Sovnarkom and Central Committee, 'On the order of removal and relocation of groups of people and valuable property'.[71]

The Evacuation Council's first chairman was transport commissar L. M. Kaganovich, and initially his deputies were deputy prime minister A. N. Kosygin and the trade union chief N. M. Shvernik. On 26 June another deputy prime minister, A. I. Mikoyan, was added to the Council as first deputy chairman, and M. G. Pervukhin became another deputy chairman on 1 July.[72] Soviet histories usually do not mention the brief reign of Kaganovich on the Evacuation Council; having set the machinery up, he was replaced as chairman on 16 July by the lesser figure of Shvernik.[73] (Kaganovich left the Evacuation Council, but remained transport commissar for the time being.)

The Council established a central apparatus of eighty to eighty-five workers drawn from the Sovnarkom, Gosplan, the trade unions and the commissariats. Eventually they formed three teams. One was responsible for the movement of productive forces: the evacuation of enterprises and employees from threatened areas and their relocation. A second team was responsible for the movement of refugees; possibly it was formed after 5 July when the first responsibilities of the Council were widened by a Sovnarkom decree, 'On the order of evacuation of the population in wartime'.[74] The third team was in charge of transport.[75]

On the ground the Council operated through plenipotentiary agents and inspectors. The plenipotentiaries were appointed from 2 July 1941 from within the commissariats (usually a deputy commissar would be picked); each plenipotentiary, assisted by a personal staff of three to five trusted aides, was responsible for establishing evacuation schedules through the collegia and specialist committees of the commissariat concerned. Local party secretaries also served as plenipotentiaries, and local authorities were instructed to set up local evacuation administrations in the interior and at road and rail centres en route from the front line.[76] The first group of plenipotentiaries to be appointed numbered thirty-five but by the end of 1941 there were three thousand of them. Their duties extended to checking trainloads, evacuation points and the condition and numbers of evacuees; they had special powers including the right to stop and unload non-priority railway freight.[77] Meanwhile at the centre the Council also set up an inspectorate headed by Kosygin, which drew its workers from the Sovnarkom, trade unions and middle-level party organisations.[78]

This was the central administrative framework under which the work of evacuation was carried out. During the autumn a few further changes were introduced in response to the rapid advance of the enemy, which continued to take the Soviet authorities by surprise.

Because of the dangerous situation being created in front of Moscow, the city began to evacuate its industries on 10 October.[79] Following a GKO discussion on 14 October Kosygin was appointed to take charge of this work.[80] Fresh German advances, however, were not confined to the Moscow sector but were taking place along the length of the central and southern fronts. On 25 October a new Committee for Evacuation was formed under Mikoyan. This committee was charged with evacuation of stocks of producer and consumer goods from the front-line zones, and of equipment belonging to a number of light industries.[81] The new committee apparently worked alongside the Evacuation Council. But by the winter the military situation had stabilised, and the immediate tasks of evacuation were considered complete. Mikoyan's Evacuation Committee was wound up on 19 December,[82] and on 25 December Shvernik's Evacuation Council was dissolved into a Committee for Freight Dispersal chaired by Mikoyan, to sort out the tangle which had been created on the railways.[83]

What were the procedures and priorities established by the Council for Evacuation? One set applied to the refugee evacuation – under the decree of 5 July civilians were subject to organised removal from regions of combat by military order, and from other regions neighbouring the front by order of the Council.[84] The main priority was attached to evacuating children through child-care organisations, and mothers with children. As explained above, it was intended to evacuate many manual workers and staff with their enterprises.[85] Detailed procedures for local authorities to follow in listing and checking the population subject to evacuation, as a basis for centralised control (and information to relatives), were not issued by the Council until early August.[86]

For the industrial evacuation we know the procedures and priorities in more detail. The decision-making procedure operated plant by plant. It is not clear where the initiative necessarily came from in each case – from the local agencies (military, political or economic) or from Moscow. Each case was processed first within the commissariat concerned, which had to forward a request to the Evacuation Council detailing transport requirements and auxiliary services needed for removal of each installation. The Council's staff was responsible for checking each request. Each case would be the subject of a Council resolution stating a schedule of evacuation, transport and relocation. The resolution would then be returned to the appropriate commissariat for action, as well as forwarded to the transport commissariat. The latter had to report daily to the Council on fulfilment of the latter's decisions, and within the commissariat an operations group of twenty-five was created for this purpose.[87] The transport side of the evacuation had to be coordinated with available rolling stock and mobilisation freights moving westward, as well as other urgent needs. From mid-July the transport coordinators operated a ten-day plan period.[88]

To be strictly accurate, this was the picture of evacuation procedures as it was seen in Moscow: all information and decisions were concentrated in the central government apparatus; nothing could be decided on the spot without the authority of a central government plenipotentiary.[89] Evidence will be found, however, suggesting that an unofficial, decentralised evacuation of industry took place side by side with the officially sanctioned movement.

To a large extent the sectoral priorities laid down by the Evacuation Council can only be inferred. To judge from results, the main priorities were attached to installations of the defence, iron and steel, engineering and power industries and agricultural stocks. An order of the Evacuation Council of 7 August 1941 instructed the transport commissariat to allocate railway trucks for evacuation of the right-bank Dnepr at the following daily rates: to the iron and steel industry 3,000 (including 1,500 for ores and metal stocks alone), to the evacuation of grain stocks 1,000 and of civilians 400, to the electricity generating industry 200, to the chemical industry 100, to other commissariats and held in reserve 380.[90] Of some 26,000 trucks (not a full account) used in the industrial evacuation of the Ukraine in the second half of 1941, just over half were allocated to the iron and steel industries, a fifth to the aircraft and armament industries, smaller but still significant proportions to power, chemicals and engineering sectors, and just over 3 per cent to all the light and food industries together.[91] On a national scale, by 20 November 1941 914,000 truckloads had been utilised in the evacuation of industry; according to incomplete data of the transport commissariat, the biggest claimants could be listed in descending order as the aircraft, iron and steel, ammunition, armament, tankbuilding and heavy engineering industries.[92]

Early top-level instructions focused on the arms industries and were not restricted to combat zones. Examples are the Politburo proposal of 24 June (formalised on 26 June) 1941 for evacuation of the

The coming of war: plans and realities in 1941

southern tank armour rolling mills, the order of 3 July 1941 for evacuation of twenty-six armament factories from Moscow, Tula and Leningrad to the Volga region and to Siberia, and the order several days later to transfer part of the aircraft industry to Western Siberia.[93]

Within each branch and enterprise priorities for evacuation were laid down as follows: first of all came finished products and equipment not yet installed, basic equipment, raw materials, cables and basic materials; then technical equipment capable of reinstallation in operating plant, power equipment and machine tools; and lastly auxiliary materials, means of transport and other objects.[94] A Sovnarkom directive of 5 July devoted to evacuation of the aircraft industry gave first place to removal of blueprints and technical drawings, and then basic metalworking equipment, with components, assemblies and assembly shops coming afterwards in order.[95]

How well did the evacuation agencies manage the process? The refugee evacuation indicates some main problems. The Belorussian party Central Committee ordered the evacuation of women and children from Minsk on the second day of the war. The Evacuation Council issued similar instructions covering Moscow and Leningrad on 6 and 7 July 1941, and by September such orders covered whole districts as far east as Tula, Orel, Kursk, Lugansk, Khar'kov, the Donets and Rostov on Don, and as far north as Murmansk. However, the appearance of foresight and prompt action is belied by results. Only a few tens of thousands were got out of Lithuania and Estonia. A quarter of a million fled Moldavia, and more than a million Belorussia. By the autumn the movement had found its stride, with 400,000 evacuated from Leningrad and 1.4 million from Moscow (on the famous night of 16–17 October the flow from the city reached 150,000).[96]

The evacuation of Leningrad (prewar population 3.2 million) encountered special problems. It began on local initiative, in advance of the Evacuation Council order just mentioned, with the departure of some 15,000 children on 29 June. It was planned at this time to evacuate 392,000 minors altogether, but only 217,000 had left by 27 August. Of the city's population as a whole, already swelled by refugees from the Baltic republics, 468,000 had left by 10 August, on which date it was planned to evacuate a further 400,000 (shortly raised to 700,000). But by 29 August a further 168,000 only had left.[97]

The next day the city was cut off by rail, and on 8 September the land siege began. Evacuation was halted until November, when heavy frosts allowed the opening of the ice road across Lake Ladoga.

This colossal movement, engulfing millions of people, has sometimes been presented in an idealised light – a train ticket, medical aid, clothing, footwear, subsistence allowances and two hot meals a day at the state's expense.[98] To travel would have been no worse than to arrive. At the point of destination 'This is the way it was,' a postwar satirist wrote, 'the workers arrived in the Urals and immediately were settled in the best cottages; pork chops were immediately placed on their tables; they went at once into warm shops, immediately found specifications, and began at once to "fulfil and overfulfil".'[99]

The contrasting reality was a violent disruption of transport, of civil life in the rear as well as at the front, and of family ties. Some early experiences of launching trainloads of refugees into the interior of the country were utterly disastrous. In June 1941 several refugee trains left the southwestern provinces and travelled as far east as Penza and even Kuibyshev; then railway officialdom caught up with them and swung them back in great loops and zigzags, eventually returning them to the Ukrainian front. Between 8 and 17 July nine passenger trains carrying 8,450 refugees were returned in this way to Khar'kov from the interior of the country.[100] An even worse fate befell many of those first 15,000 children who left Leningrad on 29 June; many were despatched to Pskov and Novgorod, but the railway lines had already been cut by the Germans. Suffering casualties, they returned to Leningrad under enemy fire. From there railway officials despatched them with unaltered instructions, returning them to the front a second time. The fortunate ones eventually reached Kirov and Sverdlovsk, far to the east.[101]

In this process families were separated, trains misrouted and held for days, and passengers deprived of food and water.[102] The dynamic of the process confused the basic distinction between transit points and points of destination. Leaderless trainloads of displaced civilians lacked clear routes and points of resettlement. The reception of refugees too lacked preparation or consultation, and evacuation bases were often short of food, hot water and medical facilities.[103] Big cities were unprepared for the reception and accommodation of thousands of homeless. In four or five months the populations of Kazan and Sverdlovsk both grew by nearly 30 per cent, and that of Kuibyshev by more; each had a prewar population around 400,000.[104] Even so,

The coming of war: plans and realities in 1941 71

cities farther to the east did not make haste to ready themselves. The Omsk city soviet, for example, set up its evacuation department only on 25 November.[105]

Perhaps in recognition of these special problems Pamfilov's team at the Evacuation Council was given the status of a separate administration on 26 September 1941 (it operated until 31 January 1942), and was allocated the staff of the former Resettlement Administration with the additional right to appoint its own plenipotentiary agents.[106] But this did not prevent difficulties building up into serious clashes between Moscow and local authorities, especially in the southeast. By the autumn of 1941 the faraway port of Makhachkala on the western shore of the Caspian sea was choked with refugees whom the local authorities could not accommodate nor absorb into the surrounding villages of Dagestan nor disperse across the Caspian into Central Asia. Not until November did the central authorities (in the person of Kosygin) intervene with water transport.[107] Meanwhile another conflict was developing in the southeastern direction in the city of Stalingrad. This city (prewar population 445,000) began to receive refugees in July 1941; by November the daily inflow had reached between 8,000 and 15,000. In nine months the city received 441,000 homeless citizens, doubling its initial population. The city defence committee, formed on 23 October, made dispersal of refugees its first priority, but was prevented from acting by Moscow until December; only then was the first contingent of 50,000 despatched to the countryside beyond the Don. By then many were squatting at the Don and Volga crossings in conditions of the utmost deprivation.[108]

An index of confusion is found in the work of a central enquiry office set up at the end of January 1942. In six months it received 900,000 enquiries concerning the whereabouts of evacuees, and it located 167,000 people (one wonders about the remainder). It answered 400,000 letters and issued papers for 1.9 million people.[109]

There are apparently conflicting estimates of the total number of people evacuated. One source states that by the spring of 1942 7.5 million people had been shifted,[110] while another gives 10 million as the number of people evacuated in this period by rail alone.[111] The figure of 10 million has also been given as the number of railway evacuees through the whole wartime period,[112] while a grand total of 25 million evacuees by all modes of transport has been given for the war as a whole.[113] Such confusion is not surprising, given that large numbers of people evidently evacuated themselves without entering a centrally directed flow within which to be counted properly. A measure of this can be gauged as follows. The Soviet 1940 population is nowadays given as 194.1 million.[114] By November 1941 the Germans had occupied the territory upon which 40 per cent of these people, or 77.6 million, had formerly resided (see Table 5 above), leaving about 116.5 million people free of enemy occupation. Assume that in wartime civilian births and deaths cancelled out, and that by 1942 this population had shared 3 million of the Soviet wartime military casualties. By 1942, then, the remaining Soviet population might have fallen to 113.5 million. But the actual total was still 130 million.[115] The difference – 16.5 million – would be a rough guide to the actual number of refugees who fled from occupied territories in 1941 and remained under Soviet control. Since the officially counted refugees of this phase of the war range from 7.5 to 10 million, we can guess that from 6.5 to 9 million people evacuated themselves unofficially. Taking both categories together, the grand total was still less than one-fifth of the population formerly living in the territories occupied in 1941.

The evacuation and relocation of the productive forces was carried out alongside this human flood. The priorities and procedures laid down were just a starting point, and they did not begin to meet many basic problems of order and timing, which had to be resolved on the spot. Often the decision to dismantle plant was left until the last moment in order to avoid unnecessary losses of current production; sometimes it was left too late, so that equipment and supplies were abandoned to the enemy or intercepted and destroyed in transit.[116] In July and September rolling and blooming mills had been removed from the Azovstal' works at Mariupol', but blast furnaces and hearths were still in operation. The evacuation of Mariupol' was ordered on 5 October, and removal of the remainder of the Azovstal' and the Kuibyshev steelworks and coking plant began the next day, but the Germans entered the town on 8 October, preventing completion of the removal.[117] From the Donbass as a whole between October and December 1941 only seventeen of sixty-four iron and steelworks were successfully evacuated.[118] At one Ukrainian metals store over 200,000 tons of rolled metals, ingots, castings, pipes and alloys were abandoned,[119] a quantity comparable to the entire strategic reserves of 177,000 tons of pig iron or 204,000 tons of rolled steel held at the beginning of 1941.[120] In mid-October German forces on the Ukrainian front turned towards Khar'kov, a centre of the tank

The coming of war: plans and realities in 1941   73

industry standing without natural defences in the middle of open steppes. The tankbuilding works carried on to the last moment; the work of dismantling and evacuation was being completed as German forces burst into the factory.[121]

Timing difficulties were compounded by contradictory instructions from above. A GKO order of 20 July 1941 on evacuation of the aircraft industry obliged commissar A. I. Shakhurin to save his threatened plants 'without violation of the current production flow plan'.[122] An especially complex situation developed in Leningrad, where factories subject to evacuation orders continued to receive urgent directives for defence production; to meet the latter, they had to leave part of their equipment behind in the city.[123] Two thousand truckloads of machinery, including equipment of the Kirov heavy tankbuilding factory, were trapped when the city's last rail link was cut on 30 August. Some had to wait for the winter to be hauled out across Lake Ladoga, while much apparently rotted in the open through the winter; in the administrative confusion no one had the authority to rescind the evacuation orders.[124]

Once there was a commitment to evacuate a region, complex issues of priority still had to be resolved. We have seen how the arms industries, iron and steel plant, and the electricity sector came at the top of the list. Electricity was in sharp deficit in the interior of the country, and generating equipment had to be saved at all costs. Once removed and relocated, it speeded up the reinstallation and restoration of productive capacity in the new industrial centres to the east. But it could not be removed too early from threatened zones, because the dismantling and evacuation of other kinds of plant and equipment themselves required electric power; without electricity other priorities would be sacrificed. For this reason electricity generating equipment was usually left until last.[125] As a result some of it was lost to the enemy although dismantled and rendered unusable – for example the Svir and part of the Dnepr hydroelectric stations.[126]

Special obstacles lay in the path of evacuation of agricultural produce and assets. There was a race against time for the 1941 grain harvest in the western regions, where harvesting work usually peaked in August. This and the next month saw a flow of emergency orders from Moscow,[127] matched by an intensive mobilisation of the local population.[128] But it is not clear how much grain was actually saved – the shortfall in the 1941 harvest compared to 1940 was later revealed to be 41 per cent,[129] but this was even more than the 38 per cent share of prewar Soviet output of the territories occupied in 1941 (see Table 5 above). Since the harvest in the interior was gathered successfully and held to its previous level,[130] little can have been rescued from the path of the invading forces. The fate of the flax harvest is also unclear. On 31 July Gosplan proposed an acceleration of harvesting work and began reporting regularly to the Sovnarkom; proposals were also made for speedy evacuation of flax harvesting and processing equipment to the east and north. But a month later, on 1 September, when the Germans were already in the heart of the flax region, Gosplan was still calling for the harvest to be speeded up,[131] and the eventual harvest was just 38 per cent of the 1940 figure.[132]

In contrast to other aspects of the evacuation, the removal of agricultural assets was organised almost entirely with local operational leadership; livestock and machinery 'travelled under their own momentum'.[133] All healthy livestock was subject to evacuation, but the logistics of fodder, shelter and exertion were far more complex than in the case of machinery. In the Ukraine most horses were transferred directly to Red Army units, and most pigs were slaughtered for meat. At first most cattle and sheep were successfully removed.[134] Through the autumn, however, difficulties of feeding, sheltering and eventually wintering the evacuation herds steadily cut away at the number of surviving animals. By the beginning of 1942 only 2 or 3 per cent of the kolkhoz herds of the occupied territories were still to be found alive in the interior of the country.[135] Most agricultural machinery had simply been abandoned; lack of fuel and parts had prevented its timely arrival at rail points for shipment to the rear, and thousands of pieces were trapped at river crossings.[136]

Once machinery and stocks were in transit, another nightmare began. Rail freight schedules were not only thrown into confusion but were twisted by distorting pressures. The Evacuation Council, concentrating on short-term results, tended to underestimate the limit beyond which installations had to be withdrawn in order to render them safe from further enemy attack. Equipment would be shifted from one part of the Ukraine to another (for example from Kiev to Poltava), where it would sit for a few days while the front approached before being reloaded and evacuated a second time.[137] In contrast, where the decision was influenced by officials of the commissariat whose assets were at stake, intent on securing maximum safety from further attack regardless of cost, assets would be despatched on journeys of extreme length – to Central Asia, Siberia, even the Far

The coming of war: plans and realities in 1941

East. Even consignments of ammunition and armament already designated for troops in the field suffered this fate.[138]

The forces at work were too strong for the railway staff of the transport commissariat to impose order. This does not mean that the railways ground to a halt altogether. A diplomatic observer who recalled their normal peacetime state of muddle considered that 'during the months of conflict the Soviet railway system has continued to function nearly as well as before and certainly better than had been anticipated'.[139] Even the Germans could not make their trains run on time on Soviet territory.[140] All the same, on the Soviet side things were bad enough. Just in July 1941 the evacuation was using almost half the trucks in the country's system.[141] Train despatchers were faced with the task of channelling them from west to east into a thinning and steadily more overloaded network. Unable to impose a coherent programme upon this task, they shuttled loaded trains backwards and forwards and from line to line in thousand-kilometre zigzags and circles far from their destinations, until local railway officials refused to accept them a third or fourth time and demanded intervention of the central authorities.[142]

A particular source of disorganisation, not the fault of the railway officials, was the growing number of loaded trains without documentation showing origin or destination.[143] Here perhaps is evidence of another side to the evacuation process, not revealed by examining only centrally sanctioned and officially recorded measures. Local initiatives, which were decided informally and without recourse to paperwork, probably resulted in trainloads of evacuated assets on a significant scale; these trainloads were not incorporated into central assessments of the situation and from the latter's point of view did not exist.

By the late autumn of 1941 the railway system was grinding to a halt. In November, compared with the preceding May, the average time required for turnover of a truck had risen from six to over sixteen days, while the distance covered in each day had halved (from over 160 to 84 kilometres); loading time and idle standing time had both risen by 70 to 80 per cent.[144] By November 58,000 loaded trucks had piled up on the main lines running to the Ural, Volga and Caucasus regions.[145] These proliferating lags intensified the shortage of empty trucks available for new evacuation trains, and rendered fine timing of evacuation orders pointless; for example, of the 13,000 trucks allocated to the evacuation of the sixty-four iron and steelworks of the

Donbass between October and December (see p. 72 above), only 3,460 could actually be made available.[146] When the situation got out of hand, empty trucks were found by dumping evacuation loads in transit in the interior of the country beside the line. In this way the rolling-stock constraint could be temporarily relaxed, at the cost of much additional labour (unloading and reloading, shunting and recoupling), while postponing the ultimate disposition of loads temporarily set to one side. This dumping was supposed to be restricted to building materials, metals, fuels and equipment which would not suffer damage from exposure.[147] But US embassy staff in Kazan reported quantities of machinery lying around the railway yards, exposed to the elements and believed ruined.[148] In these first months, of 700 evacuated enterprises only 270 reached their destinations on schedule, and a further 110 arrived on time in part only.[149]

The decisive phase of the evacuation of the productive forces was their relocation in the interior of the country. Here centralised direction of transport and allocation of final destinations became essential, but the information had first to be created for relocation to take place. One of the first wartime tasks of TsSU was to organise a census of vacant factory accommodation and other building space in the Eastern regions for the evacuated enterprises – a considerable task for which the statisticians were quite unprepared, but which they accomplished quickly and accurately.[150] The process of accounting for stocks of idle materials and equipment was also set in rapid motion. On 1 August 1941 Gosplan presented its first summary to the Sovnarkom and Evacuation Council of the freight loads removed from the front and now located in Ivanovo, Kostroma, Kirov and other rail centres, along with proposals for disposition of idle stocks of materials and machinery warehoused in various cities.[151]

Local authorities took the initiative before a central plan for the final disposition of evacuated plant was drawn up. In Western Siberia new local planning offices were set up to deal with the reception of evacuated enterprises. The first was formed by the Tomsk town soviet on 22 August 1941; trainloads started to arrive next day,[152] which suggests some lack of preparation. From Moscow's viewpoint the picture of the situation of both front and rear must have remained confused and unstable; not until 9 November 1941 was it possible to issue a central schedule for reinstalling the main arms factories evacuated from the west.[153] It was followed by a Sovnarkom directive of 29 November ordering USSR Gosplan to send many of its central

The coming of war: plans and realities in 1941

staff out into the localities to check the restoration of production of relocated plant.[154] The central authorities continued to suffer from uncertainty regarding assets actually evacuated and in transit; in the spring of 1942 there were more censuses of equipment on the railways and warehoused at intermediate points, and in March and April Gosplan workers were much occupied with allocating unclaimed assets, inviting and vetoing proposals for their use.[155]

The reinstallation of big factories did not proceed smoothly. Problems arose when equipment from a single enterprise was dispersed to several accommodations, or when several independent enterprises were crammed into a single overcrowded plant. Sometimes evacuated equipment was used to rebuild or expand existing plant, especially iron and steel complexes;[156] for example the Magnitogorsk metallurgical combine was allocated part or all of the equipment of thirty-four evacuated enterprises.[157] Often new accommodation was makeshift. Engineering factories were relocated where possible in accommodation designed for related work, but all the same one ended up in a palace of culture, another in a municipal theatre, and more than one in an agricultural MTS.[158] Other essential inputs could less easily be substituted. As a rule not more than 30 or 40 per cent of an evacuated enterprise's workforce succeeded in accompanying it to the interior,[159] most of the remainder being sucked into the army, the volunteer militia or partisan underground.[160] The bulk of the able-bodied population evacuated to the east was quickly absorbed into production or retraining,[161] but skilled working collectives had been scattered and sometimes never caught up with their enterprises. It was claimed later that most evacuated plants had restarted production within six to eight weeks of evacuation,[162] and certainly the first trainload of T-34 tanks left the Khar'kov tractor factory – now in the Ural region – on 8 December 1941.[163] Assembly plants must have been first to restart production. For basic metallurgical plant the process must have been much slower – of ninety-four iron and steelworks evacuated in the second half of 1941, fifty-four were back on stream by mid-1942.[164] At the far end of the spectrum were fifty-five evacuated enterprises which were still idle at the end of 1942 because a workforce could not be found to operate them.[165]

How can one summarise the significance of the evacuation of industry? Soviet historians have created several graphic images with which to describe it. In Belikov's words it was 'a weapon of economic struggle ... a blow struck at the enemy's plans, which aimed to deprive the Soviet army of its war industries'[166] – it was an 'economic Stalingrad' which mattered more than the great victory won later by arms on the banks of the Volga, and indeed it made the latter possible.[167] The human effort of the evacuation certainly justifies this comparison. Over a hundred aircraft factories were evacuated, but the largest of them involved 25,000–30,000 workers, 5,000–10,000 units of equipment and 150,000–200,000 square metres of factory space.[168] In six weeks 320,000 tons of equipment were shifted in 16,000 truckloads from the Ukrainian steel town of Zaporozh'e alone.[169] Nearly a hundred times this number of truckloads were involved in the evacuation as a whole – a million and a half trucks, enough to stretch in a solid line from the Pacific Ocean to the Bay of Biscay.[170]

Was the economic effectiveness of the evacuation in proportion to the effort? In the third quarter of 1941 alone 1,360 large-scale enterprises, mainly of the arms industries, were removed; by the end of the year the total had risen to 1,523 enterprises.[171] Nearly half went to the Urals, the remainder going to the Volga region, Western Siberia, Kazakhstan and Central Asia; a few travelled still further to Eastern Siberia.[172] The number of plants thus saved was rather small in comparison to the 32,000 enterprises of all sizes which, it was later revealed, were knocked out by enemy action during the years of war.[173] Their economic significance, however, was out of all proportion to their number. The assets put on wheels have been valued in a Soviet source at three years' state investments under the first Five Year Plan.[174] According to official estimates, used here for consistency, between 1929 and 1932 the fixed assets of Soviet industry grew by 3.8 billion roubles annually, or 11.4 billion roubles over three years. In comparison, by 1941 the value of all industrial assets was set at 92 billion roubles.[175] This suggests that approximately one-eighth of Soviet industrial assets were evacuated from the enemy's path. Included within this were the bulk of the defence industries and many key metallurgical, chemical and engineering works; their importance to Soviet survival in 1942 and 1943 can hardly be doubted.

Soviet historians of the home front in the initial period of the war invariably present the evacuation of industry as though it followed directly from the first wartime economic mobilisation plan adopted on 30 June 1941, and from the process of planning the eastern war economy which was initiated on 4 July. This version of events was established already in wartime, when it was stated that both the evacuation of industry and its conversion to a war footing had proceeded 'according to a single plan'.[176] Logically one should therefore give first consideration to the plans before considering the evacuation process, since the plans provided the context for the evacuation.

Examination of both plans and evacuation suggests that in reality the situation was the reverse. The evacuation agencies and procedures allowed the evacuation to be regulated from above, but it was not conducted according to an overall plan drawn up in advance.[177] The first proposals for industrial evacuation simply shattered the preconceptions of commissars and plant managers alike about the character of the war which had just begun.[178] Without contingency plans for evacuation drawn up in advance of war, planning of the evacuation had to take place 'literally en route'.[179] Lack of preparation and experience was felt so sharply that in the early days the Evacuation Council's central staff scoured Moscow's libraries and archives for any scrap of information about the evacuations of the First World War.[180] The institutions and knowledge did not exist that would have allowed the compilation of a general scheme for evacuation to follow from the start, even accepting the need to update and modify such a scheme as events unfolded. It was difficult enough just to establish administrative control from day to day.

Economic planning, therefore, took place in the context of the unforeseen need for evacuation. Evacuation provided the context of planning, and the progress of evacuation determined the extent to which early wartime economic plans would be fulfilled. This chapter is organised accordingly, and the plans are considered in the light of the evacuation, not the other way around.

A NOTE ON THE EVACUATION OF 1942

How quickly could the lessons of the 1941 evacuation be absorbed? The answer was: not quickly enough. The chance to find out came in the summer of 1942. Hitler's directive No. 41 of 5 April 1942 ordered the German forces 'to wipe out the entire defence potential remaining to the Soviets, and to cut them off, as far as possible, from their most important centres of industry'.[181] In May the Sixth Wehrmacht Army began its expedition to destroy the Soviet forces on the Don river, to take or destroy Stalingrad and to seize the oil regions of the Caucasus. On 22 June 1942 a new Evacuation Commission was set up, chaired once more by Shvernik (his deputies were Mikoyan and Kosygin).[182] The race against time began again. From the Don and Volga regions 150 enterprises (including 40 large-scale works) and hundreds of thousands of civilians were evacuated.[183] The evacuation of Voronezh district was relatively timely and successful. Of the 23,500 truckloads of equipment designated for removal from Voroshilovgrad district, however, only 8,600 got away by the end of July; the remainder were trapped, along with trainloads of assets and workers from the Donbass.[184] Except for pigs, most farm livestock was successfully evacuated from the regions involved, although as before most failed to survive the following winter; most farm machinery had to be abandoned.[185]

In Stalingrad, a major centre of tank and artillery manufacture, evacuation of the city's industries, workforce and dependent population was actively discussed during the summer. At the same time (according to A. S. Chuyanov, wartime leader of the Stalingrad district party and chairman of the city's Committee of Defence), evacuees from Leningrad and the northeastern sector were still arriving in Stalingrad despite the emergency. Thousands of vehicles and millions of farm animals piled up on the Volga's right bank, unable to cross for lack of river craft. There now began a bitter tussle between Moscow and the city authorities. River transport was mobilised by central directives to relieve congestion of the river crossings. But the evacuation of Stalingrad itself was blocked.[186] It is said that Stalin, notified by Shvernik of evacuation proposals, replied: 'We shall evacuate nothing. We must tell the army and people that there is nowhere left to retreat to. We must defend Stalingrad.'[187]

Stalingrad was bombed from the air on 23 August 1942. The civil population was unprepared and unprotected; perhaps as many as 40,000 died.[188] The departure of women and children was finally ordered the next day. A day after that, the city was under siege, but it took further bombings on 29 August and 2 September for the decision to be taken to disperse the 300,000 civilians still remaining in the burning city to the left bank of the Volga. Of the city's assets only one complete factory was saved, and that was done under fire. The rural evacuation was also left too late. Transport means were overloaded and badly coordinated, impeding military movements at a critical moment in the war.[189] For a short while the industry remaining in the town continued to serve the fighting forces; for example between 23 August and 13 September the Stalingrad tractor factory repaired 200

The coming of war: plans and realities in 1941 81

Table 6. *Soviet industrial and agricultural production 1940–2*

	1940	1941	1942
Combat aircraft, thou.	8.3	12.4	21.7
Tanks, thou.	2.8	6.6	24.4
Artillery pieces, thou.[a]	15.3	42.3	127.0
Mortars, thou.	38.5	52.5	229.9
Crude steel, mn tons	18.3	17.9	8.1
High-grade rolled steel, mn tons	3.2	4.7	3.4
Coal, mn tons	165.9	151.4	75.5
Oil, mn tons	31.1	33.0	22.0
Electricity, bn kWh	48.3	46.6	29.1
Metal-cutting machine tools, thou.	58.4	44.5	22.9
Grains, mn tons	95.6	56.4	26.7
Potatoes, mn tons	76.1	26.6	23.8
Sugar beets, mn tons	18.0	2.0	2.2
Meat and fats, mn tons[b]	4.7	4.1	1.8

[a] Excludes naval artillery.
[b] Dead weight.
Sources: For defence and industrial goods see Appendices 1 and 2. For agricultural produce see IVOVSS, v. 6, 1965, p. 67 and IVMV, v. 3, 1974, p. 378.

tanks and 600 artillery tractors. After this date further work became impossible.[190]

PART THREE: PLANS AND REALITIES

THE IMPACT OF WAR: MOBILISATION AND CONVERSION

In the first months of war the Soviet economy underwent profound structural change. The loss of territory and evacuation were just part of a larger process which also included the mobilisation of the rest of the economy and its conversion to war needs. The main features of this process are shown in Tables 6–10 and Figure 2.

Table 6 shows how the output of main products of agriculture and industry altered between 1940 and 1942. The output of military goods multiplied. The output of most producer goods was checked in 1941 (an exception was high-grade rolled steel, used for making weapons)

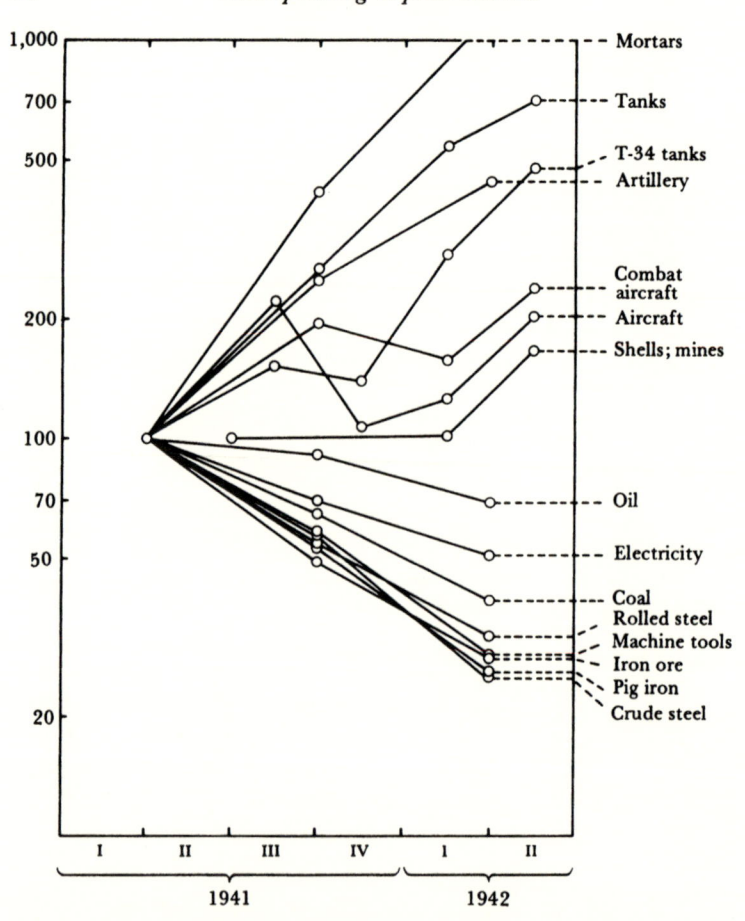

Figure 2. Changes in Soviet arms and heavy industrial production from the first half of 1941 to the first half of 1942 (indices of half-yearly or quarterly output; 1941 (first half) = 100 except for shell production, where annual 1941 = 100)

(*Source:* See Appendices 1 and 2)

and cut drastically in 1942. The output of agricultural produce had collapsed already in 1941.

For some of these series output changes can be traced through 1941 by half-years and even quarters. These are illustrated for some main military and producer goods in Figure 2. This figure shows that most of the changes suggested by the annual data in Table 6 were packed into a very short period. The discrepancy between arms mobilisation

Table 7. *Percentage shares in the USSR net material product in 1940 and 1942*

	1940	1942
Accumulation	19	4
Civilian subsistence	70	56
Military subsistence	4	13[a]
Military equipment	7	27[a]

[a] Kravchenko gives these as 11 and 29 per cent respectively, but figures given by the later source are preferred as more authoritative.
Sources: G. S. Kravchenko, 1970, p. 125; IVMV, v. 6, 1976, p. 340.

and the collapse of heavy industry is immediately apparent. The latter was a unique feature of the Soviet wartime experience – no other major power suffered such a blow at her basic industries or revealed such a decline until German economic collapse began late in 1944. At the same time it can be seen from Figure 2 that the simultaneous expansion of Soviet arms output was not problem-free; where quarterly data are available they show a break in the upward dynamic in the winter of 1941.

Such huge changes in the pattern of output were reflected in the composition of the Soviet national income. Table 7 shows that between 1940 and 1942 the share of expenditures on the armed forces grew from 11 to 40 per cent of NMP, while civilian consumption was heavily squeezed and accumulation nearly eliminated. Moreover these changes occurred within a declining total – the official index shows 1942 NMP at only 66 per cent of the 1940 level.[191]

Underlying the shifting composition of output were equally striking changes in the pattern of employment, shown in Table 8. Between 1940 and 1942 there was a net mobilisation of 6.7 million men and women into the armed forces; taking into account the military losses of the period the gross intake may have been double that number. Meanwhile the number of state employees in the economy fell by two-fifths, and the number of kolkhoz workers by three-fifths. Table 8 also reveals that, in the case of state employees, the entire weight of the blow fell upon the Western USSR, while employment east of the Urals grew significantly.

Associated with this shift in the regional composition of employment was a sharp break in the regional balance of the main industries. Tables 9 and 10 show how the Eastern USSR became the fundamental

Table 8. *The Soviet labour force in 1940 and 1942 (millions)*

	1940	1942
Armed forces	4.2	10.9
State employees	31.2	18.4
Western USSR	19.6	5.6
Eastern USSR	11.6	12.8
Kolkhoz workers[a]	35.4	15.1

[a] Able-bodied collective farm population of working age.

Sources: P. V. Sokolov, 1968, p. 215; Arutyunyan, 1970, p. 398; Mitrofanova, 1971, p. 445.

Table 9. *East–West balance of heavy industrial decline 1940–2*

	Per cent share of the Eastern USSR in			
	Output levels			Output decline 1940–2
	1940 (i)	1941 (ii)	1942 (iii)	(iv)
Pig iron	28.9	37.0	97.9	−4.0
Crude steel	32.2	39.7	82.7	−7.8
Rolled steel	28.0	39.7	85.2	−12.1
Coal	35.9	44.8	79.0	−0.1
Oil	11.6	11.5	15.9	1.9
Electricity	22.1	27.6	51.5	−22.6

Sources: (i)–(iii) from IVMV, v. 3, 1974, p. 380 and v. 5, 1975, p. 43; (iv) calculated from (i), (iii) and Appendix 2.

supplier of both military and producer goods. In the case of producer goods the decline in output was restricted to the Western USSR, and Eastern output levels grew slightly (except for oil). The war production capacity of the Eastern USSR grew more rapidly than in the country as a whole, in terms of both proportional and absolute increments. Within the Eastern USSR, however, not all regions benefited equally from the gravitational shift at work; for example, the shares of the Transcaucasus, Eastern Siberia and the Far East in capital construction declined.[192]

Table 10. *East–West balance of defence industry plant 1941–2*

	Per cent share of the Eastern USSR in defence industry enterprises	
	1941	1942
Aircraft industry	6.6	77.3
Tank industry	25.7	64.6
Armament industry	18.3	65.4
All arms industries[a]	18.5	76.0

[a] The source does not state which industries are included. The term conventionally includes the three industries named plus ammunition and sometimes shipbuilding.

Source: IVOVSS, v. 2, 1961, p. 498.

To what extent were these far-reaching changes expressed in the first wartime economic plans? The work of mobilisation could be divided into two kinds of processes. Some had been thought out before the war through lower-level contingency plans drawn up in advance, while others depended upon high-level initiatives and coordination once the war was already in progress.

Through the prewar work on industrial and plant contingency plans a system of transition from peace to war had been created. This system guaranteed that, at the moment when hostilities began, the economy would start to fight back. In the same way that troops at the front would return the enemy's fire even when leaderless or temporarily cut off, the economy's basic units would respond to emergency at this basic human level. The economy would take the first steps to realise its military–economic potential, although the steps would be uncoordinated and would not necessarily all lead in the same direction.

Throughout the economy automatic, conditioned reflexes came into operation. In Moscow leaders of the city soviet met early on the first morning of the war, calling industrial cadres to the executive the next day. Immediate measures were taken to allocate categories of defence production (ammunition, vehicles, tank repair and so on) to each plant, not waiting for the arrival of orders from above or for supplies of specialised equipment. Conversion was operated on the basis of existing contingency procedures at the municipal and enterprise levels. Operation of converted capacity had begun by the end of

June and early July. A children's bicycle factory started making flamethrowers, at a die-stamping plant teaspoons and paperclips gave way to entrenching tools and parts for anti-tank grenades, and a typewriter works began to manufacture automatic rifles and ammunition.[193] On the railways wartime schedules were introduced at 6 p.m. on 24 June, detailing new priorities and timetables; the transition was smooth and only on a single main line was disruption the result. Planned reserves of capacity were brought automatically into operation.[194] The critical human response to emergency was forthcoming.

At the highest levels the adjustment to war was far less certain. This may be judged from the other aspects of mobilisation requiring high-level initiatives and economy-wide coordination. For example, to judge from their written views, at the outbreak of war Gosplan leaders expected that sufficient reserves of arms capacity would be made available from existing defence plant, from existing conversion plans for civilian plant, from economising in strategic materials and campaigning to eliminate bottlenecks.[195] There was little discussion of practical problems which conversion would encounter.[196] The need to take into account the disruption caused by the surprise invasion and to plan in the context of industrial evacuation was not discussed in public – and the plans which we shall examine also reflected this underestimation. Nor was there discussion of the need to strike a new balance of the national economy and new sectoral and product balances. The main methods of mobilising the military–economic potential were seen as bringing into use existing reserves through harder work and economising on inputs, resulting in a qualitative improvement in input–output norms.[197]

The first wartime economic mobilisation plan for the third quarter of 1941, adopted on 30 June, was a better document than the foregoing might lead us to expect. This plan reportedly had seven main features: (1) an increase in the planned level of arms production by 26 per cent over the peacetime plan for the same quarter; (2) a curtailment of the investment plan, primarily to free metals for the current needs of arms production; (3) allocation of 14,000 metal-cutting machine tools, from a planned output of 22,000 to the ammunition, armament and aircraft industries; (4) confirmation of a list of key projects in the arms industries, fuel and energy sectors, metals and chemical production and railway building; (5) the relocation of new investment to the Eastern region; (6) abandonment of

The coming of war: plans and realities in 1941

the existing railway freight plan, except for coal, petrochemicals, metals and grain; and (7) a cut of 12 per cent in the plan for retail trade.[198]

Some aspects of this plan were good forecasts of wartime trends. It showed understanding that for the time being expanded arms output required cutbacks in civilian investment and consumption, and could not be won alongside existing objectives merely by harder work, sterner discipline and more political campaigning to eliminate slack in the economy. A new balance was required both for the national economy as a whole and for key producer goods, especially metals and machine tools. There was a readiness to cut back and rationalise the investment plan to keep the overall level of commitment of resources under control. In the meantime planners would operate a narrower set of priorities than before; some peacetime priorities would be sacrificed, and some sectors planned from the centre in peacetime would become unplannable and be cut loose.

In spite of such positive features, history dealt harshly with this first attempt at wartime economic planning. As a quantitative guide to action the plan did not take reality into account, or prove adaptable to it; 'the turn made was still insufficient,' Voznesensky wrote later.[199] As the war progressed the plan's shortcomings were speedily revealed.[200] The main problem was that the plan 'was completely insufficient to compensate for the gigantic material losses suffered by the Soviet Army during the first weeks of the war', but compounding this was a second problem not confronted in the plan: the industrial capacity on which it relied was directly threatened by the invading forces.[201] The plan was too modest compared with military needs, but too ambitious compared with industrial capabilities. Consequently the plan failed to provide a framework for economic operations. A prolonged economic crisis was initiated.

The gap between plans and reality was most severe in the aircraft and ammunition industries. In each case the immediate causes were slightly different. The Soviet air force's losses in the first hours of war had been extremely severe; its front-line aircraft were mainly destroyed, most of them on the ground.[202] At the same time, of all the arms branches its industrial base was most vulnerable to the invading forces. Within four months three-quarters of its capacity would be on wheels.[203] The terrible tension between needs and possibilities was expressed in the order of 20 July which obliged the leaders of the

88   *Soviet planning in peace and war*

aircraft industry to evacuate their plants from regions under military threat, and at the same time to follow an aircraft production plan which did not take this threat into account (see p. 73 above).

Sharp crisis also ensued in the ammunition industry, in spite of the detailed contingency and mobilisation plans drawn up before the war. Prewar plans had aimed to relax stubborn capacity limits by extending subcontracting of intermediate input needs to civilian industry (see p. 56 above). The scope of evacuation was less far-reaching than for the aircraft industry, but even so it hit hard at capacity. Early threats were directed at the industry's basic chemicals plant in the Donbass and Leningrad, and the first evacuation orders covering anti-aircraft and armour-piercing shell production were issued on 13 July.[204] By the autumn 303 ammunition works had been decommissioned, and a monthly capacity of over 13 million shell, mine and bomb bodies, millions of shell cases, detonators, fuses and hand grenades, and tens of thousands of tons of explosives had been permanently or temporarily lost.[205] In contrast the armament industry proved more resilient; a reserve of artillery capacity had been laid down in the Urals, and infantry armament capacity revealed unexpected elasticity.[206] But as a result disproportions grew rapidly. For example output of the 76 mm cannon (the basic tank and anti-tank armament) was held to its planned level, but 76 mm shell output fell to 50 or 60 per cent of plan targets.[207] A persistent and generalised 'shell famine' emerged.[208]

The leader with overall responsibility for ammunition supplies in the first months of the war was Voznesensky.[209] Even he could not lift the industry out of confusion. Ammunition targets were fixed without regard to the disruption of capacity; seemingly modest projections turned out to be infeasible. The July 1941 output plan (1 million shells) was undershot by 20 per cent, the August plan (2 million shells) by 70 per cent – an absolute decline – and the September plan (3 million shells) was also not fulfilled. The commissars concerned 'reported that they were receiving plans known in advance to be unrealistic'. Responsibility for planning the industry was taken from Voznesensky and transferred to Saburov.[210] Yet even when plans were fulfilled there could be no satisfaction. The troubles which weighed so heavily upon all the planners at this time are illustrated in the following anecdote.

'Tomorrow we'll go to the Klimov engineering works,' Voznesensky said one day to an ammunition expert.

The coming of war: plans and realities in 1941

'To the Klimov works?' The latter expressed surprise. 'Surely the factory is fulfilling its plan?'

'The front won't take our plans into account,' Voznesensky replied. 'A soldier fires a mortar shell to fit the combat situation, not the shell production plan... Mortar shells are needed, in large numbers, and we must let the front have them.'[211]

Since the first wartime economic mobilisation plan failed to provide a framework for economic operations, it was effectively replaced by a series of emergency measures adopted by the GKO, the Sovnarkom and the Central Committee in the summer and autumn of 1941. Many of these emergency measures have already been discussed. The first set concerned the evacuation of industry. Another group of measures dealt with harvesting crops in the face of invading troops;[212] among these was the extraordinary decree of 2 October 1941 ordering the harvest in the front-line regions to be divided half to the state and half to the harvesters as an incentive.[213] Further emergency measures concerned economising on iron, steel and non-ferrous metals, reallocation of petrochemicals and measures against their wastage, reallocation of vehicle parts to the military and increases in the production of spares, alterations in the electricity generating construction programme and so on.[214]

An important complementary measure was a decree of 1 July 1941 'On the extension of rights of USSR People's Commissars in wartime'. This decree gave commissars the right to reallocate materials among building sites, enterprises and agencies after consultation with those affected, and to take necessary steps to finance production orders not foreseen by the plan (including work associated with war damage, evacuation and relocation).[215] On 18 July this decree was extended to the RSFSR and Ukrainian SSR People's Commissars.[216] The measure did not devolve high-level decision-making powers upon the commissariats, but increased their discretion to act within their own sphere in order to meet their increased responsibility for emergency obligations laid upon them from above.[217]

The atmosphere within which output targets were arrived at and allocated to producers at this time is conveyed in an account of a Kremlin conference of heads of war industries with a Politburo representative early in the war:

Every report deepens the prevailing despair. The 'bottlenecks' in materials, machines, means of transport seem to grow more numerous – an impenetrable forest of 'bottlenecks'. Kasygin no longer talks, no longer asks questions.

He shrieks, orders, fixes quotas and dates, without consulting anyone ... We all know, and Kasygin knows, that the deficiences are real, that none of us can perform miracles.

By the end of the conference,

Every one of us has been loaded with instructions ... We all know that the assignments are impossible; if they can be met only by 75 per cent, there will be rejoicing and bonuses and Orders of Merit. We all know, too, that they are deliberately set higher in order to squeeze the last drop of effort from industry and that the needs are far greater than the plans.[218]

Soviet historians implicitly accept the lack of operational significance of the first wartime economic mobilisation plan by stressing that already on 4 July 1941 the GKO had appointed a commission headed by Voznesensky to draw up another wartime economic plan. This second plan was to be based upon the industries of the interior free from military threat, and the assets which would be relocated there from the regions subject to evacuation.[219] The plan eventually covered the Volga and Ural regions, Western Siberia, Kazakhstan and Central Asia for the fourth quarter of 1941 and for 1942. It was approved on 16 August and took effect on 1 October.

Few details of this plan have been released. According to the official summary, first priority lay with arms production, especially the following: (1) armaments (anti-aircraft, tank, anti-tank, regimental and corps artillery, mortars, aircraft cannon, submachine guns and rifles); (2) ammunition (shells, mines, explosives and so on); (3) aircraft (fighter, bomber and assault aircraft frames and engines), emphasising the need for forced development of new capacity, given the industry's paralysed state; (4) tanks in sharply increased numbers (tanks, tank armour, diesel tank engines and artillery tractors); (5) light naval vessels (especially anti-submarine warships and torpedo boats). At the same time the plan included a range of tasks for basic industries (oil exploration and extraction, new coal mines, new metallurgical plants and engineering works) to be pursued in the Eastern USSR, along with an eastward shift in the focus of agriculture, calling for the exploitation of all reserves of irrigated land under crops displaced from western zones (sugar beet, potatoes, vegetables, wheat). Associated with these tasks were plans for industrial and railway construction.[220] According to the capital construction programme the share of the arms industry commissariats in industrial investment in the fourth quarter of 1941 was to be 40 per

The coming of war: plans and realities in 1941 91

cent (compared to 30 per cent in the first half of the year). The number of industrial building sites projected in the third Five Year Plan was cut back from 5,700 to 614 – mainly those capable of starting production within one year. At the same time funds were set aside for restoring production at 825 relocated plants.[221]

This plan was put into operation in the most critical period of the war economy. The first battle of Moscow had just begun and would last for most of October. On 16 October Voznesensky and his secretariat joined the evacuation of Moscow, proceeding with much of the civil government apparatus to Kuibyshev; on 25 October he was appointed to represent the Sovnarkom in Kuibyshev with personal responsibility for directing the war economy being created in the Urals and beyond. He remained there until the end of November, returning to Moscow when the greatest danger had been averted.[222]

During the autumn bitter resistance of the Soviet forces gradually brought the German advance to a standstill. However, shortages of military goods had become excruciating. Marshal G. K. Zhukov at this time held a roving commission in the key sectors of combat; later he recalled how 'every time we were summoned to Supreme Headquarters we literally wheedled out of the Supreme C-in-C some 10–15 anti-tank rifles, 50–100 submachine guns, 10–15 anti-tank cannons, and the necessary minimum of artillery and mortar shells'.[223] By the winter artillery was being rationed to one or two shots per piece per day.[224] Army logistics had broken down so completely that in December horse battalions were reintroduced on a wide scale to supply the front.[225] If supplies for the front were precarious, the 10th Reserve Army numbering about 100,000 men, in formation in October and November 1941, lacked winter clothing, food, newspapers, vehicles and motorcycles, radios, maps, artillery, machine guns, mortars and anti-tank weapons.[226]

In fact, as a result of the operation of existing contingency plans and emergency measures for wartime conversion, arms output had risen more steeply than envisaged by the economy-wide plan for the third quarter of 1941. Nonetheless it fell well short of the level needed to replace battle losses of equipment. The production and wastage of military goods over a period of time can be expressed as ratios to the average stock of these goods (usually, either the first-line strength or the total strength including second and third echelons and reserves). In the period from the outbreak of war up to the end of November the average monthly output of combat aircraft was running at about 16 per cent of the average first-line air force strength, but monthly loss rates were three times as high at 45 per cent. An equally dangerous gap opened up under the armoured forces – over the same period in terms of a monthly average Soviet industry was replacing 18 per cent of the first-line tank force, but monthly losses ran at 41 per cent of the same figure. Monthly output of artillery and mortars ran at 47 per cent of the average first-line strength, but monthly losses were higher still at 57 per cent.[227] To some extent heavy losses were to be expected in the initial period of the war, given the antiquated character of the bulk of Soviet weaponry which had resulted from prewar reluctance to retire obsolete equipment. From this point of view, by the winter of 1941 the Soviet armed forces' equipment park had greatly diminished, but what was left was of a far higher technological level and far more homogeneous than before. However, the ability of Soviet industry to continue the process of force modernisation and reequipment was reaching a dangerous low point.

In the fourth quarter of 1941 output of key military goods like combat aircraft and modernised T-34 and KV tanks fell back (see Figure 2). In December only 39 per cent of the aircraft production plan was fulfilled, and only 24 per cent of the plan for aeroengines.[228] Artillery shell production was down to 20 to 30 per cent of the plan by the first ten days in January.[229] The system of material–technical supply for the arms industries was breaking down. Strategic reserves of metals accumulated at the beginning of the war had been eaten up by the acceleration in arms output.[230] Tank production, for example, was maintained only because officials were willing to break into warehouses and rob trains in their search for essential ball bearings, transformer oil, rubber and so on.[231] Freight transport was slowing to a near standstill. Industrial production as a whole declined continuously to the end of the year.[232]

As the Soviet forces struggled for the initiative, arms shortages were felt even more acutely. A discussion was held at headquarters on 5 January 1942. Stalin, flanked by Beriya and Malenkov, presented his plan for an ambitious general offensive. Zhukov advised an offensive limited to the western sector, but only after renewal of equipment and reserves.[233] Voznesensky confirmed that the arms industries could not yet supply the means for a general offensive. But in fact the decision had already been taken and the orders issued. Stalin remarked nastily of Voznesensky 'that he always brought up difficulties which would have to be overcome'.[234] Zhukov and Voznesensky

The coming of war: plans and realities in 1941   93

were overruled, and the general offensive went ahead on all fronts. In March 1942 it petered out, having exhausted the available forces and their reserves of equipment.[235]

Nonetheless at the end of 1941 the first period of the Soviet war economy's development was complete. A decisive stage of evacuation, mobilisation and conversion of the economy had been passed. A devastating blow had been absorbed, and the next stage would be one of adjustment. In the next stage the economy would bring to bear its full war potential.

A sign of recovery was that in 1942 the character of economy-wide planning would change. Arms production would remain the first priority. However, in order to meet this priority it was no longer enough to focus upon the mobilisation of the arms industries themselves. By means of the evacuation and conversion processes Soviet arms capacity had been preserved and enhanced. But the supporting and supplying industries, the basic metallurgical, energy and transport sectors were in shambles. In 1942 the binding constraints were no longer the availability of arms capacity but the supply of metals, fuels, electricity and freight capacity. The restoration of balance within the crisis-torn economy had become a precondition for continued arms mobilisation. To resolve this situation and enable the war economy to resume growth, the planners embarked on a new phase of emergency measures and rationalisations in economy-wide planning and coordination.

PLANNING AND THE REGIME OF EMERGENCY MEASURES

When war broke out Soviet administrative life underwent a complex change. A first 'change' was that the rate of change of its basic structures slowed down. From this point of view, the tendency to 'shapelessness' which had so marked the late thirties was apparently weakened and administrative forms seemed to become more stable. For example, with some minor changes affecting the administration of the mortar armament, tank and machine tool industries, the reorganisation of industrial commissariats ceased. The high peacetime rate of turnover of commissars also fell sharply. There were only five changes in commissar-level appointments in the second half of 1941, and two-thirds of the forty-three USSR People's Commissars in office in June 1941 kept their posts until the war was over.[236]

Soviet historians tend to stress the logic of administrative stabilisation in the initial period of the war. The basic institutions required to administer a full war economy had already been created before the war, and there was no need for any wholesale reorganisation. Consequently the relevance of peacetime institutions to the tasks of the moment did not diminish when war broke out. Both at the centre and in the localities the rule was to base wartime administration upon existing forms, creating new institutions only where necessary to supplement or strengthen those already in operation.[237]

The main changes in the formal structure of central government were the creation of a war cabinet (the GKO or State Defence Committee), a committee for mobilising labour (see pp. 188–90 below) and a series of temporary committees appointed to meet specific emergencies of evacuation, transport and construction. Otherwise the main prewar institutions survived, although their internal organisation usually underwent considerable change.

However, the importance of completely new institutions was actually much greater than might appear from the account above. They did not just complement or strengthen an effectively operating set of firmly established prewar institutions. In the initial period of the war there was a tendency to substitute the new bodies created to deal with the wartime emergency for the prewar administrative forms. Through these new bodies the Stalinist tendency towards dictatorial, personalised administration was initially strengthened, and the degree of 'shapelessness' of the system as a whole was from this point of view increased.

The GKO was formed on 30 June 1941. In the gap between the outbreak of war and its formation, the problems of economic mobilisation were considered daily by the Central Committee.[238] Once formed, the GKO was granted unlimited powers; its decisions carried the force of law.[239] It was headed by Stalin, whose personal deputy was Molotov. Other members were NKVD chief L. P. Beriya, Central Committee secretary G. M. Malenkov and Marshal K. E. Voroshilov. On 3 February 1942 Mikoyan and Voznesensky were added, and on 20 February Kaganovich.[240] Each member had his own party, government or military duties and, in addition, was allocated responsibility for some key branch of the national economy. Molotov was responsible for tankbuilding, Malenkov for aircraft and aeroengines, Mikoyan for consumer goods and Kaganovich for railway transport; Voznesensky was in charge of armament and ammunition production.[241] But perhaps after a short period, perhaps

The coming of war: plans and realities in 1941 95

coinciding with the difficulties of autumn 1941, the latter branch was placed under Beriya's leadership.[242] Stalin himself was Supreme Commander-in-Chief of the armed forces. Thus the GKO renewed the Stalinist political system's peacetime tendency to resolve difficulties through dictatorial measures and personal rule by decree.

Following the Stalinist style of emergency centralisation, the GKO did not create directly subordinate local bodies – the city committees of defence formed in frontal regions and in industrial centres of the interior were usually temporary bodies under the authority of the local party and soviets. Instead the GKO set up a local network of individual plenipotentiary agents – usually lower-level party and industrial leaders – which was superimposed on local government and formally independent of it.[243]

How did the GKO operate at the centre? According to Belikov the GKO held sessions from time to time to resolve current issues, extending invitations to specialists and responsible leaders. For example on 15 July 1941 there was a GKO discussion of problems of tank manufacture, involving leaders of the tank, armament and steel industries and Voznesensky as the planning chief. On 28 July a similar discussion looked at problems in the armament and ammunition industries, again with Voznesensky and a number of industrial and military leaders in attendance. GKO members and those representing other agencies would arrive at the office of the GKO chairman with fully drafted proposals for the next month's arms output, with notes on plan fulfilment for the preceding month and on available productive capacity.[244] With this kind of preparation there was no need for minutes or secretaries. From the point of view of their procedural conventions, 'There were no GKO sessions in the usual sense, i.e. with a definite agenda, secretaries and minutes. The procedure for securing agreement with Gosplan, with commissariats and agencies on questions of supplying the army, including setting up new production, was simplified in the extreme.'[245]

One guesses that this kind of informality was naturally associated with the personal style of administrative leadership. For example military–economic decisions were supposed to be supplemented or coordinated through Gosplan on the spot, and with businesslike despatch, because Voznesensky was always present in his specialist capacity and later as a GKO member when the economy was under discussion;[246] in practice Voznesensky must usually have returned to Gosplan as the boss with a *fait accompli*, around which the planners would then have to adapt existing plans, rather than involving Gosplan in the process of arriving at an operational decision. The informality of GKO sessions allowed much scope, moreover, for personal interpretation of the decisions reached. A defence industry leader observed how the outcome of such discussions was often a resolution charging someone 'to bring in revised proposals taking into account the exchange of opinions' – but since the discussion had not been minuted, whose opinions would be taken into account, and how, was left to the personal discretion of the person so entrusted.[247]

The creation of the GKO and the changes which followed in its train had considerable impact upon the Sovnarkom and commissariats. For a start, Stalin's attention was focused upon the military and diplomatic situation, so that in theory leadership of domestic government was devolved upon his Sovnarkom deputies (Beriya, Kosygin, Mikoyan, Molotov and Voznesensky).[248] But leadership of the decisive branches of the war economy was now being exercised by individual GKO members, not from within the Sovnarkom. As a result some prewar functions of the Sovnarkom could no longer be carried out from that level, and Sovnarkom subcommittees like the Economic Council and the industrial branch councils fell into disuse.[249] Such centralisation reduced the role of commissariats for priority branches, because new, shorter chains of command were being set up, bringing the key large-scale plants in the economy directly under the supervision of top-level committees and leaders; commissariat officials must have been increasingly bypassed by the decision-making process, although they continued to be responsible for dealing with the consequences of these decisions and other events which they did not control. A sign of reduced status and influence at commissariat level was the designation of such work as non-essential. Twenty commissariats yielded 50,000 workers for mobilisation.[250] Even the arms industry commissariats lost half their staff establishments.[251]

How did these changes affect the position of Gosplan? In the first weeks of the war, the planners were shut out of high-level operational decision making. The General Staff no longer had time to coordinate military–economic requirements with the current state of the economy through Gosplan itself. Instead military orders were handled directly through the GKO, which transmitted such orders in turn direct to arms plants and industrial branches. This was reflected in the internal organisation of the GKO and the distribution of responsibility for the various arms branches and transport to GKO members personally.[252] Gosplan was perhaps involved mainly through Voznesensky as an individual. At this stage, therefore, the role of Gosplan was to compile economy-wide plans which did not take reality into account and had no possibility of being put into practice, and to attempt to balance the rest of the economy around targets for the arms industries and transport which had been decided upon with reference to the situation at the front and not to economy-wide plans. Even the task of compiling the wartime economic plan for the Eastern USSR in the fourth quarter of 1941 and 1942 was formally entrusted to a special commission headed personally by Voznesensky, not to Gosplan itself, although Gosplan was surely involved as the only body competent in matters of plan compilation.

The situation in the second half of 1941 can be described as a regime of emergency measures. This regime was marked by a sharp increase in the elements of personalised, dictatorial administration which tended to set aside existing institutions and formal lines of command. The regime of emergency measures involved a combination of unplanned improvisations and panic measures undertaken at the centre, with the operation of previously planned contingency procedures in the economy's basic units. It was this regime which directed the evacuation, conversion and mobilisation processes and ensured the survival of Soviet arms capacity. Suited to rapid mobilisation for a limited set of short-run priorities, it failed at this time to take into account the broad situation evolving in the economy as a whole. Government economic policy concerned itself with factors directly influencing arms production, but indirect influences, no matter how important, were set to one side. It follows that, from the point of view of understanding economic operations in these first months, the drafting of economy-wide plans for coordinating and balancing the economy's branches and sectors was virtually irrelevant. Such a situation, however, could not be sustained for long.

By the spring of 1942 better coordination of the arms industries with their heavy industrial base had become essential. Crisis measures under the emergency regime had saved the basic components of Soviet arms capacity, but were now being overtaken by further rapid changes in the military and economic context. From the military standpoint Stalin was seeking an offensive against the invading armies, but to take the offensive implied raising Red Army force levels and accepting more rapid force attrition. Demands upon the arms industries could only increase. From the economic standpoint the ability of the arms industries to sustain existing output levels was being destroyed by the downward slide of the basic industries.

On the surface, therefore, 1942 would be dominated by the same urgent needs which had come to the fore in 1941, namely the needs of the military for as many guns, shells, tanks and aircraft as possible. At a deeper level the problem of meeting these needs took a different and more complex character. They could not be met without rebalancing the arms and basic industries within the national economy as a whole. Without the restoration of economic balance, resource mobilisation for war could not be sustained.

Basically the regime of emergency measures would continue unabated through 1942, but by the end of 1941 its character had already begun to change. An essential aspect of this change was the restored prominence of Gosplan, because resource mobilisation depended increasingly on what the planners did, and because emergency measures had to be coordinated increasingly through the planning system. This could be observed at both higher and lower levels. For example from the end of 1941, the GKO member responsible for armament and ammunition output (Beriya, presumably) ended the exclusion of planners from operational decisions by setting up a working group of Sovnarkom and Gosplan staff to mediate between the Red Army's chief artillery administration and industry.[253] At lower levels there was a process of integration of mobilisation work and current planning; in Moscow, for example, until November 1941 these two aspects of wartime economic administration had been carried out independently from separate offices, but were now brought under one roof.[254]

Gosplan's own internal organisation changed. The Gosplan department responsible for arms industries was subdivided to deal separately with armament, ammunition, aircraft, and tank and shipbuilding; to these new departments were subordinated all relevant plants in the country, regardless of their formal attachment to particular commissariats or other agencies.[255] Tasks were being increasingly allocated directly from the centre to enterprises, and Gosplan shared in this centralisation by developing quarterly supply plans for 120 large industrial users. The number of planned production indicators increased to over 30,000.[256] There was also an increase in the frequency of fulfilment checks – the five-day and ten-day reports of plan fulfilment progress in basic industries, initiated in 1938, were stepped up to a daily basis when war broke out.[257] In addition the number of centrally planned products doubled.[258]

All these measures were designed to increase the authority of central plans through shorter chains of command, tighter controls and increased mobilisation of reserves. Whether they were successful in this did not depend on them alone. For example plan fulfilment checks depended to a high degree upon the accuracy of statistical data collection, and at the beginning of the war TsSU was scarcely equipped for such an additional burden, being preoccupied by work for the relocation of industry – censuses of materials and equipment and of industrial accommodation. Basic statistical reporting remained in a mess until March 1942, and full reporting was not restored until the end of that year.[259] Early centralisation in the planning process must have been more apparent than real, given the irrelevance of the plans to what was actually taking place. However, as time passed and the situation changed, the planners recovered their authority and the economy really did become more centralised.

Centralisation measures directly affected the arms and basic industries. They were complemented by decentralisation of 'residual' areas of economic life. As early as 7 July 1941 a Sovnarkom decree stressed the need for increased utilisation of 'local resources' (i.e. resources not supplied on the basis of central plans) to meet demand for both rationed and non-rationed consumer goods. Measures were taken to cut their production loose from central plans, to reduce the volume of centrally planned commodity stocks, and to devolve consumer supply upon the resources and initiative of local industries, suppliers and trade organisations.[260] At the same time of course the real scope for exercise of local initiative and discretion over local resources was being greatly limited by the centralising forces at work. As far as the local economy was concerned these centralising forces were of two kinds. Plan centralisation directly increased pressure on local resources by reducing the availability of central resources to local users and consumers. At the same time financial centralisation, mainly sharp increases in direct taxes and cutbacks in local government budgets in favour of central government,[261] tended to reduce the pressure of autonomous monetary demand on the local economy.

In summary, in the opening period of the war, Gosplan was temporarily displaced from the centre of the planning and management process. But as the national economic balance and the demands upon it evolved, this position was reversed. The basis was laid for a powerful accumulation of authority within Gosplan. Parts of the economy, however, were necessarily left outside the sphere of centralisation.

CONCLUSIONS

Nineteen-forty-one witnessed a sharp confrontation between Soviet economic plans and reality. During the confrontation the Soviet economic system did not collapse; some elements of it just went into higher gear. Other elements worked badly or not at all. The mix of elements changed drastically. The importance and nature of plan compilation and control over plan fulfilment began to evolve at high speed.

The clash between plans and reality would have been severe, given the most farsighted leadership. Uncertainty, shock and disruption were inevitable. The predicament of 1941 was sharpened, however, because those responsible for Soviet war preparations had failed – or not been allowed – to grasp and take into account the likely losses and disruption which would follow a full-scale German attack. Conversion of the economy to a war footing had to proceed 'when the fascist hordes had already crossed our frontiers, had brought down upon [our] industrial centres massive blows of air power and tank formations, and were beginning to advance into the depths of the country, towards vitally important regions'.[262] Experience alone demonstrated 'what a huge task, unforeseen by plans, the Soviet people would have to accomplish'.[263] Under these circumstances the process of adaptation of the economy as a whole to the real conditions and requirements of war was regulated with great difficulty.

Soviet commentators sometimes suggest that the very rapidity of structural change in the Soviet economy in the second half of 1941, especially the great divergence between growing arms output and contracting basic industries, showed the superior flexibility and manoeuvrability of an economy based on central planning.[264] In fact it is hard to support this conclusion. The structural change of this period reflected several factors. The decline of the Soviet civilian economy was mainly brought about by the Wehrmacht. The Soviet arms mobilisation was partly improvised and partly planned. The part of it which was planned in advance reflected the operation of plant and industrial branch contingency plans. But during the period of most violent structural change, central planning was really absent from the stage.

The regime of emergency measures was essential to Soviet survival in 1941. A key to its success were the years of contingency planning at lower levels in the economy which ensured that its basic units would have an automatic, conditioned response to emergency. They would not succumb to shock, and would initiate economic resistance to the enemy at this basic human level. The sum of lower-level responses would not be coordinated, efficient or tailored to an unforeseen strategic environment. They would not add up to a balanced economy-wide whole. But they would begin to mobilise the economy's war potential.

The other key to the success of the emergency regime was the ability of the central authorities to improvise new policies under extreme pressure. It was these policies which managed the evolution of the economy as a whole in the autumn and winter of 1941. The outstanding example was the evacuation and relocation of industry. From one point of view the evacuation was a messy, unplanned operation which incurred substantial inefficiency costs. From another viewpoint the important thing is that the evacuation was an imaginative stroke of policy which worked. However, the results of emergency improvisation could be learnt and transferred to new circumstances only with great difficulty, as the second (Stalingrad) evacuation showed in 1942.

The emergency regime of 1941, however imaginative and experimental in practical detail, did not mark a new departure for the Soviet economic system. As a method of mobilising resources under extreme pressure, it shared many features in common with previous peacetime episodes of rapid economic mobilisation under the stresses of food shortage, trade sanctions and rearmament. It carried these common features to a new extreme.

Among such common features, the emergency regime of 1941 shared with prewar systems of emergency economic management a central defect. It was solely a method for securing rapid resource mobilisation, regardless of the costs incurred. Dictatorial administration from above plus conditioned responses from below could not provide the balance functions necessary to sustain economic life over a long period or through a protracted war. They bought time and space for economy-wide plans to adapt to the radically changed environment, but they could not take the place of economy-wide planning. The emergency regime of 1941 averted Soviet defeat, but it could not supply the means of Soviet victory. In the summer and autumn of 1941 resource mobilisation was pursued without regard to economic balance, and by the winter the imbalances in the economy had reached an extreme pitch of crisis. This set the context for a change in the nature of the emergency regime, as it strove now to restore economy-wide equilibrium.

NOTES

1 Cited by Gorbunov, 1981, p. 15.
2 Holloway, 1980, p. 131.
3 Sorokin, 1975, p. 3.
4 Tupper, 1982, pp. 5, 10–12.
5 Carr, 1976, p. 331.
6 Stalin, 1940, pp. 365–6 ('The Tasks of Business Executives').
7 For expressions and accounts of this ideology in the 1930s see Knickerbocker, 1931, pp. 3–4; Scott, 1973, p. 5; Lewin, 1975, p. 102; Bialer, 1980, p. 22.
8 Shvernik, 1940, pp. 6–7.
9 Milward, 1977, pp. 29–30.
10 Clausewitz, 1968, p. 164.
11 Ibid., p. 167.
12 Belov, 1939, pp. 60–1; 1940a, p. 56.
13 Both these projects had been planned since the twenties and even before; see Clark, 1956, p. 232; Kirstein, 1980, pp. 1–2.
14 Clark, 1956, pp. 233–4.
15 Bardin, 1944, pp. 46–7.
16 Cooper, 1976, p. 15.
17 Bardin, 1943, pp. 20–2.
18 Chadaev, 1965, pp. 59–60.
19 Kas'yanenko, 1972, pp. 209–10.
20 Ibid., pp. 214, 217–19.
21 The assessment appeared in *Pravda* and excited diplomatic comment; see FRUS 1940, v. III, 1958, pp. 181–2.
22 Kas'yanenko, 1972, pp. 215–16.
23 IVOVSS, v. 1, 1963, p. 412.
24 IVMV, v. 3, 1974, p. 387.
25 Voznesensky, 1948, p. 123.
26 IVMV, v. 3, 1974, p. 387. Estimates for petrochemicals, iron and steel are derived by comparing absolute stock levels given in the source with the 1940 output levels given in Appendix 2.
27 Ibid., pp. 387–8.
28 Khrulev, 1961, pp. 65–6; Erickson, 1975, p. 61.
29 Ist. KPSS, v. 5(i), 1970, p. 120.
30 Cooper, 1976, pp. 5–8; Zaleski, 1980, p. 15. This body should not be

confused with the defence industry subcommittee of the Sovnarkom Economic Council set up in the spring of 1940 (see p. 28 above).
31 IVMV, v. 2, 1974, p. 189.
32 Cooper, 1976, pp. 26–7.
33 Ist. KPSS, v. 5(i), 1970, p. 121.
34 Aleshchenko, 1980, p. 11.
35 Zhukov, 1971, p. 214.
36 Belikov, 1966, p. 32.
37 Voznesensky, 1948, pp. 65–6.
38 ISE, v. 5, 1978, pp. 95–103.
39 Nikitin, 1960, p. 23.
40 Pervukhin, 1974, p. 24.
41 Tupper, 1981, p. 7.
42 Nikitin, 1960, p. 24.
43 Yakovlev, 1981, p. 66.
44 Tupper, 1981, pp. 9–10.
45 Berri, 1940, p. 148.
46 Tupper, 1981, p. 9.
47 Tupper, 1982, p. 146.
48 Ibid., p. 188.
49 Clark, 1956, pp. 17, 25.
50 Tupper, 1982, p. 222.
51 Koopmans, 1957, p. 189.
52 Belikov, 1961, p. 37; 1966, p. 31; Ist. KPSS, v. 5(i), 1970, p. 282; Zalkind and Miroshnichenko, 1980, p. 204.
53 Van Creveld, 1977, pp. 210, 236.
54 Belov, 1940a, pp. 58–9.
55 Medvedev, 1972, pp. 456–7.
56 Ibid., pp. 458–9. See also Erickson, 1975, pp. 1–7, 80–1.
57 Tupper, 1982, ch. 5.
58 Bialer, ed., 1970, p. 584.
59 Voznesensky, 1941, p. 8.
60 Belov, 1940a, pp. 58–9.
61 FRUS 1940, v. III, 1958, pp. 195–6.
62 Kumanev, 1966, p. 119.
63 V. Kravchenko, 1947, p. 363.
64 Shakhurin, 1975, p. 134.
65 ISE, v. 4, 1978, p. 103.
66 Resheniya, v. 3, 1968, p. 39.
67 Stalin, 1945, p. 15.
68 The quotation is from Belikov, Kumanev and Mitrofanova, 1976, p. 259. In fact the phrase 'a coherent and rapidly growing war economy' was first used by Stalin in a speech in November 1943; see Stalin, 1945, p. 97.
69 Resheniya, v. 3, 1968, p. 42.
70 Chalmaev, 1981, p. 151.
71 Strizhkov, 1980, p. 21.
72 Pogrebnoi, 1966, p. 201. Initially the Council had six other members:

Marshal B. M. Shaposhnikov, N. F. Dubronin, P. S. Popkov, S. N. Kruglov, A. I. Kirpichnikov and its secretary, M. R. Kuz'min.

73 Kumanev, 1966, p. 117. Kaganovich's place on the Council was taken by his deputy at the transport commissariat, B. N. Arutyunov; other members now included M. Z. Saburov of Gosplan, Major-General M. V. Zakharov and 'one representative of the NKVD': Pogrebnoi, 1966, p. 202.
74 Belikov, 1961, p. 43. On 26 September 1941 this second team became a separate Administration for Evacuation of the Population: Belonosov, 1966, p. 16.
75 Pogrebnoi, 1966, p. 202. The first team was headed by I. F. Semichastnov (defence industries) and A. M. Protasov (civilian industries), the second by RSFSR prime minister K. D. Pamfilov, and the third by F. T. Izmailov.
76 Pogrebnoi, 1966, p. 203; Pervukhin, 1974, p. 14.
77 Belonosov, 1970, p. 49.
78 IVOVSS, v. 2, 1961, p. 143; Pogrebnoi, 1966, p. 203.
79 Aleshchenko, 1980, pp. 33-4.
80 Ist. KPSS, v. 5(i), 1970, pp. 291-2.
81 IVOVSS, v. 2, 1961, p. 148.
82 Ist. KPSS, v. 5(i), 1970, p. 292.
83 G. S. Kravchenko, 1970, p. 115.
84 Belikov, 1961, p. 43.
85 Belonosov, 1966, p. 18.
86 Munchaev, 1975, p. 134.
87 Dubronin, 1966, pp. 209-10.
88 Kumanev, 1976, p. 93.
89 Chalmaev, 1981, pp. 152, 200.
90 Belikov, 1966, p. 39.
91 Ibid., p. 44.
92 Kumanev, 1976, p. 114. Incompleteness of the data may be judged from the fact that the industries listed accounted for only 15 per cent of the grand total of trucks loaded. The source refers not to 'heavy engineering' but to the 'heavy industry' commissariat – clearly an anachronism.
93 Belikov, 1966, p. 35.
94 G. S. Kravchenko, 1970, p. 113.
95 Belikov, 1966, p. 35.
96 Belonosov, 1966, pp. 19-20; Dubronin, 1966, p. 214.
97 Gouré, 1964, p. 53. Of the total of 636,000 evacuated by 29 August 1941, 148,000 were refugees from the Baltic republics, and 10,000 were accompanying equipment or livestock.
98 Belikov, 1961, p. 43.
99 Cited by Gallagher, 1963, p. 110.
100 Kumanev, 1966, p. 132.
101 Gouré, 1964, p. 53.
102 Ibid., p. 54.
103 Belonosov, 1966, p. 26; Kumanev, 1966, p. 118; Munchaev, 1975, p. 138.
104 Munchaev, 1975, pp. 138-9.

105 Kupert, 1977, p. 86.
106 Belonosov, 1966, pp. 16–17.
107 Munchaev, 1975, pp. 137–8.
108 Chuyanov, 1966, pp. 233–8.
109 Belonosov, 1966, p. 26.
110 Ibid.
111 Munchaev, 1975, p. 137.
112 Belikov, 1961, p. 43.
113 Belonosov, 1966, p. 28.
114 Nar. khoz., 1972, p. 9.
115 IVMV, v. 7, 1976, p. 41
116 Pogrebnoi, 1966, p. 206.
117 Belikov, 1966, p. 40; Morekhina, 1974, pp. 87–90.
118 Morekhina, 1974, p. 91.
119 G. S. Kravchenko, 1970, p. 114.
120 IVMV, v. 3, 1974, p. 388.
121 Chalmaev, 1981, pp. 200–2.
122 IVMV, v. 4, 1975, p. 137.
123 Zinich, 1971, p. 94.
124 Gouré, 1964, p. 51; Belonosov, 1970, p. 54.
125 IVOVSS, v. 2, 1961, p. 144.
126 Belikov, 1966, p. 38.
127 Strizkhov, 1980, p. 31.
128 Arutyunyan, 1970, pp. 35–42.
129 IVOVSS, v. 6, 1965, p. 67.
130 Arutyunyan, 1970, p. 44.
131 Zalkind and Miroshnichenko, 1980, p. 208.
132 IVOVSS, v. 6, 1965, p. 67.
133 Arutyunyan, 1970, pp. 45–6.
134 Ibid., p. 50.
135 Ibid., p. 53.
136 Ibid., pp. 49, 51.
137 Pogrebnoi, 1966, p. 206.
138 Kumanev, 1966, p. 118.
139 FRUS 1942, v. III, 1961, p. 429 (report of Walter Thurston, 20 March 1942).
140 Van Creveld, p. 77, pp. 157–61, 165–6, 172–4.
141 Kosygin, 1980, p. 47.
142 Kumanev, 1966, p. 132.
143 Pogrebnoi, 1966, pp. 206–7.
144 Kumanev, 1976, p. 141.
145 Ibid., p. 112.
146 Kumanev, 1966, p. 127.
147 Dubronin, 1966, pp. 210–11.
148 FRUS 1942, v. III, 1961, pp. 425–6. The practice was condemned in a GKO resolution of 9 November 1941; see Resheniya, v. 3, 1968, pp. 52–4.
149 Kumanev, 1966, p. 132.

150 Starovsky and Ezhov, 1975, p. 5.
151 Zalkind and Miroshnichenko, 1980, p. 206.
152 Kupert, 1977, p. 86.
153 Belikov, 1961, p. 44.
154 Arsen'ev, 1972, p. 22.
155 Ibid., pp. 24–5.
156 D'yakov, 1978, p. 47.
157 Belikov, 1966, p. 36.
158 Zinich, 1971, pp. 95–6.
159 IVOVSS, v. 2, 1961, p. 150.
160 Tel'pukhovsky, 1958, p. 32.
161 Belonosov, 1966, p. 28.
162 Kosyachenko, 1944, p. 7.
163 Belonosov, 1970, p. 53.
164 D'yakov, 1978, p. 47.
165 G. S. Kravchenko, 1970, p. 115.
166 Belikov, 1961, p. 41.
167 Ibid., pp. 48–9.
168 Shakhurin, 1975, p. 139.
169 Belonosov, 1970, p. 52.
170 Kumanev, 1974, p. 215.
171 Voznesensky, 1948, p. 36; Belikov, 1966, p. 47; G. S. Kravchenko, 1970, p. 113. A larger figure of 2,593 is sometimes given, for example by Kumanev, 1974, p. 215 and Strizkhov, 1980, p. 30. According to Belikov, 1966, p. 48, this was the number of requests for railway trucks received from enterprises and industry commissariats by the transport commissariat.
172 Voznesensky, 1948, pp. 42–6.
173 Nar. khoz., 1972, p. 55.
174 Lipatov, 1966, p. 187.
175 For both figures see ISE, v. 5, 1978, pp. 52–3.
176 Kosyachenko, 1944, pp. 5–7.
177 Zaleski, 1980, p. 293.
178 Chalmaev, 1981, p. 151.
179 Kumanev, 1966, p. 119.
180 Dubronin, 1966, p. 209.
181 Trevor Roper, ed., 1966, p. 178.
182 Other members were Saburov of Gosplan, Arutyunov of the transport commissariat, P. A. Ermolin and 'a representative of the NKVD': Mitrofanova, 1971, p. 170.
183 Belonosov, 1966, p. 27; IVMV, v. 5, 1975, p. 39.
184 Morekhina, 1974, p. 137.
185 Arutyunyan, 1970, pp. 55–7.
186 Chuyanov, 1966, pp. 238–42.
187 Pervukhin, 1974, p. 30; see also Chalmaev, 1981, p. 253.
188 Werth, 1964, p. 1062.
189 Chuyanov, 1966, pp. 242–4.
190 Chalmaev, 1981, pp. 270–1; see also Morekhina, 1974, pp. 138–9.

The coming of war: plans and realities in 1941

191 IVOVSS, v. 6, 1965, p. 45. For explanation of the net material product measure see Appendix 5.
192 V. Sokolov, 1946, p. 20; see also Dunmore, 1980, pp. 35–6.
193 Aleshchenko, 1980, pp. 28–9.
194 Kumanev, 1976, pp. 73–4.
195 Dobrov, 1941; Kursky, 1941b, p. 25; Sonin, 1941; Sukharevsky, 1941, p. 33.
196 Sen'ko, 1941 was the exception.
197 Kursky, 1941b, pp. 20–2; Notkin, 1941; Shelekhov, 1941, pp. 38–42; Sukharevsky, 1941, pp. 28–31.
198 Voznesensky, 1948, pp. 33–4.
199 Ibid., p. 34.
200 IVOVSS, v. 2, 1961, p. 139.
201 Belikov, 1961, pp. 37–8.
202 Bialer, ed., 1970, p. 205.
203 IVMV, v. 4, 1975, p. 150.
204 Ibid., p. 151.
205 Voznesensky, 1948, p. 37.
206 Vannikov, 1968, pp. 119–20.
207 IVMV, v. 4, 1975, p. 151; also Arsen'ev, 1972, p. 19.
208 Yakovlev, 1981, pp. 84, 117.
209 Kolotov and Petrovichev, 1963, p. 32.
210 Khrulev, 1961, p. 66.
211 Kolotov, 1976, p. 267.
212 Strizkhov, 1980, 1931.
213 IVOVSS, v. 2, 1961, p. 165.
214 Zalkind and Miroshnichenko, 1980, pp. 206–7.
215 Resheniya, v. 3, 1968, pp. 40–1.
216 Ibid., p. 44.
217 Arsen'ev, 1972, p. 12; Strizhkov, 1980, pp. 24–5.
218 V. Kravchenko, 1947, pp. 410–11. 'Kasygin', identified as 'one of Stalin's most powerful assistants', with the given names Aleksei Nikolayevich, was surely deputy prime minister Kosygin.
219 Resheniya, v. 3, 1968, p. 42; IVOVSS, v. 2, 1961, p. 139. Other members of Voznesensky's commission were the tank expert and medium engineering commissar V. A. Malyshev, deputy prime minister and Evacuation Council member M. G. Pervukhin, and Gosplan chief Saburov; see Ist. KPSS, v. 5(i), 1970, p. 288. The last source wrongly lists Voznesensky, not Saburov, as head of Gosplan at the time.
220 Resheniya, v. 3, 1968, pp. 44–8; details also from Voznesensky, 1948, pp. 34–5; G. S. Kravchenko, 1970, pp. 107–8; Zalkind and Miroshnichenko, 1980, pp. 205–6, 211, 213.
221 IVOVSS, v. 2, 1961, p. 142. The arms industries took 25 per cent of industrial investment in the prewar years 1938–41; see p. 9 above.
222 Kolotov, 1976, pp. 263–5. The official order of government evacuation was issued by Khrulev only on 5 November; see Erickson, 1975, pp. 9 228–9.
223 Cited in Bialer, ed., 1970, pp. 333–4. See also Tyl SVS, 1977, p. 160.

224 Arsen'ev, 1972, p. 20.
225 General A. V. Khrulev, cited in Bialer, ed., 1970, p. 374.
226 Marshal F. I. Golikov, cited in ibid., pp. 314–17.
227 For more discussion of these figures and their meaning see pp. 110–15 below. For sources, methods and due qualifications see Appendix 3.
228 IVMV, v. 4, 1975, p. 150.
229 Zhukov, cited in Bialer, ed., 1970, p. 334.
230 Morekhina, 1974, pp. 56–7.
231 Chalmaev, 1981, p. 206. Again the practice was condemned in the GKO resolution of 9 November 1941; see Resheniya, v. 3, 1968, pp. 52–4.
232 Sorokin, 1975, p. 8.
233 Zhukov, 1971, pp. 352–3.
234 Erickson, 1975, p. 298.
235 Marshal A. M. Vasilevsky, cited in Bialer, ed., 1970, p. 401.
236 See Appendix 4.
237 Rubin, 1969, p. 138; Arsen'ev, 1972, p. 6; Zverev, 1973, p. 205; Belikov, 1974, p. 75; Kupert, 1977, p. 82; Strizhkov, 1980, pp. 21–2.
238 Belikov, Kumanev and Mitrofanova, 1976, p. 259.
239 Resheniya, v. 3, 1968, p. 40.
240 Later in the war, on 20 November 1944, Voroshilov was dismissed and replaced by General N. A. Bulganin. The committee was dissolved on 4 September 1945. See Fainsod, 1963, pp. 391–2.
241 IVMV, v. 4, 1975, pp. 52, 133.
242 V. Kravchenko, 1947, p. 404.
243 Belikov, 1974, p. 76.
244 Ibid., pp. 72–4.
245 Khrulev, 1961, pp. 66–7.
246 Belikov, 1974, p. 74.
247 Vannikov, 1962, p. 78.
248 Strizkhov, 1980, p. 23.
249 Ibid., p. 22. The last reported decision of the Economic Council was apparently dated 14 September 1941; see Belikov, 1966, p. 40.
250 Arsen'ev, 1972, p. 11.
251 Strizkhov, 1980, p. 25.
252 Yakovlev, 1981, pp. 111–12.
253 Ibid., p. 112.
254 Aleshchenko, 1980, p. 43.
255 Kolotov, 1976, p. 255.
256 Chadaev, 1971, p. 55.
257 Zalkind and Miroshnichenko, 1980, p. 203.
258 Ibid., p. 202.
259 Starovsky and Ezhov, 1975, p. 6.
260 Lyubimov, 1968, p. 11.
261 Zverev, 1943, p. 26.
262 Chadaev, 1965, p. 61.
263 P. V. Sokolov, 1968, p. 213.
264 IVMV, v. 12, 1982, p. 170. See also Chapter 5, p. 243 below.

3

The Soviet productive effort

We must evaluate the economic efforts of each participant in the anti-Hitler coalition, first of all, not by the achieved level of output and the volume of armament produced, but by the degree of its utilisation in the course of combat. The share and significance of [their] real contribution to the attainment of overall success are determined by how effectively and purposefully the material and human resources of one or another country are utilised for the production of military equipment, and to what degree, where and when the weaponry produced is applied.

(The official Soviet history of World War II)[1]

INTRODUCTION

Germany went to war on the basis of a limited economic mobilisation. But this was a style of warfare which her adversaries could not copy. German leaders planned for speedy victories, which could be achieved without prolonged commitment or substantial losses of troops and equipment in the field. There was little special mobilisation of German industry for the invasion of the USSR, and with the invasion under way German defence production actually declined. This was a logical development, given the intention to defeat the Red Army in time for Christmas.[2] Germany's adversaries, in contrast, could place no confidence in their chance of an early victory. Once war had broken out their only option was to subject their economies to a progressive and unprecedented mobilisation for a protracted, unlimited war. They had to fight first to deny Germany her lightning victory. Once they had successfully imposed on Germany a protracted war, they had then to mobilise further and fight to win it.[3]

The frustration of Germany's blitzkrieg strategy in Russia in 1941 had economic aspects which formed the subject of Chapter 2. By the beginning of 1942 the Soviet economy had met the test of survival. A first phase of arms mobilisation had been accomplished, but in the process the economy's internal balances had been loaded to the point of breakdown. In the following period economic balance was improved and arms mobilisation resumed. As a result, during the war the output of military goods and of strategic industries reached a colossal volume. For every combat aircraft, cannon and tank produced in 1940, in 1944 Soviet industry produced four, eight and ten respectively. The hugely expanded Soviet forces were successfully supplied with munitions and fuelled, clothed and fed. The arms mobilisation of the economy was, moreover, achieved on the basis of a capital stock and workforce much smaller than before the war.

The subject of the present chapter is the changing proportions assumed by the Soviet economy during these years. Part One takes a long view of the direct demands placed on the economy by the battle losses and replacement needs of the Red Army. In Part Two we turn to the resulting changes in the overall structure of production and in the reproduction of productive assets and labour. Part Three goes on to examine summary measures of the degree of mobilisation of the Soviet economy for wartime needs. Connected with this latter question is the changing character of mobilisation to be associated with the different phases of the Soviet war economy. By 1942 a first phase had been accomplished, but the real turning point had not yet been reached.

PART ONE: THE TIDE OF COMBAT

BATTLE LOSSES AND ARMS BALANCES

When Hitler launched his invasion of the Soviet Union on 22 June 1941 the German forces enjoyed not only tactical and strategic surprise but also quantitative superiority over the defending first-line forces with respect to combat-ready personnel, armament and modernised tanks and aircraft. At the same time the Red Army approached equality with the German forces counting its reserve personnel, and exceeded them over a wide range of obsolete equipment. During the following months both armies encountered unexpectedly heavy losses, and for the Red Army at first glance the scale of losses was annihilating. However, the Soviet Union replaced these losses at a rate sufficient to win first parity and subsequently

Table 11. *Balance of combat forces on the Soviet–German front 1941–5*

		1941 June	1941 Dec.	1942 May	1942 Nov.	1943 July	1944 Jan.	1944 June	1945 Jan.
Service personnel, thou.	USSR	2,900[a]	4,200	5,500	6,124	6,442	6,165	6,500	6,000
	Germany	5,500	5,000	6,200	6,270	5,325	4,906	4,000	3,100
Artillery and mortars[b]	USSR	34,965	22,000	43,640	72,500	98,790	88,900	83,200	91,400
	Germany	47,260	26,800	43,000	70,980	54,300	54,000	49,000	28,500
Tanks and self-propelled guns	USSR	1,800[c]	1,730	4,065[d]	6,014	9,580	4,900	8,000[e]	11,000
	Germany	2,800[f]	1,500	3,230	6,600	8,550	5,400	5,200	3,950
Combat aircraft	USSR	1,540[g]	2,495	3,160	3,088	8,290	8,500	11,800	14,500
	Germany	4,950	2,500	3,400	3,500	2,980	3,000	2,800	1,960

[a] In 1960 N. S. Khrushchev reported that by the beginning of 1941 the total Red Army strength had reached 4,207,000 (including rear echelons and reserves); see Bergson, 1961, pp. 365–6. With recruitment in the first half of 1941 the total might have reached 5,000,000 by the outbreak of war.

[b] Excludes 50 mm mortars and rocket mortars. Fifty-mm mortars were widely deployed by the Soviet forces at the outbreak of war, but were found to be ineffective and were shortly withdrawn from service. Rocket mortars were pioneered in 1941 but were only brought into serial production in June 1941.

[c] Excludes light tanks, also widely deployed in 1941 but found to be of little value in combat with the German forces. The figure includes 1,475 tanks of modern design (this means KV heavy and T-34 medium tanks). Light tanks went on being produced until the end of 1943; see Milsom, 1971, p. 95. The total number of Soviet tanks held in the forward area at the outbreak of war is put at 7,000; estimates of the entire Soviet tank park, including rear echelons and reserves, range from 15,000 to 24,000; see ibid., p. 58. Ogorkiewicz, 1970, p. 227 favours the upper limit (21,000 to 24,000); and there is some support for this in the known 1939 figure of 23,930 tanks; see Milsom, 1971, p. 180.

[d] Includes 1,995 light tanks; see Chalmaev, 1981, p. 245.

[e] Excludes light tanks.

[f] This corresponded to a figure for reserves of 9,500 tanks; see Milsom, 1971, p. 68.

[g] Excludes obsolete aircraft. Since according to Tupper, 1982, p. 200 new types accounted for 19 per cent of first-line strength, total combat forces must have been 8,105 aircraft. In 1938 the ratio of first-line forces to the total air park, including transport aircraft, trainers and reserves, was about 68 per cent (ibid., pp. 110–11), which would suggest a total air park at the outbreak of war of 11,920 aircraft, but this may well be a considerable underestimate.

Source: VO voina, 1970, p. 579.

quantitative superiority over the invader. These trends in the balance of fighting forces are shown in Table 11.

Behind the changing Soviet first-line strength shown in this table lie extremely high rates of turnover of the stock of personnel and equipment. In the first six months of the war the number of Soviet soldiers killed or captured equalled the entire Red Army strength of June 1941, including reserves and rear echelons. The rate of human loss was naturally far higher than the few hundred thousand Soviet males who reached the age of military service in the same period. The economic consequences of such a human loss are considered in more detail in Part Two of this chapter.

Associated with the withering losses of personnel were extremely high rates of loss of military equipment. The Soviet armed forces suffered these heavy equipment losses in every period of the war. The rate of loss was notably insensitive to the degree of Soviet advantage or disadvantage; that is, there was no simple rule whereby losing the war meant losing equipment, and winning meant loss avoidance. When forced onto the defensive Soviet forces lost heavily because they were taken by surprise, outmanoeuvred and decimated or annihilated. They lost no less heavily in the counteroffensive because, with the odds more evenly balanced, they had to expose themselves to enemy defences and take substantial risks. Nor was the rate of attrition particularly sensitive to comparative force levels. When equipment was scarce, Soviet commanders would husband their resources and seek to avoid risking them in battle. As their force levels were expanded by additional supplies, commanders would take more initiatives and their echelons would become more exposed. Rapid force accumulation also brought lowered standards of experience, training and maintenance and higher equipment losses both on and off the battlefield.

Thus, whether they were winning or losing, the Soviet armed forces lost thousands upon thousands of aircraft, tanks and artillery pieces in every month of the war. The rate of attrition did vary within limits. But it was responsive only to extreme changes in the strategic and tactical environment and in the intensity of warfare.

For some main types of military equipment, balances can be compiled to show the relationship among first-line force levels, new supplies made available from domestic production and imports, and losses from first-line forces due to all causes (battlefield attrition, operational wear and tear, accidental damage, other withdrawals from the front line). The sources and methods for compiling these arms balances are shown in Appendix 3. The reliability of the results is subject not only to the accuracy of the original sources, but also to unavoidable problems such as the difficulty of fitting together disparate kinds of information on force levels, production levels and aid shipments, and allowing for altogether missing information on the allocation of new supplies between front-line and rear echelons and reserves. Nonetheless the results can throw some light on the demands being placed on Soviet industry (and Soviet allies) at different periods of the war to make good equipment losses and allow force accumulation.

Soviet losses of first-line military equipment over a given period can be estimated at monthly rates and expressed as proportions of the average first-line strength within the period. These estimates show that in the first and militarily most disastrous five months of the war Soviet losses of first-line combat aircraft averaged 45 per cent monthly, with losses of first-line tanks and artillery (including mortars) at 41 and 51 per cent respectively. Of course these losses were not spread evenly over the five months, as such averages imply – what tended to happen was that Soviet losses were concentrated at the beginning of the period, resulting in extremely rapid reduction of force levels; after this, the remainder was committed to defensive battles in which the aim was to wear the enemy down, not to risk further substantial Soviet losses.

This was the most disastrous period of the war, but Figure 3 shows that it did not result in the heaviest equipment losses. For example, although monthly loss rates were already devastatingly high, when the Red Army dug its heels in and committed itself to an offensive in December 1941, loss rates actually rose. For the artillery and tank forces this was the heaviest period of the war. After the spring of 1942, artillery loss rates fell steadily throughout the war. Tank loss rates fell only a little, staying at over 40 per cent per month until the end of 1943, except for a brief respite after the climax at Stalingrad. For the air forces the battle for command of the skies really began in the summer of 1942, and monthly loss rates climbed to nearly 80 per cent in this period. After June 1944 the outcome of the war was in little doubt, but absolute monthly loss rates were still very high at over 2,000 tanks, nearly 3,000 aircraft and nearly 10,000 artillery and mortar pieces per month.

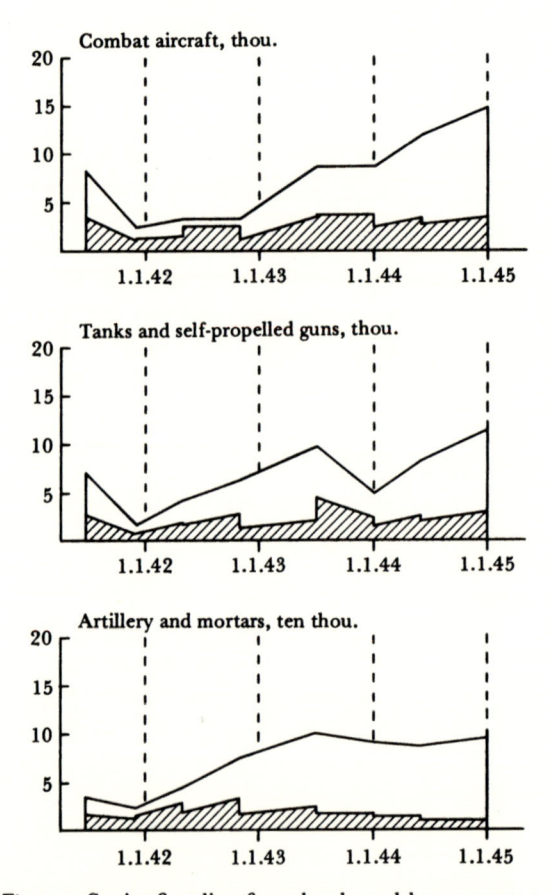

Figure 3. Soviet first-line force levels and losses 1941–5

Notes to Figure 3
Force levels

First-line force levels between benchmark dates given in Table 11 above. All data are as in Table 11, except that figures for first-line combat aircraft and tanks on 22 June 1941 are adjusted upward to 8,105 and 7,000 respectively to take into account estimates for numbers of older types, in line with notes to Table 11.

Force losses

First-line equipment losses from all causes, calculated as constant proportions of average force levels between benchmark dates and expressed in monthly rates. Loss estimates are taken from Appendix 3 below.

The Soviet productive effort

What can be learnt from Figure 3 about the development of the war economy? First, in spite of a decade and more of rearmament, the Soviet forces could not have fought the invader for more than ten to fifteen weeks with the weapons deployed in forward areas before the war, given the losses actually encountered. Without fresh supplies, Soviet commanders could only seek to protect their forces and could not risk them in battles of their own choosing. Secondly, the productive capacities of the arms industries in operation before the war were insufficient to supply the immediate combat needs of the Red Army – the entire Soviet output of combat aircraft, tanks, artillery and mortars in the first half of 1941 represented no more than one to three months' losses in the war up to December. Thus Figure 3 shows why arms production became a top priority from the first moment of the war to the last. Thirdly, it shows how Soviet losses climbed once the Soviet counteroffensive started, and it shows the necessity of expanding existing arms capacities and supplying them with greatly increased quantities of metals, fuels, machinery, transport services and labour.

THE ROLE OF SUPPLY

In illustrating Soviet arms balances in wartime we must now turn to the role of supply. Figure 4 shows how domestic production and

Note for fig. 3 (*cont.*)
In referring to Figure 3, the reader should take into account the important qualifications noted in the text. In addition the reader should note that, in order to arrive at the given estimates of monthly force losses, the underlying data have been extensively manipulated to fit them to the chosen arms categories and time periods. The extent of manipulation is explained in Appendix 3. The reader who does not wish to refer to Appendix 3 should further be aware of the underlying method of calculating the force losses shown in the diagram. In each period the actual increase in first-line equipment is subtracted from the increase potentially available as a result of domestic production and imports over the same period. The 'missing' residual measures losses from all causes, plus additions to rear formations and reserves. In general changes in rear formations and reserves are not known, but clearly they may have been considerable over short periods of time – for example during preparations for an offensive. However, if we assume that over a period of months changes in rear formations and reserves could be netted out at zero, then the difference between the potential and actual increase in first-line strength will approximately measure first-line force losses.

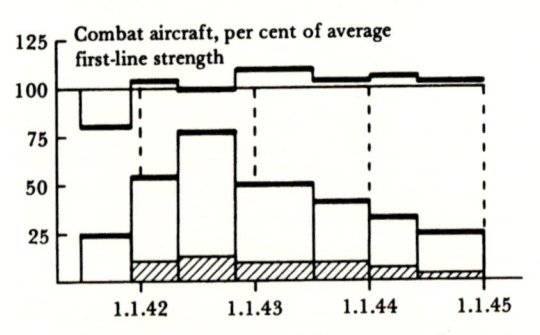

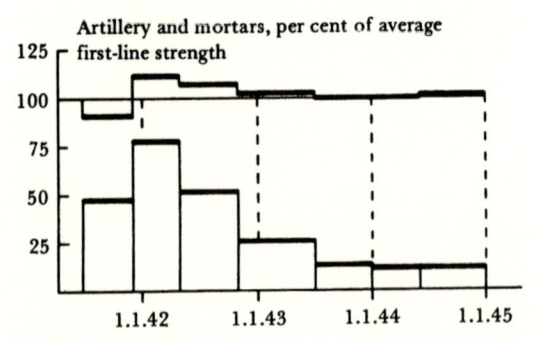

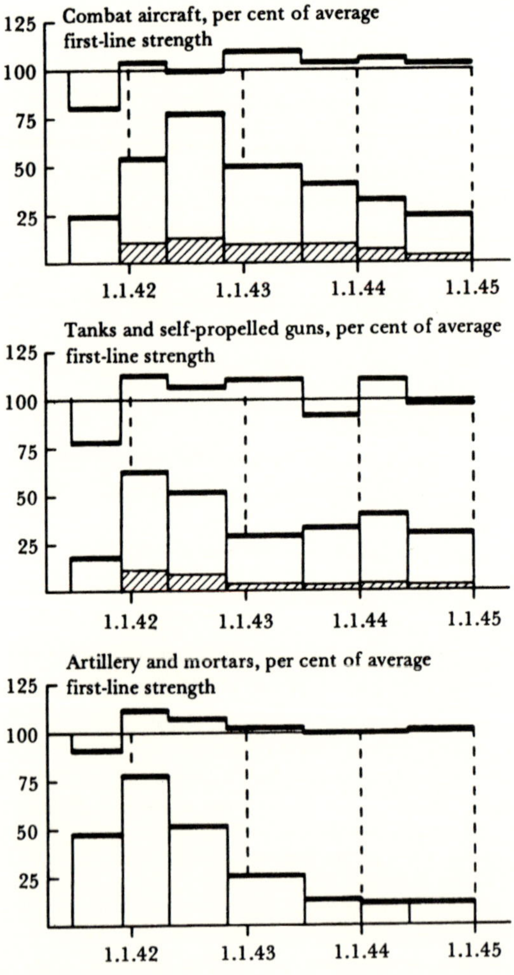

Figure 4. Soviet first-line force replacement and growth 1941–5

Notes to Figure 4
Force replacement

New supplies becoming available for domestic production (white blocks) and from imports (shaded blocks), expressed as monthly rates and calculated as proportions of average first-line forces between benchmark dates. Supply estimates are taken from Appendix 3 below.

imports together made up for losses of aircraft, tanks and artillery in various periods. For all categories the first five months of fighting resulted in heavy net losses – arms production, although already much higher than in peacetime, had not yet grappled seriously with the needs of war. In 1942 climbing domestic output and the first Allied aid shipments together converted the situation to one of rapid net expansion of ground tank and artillery forces; the air forces faced a heavier burden of continuing losses, and in spite of a high rate of domestic output and overseas supplies the losses of 1941 were not made good until 1943.

The role of Allied equipment made available for Soviet arms balances deserves separate consideration. In 1942 arriving shipments ran at much lower levels than in 1943 or 1944, but were composed predominantly of military goods – tanks, aircraft and explosives. They made an important contribution to Soviet firepower in 1942 – over 20 per cent of newly available combat aircraft and tanks. In 1943 and 1944 imports of aircraft continued to make an important addition to Soviet supplies. At the same time the role of imports in Soviet tank power fell back to about 10 per cent of total supplies. Allied shipments of artillery (except anti-aircraft guns) and mortar armament were insignificant at all times. Of course this does not allow us to make a general assessment of the significance of Allied aid in the Soviet war effort, since we have not considered the Allied contribution to other arms balances, to the Soviet transport balance, to the food and clothing balance or to material balances. Nor have we considered the Soviet contribution in terms of non-tradable military goods, the range of which is even broader and less easily defined. Such questions are touched upon again in Part Three of this chapter.

By how much did Soviet arms output have to grow to achieve these increases in force levels? Table 12 shows the output of some principal weapons from 1940 to 1945. By the outbreak of war the slowdown of rearmament in 1939 had been overcome, and production accelerated during 1941. In spite of the hesitation in arms capacity mobilisation

Notes to Figure 4 (cont.)
Force growth

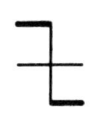

Average net monthly change in first-line forces between benchmark dates, calculated as a proportion of average first-line forces over the same period. Data used are from Table 11, with figures for 22 June 1941 adjusted as in Figure 3. Increases in force levels are shown as blocks above the 100 per cent line; decreases are shown below the line.

Table 12. *Soviet arms production 1940–5*

	1940	1941	1942	1943	1944	1945[a]
Aircraft	10,565	15,735	25,436	34,845	40,246	20,102
Tanks and self-propelled guns[b]	2,794	6,590	24,446	24,089	28,963	15,419
Artillery and mortars, thou.	53.8	67.8	356.9	199.5	129.5	64.6
Rifles and carbines, thou.	1,461	2,660	4,049	3,437	2,450	574

[a] First six months only.
[b] Self-propelled guns entered production in 1943.

Sources: See Appendix 1.

at the end of 1941 (recorded in Figure 2 on p. 82 above), dramatic increases were achieved in all categories. For the main weapons platforms, aircraft and tanks, a substantial rate of increase was recorded throughout the war, although the most rapid growth occurred before 1943. Tank production in the first half of 1943 was adversely affected by successful bombing of the Gor'ky tank factory. For weapons and ammunition of all kinds the first twelve to eighteen months saw a breathtaking production surge. Output peaked in 1942 or early 1943 – the ground forces had achieved sufficiency of armament, and loss rates were declining, so the peak was followed by sharp reductions in output, enabling resources to be switched elsewhere.

Is there any one useful measure of growth in the volume of domestic arms supplies during the war? An official index of wartime output of four defence industry commissariats, first published in 1965, is shown in Table 13 (the main arms branches omitted under this classification are mortar armament and naval vessels). Table 13 confirms that armament and ammunition output accelerated most rapidly at the outbreak of war, while tank and aircraft production took longer to gather momentum. Both the aggregate index and its components grow continuously through 1944, although only for tank and ammunition output is growth substantial at this late stage in the war. Arms production is shown to have doubled towards the end of 1942 or early 1943, and in the peak year of 1944 was 2.5 times higher than in 1940. The latter fact may be compared with Voznesensky's statement that 'war production in the eastern and central areas of the U.S.S.R. alone increased during the Patriotic War two and a half times over in comparison with the 1940 production level for the whole of the U.S.S.R.'[4]

Table 13. *Changes in arms production by commissariat 1941–5 (1940 = 100)*

	1941	1942	1943	1944	1945
Aircraft industry	126	178	223	239	177
Tank industry	112	184	234	296	276
Armament industry	145	191	200	206	156
Ammunition industry	152	218	264	310	171
Total (four commissariats)[a]	140	186	224	251	—

[a] This index moves roughly with the indices for the four industries which it combines, but it cannot be derived directly from them (in the sense that there is no unique set of non-negative fractions summing to unity with which the components can be weighted to arrive at the sum given for each year). There are three possible explanations. There may have been errors in computing the overall index. The overall index may have been computed using variable weights. Or the overall index may be based on unpublished real quantity time series underlying the industry output indices.

Source: IVOVSS, v. 6, 1965, pp. 45, 52. For a recent, authoritative citation of this table see ISE, v. 5, 1978, pp. 189, 258.

Table 13 poses its share of problems. Its component series are usually interpreted as volume indices calculated in terms of the fixed prices of a common base year, i.e. as measures of 'real' arms production. An indirect confirmation of this may be found in the work of Bergson, who, having isolated weapons procurement within the defence budgets for 1940 and 1944, and estimating that weapons production costs had fallen by 20 per cent between these two dates in terms of the 1937 pattern of procurement, calculated 1944 'real' defence spending on domestically manufactured arms as 2.3 times the 1940 level.[5] This could be compared with the results for 1944 shown in Table 13.

Unfortunately it is difficult to reconcile the detail of Table 13, understood in this way, with the detail of Table 12. Table 13's indices of industrial output rise far less rapidly between 1940 and 1942 than the recorded numbers of planes, tanks, guns and shells produced. In this period the number of aircraft built rose by 141 per cent, but the industry's output index shown in Table 13 increases by only 78 per cent. More strikingly the number of tanks produced rose by 775 per cent over the same two years, yet the index of tank industry output increases by a mere 84 per cent. With regard to the supply of armament and ammunition similar discrepancies are suggested (although with less precision) when Table 13 is compared either with Table 12 or with more detailed time series in Appendix 1.

Given the discrepancies between Tables 12 and 13, which provides us with the more reliable picture of the changing volume of Soviet arms supplies in wartime? Our answer to this must depend on the reasons for divergence. There are three possible reasons, each with different implications. The first may arise if the changes in the numbers of units produced, shown in Table 12, conceal significant changes in the composition and quality of output; this might prove a reason for preferring the information in Table 13. In the aircraft industry, for example, the war saw a rapid shift away from building heavy, complex and expensive bombers towards lighter, simpler and cheaper fighters and ground-attack aircraft (for this and other more detailed information about the changing composition of arms supplies, see Appendix 1). This would suggest deflation of the change in the volume of output suggested by Table 12 towards that suggested by Table 13. But no such factor could explain the huge gap between the changes in the tank industry's output index and the far larger expansion in the number of tanks produced in each year, since the main change in the composition of output was the discontinuation of light tank manufacture and appearance of heavy self-propelled artillery in 1943. Again less precise data on wartime output of the main types of armament and ammunition similarly suggest rejection of the hypothesis that Table 13 represents Table 12 properly deflated for changes in the composition and quality of output.

The second and third possible reasons for divergence between Tables 12 and 13 are that Table 13 may incorporate changes in inputs as well as outputs – the information may reflect changes in current values, not constant-price volumes; or that the information in Table 13 may reflect changing administrative boundaries as well as the changing volume of outputs. Either of these would encourage us to prefer the information in Table 12 as clearer and less ambiguous in its meaning. As far as input values are concerned, between 1940 and 1943 the prices of machinery, materials and labour for arms production all increased, but the economies arising from mass production and process innovation were so great that unit costs in the defence industries fell substantially. For 1942 Voznesensky set the transfer prices for defence industry output at 72 per cent of the 1940 level.[6] In 1943 they may have fallen further.[7] But in 1944 production costs probably increased; for this year Bergson set the cost deflation compared to 1940 at a 'conservative' 20 per cent. If the information shown in Table 13 indicates changes in values, not volumes, it would be necessary to apply an upward correction of perhaps 30 per cent to 1942 and 1943 and 20 per cent to 1944 in order to approximate to changes in 'real' output.

Lastly, the industry-based indices of Table 13 may have been influenced by the changing administrative definition of industries. Let us take tank production as an example. The tank industry was formed as a ministerial unit only in September 1941, and combined tankbuilding with various kinds of non-military engineering ranging from locomotive building to machine tool manufacture. Its plants shut down civilian output and concentrated on tanks; this may explain why initially tank output grew so rapidly while the industry's total production measured in Table 13 grew so much more modestly, reflecting the loss of civilian lines. A further loss to the industry's production measured in Table 13 may have occurred in February 1942, when the industry's machine tool capacity was split off to form a new ministerial unit.[8] Perhaps too throughout this period the tank industry's output as measured in Table 13 was being deflated by the growth of value added among the industry's subcontractors outside its accounting jurisdiction. In this case the opposite may have been at work during 1943, when the industry's output measured in Table 13 rose in spite of a fall in the number of tanks produced.

The profound uncertainties attached to Table 13 suggest a serious danger of underestimating the 'real' increase in Soviet arms supplies during the war. The response of Soviet industry to the battle losses and replacement needs of the Red Army is better gauged from Table 12 and Appendix 1. In the next part of the chapter we turn to examine the context of rapidly growing arms supplies – the changing structure of outputs, inputs and capacity in the economy as a whole.

PART TWO: OUTPUTS AND INPUTS

THE STRUCTURE OF PRODUCTION

Supply of the Soviet arms mobilisation rested upon a complex economic system. Each shell fired at the enemy had been machined by engineers, it had been manufactured out of metals and chemicals, and the process of its manufacture had required the transformation of fuels into energetic power; it had been transported physically through the stages of production and then to the front line. At each stage the capacity to do these things had been erected by builders. The workers and soldiers who converted the raw materials into fighting power had been fed, clothed and sheltered. Had any element of this many-sided combination been missing, the fighting power of the Soviet Army could not have been realised.

In this section we look at the changing proportions in which different industries were combined under wartime conditions. We start with the centrally important complex of heavy industries, and then we proceed to incorporate the light industries and agriculture. In following sections we consider the role and reproduction of the economy's fixed assets and workforce.

The most complex interactions among specialised industrial sectors were found in the sphere of the defence and heavy industries. A simplified picture of their interaction is found in Figure 5. The diagram can be read starting from the left-hand side. The armed forces were the final consumer – they received weapons and other military equipment from the arms industries. They also depended directly upon the fuel and energy sector for the power to operate them. Arms industries, comprising specialised defence-related engineering and assembly plants, manufactured military goods. For this they depended on all the heavy industries for supplies of machine tools, machinery and components, chemicals, metals and energy. At one more remove the civilian engineering sector required more chemicals, metals and energy for operation. The chemicals, metals and energy sectors used raw materials and each others' products for their needs together with inputs of machinery. The whole system was bound together by a transport network which it supplied with machinery and fuel and without which it could not function. In particular the world of the 'basic industries' (primarily metals, fuels and transport) was a tightly interlocking sub-system within which disturbances could be transmitted and amplified nearly without limit.

The wartime performance of the main sectors of heavy industry and transport can be gauged from Tables 14 and 15. The shock to output, which lasted through 1942, is clearly visible in all sectors. The rate, depth and persistence of decline varied among sectors, reflecting the various causes at work. Civilian engineering output (represented in Table 14 by machine tools and agricultural and road vehicles) fell

The Soviet productive effort 123

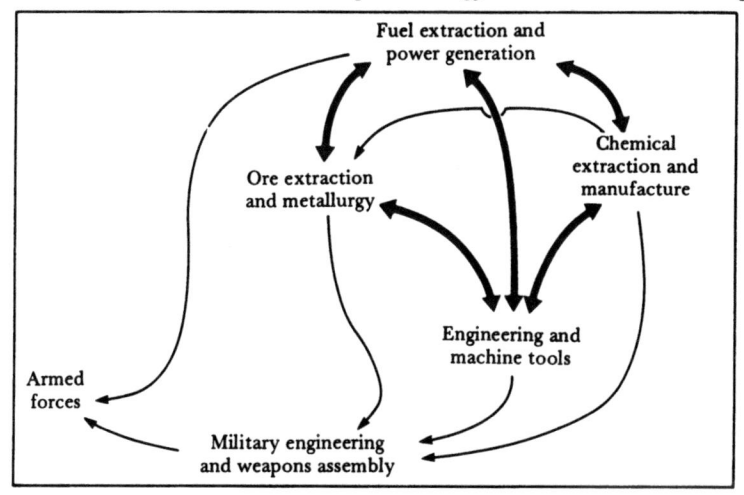

Figure 5. Input–output interaction of the arms industry and heavy industry

Key: A thin arrow pointing in a single direction ⟶ indicates a one-way flow of products from supplier to user. A broad arrow pointing in both directions ⟷ indicates a two-way product flow with each sector consuming part of the other's output.

Notes: In order to read the diagram, start on the left-hand side with the armed forces and follow each product flow backwards to its source. Two sectors – the transport and construction industries – are not represented explicitly but are implicitly present. Each arrow represents spatial flows requiring transport services for their realisation; to deliver its services the transport industry requires inputs of machinery and fuel. Moreover each of the supplying sectors in the diagram requires receipt of built capacity from the construction industry before it can use current inputs or supply outputs.

sharply. The binding constraint, however, was not cuts in capacity but the shortage of metals and fuels and their diversion to defence engineering. Cuts in the supply of metals, coal and electric power were primarily due to cuts in capacity as territory was yielded to the German advance (the capacity was either lost permanently or temporarily decommissioned for evacuation). Reductions in the supply of transport services reflected both the loss of transport assets and their progressive scrambling during the transition to new wartime tasks. Initial output losses interacted to produce a cumulative circle of disruption which proved extremely difficult to reverse as coordination, morale and working conditions declined. The story of how this was eventually achieved is told in Chapter 4.

Table 14. *Soviet heavy industrial production 1940–5*

	1940	1941	1942	1943	1944	1945
Iron ore, mn tons	29.9	24.7	9.7	9.3	11.7	15.9
Pig iron, mn tons	14.9	13.8	4.8	5.6	7.3	8.8
Crude steel, mn tons	18.3	17.9	8.1	8.5	10.9	12.3
Rolled steel, mn tons	13.1	12.6	5.4	5.7	7.9	8.5
High-grade	3.2	4.7	3.4	4.2	—	4.1
Ordinary	9.9	7.9	2.0	1.5	—	4.4
Copper, thou. tons	—	—	118	105	—	135
Aluminium, thou. tons	—	—	51.7	62.3	82.7	86.3
Coal, mn tons	165.9	151.4	75.5	93.1	121.5	149.3
Oil, mn tons	31.1	33.0	22.0	18.0	18.2	19.4
Electricity, bn kWh	48.3	46.6	29.1	32.2	39.2	43.3
Machine tools, thou.[a]	58.4	44.5	22.9	23.3	34.0	38.4
Tractors, thou.	31.6	—	3.5	1.1	3.2	7.7
Trucks, thou.	136.0	—	30.9	45.5	52.6	68.5

[a] Metal-cutting machine tools only.
Sources: See Appendix 2.

Table 15. *Changes in Soviet freight transport volumes 1940–5 (1940 = 100)*

	1941	1942	1943	1944	1945
Railways[a]	93	52	58	68	76
Sea craft	85	66	137	144	144
River craft	95	60	62	62	52
Motor vehicles	70	31	31	39	56
Aircraft	74	61	78	148	275
Oil pipeline	69	39	43	70	71
All types	92	53	61	77	77

[a] The source does not indicate the base-year weights used to combine different kinds of transport services into the aggregate index, which (as in Table 13) cannot be derived directly from the component indices shown. However, according to Kumanev, 1976, p. 393, taking the war years as a whole railway services accounted for over 83 per cent of all freight transfers and over 70 per cent of all military freights.
Source: IVOVSS, v. 6, 1965, pp. 45, 70.

Table 16. *Output declines and territorial losses 1940–2 (percentages)*

	Productive capacity located on territory lost between 22 June and November 1941	Output decline 1940 to 1942	Margin of output decline over 'lost' capacity[a]
Iron ore	71	68	3
Pig iron	68	68	0
Crude steel	58	56	2
Rolled steel	57	41	16
Coal	63	54	9
Electric power	42	40	2
Railway lines	41	48	−7

[a] The difference between the first two columns; 'lost' means lost to the enemy or decommissioned for evacuation.

Sources: Table 5 and calculated from Tables 14 and 15.

For the main sectors (except engineering) shown in Tables 14 and 15 we can crudely compare output declines up to 1942 with capacity lost or decommissioned as a result of German advances in 1941. The result helps us to measure the ability of the Soviet economy to compensate for output losses caused directly by enemy action. Table 16 shows us that in nearly all cases Soviet output in 1942 was higher than would have been predicted simply from studying the pattern of German advances up to the end of 1941 – and this was in spite of further German advances in the summer and autumn of 1942. The exception was railway transport, where the provision of services fell somewhat below this crude benchmark. By such standards the short-term performance of Soviet heavy industry was good under the circumstances. It was made possible by concentrating human and material resources upon these sectors, and it can easily be understood that this was to the detriment of the rest of the civilian economy.

Finally, Tables 14 and 15 show us that throughout heavy industry 1943 was a year of stabilisation or even recovery, while 1944 saw further expansion. However, 1945 output remained far below prewar levels.

Is it possible to find useful summary measures of the expansion of Soviet heavy industry in wartime? Table 17 shows official industry-based indices of real output, and these may be compared with unit production series in Table 15. A remarkable feature of Table 17 is the

Table 17. *Changes in Soviet heavy industrial production 1940–5 (1940 = 100)*

	1941	1942	1943	1944	1945
Ferrous ores and metallurgy[a]	105	62	70	88	89
Fuels[a]	94	53	59	71	75
Coal extraction	87	43	54	71	88
Oil extraction	102	61	63	72	68
Electrical and thermal power	97	62	67	81	91
Engineering and metalworking[b]	112	119	142	158	129
Timber and woodworking	88	48	51	55	55
Industrial building materials[a]	79	26	29	35	41

[a] Chadaev, 1965, p. 67 gives the same series for 1940–3 but with some small discrepancies for the indicated rows, as follows:

	1941	1942	1943
Ferrous ores and metallurgy	109	69	76
Fuels	93	50	56
Industrial building materials	80	27	31

[b] Includes armament and ammunition production.
Source: IVOVSS, v. 6, 1965, p. 59.

buoyancy of the index for ferrous ores and metallurgy, which shows 1942 output at 62 per cent of 1940 when the physical tonnage of pig iron and of crude and rolled steel products had fallen by one-half to two-thirds. This apparent discrepancy is explained only by the drive to maintain output of high-value, high-grade rolled steel for arms production (see Table 14) in spite of the industry's overall decline. The arms mobilisation is also visible in Table 17 in the expansion of the index for engineering and metalworking, which includes the armament and ammunition industries. With these exceptions Table 17 shows a pattern for the heavy industries consistent with what we already know.

For accounting purposes Soviet statisticians do not generate a production index for heavy industry as a whole. Instead they use the classification of industrial output by end use into group 'A' (means of production, or industrial goods) and group 'B' (means of consumption). From an input–output perspective the distinction between groups 'A' and 'B' should be illuminating, but is prone to operational

Table 18. *Changes in Soviet industrial production 1940–5 (1940 = 100)*

	1941	1942	1943	1944	1945
Industrial output group 'A'[a]	111	100	119	136	112
Arms output (four defence industry commissariats)	140	186	224	251	—
Output of means of arms production[b]	150	156	167	174	166
Industrial output group 'B'	77	41	45	54	59
Gross industrial output	98	77	90	104	92

[a] In this table group 'A' has an implicit 1940 weight in gross industrial production of 61 per cent.
[b] Said to be calculated at 1971 prices.

Sources: Indices for groups 'A' and 'B' and for gross industrial output are from Chadaev, 1965, p. 66; the index for gross industrial output is the same as that given by IVOVSS, v. 6, 1965, p. 45. The arms output index, also from the latter source, is reproduced from Table 13 above for purposes of comparison. The index of output of means of arms production is a comparatively recent one published by Avramchuk, 1975, p. 7.

distortions. For example military goods are classified as industrial, and included in group 'A' output, although they are clearly not means of production – a practice long criticised by a number of Soviet economists.[9] In addition the definition of group 'A' does not normally distinguish between industrial goods destined for defence and civilian industries.

Table 18 shows indices of output for groups 'A' and 'B' and for gross industrial output. Group 'A' output rose substantially in 1941 under the impact of the arms mobilisation, then fell back in 1942 as heavy industry faltered. Meanwhile, according to other information in this table, arms production had grown by 86 per cent over 1940 (recall that this is a likely underestimate) while the output of industrial goods for the arms industries had grown by 56 per cent. A very substantial fall is implied in the output of means of civilian production up to 1942, but the extent of it cannot be calculated from the data available. Group 'A' output resumed expansion in 1943 and by 1944 was more than one-third up on prewar levels. But Table 18 also shows that in the same year industrial production as a whole was barely higher than in 1940, while the output of consumer goods had sunk to around half the prewar level.

Table 19. *Comparative resource mobilisation: a Soviet view of 1942*

Units produced in 1942	USSR	Germany[a]	USA	Britain
Per mn tons crude steel				
Aircraft	3,179	717	614	1,820
Tanks	3,083	453	306	666
Per bn kWh electricity				
Aircraft	877	204	206	495
Tanks	851	129	103	180
Per thou. machine tools[b]				
Aircraft	1,106	137	156	247
Tanks	1,073	87	78	90

[a] Excluding colonial and conquered territories.
[b] Metal-cutting machine tools only.
Source: G. S. Kravchenko, 1970, p. 208.

One Soviet historian has constructed some measures of comparative wartime resource mobilisation from the internal coefficients of the defence and heavy industry complex. G. S. Kravchenko uses 1942 outputs of main types of weapons in proportion to the production of principal industrial goods in that year for the four great powers. Although this means anticipating some later discussion, his results are shown here in Table 19. This table shows that the USSR devoted her supplies of industrial goods to defence production far more intensively than her main allies or main enemy. Relative to her available steel, energy and engineering capacity the Soviet Union produced far more aircraft and tanks in 1942 than the other powers. Unfortunately this table does not tell the whole story. In 1942 neither Germany nor the United States had geared its economy for unlimited war. Moreover wartime mobilisation of the other powers was directed towards military goals which the USSR did not attempt – for example motorisation of the ground forces and strategic sea and air power. Soviet industry did not try to build large numbers of heavy long-range bombers, battle cruisers and aircraft carriers, cargo vessels or heavy goods road vehicles. Consequently the value of the indices shown in Table 19 for cross-country comparisons is limited.

The concepts behind Table 19 can more usefully be applied to study of Soviet mobilisation of basic industrial goods over time. Figure 6 takes the example of steel utilisation from 1940 to 1945, broadening

The Soviet productive effort 129

Output per thousand tons of domestic crude steel supplies

Aircraft

Tanks and self-propelled guns

Artillery pieces

Metal-cutting machine tools

Trucks

Tractors

1940　1941　1942　1943　1944　1945

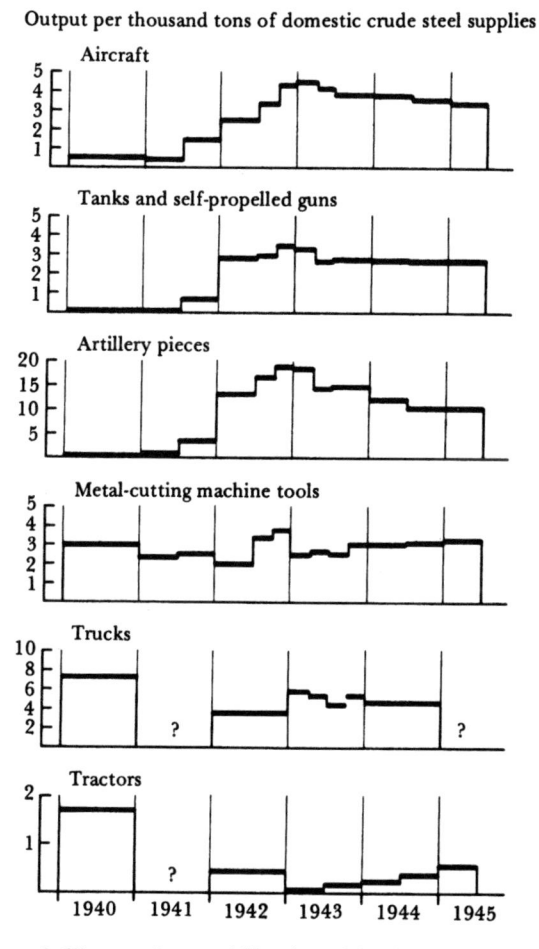

Figure 6. The wartime mobilisation of Soviet steel 1940–5

Notes to Figure 6
What is measured in the diagrams is the number of units of each item of military or industrial goods produced per thousand tons of crude steel produced over the same period. The period over which this rate is measured varies, and is shown in as much detail (half-yearly, quarterly) as possible given the need for comparability of data. Thus in 1940 0.6 aircraft were built for every thousand tons of crude steel produced, but in the first half of 1941 the rate fell slightly to 0.5 aircraft; the wartime peak was 4.5 aircraft per thousand tons of steel produced (in the first quarter of 1943). Data are calculated from Appendices 1 and 2.

the scope to six main steel-consuming products (three military goods and three industrial goods). Relative to available steel supplies, aircraft, tank and artillery production grew continuously from the outbreak of war until the last quarter of 1942. After that steel output expanded while arms output stabilised, so that the intensity of utilisation of steel for military goods declined somewhat. The production of non-military metal-using industrial goods in wartime fell relative to steel supplies. In the case of such goods as machine tools or trucks the fall was substantial, but, given their continued significance for wartime industry, there was some kind of floor which prevented the fall from being too deep or too sustained – even under the conditions of wartime steel famine. But for agricultural machinery such as tractors (and, by extension, other consumer-oriented industrial goods) no such floor existed and supplies of steel were virtually shut off completely.

The fates of light industry and agriculture in wartime are shown in Tables 20 and 21. For manufactured consumer goods 1942 was the worst year, and the rest of the war saw only marginal improvements; most civilians finished the war with the same crockery, clothing and footwear – patched with glue and thread – with which they began it. For agriculture 1942 was a dreadful year, with output down over 60 per cent compared to 1940. But at least the population which it had to support had also fallen, although only by one-third. Nineteen-forty-three was even worse – farm output stagnated or fell further, while the population recovered from 130 to 143 million.[10] Improvements followed, but were far less than needed to restore the Soviet diet. In wartime Soviet workers ate much less meat and vegetables, and hardly any sugar or preserves, making up for these with some extra fish and potatoes.[11] Soviet food supplies were also supplemented by foreign aid in 1943 and 1944.[12]

In summary, when war broke out the Soviet economy staggered under the blow. Recovery from the blow meant shifting into a new gear – resources were poured into the defence industries, and then into the heavy industries which supported them. Defence output multiplied although the availability of basic industrial and engineering goods for current inputs had sharply contracted. Defence output grew most rapidly during 1942, and during 1943 the heavy industries began their recovery. In the consumer sector and agriculture the decline had been precipitous and was barely stopped in 1943. Some recovery took place in 1944, but the situation remained disastrous throughout the war.

Table 20. *Changes in light industry and food industry output 1940–5 (1940 = 100)*

	1941	1942	1943	1944	1945
Light industry output	*88*	*48*	*54*	*64*	*62*
Cotton textiles	91	36	38	43	41
Woollen textiles	74	32	35	40	42
Silk weaves	77	41	50	55	50
Sewn goods	94	73	86	107	103
Leather; furs; footwear	85	47	54	64	60
Food industry output	*80*	*42*	*41*	*47*	*51*
Meat	80	52	48	46	45
Fish	92	68	86	90	79
Milk products	87	52	62	78	73
Sugar	44	5	6	11	20

Source: IVOVSS, v. 6, 1965, p. 63.

Table 21. *Changes in agricultural output 1940–5 (1940 = 100)*

	1941	1942	1943	1944	1945
Gross agricultural output	62	38	37	54	60
Crop harvests (barn yields)					
Grains	59	31	31	51	49
Sugar beets	11	12	7	23	30
Raw cotton	111	59	32	51	52
Flax; hemp	38	60	45	48	43
Sunflowers	34	11	30	38	32
Potatoes	35	31	46	72	77
Livestock products					
Meat and fats	87	39	38	42	55
Milk	76	47	49	66	79
Wool	100	78	62	64	69
Eggs	76	37	28	29	40

Sources: IVOVSS, v. 6, 1965, pp. 45, 67.

132　　　　　　*Soviet planning in peace and war*

Table 22. *Industrial output in the liberated regions 1940–5*

	1940	1942	1943	1944	1945[a]
Iron ore, thou. tons	20,200	283	223	1,200	1,800
Pig iron, thou. tons	9,600	69	270	1,100	700
Crude steel, thou. tons	9,100	81	80	1,100	750
Rolled steel, thou. tons	6,700	—	5	600	560
Coal, thou. tons	48,600	12,400[b]	18,600	39,100	26,600
Oil, thou. tons	—	—	2	44	—
Electricity, mn kWh	—	158	810	3,010	—
Coal-cutting machines	1,185	—	11	282	375
Tractors	10,400	—	0	417	1,503
Leather footwear, thou. pr	—	747	1,300	2,600	—
Woollen textiles, mn m²	13	1	—	—	—
Lump sugar, thou. tons	1,343	5	20	174	—
Animal fats, thou. tons	—	5	—	21	—

[a] First six months only.
[b] The source gives this number as 12.4 thousand tons, but the 1942 output of the Moscow coal basin alone was 8.6 million tons, which should be included in the figure estimated; see Sov. ekon., 1970, p. 91.

Sources: Prikhod'ko, 1968, pp. 12, 14, 16, 19, 22; 1973, pp. 50, 72, 111, 132.

Table 23. *The liberated regions' share in industrial growth 1942–5*

	Per cent share of the liberated regions in output levels				Per cent share of the liberated regions in the increase in outputs		
	1942	1943	1944	1945[a]	1942–3	1943–4	1944–5[b]
Pig iron	1.4	4.8	15.1	16.7	25.1	48.8	27.3
Crude steel	1.0	0.9	10.1	12.7	−0.3	42.5	44.4
Rolled steel	—	0.1	7.6	13.7	—	27.0	173.3
Coal	16.4	20.0	32.2	37.7	35.2	72.2	71.6
Electricity	0.5	2.5	7.7	—	20.4	31.7	—
Tractors	—	0.0	13.0	44.2	—	19.9	57.5

[a] First six months only.
[b] First six months of 1945 at annual rate.

Sources: Calculated from Tables 14 and 22.

The Soviet productive effort 133

Above (pp. 84–5 and 125) we took care to establish the spatial component of the changing structure of production in 1941 and 1942 – the extent to which declines in the output of particular commodities could be explained by the transfer of territory from Soviet to German control. In considering the uneven pattern of industrial recovery, what contribution to Soviet output was made by the liberation of territory as the war progressed?

Table 22 shows available data for industrial production in the regions classified as 'liberated' upon recapture from the German forces, counting only the periods during which they were under Soviet control. In Table 23 these data are compared where possible with nationwide wartime output in order to show the relative importance of the liberated regions in all-Union output growth. The picture is incomplete but striking. Rehabilitated capacity accounted for nearly half the output growth in ferrous metallurgy and about three-quarters of the growth in coal extraction in the years 1943 to 1945. All the same the contribution of the liberated regions to industrial output in 1945 fell considerably short of the prewar position.

FIXED CAPACITY AND NEW INVESTMENT

The availability of fixed capacity to the Soviet wartime economy was determined by three factors. These were first of all the effects on existing capacity of territorial losses and gains and, secondly, the offsetting effects of evacuation of existing assets from war zones and later their return; thirdly, there was the creation of new capacity through fixed investment during the war years. However, when war broke out investment activity was reined sharply back; according to the official index in 1942 and 1943 it ran at only 53 per cent of the 1940 level and had not yet fully recovered by 1945.[13]

As far as the first two processes are concerned, their relative importance in 1941 and 1942 (the loss of territory and evacuation of assets) has been extensively discussed above. When taken together, the net results of territorial change greatly outweighed the significance of new investment. For example during 1941 and 1942 the Soviet stock of fixed assets apparently fell by 37 per cent, but new investment should have added to it by 9 per cent, so that the net results of territorial change had deprived the Soviet economy of about 46 per cent of its end-1940 fixed capital stock. During 1943 and 1944, on the other hand, the stock of fixed assets grew by 38 per cent of the end-1942 level, but 25 to 26 per cent (about two-thirds) reflected the results of territorial gain, while new investment added only 12 to 13 per cent to the end-1942 capital stock.[14]

If we look only at the net significance of new investment in the make-up of the country's fixed assets, we understate the importance of the investment process taken as a whole. For example, during the second and third Five Year Plans new plant had been constructed at the rate of 800 to 900 per year. In the war years the rate fell to a little below 800 per year,[15] and we shall see below that in industry the average size of new plant apparently declined. But as well as building new plant, the investment effort included the relocation of more than 1,500 evacuated factories in 1941 and 1942; in 1942 for example the value of newly invested industrial equipment only slightly exceeded that of relocated equipment.[16] The investment effort also included the restoration of 7,500 recaptured plants on previously occupied territory; this accounted for 16 per cent of industrial investment in 1943 and 41 to 42 per cent in 1944 and 1945.[17]

There is evidence that wartime investment was more effective than investment in the preceding peacetime years in commissioning new fixed capacity. If we compare newly finished capacity with the volume of current investment, then the average annual rate of completion of investment during the second and third Five Year Plans was 87 and 89 per cent respectively. In the war years the completion rate rose slightly to 91 per cent.[18] There is evidence, moreover, of substantial variation from year to year. According to contemporary sources the completion rate was only 86.5 per cent in 1940; in 1942 it rose to 106 per cent, and in 1943 to 112 per cent.[19] Presumably investment completion fell sharply in 1941 when many existing projects were frozen at the outbreak of war. At the same time new projects were cancelled and new investment concentrated on those existing projects protected by some degree of wartime priority. Thus it was mainly plant construction activity which fell, while in the first eighteen months of the war assembly and installation of equipment ran 30 per cent higher than in the prewar year and a half from January 1940.[20] The militarisation of work under the construction commissariat and the relaxation of peacetime building standards and regulations also helped to speed up the investment process.[21] Also important was more modest project design. For example the average size of newly commissioned plant in the iron and steel industry fell sharply at the outbreak of war and, for some kinds of plant, fell continuously throughout the war years.[22] In the electric power industry priority was given first to finishing projects already near completion, then to building new small and medium-sized plant.[23] These were the foundations of comparatively high completion rates in 1942 and 1943. By the end of 1943 the 1940 backlog of unfinished investment had been halved.[24] However, uncompleted investment possibly grew again in 1944 and 1945 as new long-term reconstruction projects were begun.

Thus if we take the war years as a whole, the average volume of new and reconstructed capacity in the main sectors of the iron and steel, coal and electrical power industries commissioned in each year substantially exceeded the average volume of new and reconstructed capacity completed annually under the third, and in some cases the second, Five Year Plan.[25]

Of course the composition of investment altered sharply when war broke out, and the changing regional and sectoral breakdown may also affect our view of its significance. The regional composition of investment followed a predictable pattern. The interior regions of the country (the Ural region and Western Siberia, Central Asia and Kazakhstan, and the southeastern region of the European USSR) increased their share in total investment from 26 per cent in 1940 to 61 per cent in 1942 and the same in 1943. The rest of the European USSR (including the Transcaucasus) and Eastern Siberia and the Far East all lost. In 1944 the centre of gravity of investment activity shifted westward again, but it was the central and southern regions of the European USSR which gained from the swing; the Far East and Eastern Siberia, the Transcaucasus, and the northern and western regions of the European USSR (the latter still partly under enemy occupation) remained starved of new investments.[26]

Of equal interest is the industrial composition of investment. Sweeping changes are revealed in Table 24. Investment in heavy industry, including the arms industries, stood at about 30 per cent of total investment under the third Five Year Plan, rising to 41 per cent in 1940. This share was sustained taking the war years together, but in 1942 alone it rose to 59 per cent. As a result, if we compare 1942 with the prewar pattern, total investment had fallen by nearly half, but investment in heavy industry must have remained stable.

Within heavy industry a number of sectors gained still greater prominence. Among these were the basic industries and construction, while engineering showed a modest increase in its share. But within

Table 24. *The industrial composition of investment 1938–45 (percentage shares)*

	1938–June 1941	July 1941–5	1940	1942
Heavy industry	29.9	41.6	41	58
Fuels; energy	7.6	10.7	—	11
Iron and steel	2.5	5.3		
Chemicals	1.7	1.6		
Engineering[a]	11.8 } 22.3	15.3 } 30.8	—	47
Construction	1.6	2.5		
Other heavy	4.7	6.1		
Transport	17.5	14.7	20	15
Light industry	5.5	3.0		
Agriculture	11.4 } 52.5	9.7 } 43.7	39	27
Residential construction	17.5	16.0		
Service construction	18.1	15.0		
Total investment	99.9	100.0	100	100

[a] This must include the bulk of the arms industries; part (but not all) may be included under 'other heavy' industries.

Sources: 1938–June 1941 and July 1941–5 calculated from Kap. str., 1961, pp. 56–7, 66–7; shares for 1940 and 1942 are from Kromov, 1943, p. 28 and Lersky, 1945, p. 10 (Lersky, 1943, p. 2 gives slightly different figures).

Table 25. *The ministerial composition of investment 1940–4 (percentage shares, by commissariat)*

	1940	1943	1944
Defence industries	13.2	21.4	15.0
Iron and steel industry	5.0	8.4	10.6
Coal industry	5.5	7.1	9.1
Electric power industry	3.9	5.5	4.8

Source: V. Sokolov, 1946, p. 19.

the engineering industry there was presumably a dramatic change from investment in civilian plant to war-related engineering and weapons factories. The rising claim of the defence industries on investment resources is not identified directly in Table 24, but is shown clearly in Table 25 for 1943 and 1944. In 1943, when investment as a whole was still just over half its 1940 level, the share of the arms industry commissariats in investment was over 21 per cent, and this was over one and a half times their 1940 share. The main basic industries' share had also risen by a similar proportion. In 1944, as investment recovered, the share of the defence industries fell back, while the basic industries were the main beneficiaries. No comparable data are available, however, for 1942.

Light industry, agriculture and residential and service construction were starved of investment resources during the war years. The impact on equipment budgets for non-priority sectors was even greater than Table 24 would suggest. If, for example, we compare 1942–5 with 1938–41, agriculture in wartime received one-tenth of the supply of tractors and trucks made available annually in the prewar years, and one-hundredth of the supply of combine harvesters.[27] This was the price of sustained investment in the economy's wartime priorities.

THE WORKFORCE AND LABOUR INPUTS

In a postwar review of German wartime experience Nicholas Kaldor posed the question of the role of labour in limiting a country's war effort. Any country's 'war potential', he considered,

> must be determined by at least one of the following four factors: the capital equipment of its industry, its available man-power, its supply of raw materials, and finally, the ability and skill of its industrial organisers, engineers and technicians. Some of these, however, are limited only from a short-term view point. Assuming that there is time enough to build up the capital equipment of its industries, in all stages, to the requirements of war, the ultimate limits to a country's war potential are set simply by the quantity and skill of its man-power, and by the richness of ores and minerals of the areas under its control or with which it is capable of trading. These two are the ultimate bottlenecks which must become operative if and when all other temporary bottlenecks have been overcome.[28]

Kaldor's experience, moreover, was that of the two 'ultimate bottlenecks' it was the limit set by manpower which became operative among the main belligerent economies of World War II.[29]

The Soviet labour balance was already under strain when war broke out, a factor which sharply differentiated it from the position in Britain, the United States or Germany. In the first year of the war the Soviet authorities had to find 11–12 million young men and women for the armed forces (about a million women served) in order to make good the heavy losses of killed and captured and to lift force levels

Table 26. *The Soviet labour force 1940–5 (millions)*

	1940	1941	1942	1943	1944	1945
Armed forces	4.2	—	10.9	—	11.2	11.6
Employees[a]	31.2	27.5[b]	18.4	19.4	23.6	27.3
Western USSR	19.6	—	5.6	6.1	10.5	14.1
Eastern USSR	11.6	—	12.8	13.3	13.1	13.2
Industrial	11.0	—	7.2	7.5	8.2	9.5
Nonindustrial[c]	20.2	—	11.2	11.9	15.4	17.8
Kolkhoz workers[d]	35.4	16.5	15.1	16.6	22.0	23.9
Participant population[e]	70.8	—	44.4	—	56.8	62.8

[a] 'Workers and staff', excluding collective farm workers.
[b] The third-quarter figure was 26.2, and for November 19.8.
[c] Total of employees, minus industrial employees.
[d] Able-bodied collective farm population of working age.
[e] Armed forces plus employees plus kolkhoz workers. By 1945, however, the total of Soviet manpower resources had been increased above the figure given here by approximately 5 million German prisoners of war.

Sources: P. V. Sokolov, 1968, p. 215; Arutyunyan, 1970, p. 398; Mitrofanova, 1971, pp. 439, 445.

from the prewar 4–5 million to the 10.9 million of 1942. Mobilisation of resources into the arms industries required more millions of workers to supply the military equipment appropriate to such force levels and to replace equipment losses; and to supply, evacuate if necessary, add to and operate the industrial goods upon which the arms industries depended. At the same time, as Table 26 shows, the country's total of manpower resources fell by over 26 million people.[30] As we saw in Chapter 2, where state employees are concerned the entire weight of the blow fell upon the Western USSR.

Behind the changing numbers of workers at work or in the services lay a complex picture of a rapidly changing population, together with changing participation rates for different groups within the population. In 1941 and 1942 tens of millions were cut away from the population by enemy action. These losses were offset only to a very small extent by increased participation of women, of the very young and the very old, and of the rural population. For example in the second half of 1941, before introduction of the chief instruments for compulsory mobilisation of labour, 500,000 housewives volunteered for war work along with 300,000 schoolchildren from the eighth, ninth and tenth classes and thousands of students and veterans.[31] Again, between mid-February 1942 and the end of November, 515,000 additional workers were found from the previously non-employed urban population for wartime employment.[32] But these additions to the workforce were dwarfed by wartime losses over the same period and by the increased scale of military recruitment. Meanwhile more thousands were being recruited for war work from the rural population, but we shall see that by 1942 this was largely at the expense of agricultural labour and did not result in additions to the total of manpower resources.

As a result of the recruitment of young males into the services, together with the increased participation of other groups within the population, the composition of the workforce changed markedly. Among industrial employees the share of women rose from 41 per cent at the beginning of 1940 to 53 per cent on 1 October 1942.[33] In rural localities their workforce share rose from 52 per cent in 1939 to 71 per cent by the beginning of 1943. Within state employment as a whole the combined share of the under-nineteens and the over-fifties rose from 15 per cent in 1939 to 27 per cent in 1942.[34] However, at the same time the decline in both population and workforce was so rapid that only in the case of youth employment did an increased share mean bigger absolute numbers.

The Soviet workforce changed rapidly not only as regards its age–sex and social composition, but also in its level of skills and work experience. As in other contemporary war economies the diversion of young adult males to the forces placed severe strain upon the supply of skilled labour. The protection of essential workers against military conscription could guard against this only to a limited extent. As a result industrial training took on new vigour in wartime, and something of its dimensions is indicated in Table 27. Between 1940 and 1942, for example, the share of the manual industrial workforce undergoing some form of training nearly doubled, reaching 80 per cent in the latter year. Taking the war years as a whole (and subject to the uncertainties indicated in the table) some 2.8 million school-leavers received vocational training, perhaps 14.2 million new workers were trained on the job and 13.7 million workers raised their craft qualifications, also on the job. Of course the membership of these three groups may have overlapped to a considerable extent, but taken separately each must also have comfortably exceeded the prewar rate of participation in industrial training. Among the results

140   *Soviet planning in peace and war*

Table 27. *Reproduction of the industrial workforce 1940–5 (thousands)*[a]

	1940	1941	1942	1943	1944	1945
Industrial workforce[b]	8,290	7,827	5,491	—	—	—
Training of new workers	1,655	1,244	1,260	3,417	3,936	4,360
Skill promotion of workers	1,950	1,521	2,512	1,717	3,433	4,561
School-leavers' vocational training[c]	61	485	617	653	494	523
All industrial training	3,666	3,250	4,389	5,787	7,863	9,444
All training as percentage of workforce	44.2	41.5	79.9	—	—	—

[a] This table is compiled from two different places in the given source, and differences of definition between the two greatly reduce its usefulness. For 1940–2 the table refers to manual workers 'of the mass trades' (*rabochie massovykh professii*), and the mid-year industrial manual workforce is given as the appropriate population of workers to which such training related. For 1943–5 the table refers to manual workers *and other employees* of the mass trades (*rabochie i drugie rabotniki*; a *rabotnik* is a worker by hand or by brain, not necessarily a manual worker), and the source does not indicate whether the same or a different workforce population would be appropriate for measuring participation in training schemes. Had the table been compiled using a consistent definition for the war years, it would have been possible to use it for other purposes than those intended – for example to estimate trends in recruitment rates and implied turnover of workforce; quit rates (including the impact of normal turnover, promotion, invasion and conscription) could also have been estimated by comparing recruitment with the net change in the workforce. As it is we cannot say whether the apparent leap in training of new workers in 1943, for example, was due to greatly increased recruitment possibilities as a result of satisfaction of the manpower needs of the Red Army, or whether it is just due to a broader definition of the workforce population.

[b] Mid-year data; for further definition see note a.

[c] This included training in the colleges of various economic agencies and commissariats, but after 1940 the great bulk of vocational training was carried out in the State Labour Reserve system set up in that year.

Source: G. S. Kravchenko, 1970, pp. 112, 225.

was a striking increase in the access of women to skilled trades in engineering, transport and the electric power industry.[35]

An unknown influence on the composition of the workforce in wartime was the role of forced labour held by the NKVD chief administration of labour camps (GULag). Victor Kravchenko, who worked at the RSFSR Sovnarkom from May 1942 to April 1943, claimed later that few war plants 'were without decisive *cadres* of compulsory labour' and that 'in dozens of them coerced labor was the principal or sole reliance'.[36] But we must treat this picture of forced labour everywhere circumspectly, since it is associated with his greatly exaggerated figure of 20 million as the rumoured 'official' estimate for forced labourers in wartime. No other estimate exceeds 12 million, and cautious study points to 4–5 million (still a very large number, of course) as a maximum figure for 1939.[37] Between 1939 and 1941 this figure was swelled by the internment of deportees from Poland and the Baltic republics, then deflated sharply when war broke out by mass executions, losses to the enemy and releases. The true number of forced labourers in wartime remains hidden.

In wartime the total of workers at work was reduced, but those who remained worked much harder than before. A decree of the Presidium of the USSR Supreme Soviet dated 26 June 1941 abolished normal holidays and leave from work, and introduced up to three hours' compulsory overtime per day.[38] Increased hours and intensity of work, however, were associated with varying results of work in different sectors of the economy. In industry the longer hours and abolition of time off is said to have directly increased capacity loading by a third.[39] Between 1940 and 1942, according to Voznesensky, hours of work rose by 22 per cent and output per hour worked by 7 per cent;[40] Table 28 shows the resulting 30 per cent increase in industrial output per worker. According to the same table, by 1944 industrial output per worker had risen 42 per cent above the prewar level, and most of the gain over 1942 must have been in output per hour worked. Much of the gain in industry, however, must have been transitory – it resulted from shifting workers from low-productivity civilian trades to high-productivity war work, from increased intensity of workforce utilisation, and from reaping economies of scale in arms manufacture. All these would be reversed once reconversion to peacetime needs began in 1945. While the war lasted, however, substantial improvements were recorded in labour requirements for various types of weapons production and assembly.[41]

In other sectors of the economy output per worker employed failed to improve in wartime in spite of the longer hours and greater intensity of work. Table 28 shows that in construction output per worker fell in 1942, and thereafter failed to show sustained recovery. In transport output per worker declined in each year of the war until 1945. In agriculture the picture was especially serious. In the kolkhoz

Table 28. *Trends in output per worker employed 1940–5 (1940 = 100)*

	1941	1942	1943	1944	1945
Industry	110	130	139	142	114
Transport	98	79	74	67	68
Construction	100	91	96	95	89

Source: IVOVSS, v. 6, 1965, p. 74.

sector the able-bodied population fell by nearly three-fifths, but output fell by even more – and this was in spite of the fact that each kolkhoz household and worker farmed more land than before and in spite of the fact that the number of workdays contributed by each farmer to the kolkhoz increased by nearly two-fifths.[42]

In summary, to sustain the increased output of arms and of basic industrial goods required for the war, the Soviet economy poured available investment and manpower resources into heavy industry. Throughout the economy human and non-human resources of all kinds were being utilised more intensively than before the war, but only in industry was there any sign of increased efficiency of utilisation.

PART THREE: MEASURES OF MOBILISATION

MOBILISATION OF THE WORKING POPULATION

In principle one may define four distinct stages of mobilisation of a country's working population for war. At the first stage there exist substantial reserves of unemployed or underemployed labour – even by peacetime standards. Mobilisation for war is accompanied by expansion of the whole economy and growing prosperity of the population. At the second stage rearmament and military supply begin to bite into leisure and into both present and future consumption – there is something like full employment, and the workers must work harder and eat less while the economy is being converted to a war footing. There is a degree of strain on aggregate supply, but each new military priority can be met by civilian sacrifices – the civilian economy contains reserves still to be converted to wartime purposes, and wartime needs do not yet have to be ranked in order to establish 'priorities within priorities'.

The Soviet productive effort 143

The third stage marks the creation of a fully mobilised war economy. Wartime conversion has been completed, and the civilian economy has been stripped to the bone. No more resources are available for the war effort from peacetime investment and consumption. Each new wartime priority can be met only by sacrificing existing ones, at least in the short run. Output can be increased at all only by organising existing workers more efficiently or by diverting existing workers from some other purpose to produce new labour-saving producer goods. Even the commitment of manpower to the fighting forces must be strictly limited in order to ensure sufficient labour supplies for the reproduction of the war economy and the replenishment of the civilian population. Should this limit have to be breached, a fourth stage is reached. An ultimate crisis would be at hand when the need for manpower for hand-to-hand fighting would overwhelm the claims of the war economy, 'when manpower to hold weapons became more important than manpower to make them'.[43] Everyone would become a soldier. If the situation is not quickly resolved, allowing the economy to revert to the third stage, the army would now fight to its last ration of arms and subsistence, and military collapse would follow.

Measured against this crude set of benchmarks, how intense was the wartime mobilisation of Soviet labour? At the outbreak of war the mobilisation of labour was already at the second stage – there was full employment, and rearmament had already resulted in substantial losses of civilian output and leisure of the population. Still, the civilian economy retained very large reserves. By the end of 1942 these reserves had been fully mobilised for war, and at a national level completed conversion to a war footing had brought labour mobilisation to the third stage.

The conversion process was not smooth, nor was it evenly enacted across the country. In fact, when the German invasion started, in some western regions the workforce was jolted immediately onto the fourth stage – mobilisation for hand-to-hand fighting. Home defence militias were recruited from mass volunteers in the big factories in Leningrad and Moscow (twenty-four divisions), in Tula, in Kiev (29,000 men by mid-July 1941), in the mining and steel towns of the Donbass (three divisions), in the Black Sea ports and other threatened cities.[44] Their establishment and training were supposed to be accomplished in addition to meeting current labour obligations, but inevitably with the approach of the front production took second place. The indiscriminate character of recruitment put skilled munitions, engineering and metal workers in the front line.[45] Heavy losses among the workforce cadres were the result. This was associated, for example, with the previously noted fact that of the workers subject to evacuation with their enterprises, typically only 30 to 40 per cent reached the interior of the country and were successfully relocated. The majority of the workers involved had volunteered for the home defence militia or the Red Army itself, or remained behind German lines to fight as partisans.[46]

In the interior of the country the diversion of industrial manpower to fighting and the climbing demand for military and industrial goods with which to equip them combined together to generate huge shortages of labour. By the first months of 1942 the commissariats covering the metallurgical, engineering, machine tool and defence industries were short of 472,000 workers (nearly half of this number was accounted for by the aircraft industry alone; the tank, armament, ammunition and shipbuilding industries made up another third).[47] To meet such needs a violent redistribution of the workforce took place.

The organisation of this movement will be considered in detail in Chapter 4. Here we shall outline briefly the results. In the first months of the war, as we have already seen, there was mass recruitment to industry from the previously non-employed population of housewives, school students and pensioners, totalling 800,000 in the second half of 1941. This movement was largely voluntary. At the same time the compulsory redirection of labour began under a Manpower Committee established on 30 June 1941. In the second half of 1941 69,000 workers were transferred from the food and light and local industries to heavy industry and construction, and 59,000 to the arms industries.[48] Just in the Moscow city department of industrial commerce a thousand skilled workers, mainly metalworkers, were identified and in the city's cafeterias and restaurants another 1,500 metal and building workers. Eleven thousand skilled workers (metalworkers, builders, drivers and others) were drawn from state and economic agencies, trade and catering.[49]

As the war progressed, compulsory direction of labour assumed a much larger scale. According to Table 29, three-quarters of a million workers were redirected to industry, construction and transport in 1942 through the Manpower Committee alone, and taking 1943 and 1944 together about a million workers a year flowed through the same

Table 29. *Direction of labour through the Manpower Committee 1942–5 (thousands)*

	1942	1943	1944	1945[a]	Total
Into industry, construction and transport	734	891[b]	1,113	273	3,010
Per cent share by commissariat[c]					
Arms industries	27.2	—	—	—	16.2
Engineering industries	7.0	—	—	—	5.6
Ferrous and nonferrous metals	12.2	—	—	—	13.7
Fuels and power	10.1	—	—	—	19.0
Chemical industry	1.4	—	—	—	1.2
Construction	1.5	—	—	—	6.4
Transport	2.9	—	—	—	7.0
Food and clothing industries	7.3	—	—	—	4.5
Into vocational training	826	771	500	25	2,121
Into seasonal work	1,396	2,039	2,227	1,089	6,751
Total	2,956	3,700	3,840	1,387	11,883

[a] First seven months.
[b] In the same year another 429,000 workers were directed into industry, construction and transport through other channels.
[c] These shares are calculated from the given source. They do not cover all commissariats involved in industry, construction and transport. The ones listed here covered 511,000 of the 734,000 mobilised in 1942, and 2,216,000 of the 3,010,000 mobilised over the period as a whole. Where commissariats are grouped together in this table, the industry groups are made up as follows. Arms industries: aircraft, tanks, armament, ammunition, shipbuilding, mortar armament. Engineering industries: heavy and medium engineering, machine tools, electrical industry. Fuels and power: coal, oil and electrical power.

Sources: Taken or calculated from Mitrofanova, 1971, pp. 193, 428, 433.

channel. To judge from the incomplete data in Table 29 regarding their destination, two-thirds of them were poured into the complex formed by the defence industries with the main heavy and basic industries (both for the war years as a whole and for 1942 alone). In 1942 the defence industries took 27 per cent of available redirected labour, falling to 16 per cent taking the period as a whole, while the share of the heavy and basic industries gained correspondingly as the infrastructure supporting arms manufacture grew in importance.

The sources of mobilised labour also changed as the war progressed. We have seen that in the first months of the war the main sources were the previously non-employed population and those engaged in nonessential work in services and light industry. At the same time conscripts drawn mainly from agriculture and local industries, and judged unfit for active service, were directed into heavy industry and construction on a large scale – 700,000 in the second half of 1941 alone.[50] As reserves in industry and services became exhausted, agriculture became the main recruiting ground for the war economy. Rural localities provided 23 per cent of those mobilised for war work by the Manpower Committee in 1942, 59 per cent in 1943 and 62 per cent in 1944.[51]

In the course of 1942 all significant labour reserves became exhausted. In low-priority agriculture the drain of manpower had become so acute that in April a Sovnarkom and Central Committee decree ordered a reverse mobilisation of remaining pockets of the non-employed population back into farm work.[52] In a high-priority sector like transport the shortage of skilled workers had become sufficiently alarming for it to take precedence even over military needs – in May 1942 the State Defence Committee called a halt to further army recruitment of railway workers and even ordered a return to railway work of mechanics, despatchers and station staff on active service.[53] By the end of 1942 the Red Army had neared its wartime ceiling of 11.5 million, and a system of reservation (protection from military service) of those in essential war work now operated in the defence, heavy and basic industries.[54] From now on there were no more reserves of labour in inessential employment in low-priority sectors to be yielded up for the war. All kinds of work acquired high priority, and the ordering of priorities became more and more finely graded, so that the redirection of handfuls of soldiers from the front to the essential industries eventually rose to be the concern of the very highest authorities.[55] And a last milestone was reached on 4 May 1944, when in many parts of the country further transfers of labour out of agriculture to industry and construction were prohibited by the State Defence Committee,[56] effectively giving farming the status of essential war work.

In summary, the period from June 1941 to the end of 1942 marked the transition of the labour force from peacetime full employment to all-out wartime mobilisation. During the transition itself a spectrum of degrees of mobilisation was visible across the country. In the western theatres of war, there was an immediate transition to mobilisation of workers for combat, which took precedence over the needs of the war economy. In the Far East, at the other end of the country, an American observer detected a degree of unmobilised slack in the male labour force, which he thought was being held in reserve against the contingency of an outbreak of war with Japan.[57] Between these two extremes, the rest of the country was travelling the path of conversion from peacetime to wartime economic priorities. By 1943, of the adult able-bodied population everyone was either serving in the forces or serving in some essential category of war work in the national economy, and every kind of inessential work had been eliminated.

In the closing stages of the war the Soviet labour balance began to relax. The armed forces did not contract – in fact they expanded slightly, touching 11.6 million in 1945. But the civil and military casualties of 1941 and 1942 were not repeated on the same scale. Moreover in 1943 and 1944 significant increments to the workforce began to accrue from recovered territory, repatriated citizens and demobilised soldiers,[58] and additionally from German prisoners of war. By the second half of 1944 some form of labour market had been restored. Enterprises began once again to recruit workers direct from the population,[59] and significant voluntary – if unauthorised – turnover was being reported in the defence and heavy industries.[60] Thus it seems clear that 1943 marked the peak for wartime mobilisation of Soviet labour, and that this peak was close to the maximum which could have been achieved.

How did the intensity of mobilisation of Soviet labour compare with that of other belligerents in World War II? For this we need a quantitative measure, which in the Soviet case can only be estimated indirectly. Moreover there is no single satisfactory measure, since different definitions of war-related employment may be applied. The numbers in military service are unambiguous enough, but civilian war employment may be measured either on a broad or a narrow basis. For example a narrow definition might include only workers supplying military equipment and subsistence (counting all stages of production, of course). A broader definition would extend to war-related construction and transport and other kinds of equipment.

We shall take the British economy as the standard of comparison, since Britain provided the most successful economic mobilisation among the capitalist countries at war. On the broad definition, in Britain in June 1944 the armed forces plus civilian war employment accounted for 55 per cent of the working population.[61] A narrower definition would be provided by the armed forces plus group I industries, and an advantage here is that we can follow this narrower measure through time. On the narrow basis, Britain had committed 18 per cent of her working population to war in June 1939, and this share had risen to 38 per cent by June 1941. Between June 1942 and 1944 it stood still higher, fluctuating only marginally between 43 and 45 per cent.[62]

In the Soviet case there are no official measures of the intensity of labour mobilisation, because of the absence of employment series for the defence (and many civilian) industries. These can only be estimated from the known shares of net material product devoted to the war effort (these are analysed in more detail in the following section). We assume that war workers were perhaps one and a half times or twice as productive as others in terms of current roubles – the productivity of non-war workers was held down by lack of priority in the supply of inputs and by the low productivity of agriculture. On this basis, using the narrow definition of civilian war employment, the Soviet Union had committed perhaps 11–13 per cent of her working population to war by 1940. This figure jumped to between 43 and 48 per cent in 1942, and peaked in 1943 at between 45 and 48 per cent. On the broader definition of civilian war employment, however, the Soviet commitment of manpower to war rose from 14–16 per cent in 1940 to reach the 55–60 per cent range already in 1942.[63] These rough approximations suggest that the Soviet and British records of success in mobilising labour for war were fully comparable, in spite of the Soviet Union's much narrower margin of economic and military survival in terms of national income per worker.

MOBILISATION OF THE NATIONAL INCOME

What were the financial implications and results of the mobilisation of physical resources for war? In wartime increased defence spending was financed in five main ways. First, central government spending on the economy, on social and cultural activities and on administration was sharply cut back. Secondly, local government spending was also cut, and the prewar trend to growing financial autonomy of local government was also reversed. Thirdly, although revenues from indirect taxation and from direct taxation of enterprise incomes fell in line with economic activity as a whole, direct taxation of wage

Table 30. *The USSR state budget 1940–5 (billion roubles)*

	1940	1941	1942	1943	1944	1945
Total government spending on goods and services	*171*	*188*	*181*	*208*	*261*	*295*
Defence	57	83	108	125	138	128
Economic	58	52	32	33	54	74
Socio-cultural	41	31	30	38	51	63
Administrative	7	5	4	5	7	9
Unidentified	8	17	7	7	11	21
Total current government revenues	*169*	*163*	*150*	*179*	*236*	*270*
Indirect taxes	106	93	66	71	95	123
Enterprise taxes	27	48[a]	18	24	25	21
Household taxes[b]	20	22	37	47	62	57
Other current	4	5	3	4	5	6
Unidentified	12	−5	26	33	49	63
Government borrowing requirement[c]	*2*	*15*	*31*	*29*	*25*	*25*
Bond finance	9	8	14	23	30	25
Monetary finance	−6	21	20	9	−5	−3
Unidentified	−1	−14	−7	−3	0	3

[a] This included an exceptional transfer to the government of 20 billion roubles of cash balances held in the socialised sector.
[b] Including war lottery receipts, money donations and collections, and social insurance contributions.
[c] This is Millar's lower bound for the budget deficit (his upper bound being calculated to take into account only identified uses and sources of funds).
Source: Millar, 1980, pp. 190–11.

incomes increased sharply. Fourthly, the importance of revenues from unidentified sources increased throughout the war. Fifthly and last, government was operated at a deficit throughout the war; in 1941 and 1942 the deficit was financed mainly by means of monetary expansion, but by 1943 the deficit was mainly – and thereafter entirely – bond-financed.[64]

Some main trends in wartime government finance are confirmed in Table 30. A point of special interest is to establish the role of Lend–Lease in the wartime budget. A 1944 British embassy analysis suggested that Lend–Lease could be detected in the large and growing difference between total revenues and the sum of the identified subtotals for revenue given in the budget (in Table 30, unidentified revenues).[65] Probably it would be incorrect to ascribe the entire residual of unidentified revenues to Lend–Lease – for example, taking 1944 Bergson valued Lend–Lease to the Soviet Union to 30 to 35 billion 1937 roubles, compared with total unidentified revenues in that year of 49 billion roubles.[66] Moreover in 1945 unidentified revenues grew, while Lend–Lease declined and was then cut off. Nonetheless it seems possible that in the peak year of 1944 Lend–Lease financed up to 13 per cent of total government spending and up to a quarter of defence spending.

How was the war effort financed in terms of the Soviet national income? How did the mobilisation of the Soviet national income compare with that of other belligerent powers? In order to answer such questions we must distinguish, as before, the 'broad' and 'narrow' definitions of war-related economic activity. In addition, in tracing and comparing the mobilisation of national income we face the further problem of its valuation (the alert reader will be aware, however, that we had to presume the solution to this problem in order to estimate the measures of workforce mobilisation presented above). The appropriate valuation is found in the current domestic factor costs of output in each country – not the fixed prices of a given base year, nor the standard of factor costs derived from a single country. The fixed prices of a given base year would be appropriate for measurement of changes in the 'real' volume of national income or its components through time – for example it is clearly relevant that between 1940 and 1942 the real national income of the Soviet Union fell by one-third, whereas that of the UK remained stable or fell only slightly between 1939 and the peak of economic mobilisation in 1943.[67] Alternatively revaluation of the Soviet national income at British factor cost (or of British national income in Soviet roubles) would be appropriate if we wished to compare directly the 'real' volumes of economic activity in these two countries, war-related and otherwise. But neither of these is the present task. We just want to establish how much of its own national income, measured in terms of its own current valuations, each nation was able to divert to its own war effort at some point in time.

A separate problem lies in the fact that Soviet prices did not necessarily correspond to Soviet factor costs, while the Soviet national income concept diverged from the UN System of National Accounts, which owes much to the British practice of the 1940s and 1950s. The Soviet national income measure includes indirect taxes and subsidies,

Table 31. *Volume and structure of Soviet national income 1940–5*

	1940	1941	1942	1943	1944	1945
Net material product (1940 = 100)[a]	100	92	66	74	88	83
Per cent share in NMP[b]						
Accumulation	19	—	4	7	15	13
Civilian subsistence	70	—	56	49	50	62
Military subsistence	4⎫11	—	13⎫40	11⎫44	11⎫35	7⎫25
Military equipment	7⎭	—	27⎭	33⎭	24⎭	18⎭

[a] *Natsional'nyi dokhod* ('national income') measured at 1926/7 market prices.
[b] These data seem to be authoritative on the basis of narrow definitions of military outlays. However, other data also exist. For 1942 G. S. Kravchenko, 1970, p. 125 gives a slightly higher share for military equipment (29 per cent), but he still gives the total of military outlays as claiming 40 per cent by reducing the share of military subsistence to 11 per cent. P. V. Sokolov, 1968, pp. 249–50, on the other hand, gives the higher share for military equipment and a much higher share for military subsistence too (26 per cent), raising the overall share of military outlays in 1942 to 55 per cent – a figure also given in IVOVSS, v. 6, 1965, p. 46 as reflecting the overall share of resources to 'wartime needs'. So in the latter case the broad definition of war-related activity is involved, and Sokolov may have defined 'military subsistence' to include the subsistence of more than strictly military personnel.

Sources: For the NMP index see IVOVSS, v. 6, 1965, p. 45; this index is more recently cited in IVMV, v. 12, 1982, p. 166. For shares in NMP see Voznesensky, 1948, p. 56; Chadaev, 1965, p. 380; G. S. Kravchenko, 1970, pp. 125, 228; IVMV, v. 6, 1976, p. 340 and v. 12, 1982, p. 161.

and excludes the output of the 'nonproductive' sphere. Soviet defence output (in common with the output of investment goods) was subsidised and prices held below cost. Indirect taxes, included in the price of consumer goods, financed these subsidies and in addition much of the employment in the 'nonproductive' sphere.[68] The share of subsidised non-consumption in output is attributed to the output of consumption goods. Measurement at current prices undervalued the factor cost of producing weaponry. Consequently the use of current prices below sets a lower bound on the true share of the Soviet national income mobilised for war, in comparison with the share of spending on warfare out of the British national income measured at current factor cost.

What degree of national income mobilisation was achieved in

Table 32. *The output share of Soviet wartime needs in 1940 and 1942 (percentages)*[a]

	1940	1942[b]
Net material product	15	57–8
Gross industrial output	26	68[c]
Gross agricultural output	9	24
Transport services	16	61

[a] 'Wartime needs' (*voennye nuzhdy*) are thus defined more broadly than the categories of military subsistence and equipment used in Table 31.

[b] There is a certain history to these figures. The first comparable published statistic was the claim in IVOVSS, v. 6, 1965, p. 46 that in 1942 'wartime needs' claimed 55 per cent of the Soviet NMP (see also the notes to Table 31). Then new data appeared when, in Sorokin, 1971, p. 51 and Po ed. plan., 1971, pp. 87–8, it was claimed that 'in the course of the war' (but not specifying a particular year) '57–8 per cent of the national income, 65–8 per cent of industrial production and about a quarter of agricultural production were used for wartime needs'. Whether these were intended as average or peak values is not known. But their similarity with the figures now claimed for 1942 is surely not a coincidence.

[c] A slightly lower figure of 64 per cent, along with figures for 1943–5, is given by G. S. Kravchenko, 1970, pp. 351–2. According to Kravchenko the share of wartime needs in industrial output peaked in 1942, falling to 58 per cent in 1943, 51 per cent in 1944 and 40 per cent in 1945. In spite of the apparent precision of these figures there is still some doubt about coverage. For example, taking the first half of 1942 alone, the arms industry commissariats are said to have contributed about half of gross industrial output, but this does not include military orders contracted to other civilian industry commissariats; their inclusion would raise the figure to 70–80 per cent (IVMV, v. 4, 1975, p. 162).

Source: ISE, v. 5, 1978, p. 183.

Britain? The share of government spending on war in the UK's net national income, measured at current factor cost, rose from 15 per cent in 1939 to a peak of 55 per cent in 1943.[69] This appears to correspond to a broad definition of the war effort. Bearing in mind the qualifications already noted, we can compare this with Soviet national income data, which are presented both on narrow definitions (Table 31) and on a broader basis (Table 32).

On a narrow definition of the resource costs of war the Soviet Union did not mobilise as large a share of her national income for war as did Britain. According to the data in Table 31, counting only expendi-

The Soviet productive effort

tures on the subsistence and equipment of the armed forces, 11 per cent of the Soviet net material product had been mobilised for war in 1940. This share rose to 40 per cent in 1942 (out of a much reduced total) and peaked at 44 per cent in 1943. The absolute volume of resources devoted to war was also at a maximum in 1943. As the economy continued to recover, the share of the war effort dipped sharply, falling to only 35 per cent in 1944.[70] The increase in military spending between 1940 and 1942 was financed equally by cuts in accumulation and in civilian consumption. In 1943 as the national income began to recover, civilian consumption was held back so that both military spending and accumulation could increase their shares together. But only in 1944 was there a major recovery in the share of accumulation, and civilian consumption did not really begin to come back until 1945.

When a broader definition of war-related economic activity is used, the Soviet mobilisation of national income for war is seen to be equivalent to the British record. More broadly based Soviet data are available only for 1940 and 1942, and are shown in Table 32. In 1940 war purposes generally preempted 15 per cent of the national income (not 11 per cent, which corresponded to the narrower concept), and by 1942 the share had jumped to 57–8 (not 40) per cent. Table 32 also allows us to see that the share of output taken up by wartime needs was rather less than the national average in agriculture, about the same in the transport sector, and substantially more in industry.

In order properly to compare the output shares committed to war in different countries, the relationship between military and economic factors must be fully taken into account. One of the first estimates of comparative Allied national income mobilisation appeared in a chart in a June 1945 United States official report on Lend–Lease. It showed, on the basis of the information then available, that by 1943 all the main Allies had committed between 46 and 53 per cent of their national income to war; the USSR appeared toward the bottom of this range.[71] The American comment was that the military burdens of war had been shared extremely unequally, but that the economic burdens had been shared among the Allies in proportion to their wealth through Lend–Lease and mutual aid.[72]

Certainly Lend–Lease was more important to the Soviet economy than Soviet historians commonly recognise. Its volume was slight in relation to the cumulative economic effort of 1941–5,[73] but in the peak years of 1943 and 1944 it amounted to a significant proportion of the

Soviet GNP.[74] Even so the economic importance of Lend–Lease was still less than its diplomatic significance (not to mention its role as a catalyst for postwar recrimination). Moreover the American comment did less than justice to the contribution of the Soviet domestic economy. This is because the fighting front cut through the Soviet economy to a greater degree than for the other Allies, even for Britain. In the judgement of the authoritative historians of the British war economy,

> War efficacy and effort signify not merely the accumulation of men and material but the intensity of their use in combat with the enemy... A higher rate of production in areas thousands of miles distant from the battle fronts may have smaller value than a lower rate of output in an advanced base...
> Inevitably, war production in an advanced base has to struggle against acute difficulties which depress the rate of output. The direct destruction of materials and plant by air bombardment, the dispersal of production units, interruption of the flow of production through damage to the transport system, exhaustion of the workers through the black-out conditions in the factories and through the extra strain of night duty in the Home Guard or Civil Defence – all these drawbacks have to be set against the advantages of producing weapons close to the front line, or in it.[75]

In a direct comment on the American estimate of comparative Allied national income mobilisation, they concluded:

> No person possessing either military or economic knowledge would be rash enough to declare the war effort of devastated Russia inferior to that of Britain or Canada, simply because the lines on the chart show that Russia – with its much lower national income per head of the population – devoted a smaller proportion of the total to direct war purposes.[76]

This conclusion carries even greater force today, when, in the light of subsequent research, it seems likely that the USSR mobilised no less a share of her national income than Great Britain or Canada, and rather more than the United States. Thus the magnitude of the Soviet economic achievement, taken together with its military circumstances, remains a unique feature of the Soviet wartime experience.

CONCLUSION: PHASES OF ECONOMIC MOBILISATION

When the main economic indicators are taken together, we can agree that 1943 marked a turning point for the Soviet economy. Before 1943 economic mobilisation for war relied mainly upon conserving existing arms capacity, converting existing resources from civilian to war-related uses, and taking up slack in the civilian economy. War production grew rapidly, but the sources of its expansion were transitory. By 1943 economic mobilisation had peaked. From now on further expansion of the war economy depended upon the generation or acquisition of new resources. Accordingly Soviet historians divide the war into two main economic phases – a mobilisation phase, followed by an expansion phase – with a turning point in between.

The origin of this convention is not without interest. In effect it was Stalin who introduced it into public discourse in a speech of November 1943, when he remarked that '*The past year marked a turn* not only in the progress of hostilities, but also in the work of our rear. We were no longer confronted with such tasks as evacuating enterprises to the east and of switching industry to the production of armaments. The Soviet state now has *an efficient and rapidly expanding war economy*.' And a few minutes later, speaking of the war effort in general rather than merely in its economic aspect, he added: 'During the past year the Red Army and the Soviet people have achieved great successes in the struggle against the German invaders. We achieved *a radical turning point* in the war in favor of our country, and now the war is heading for its final outcome.'[77] Exactly who originated these ideas behind the scenes is not known, especially since the Stalinist occasion of their first public utterance has not been acknowledged by Soviet historians for many years. The only hint to their possible origin can be found in their attribution by the former Gosplan member G. M. Sorokin to an unpublished Gosplan report in the Soviet archives, with perhaps the veiled implication that this was Stalin's source.[78] In any case, whoever first developed them, these ideas were quickly taken up and expounded by political and economic commentators.[79]

In fact by the end of the war most of the analytical content of Stalin's periodisation, as it is used today in Soviet historiography, had already been brought into being. Its most important exponent was another Gosplan member, B. Sukharevsky. He defined the first phase as lasting eighteen months, to the end of 1942. In this phase the expansion of arms output depended mainly upon evacuating and relocating existing capacity, transferring workers and investment resources from civilian to military industries, and making workers work longer hours. In 1943 these sources of expansion were exhausted. A new interdependence had to be found between the arms industries and the civilian economy, and in particular the basic and arms industries had now to grow simultaneously. Arms manufacture kept on spilling out into the civilian branches of heavy industry. On the other hand the availability of new inputs from heavy industry was a critical factor in continued expansion of arms manufacture. The normal or peacetime sources of economic growth had now to reassert themselves – that is, the creation of new capacity and resource-saving innovation.[80]

After the war a little more was added by Voznesensky in his celebrated book. In one respect Voznesensky took Stalin's formula a little further, when he defined 1943 as 'the year of *a radical turn* in the development of the war economy';[81] Stalin had referred only to 'a turn ... in the work of our rear', reserving the term 'radical' for the breakthrough in the whole military, diplomatic and economic situation. In other respects Voznesensky somewhat blurred the picture; for example he declared that conversion of the economy to a war footing had been effected by the middle of 1942.[82] And in place of Stalin's concept of 'an efficient and rapidly expanding war economy' brought into being during 1943, Voznesensky wrote about expanded reproduction or 'reproduction on an extending scale' starting in the eastern territories at the end of 1941.[83]

All this naturally left substantial room for ambiguity, not to be resolved until serious historical research began again in the late fifties. There was agreement that the work of economic conversion had been roughly completed by mid-1942.[84] Some now therefore favoured bringing the economic turning point (whether or not it was 'radical') forward to the summer of 1942; this would have the added advantage of enabling the economic turning point to correlate with the military breakthrough at Stalingrad, rather than to come after it.[85] More recent authorities hold, however, that conditions in the second half of 1942 were too difficult to allow the economy to achieve a turnaround; conversion had been completed, but expansion faltered and some sectors of the economy still recorded declines. The 'radical turning point' would come only in 1943.[86] Nor did a turning point occur in all sectors of the economy simultaneously; for example in agriculture it was delayed until 1944.[87] This leads some to argue that the term 'radical' is too grand to have been appropriate for the economic events of 1943 – there was a turning point, but it was too modest and too complicated to be called radical.[88]

The economic indicators and analysis so far put forward in this book suggest acceptance of the idea of a mobilisation and an expansion phase with the turning point in 1943, subject to some small but

The Soviet productive effort 157

important qualifications. From the point of view of economic planning and coordination the first phase lasted eighteen months, to the end of 1942, and within it two sub-periods may be defined. In the first six months of the war everything was concentrated on the conservation of existing arms capacity and the conversion of civilian capacity to arms manufacture. The rest of the economy declined. Although the last prewar economic crisis of 1937–40 had only just been resolved, a new economic crisis was quickly formed. Although it was not in origin a crisis of excessive accumulation, it comprised similar elements of overcommitment of the economy, of a widening gap between ends and means and of multiplying imbalances between outputs and inputs. As in peacetime, the symptoms of economic crisis in time of war could be repressed only up to a point. In the first six months of the war the only imbalance which mattered was the gap between the need for arms and the available arms capacity. However, once this gap began to narrow, it was immediately overtaken in importance by the gap which had opened up between rising arms output and the crumbling heavy industrial infrastructure. In the next sub-period, which lasted for the whole of 1942, the heavy industries were stabilised, rationalisation took place in the fields of capital construction and labour mobilisation, and the economy was rebalanced around new priorities.

By peacetime standards the economy remained in deep crisis, but from a wartime perspective 1942 was the year of crisis resolution. Arms mobilisation was resumed and by 1943 had begun to peak in proportion to the rest of the economy. The new coherence of the war economy was reflected in its continued expansion, in spite of the fact that the transfer of labour and fixed capacity from the civilian economy to wartime uses was at an end. The generation of new resources for expansion of the economy's production frontier was resumed. In 1943, however, expansion was still very tightly constrained, and focused exclusively on the production of military and basic industrial goods. It would make sense, therefore, to recognise a further division between sub-periods during 1944 when the liberated territories began once again to contribute significantly to overall economic activity, the labour balance showed signs of relaxation, and agriculture began to indicate the first promise of recovery.[89]

To conclude, the development of the Soviet war economy may be divided into a mobilisation phase and an expansion phase, with the turning point in 1943. In more detail, each phase is sub-divided into two periods. Nineteen-forty-one saw the period of emergency arms mobilisation and the onset of economic crisis. In 1942 the arms mobilisation continued, but the emergency shifted to the condition of the basic industries. This was the second period. The third period, 1943, saw arms mobilisation reach a peak, while economic expansion resumed. The fourth period began during 1944 when expansion penetrated even the most devastated regions and sectors. The organisation of the process of crisis resolution and recovery from the beginning of 1942 forms the subject of the next chapter.

NOTES

1 IVMV, v. 12, 1982, p. 145.
2 Milward, 1965, pp. 41–2.
3 Milward, 1977, p. 56.
4 Voznesensky, 1948, p. 63.
5 Bergson, 1961, p. 74 and Appendix E ('"Real" Defense Outlays').
6 Voznesensky, 1948, p. 102.
7 For several principal aircraft types, tanks and guns, transfer prices in 1943 had been reduced by one-half to two-thirds compared with 1941, according to data in Tyl SVS, 1977, p. 350.
8 See Appendix 4.
9 G. S. Kravchenko, 1970, pp. 13–17. Nove, 1977, p. 331 also cites the late S. G. Strumilin as a proponent of this criticism. See further Appendix 5.
10 IVMV, v. 7, 1976, p. 41.
11 IVOVSS, v. 6, 1965, p. 77.
12 See Appendix 3.
13 IVOVSS, v. 6, 1965, p. 45. For more detail see n. 14.
14 These estimates are very rough and were reached by a hazardous path. Authoritative sources provide us with various indices based on 1940 for productive and nonproductive fixed assets and for investment in the war years. Unfortunately they do not tell us the relative proportions of these series in the initial year, but we can estimate this for the sake of argument as follows. Chadaev, 1965, p. 378 gives the following indices for productive and nonproductive fixed assets in each year (it would be consistent with Soviet practice, and with the internal evidence of the indices' behaviour, for these to be end-year estimates):

	1940	1941	1942	1943	1944	1945
1. Productive fixed assets	100	72	68	76	84	88
2. Nonproductive fixed assets	100	64	58	75	90	93

Assume that the productive and nonproductive sectors laid claim to equal shares in 1940 (in 1981 nonproductive fixed assets were only one-third of the total, but they had multiplied by 9.4 times since 1940, whereas productive fixed assets had multiplied by 17 times over the

The Soviet productive effort

same period; see Nar. khoz., 1982, pp. 68–9). This means that we can use their unweighted average for an index of the total stock of fixed assets:

	1940	1941	1942	1943	1944	1945
3. Total fixed assets $((1) + (2)) \div 2$	100	68	63	75.5	87	90.5

Taking these to be end-year estimates, we find the following:

4. Net change in fixed assets as percentage of 1940 fixed assets	—	−32	−5	12.5	11.5	3.5
		−37		24		
5. (4) as percentage of 1942 fixed assets	—	—		38.10		—

IVOVSS, v. 6, 1965, p. 45 gives us an index of state and cooperative investment (excluding the collective farm sector and investment by the population) at constant 1955 prices, as follows:

6. Investment	100	86	53	53	72	89

We use this as our estimate of fixed investment, although of course it includes additions to finished goods and work in progress as well as to fixed assets. According to Voznesensky, 1948, p. 56 in 1940 the share of accumulation in net material product was 19 per cent; again accumulation as a whole includes additions to working as well as to fixed capital, so here an upward bias is imparted to our estimate of the role of fixed investment. Assume a 1940 ratio of all fixed assets, productive and nonproductive, to net material product of 3 (in theory NMP excludes income generated by nonproductive assets, but it is measured at market prices rather than factor cost, and so includes the indirect taxes which finance the bulk of nonproductive sector factor incomes; see Nove, 1977, pp. 326–7). On this basis 1940 investment was 19 per cent of net material product, which in turn was one-third of productive and nonproductive fixed assets taken together. Row (6) can now be scaled comparably with (3):

7. Investment as percemtage of 1940 fixed assets $((6) \times 0.19) \div 3$	6.33	5.45	3.36	3.36	4.56	5.64
			8.81		7.92	
8. Investment as percentage of 1942 fixed assets	—	—	—	12.57	—	

The relative importance of territorial changes and of new investment in changes in the stock of fixed assets can now be estimated as follows:

9. Net change in fixed assets, less investment, as percentage of 1940 fixed assets $(4)-(7)$	—	−37.45	−8.36	9.14	6.94	−2.14
		−45.81		16.08		
10. (9) as percentage of 1942 fixed assets	—	—		25.52		—

Of course these calculations are very crude. A possible confirmation is obtained in the following way. Summing across row (9) should give us an estimate of the net loss of fixed assets directly attributable to the actions of the enemy on enemy-held territory. The sum amounts to 32 per cent of the 1940 stock of fixed assets. An official estimate of war damage to property is 679 billion prewar roubles (Nar. khoz., 1982, p. 57), or 'approximately 30 percent of the prewar capital stock' (Millar and Linz, 1978, p. 959).

15 Nar. khoz., 1961, p. 603 and D'yakov, 1978, p. 63.
16 Lersky, 1945, p. 17.
17 D'yakov, 1978, p. 63.
18 Calculated from Kap. str., 1961, pp. 34, 144. If the typical investment project takes two years to complete, with investment spending divided equally between the two years, and if annual investment grows at 20 per cent per year, the steady-state investment completion ratio will be just over 90 per cent.
19 Lersky, 1943, p. 40 gives figures up to 1942, and V. Sokolov, 1946, p. 25 up to 1943. Lersky gives 86.5 per cent for 1941, whereas Sokolov gives the same figure for 1940. I assume that 1940 was intended, since 1941 is an unlikely benchmark year. ISE, v. 5, 1978, p. 247 unhelpfully attributes 112 per cent to 1942 and 120.8 per cent to 1943.
20 Lersky, 1943, p. 40.
21 Ginzburg, 1974, pp. 139–41.
22 Calculated from D'yakov, 1978, p. 50.
23 Ibid., p. 43.
24 V. Sokolov, 1946, p. 26.
25 Kap. str., 1961, p. 136.
26 V. Sokolov, 1946, p. 20; where Sokolov refers to the northeastern region Lokshin, 1964, p. 61 correctly refers to the southeastern.
27 Kap. str., 1961, pp. 134–5.
28 Kaldor, 1945/6, p. 34.
29 The term 'manpower' is used here with apologies, since in all the war economies manpower was composed predominantly of womanpower.
30 See also P. V. Sokolov, 1968, p. 215.
31 Mitrofanova, 1971, p. 186.
32 Ibid., p. 190.
33 IVMV, v. 5, 1975, p. 50. According to IVMV, v. 7, 1976, p. 43, the share of women in state employment was 53 per cent in 1942 and 57 per cent in 1943.
34 Voznesensky, 1948, p. 90.
35 Ibid., p. 89.
36 V. Kravchenko, 1947, pp. 403–5.
37 Wheatcroft, 1981, p. 286.
38 Resheniya, v. 3, 1968, pp. 37–8. Sick leave and maternity leave were protected, however. The new regulations came on top of the lengthening of the working day and week exactly a year earlier.
39 Tel'pukhovsky, 1974, p. 175.
40 Voznesensky, 1948, p. 91.
41 We can classify the data provided by Voznesensky, 1948, p. 92 to show the

economies achieved in labour time required for the manufacture of each unit of various weapons over the period 1941–3, as follows: at 25 per cent the TT cartridge, from 31 to 40 per cent the Il-2 and Il-4 aircraft and 76 mm regimental gun, from 41 to 50 per cent the Pe-2 bomber, the 152 mm howitzer and large-calibre machine guns, from 51 to 60 per cent the T-34 and KV tanks, and at 73 per cent divisional guns.

42 Voznesensky, 1948, p. 76 positively evaluates agriculture's wartime performance on the basis of the increase in inputs per collective farmer. Arutyunyan, 1970, pp. 5–18 attacks this assessment on the basis of the decline in output per unit input – on average the kolkhoz population disposed of more land, worked harder and produced less. He also notes (p. 6) that labour input figures based on the population specialised in agriculture underestimate total labour inputs, because of the involvement of urban workers in farming on the side.

43 Milward, 1965, p. 129. These paragraphs draw extensively on Milward's analysis of the German war economy.

44 Belonosov, 1970, pp. 21–36.

45 Gouré, 1964, p. 46; Morekhina, 1974, p. 44.

46 Tel'pukhovsky, 1958, p. 32. This was the official version. Doubtless some remained for less honourable reasons.

47 Data in G. S. Kravchenko, 1970, p. 109 with addition of data for the machine tool industry from Mitrofanova, 1971, p. 189. For the aircraft and tank industries 60 per cent or more of the vacancies were for skilled workers.

48 ISE, v. 5, 1978, p. 203.

49 Tel'pukhovsky, 1958, p. 35.

50 G. S. Kravchenko, 1970, pp. 110–11; a quarter of a million each went to the arms industries and to construction, the remainder to the metallurgical, fuel and power industries. See on sources and organisation of recruitment into construction D'yakov, 1978, p. 60.

51 ISE, v. 5, 1978, p. 203.

52 Kursky, 1975, p. 16.

53 Ist. KPSS, v. 5(i), 1970, p. 307.

54 Mitrofanova, 1971, pp. 424–5, 434.

55 See Resheniya, v. 3, 1968 for the following published decisions on this subject. On 22 February 1943 the State Defence Committee forbade military recruitment of manual workers and technicians engaged in restoration of the Donbass coalfield (p. 96); on 26 October 1943 it ordered the defence commissariat to direct 50,000 conscripts from the liberated regions, unfit for active service by reason of age, to restoration work in the Donbass, to protect from conscription Donbass miners and others engaged in restoration work, and even to demobilise 600 former mining engineers from the Red Army (pp. 175–6). On 18 February 1944 the Sovnarkom and Central Committee ordered the demobilisation of 300 former agricultural machinery technicians and 12,500 conscripts unfit for active service to work in the farm machinery industry (p. 185). On 28 February the State Defence Committee ordered demobilisation of 150 technicians for the machine tool industry (p. 193), on 3 September

162 Soviet planning in peace and war

demobilisation of 150 drivers for work in connection with the Moscow–Saratov gas pipeline (p. 210) and on 19 September redirection of 4,000 conscripts unfit for active service to work in the Krivoi Rog iron ore basin (pp. 218–19).

56 Mitrofanova, 1971, p. 427.
57 FRUS 1942, v. III, 1961, p. 456: report from Vladivostok of United States consul General Alexander I. Ward.
58 Mitrofanova, 1971, pp. 424–5.
59 Ibid., p. 428.
60 Ibid., p. 436.
61 Hancock and Gowing, 1949, p. 370. The equivalent figure for the less fully mobilised United States war economy in June 1944 was 40 per cent.
62 Calculated from ibid., pp. 77–8, 202–3, 350–1. With the armed forces are included civil defence workers and police. Group I industries included munitions, shipbuilding, engineering, chemicals and metallurgy, but not fuels and power, transport, light industries or agriculture.
63 Our starting point is the shares of the Soviet net material product devoted to war purposes, given officially as follows:

	1940 (narrow basis)	1940 (broad basis)	1942 (narrow basis)	1942 (broad basis)	1943	1944	1945
Per cent shares	11	15	40	57–8	44	36	25

For sources and further analysis the reader may turn to pp. 151–2 above. These percentages can now be used to calculate the share of the workforce in war-related employment in each year. If war workers were just as productive as others, the output and employment shares devoted to war would be the same. Probably war workers were more productive, so we assume a productivity differential in the range of 1.5 to 2 in their favour. This gives us estimated employment shares for war workers as follows:

War workers, per cent of workforce	5.8–7.7	8.1–10.5	25.0–30.8	40.3–47.4	28.2–34.4	21.2–26.4	14.3–20.0

The rest of the required data are found in Table 26 above.

Total workforce, mn	66.6	66.6	33.5	33.5	36.0	45.6	51.2
Estimated war workers, mn	3.9–5.1	5.4–7.0	8.4–10.3	13.5–15.9	10.2–12.4	9.7–12.1	7.3–10.2
Armed forces, mn	4.2	4.2	10.9	10.9	(11)	11.2	11.6

Our final assumption has been to interpolate an estimate of 11 million for the Soviet armed forces in 1943. Calculation of the share of Soviet labour resources committed to war is now straightforward.

Armed forces plus estimated war workers, mn	8.1–9.3	9.6–11.2	19.3–21.2	24.4–26.8	21.2–22.4	20.9–23.3	18.9–21.8
Working population, mn	70.8	70.8	44.4	44.4	(47)	56.8	62.8
Armed forces plus estimated war workers, per cent of working population	11.4–13.1	13.6–15.8	43.4–47.7	55.0–60.3	45.0–47.6	36.7–40.9	30.1–34.8

64 Millar, 1980, pp. 108–18.
65 Public Record Office, Kew, FO 371.43314 N2122/42/38 for 1944.
66 Bergson, 1961, p. 99.
67 Over the period net national income at current factor cost rose by about 60 per cent (Hancock and Gowing, 1949, pp. 75, 347), while wholesale prices rose by 64 to 73 per cent (Pollard, 1969, p. 324).
68 See Appendix 5, 'Net material product'.
69 Hancock and Gowing, 1949, pp. 75, 347.
70 For comparison Bergson, 1961, p. 237 estimated the share of defence in the 1944 Soviet GNP at current factor cost at 37 per cent.

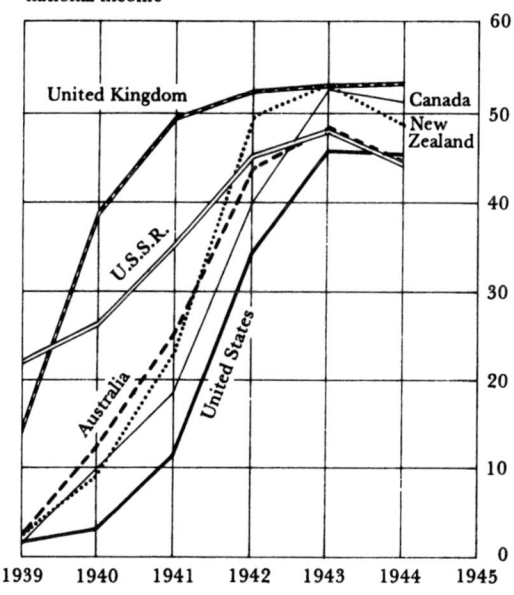

71

War expenditures in percent of national income

[Chart showing war expenditures as percent of national income for United Kingdom, Canada, New Zealand, U.S.S.R., United States, and Australia from 1939 to 1945]

National income statistics are for net national income, at market prices

This chart, attributed to the Foreign Economic Administration, is copied from US President, no. 20, 1945, p. 41.

72 Ibid., p. 40.
73 A point made frequently by Soviet historians, for example Rzheshevsky, 1971, pp. 613–18.
74 According to Bergson, 1961, p. 99 Lend–Lease in 1944 amounted to 10–12 per cent of Soviet 1944 GNP measured in 1937 roubles. In the British case net borrowing from abroad amounted to 13 per cent of UK net national income at current factor cost in 1940 and 12 per cent in 1941, falling to 8 per cent in 1943; see Hancock and Gowing, 1949, pp. 199, 347.

75 Hancock and Gowing, 1949, p. 368. See also the quotation from IVMV, v. 12, 1982, p. 145 which heads this chapter.
76 Hancock and Gowing, 1949, p. 370.
77 Stalin, 1945, pp. 96–7, 106. Emphasis added.
78 Sorokin, 1968, p. 122.
79 Bol'shevik, 1943, p. 3.
80 Sukharevsky, 1945a, pp. 3–7; 1945b, p. 9.
81 Voznesensky, 1948, p. 27. Emphasis added.
82 Ibid., p. 33.
83 Ibid., p. 39.
84 IVOVSS, v. 6, 1965, p. 47; Chadaev, 1965, pp. 381–2.
85 Komkov, 1968, pp. 226–7; G. S. Kravchenko, 1970, pp. 349–50. Kravchenko, however, rejected the idea of a necessary identification between economic and military turning points.
86 IVMV, v. 6, 1976, p. 339.
87 Arutyunyan, 1970, p. 21; IVMV, v. 8, 1977, p. 361 and v. 9, 1978, p. 392.
88 This view was put to me in conversations at the Institute of USSR History of the USSR Academy of Sciences in Moscow in 1982.
89 Plan. khoz., 1944, p. 4.

4

The search for economic balance in wartime

> Friction is the only conception which in a general way corresponds to that which distinguishes real War from War on paper. The military machine, the Army and all belonging to it, is in fact simple and appears on this account easy to manage. But let us reflect that no part of it is in one piece, that it is composed entirely of individuals, each of which keeps up its own friction in all directions. Theoretically all sounds very well: the commander of a battalion is responsible for the execution of the order given; and as the battalion by its discipline is glued together into one piece, and the chief must be a man of acknowledged zeal, the beam turns on an iron pin with little friction. But it is not so in reality...
>
> (Carl von Clausewitz)[1]

INTRODUCTION

In Chapter 1 it was stated that the real purpose of planning is to enable the continuous adaptation of the economic system to changing reality according to permanent objectives. The most important problem of central planning in the Soviet Union was given as the failure to adapt plans smoothly and continuously to the resources really available and to the real conditions under which they would be supplied. Adaptation of plans does take place, but it occurs discontinuously under the pressure of accumulated imbalances. Plans are formulated on the basis of existing knowledge and put into operation. In the course of implementation possible difficulties are revealed and new information is generated. But because of a multitude of frictions the information is at first discounted, the difficulties denied by those in charge of the plan. Consequently adaptation is postponed. Only when one or another social tolerance limit is breached by the resulting stress will the system react to accumulating evidence of disproportion.

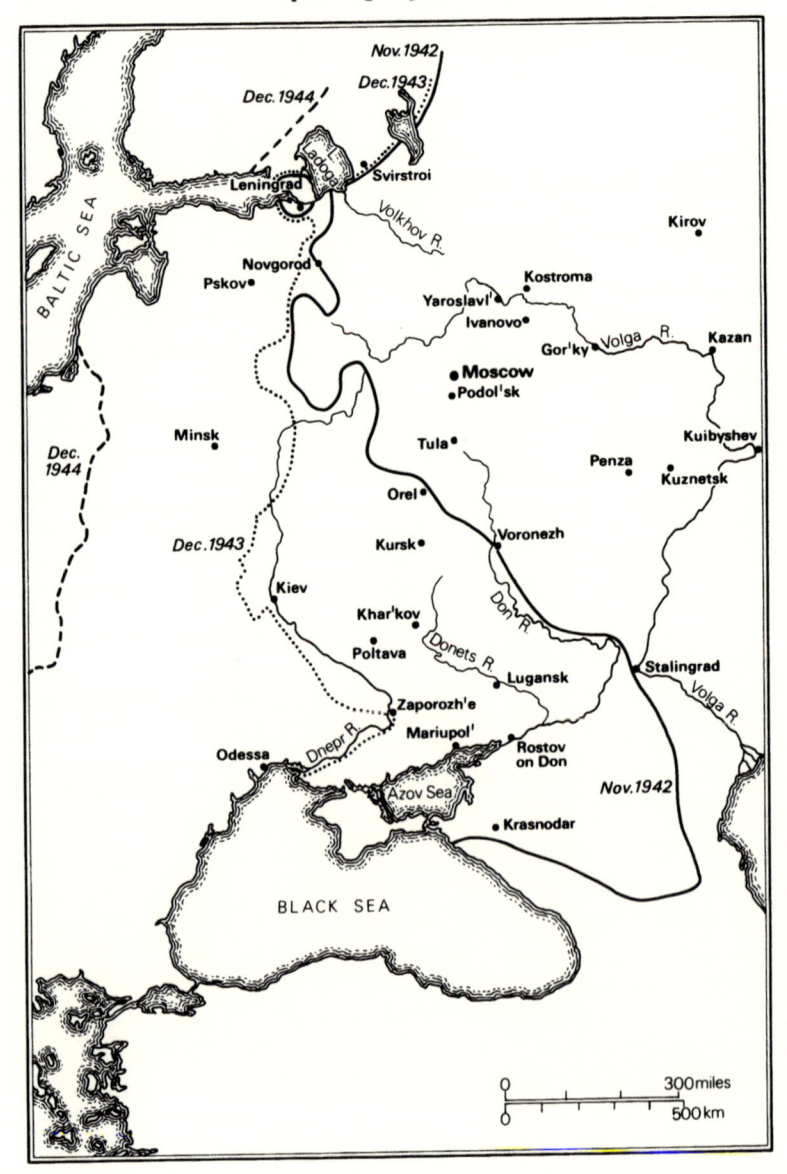

The Soviet–German front 1942–4

When considered from the point of view of how new resources are allocated at a sectoral or local level, the resulting adaptive cycle is described by János Kornai as 'postponement, putting out the fire'. This is the cycle which operates at lower levels of the economy, under conditions of investment hunger generated by the macroeconomic investment cycle which we have already considered. The term 'firefighting' is borrowed from modern control theory.[2] When investment goods are in short supply, and in the absence of other allocative criteria, new resources are denied to any sector of the economy until fire 'breaks out'. This is the point at which the results of postponement and neglect breach the limit of social tolerance. At this point new resources will be pumped in to cool down the local crisis. But this is at the cost of postponement elsewhere. 'Putting out the fire' therefore

creates a vicious circle. It pre-empts the available uncommitted resources for the fields (subsectors, regions, etc.) in which problems are accumulating. Therefore nothing or hardly anything is granted to areas in which the situation is still tolerable. There the utilization of fixed capital is constantly on the increase; among other things, quantity drive and the continuous expansion prevailing everywhere in the economy promote this increase. Postponement begins, which sooner or later leads to difficulties there as well. Exactly this – the overstepping of their own tolerance limits – will give them the right to obtain investment resources not yet committed. *Thus, 'putting out the fire' permanently reproduces itself.*

Such an adaptive routine, Kornai concludes, 'may be a painful form of progress, but not "irrational"... experience shows that it is *viable*'.[3]

The 'firefighting' model provides an apt description of the means whereby the Soviet economic crisis of 1941–2 was tackled at a sectoral and industrial branch level. At the same time, to convey a sense of the historical process, we need to add further dimensions to that of Kornai's picture.

First, like the emergency regime of which it formed an element, the 'firefighting' model did not mark an entirely new departure in Soviet economic life. It found precedents in previous Soviet episodes of extreme mobilisation and crisis management, during the civil war and later under the prewar Five Year Plans for rapid industrialisation.

Secondly, resort to the 'firefighting' model stimulated institutional change in the economic system. This is because pumping resources from each successive overheated crisis point to the next could not be implemented within a fixed set of institutions. For example, during

1942, as the locus of crisis shifted from arms capacity to iron, steel, energy and transport, the instruments of management, the role of planning and the locus of authority all continued to evolve. As a result the economic system which had evolved by 1943 or 1944 was significantly different from that of 1941 and 1942.

This chapter is divided into three parts. In Part One we examine in detail the process whereby the economy was rebalanced in 1942. In Part Two we go on to look at the resumed search for a coherent planning system in 1943–5. In Part Three we come to some general conclusions about the role of planning in the wartime economic system. The more general question about what was learned in the process from the wartime economic experience is left to Chapter 5.

PART ONE: THE RESTORATION OF ECONOMIC BALANCE

ARMS AND THE BASIC INDUSTRIES

The decline of the basic industries in the autumn and winter of 1941 proved extremely difficult to reverse. This reflected the interlocking character of exchange of basic goods and services among them, which resulted in a vicious circle of decline. The extraction of fuels for the output of energy, the supply of iron and steel products and the availability of transport services formed a complementary bloc at the heart of the industrial economy. The dislocation of this bloc's internal harmony coincided with the multiplication of external demands upon it for the current and capital needs of the defence industries, for the conversion of civilian industry, for evacuation to the rear and for the supply of the front.

Thus by 1942 it was the metals–energy–transport balance which had become most tightly constrained. In the arms industries fixed capacity was no longer a binding limit on output;[4] current shortages of metals, fuels and labour were the problem. One step further back along the supply line lay the civilian engineering industry, but here too output was limited by shortages of metals, fuels and labour, not by fixed capacity.[5] The construction industry too faced grave difficulties over the supply of labour and of building materials,[6] especially structural steel, but fixed capacity was not the problem. But the fixed assets of the metals–energy–transport bloc had been stripped away.

This was where allocative priorities had to be most strictly defined, and where correct or incorrect decisions would have the most permanent effect.

Of all resources none are less movable than minerals in the ground. The lines of German advance, aimed at the location of the Soviet Union's major coal and oil reserves, created immediate problems of fuel supply. During the autumn of 1941 German troops occupied the coal–metallurgical region of the Donbass. As they approached the capital, output of the Moscow coal basin dwindled to zero. Nearly two-thirds of the country's prewar mining capacity was in enemy hands.[7] By 27 January 1942 coal stocks in the central region of the European RSFSR had fallen to only twenty-four hours' productive utilisation.[8] Even in the high-priority iron and steel industry coal stocks held at plant level in January amounted to only three or four days' consumption for coking coal and eight days' for general-purpose fuel.[9] Meanwhile output continued to fall. In the biggest coalfield of the interior, the Kuzbass, output declined in face of a growing shortage of workers.[10] For the country as a whole coal extraction in the first half of 1942 ran at under 40 per cent of the same period in the preceding year.[11]

During 1942, in consequence, coal temporarily lost its position as supplier of the greater part of the country's fuel needs.[12] The share of oil and wood fuels rose.[13] Abundant timber was available from the forest zones of the north. But oil supplies were also under threat. In the third quarter of 1941 oil extraction was still buoyant – higher than in the same quarter of the previous year. Then a sudden decline set in. By December the flow was a third below the June rate of extraction. Combined with the disruption of transport, a major factor was a shortage of drilling and piping equipment.[14] The Soviet oil industry's prewar pattern showed an average well life of ten years or less and high turnover of exhausted wells. A variety of features followed from this. The first requirement was a high level of new drilling to maintain output expansion. Once located by costly exploration, new wells could be opened within months at comparatively small initial capital cost. But after the first phase of exploitation the typical well required a series of equipment changeovers from free-flowing to pumping and compression methods of extraction.[15] Without regular renewals of machinery and equipment new wells could not be opened nor existing ones maintained in exploitation. In the Caucasus growing transport difficulties were also beginning to hinder removal of extracted oil from the region.

In the electricity generating industry cutbacks in fuel and capacity took effect simultaneously. By the end of 1941 over 40 per cent of nationwide capacity had been decommissioned because of the enemy advance.[16] Capacity still in operation in the interior faced increased demands as the relocation of evacuated industries became a reality (of course the relocated assets included some power generating equipment). In spite of this capacity utilisation was actually lower by 8 per cent in 1942 than in 1940.[17] Even in the Urals, the region of greatest additional demand, electricity generation was running at 15 per cent below capacity in the first months of 1942, and in the Moscow region electricity generation fell 60 per cent below the plan on some days.[18] In this fuel shortages were a critical factor. Of course the industry also had a significant hydroelectric component not dependent on mineral fuel supplies, but many of the prestige projects of the prewar period had fallen into enemy hands.

The decay of the fuel and power system was hastened at every point by disruptions of transport. By 1942 major road and rail links had been broken. Under the burden of new tasks the railways were winding down. Between May and December 1941 the speed of movement of railway trucks had fallen by a third, and loading and waiting time had both doubled. As a result the daily travel of each truck had fallen by more than half. Together with more protracted east–west hauls between the frontal and interior regions, this meant that the period of circulation of trucks had nearly trebled.[19] With the eastward retreat the density of the rail network declined sharply; as the channels thinned out to the rear of Moscow, and especially behind Kuibyshev in the Urals, they became clogged and overloaded. An essential part of the solution would be the construction of new lines.[20] At the same time, however, material supplies to the railways were cut right back. In the third quarter of 1941 the railways were provided with almost 90 per cent of the 64,000 tons of rail required by the railway managers; in the fourth quarter they were given a paper allocation of only 20 per cent of the 189,000 tons now demanded. Just to replace wear and tear they asked for 846 kilometres of rail in early December 1941 and received 8 kilometres. In the same month they received 30 per cent of the sleepers they had asked for, and 5 per cent of the iron castings.[21] In 1942 as a whole they would be supplied with just over 300,000 tons of iron and steel (compared to 2.9 million tons in 1940), eight new locomotives and no new railway trucks at all.[22]

At the centre of the planning system it was the drop in iron and steel supplies which provoked gravest concern in the spring of 1942.[23] Here the biggest cutbacks in capacity and output were registered. By the end of 1941 nearly 70 per cent of iron mining and smelting capacity and nearly 60 per cent of steel forging and rolling capacity had been decommissioned. Utilisation of remaining capacity fell,[24] while fuel costs rose per ton of crude steel produced.[25] Soviet rolling mills were being rapidly converted to high-grade rolled steel products essential to arms manufacture, boosting high-grade output by 47 per cent in 1941 as a whole compared with 1940 (meanwhile the output of ordinary rollings fell by a fifth). But the disruption of rolling capacity in the autumn and winter of 1941 was so great that high-grade output was 28 per cent lower in 1942 than in the previous year, and the output of ordinary rollings fell by three-quarters.[26]

Already in a critical state, the metals–energy–transport balance was further destabilised in the late spring and summer of 1942 by the German offensive against Stalingrad and the Caucasus. Hitler's directive No. 41 of 5 April 1942 ordered the German forces 'to wipe out the entire defence potential remaining to the Soviets, and to cut them off, as far as possible, from their most important centres of industry'.[27] At the centre of this operation was the expedition of the Sixth Wehrmacht Army to destroy Soviet forces on the Don river, to take or destroy Stalingrad and to seize the Caucasian oilfields. On 22 June 1942 the second wave of evacuation of Soviet industry, this time from the Don and Volga regions, was marked by formation of a new Evacuation Commission.[28] Equipment was ordered out of the Caucasian oilfields, drilling was cut back, and only the most productive wells were retained in operation. Oil extraction fell back sharply in Azerbaidzhan,[29] halved in Georgia and ceased altogether in Krasnodar.[30] Nationwide yields fell steadily through 1942 and by the first quarter of 1943 were running at just under half the rate established in the last six months of peace.[31] At the same time the German approach to the Caucasus blocked off oil transit routes, making necessary huge detours. Baku oil had to travel a great arc across the waters of the Caspian to Krasnovodsk and up through Turkmenia to Orenburg in order to arrive back in the country's interior.[32] Extracted oil was held up within the region for lack of transport, and in turn extraction had to be slowed down for lack of storage facilities.[33]

The Soviet coal industry, supplying the country's most important mineral fuel, had already suffered its most grievous wounds in 1941. In 1942 things improved little. The Kuznetsk coalfield failed repeatedly to match either prewar performance or wartime plan targets. And the same was marked in the Karanganda coalfield, in spite of the opening up of new pits.[34] Here the problem was not the direct actions of the enemy but failure to secure necessary inputs, poor workforce organisation and training, and the failure of morale arising from poor living conditions and leadership.[35]

Such problems of supply were exacerbated by new strains on railway transport. The tasks of the 1941 evacuation had been accomplished, but now began the period of the great offensives. The biggest Soviet military operations, such as at Moscow, Stalingrad and Kursk, required huge westward concentrations of 300,000 or so railway trucks on super-long hauls of thousands of kilometres from the interior, converging upon a common front. Organising their convergence and prompt dispersal was a task fraught with difficulty.[36] German success on the southern front in the summer of 1942 added new complications. On top of the tasks of a second evacuation, the rail and sea route from the Urals through Central Asia to Krasnovodsk and Baku now had to bear military supplies for Soviet troops fighting in the Caucasus,[37] in addition to the reverse flow of oil.

Improvements in the indices of railway utilisation had been won in June and July 1942, but in August and September the trend was reversed.[38] Through the autumn the railways struggled successfully with the requirements of the Stalingrad operation, but this was at the expense of the expanding war economy. In the summer of 1942 coal stocks held at iron and steel plants had been lifted above the crisis levels of the previous January;[39] in the following winter they fell back again, and by January 1943 large parts of the industry were standing idle for lack of fuels and energy.[40] Yet so extreme was the shortage of transport that in February 1943 iron and steel plants were reported to be choked with stockpiled products.[41] At Gosplan those concerned with the 1943 first-quarter plan considered that the problems of coal, steel and railway freight posed a danger for the whole economy, especially for continued expansion of the arms industries.[42] The last straw was apparently the railways' first-quarter performance, which fell more than 10 per cent below plan in March 1943.[43]

Figure 7 shows differential growth of different products of the arms and heavy industries during 1942 and 1943. In 1942 the heavy

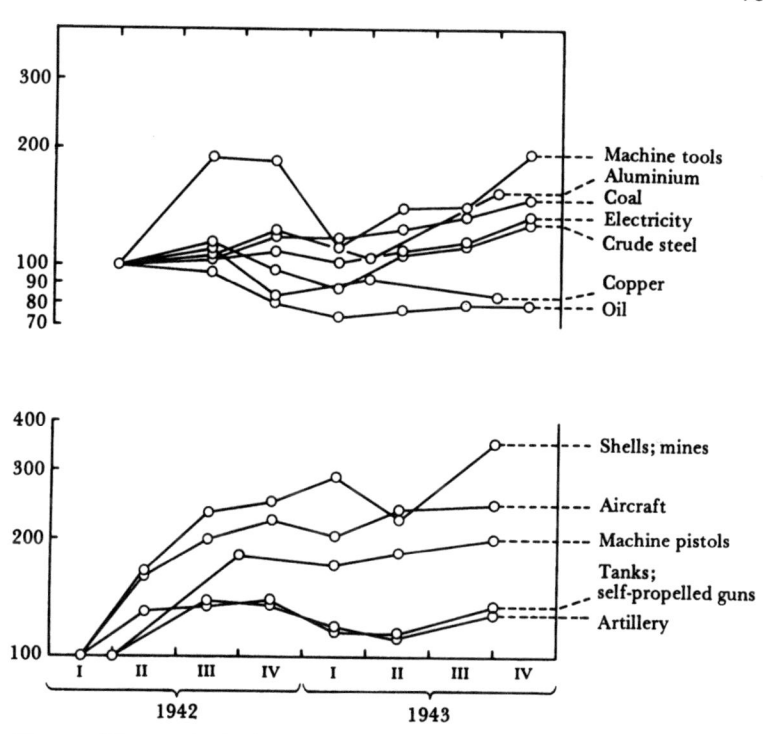

Figure 7. Changes in Soviet arms and heavy industrial production from the beginning of 1942 to the end of 1943 (indices of half-yearly or quarterly output; 1942 (first half) = 100 except for aircraft, shells and mines, and tanks and self-propelled guns, for which 1942 (first quarter) = 100)
(*Source:* Appendices 1 and 2)

industries (except machine tools) failed to restore the output losses sustained in the initial period of the war. The winter was a particularly difficult time in basic industry. Output faltered nearly everywhere and oil and steel products showed declines beneath previous low points. Under the circumstances of acute metal shortage and the needs of arms manufacture the recovery in toolmaking, too, was reversed. Only in 1943 did a sustained recovery emerge in most sectors.

Arms production expanded throughout 1942, but the expansion decelerated. For all the main categories there was a peak in output levels in late 1942 or early 1943, followed by a temporary contraction. Probably this reflected factors on both the supply and the demand side. The supply side would have registered the knock-on effects of

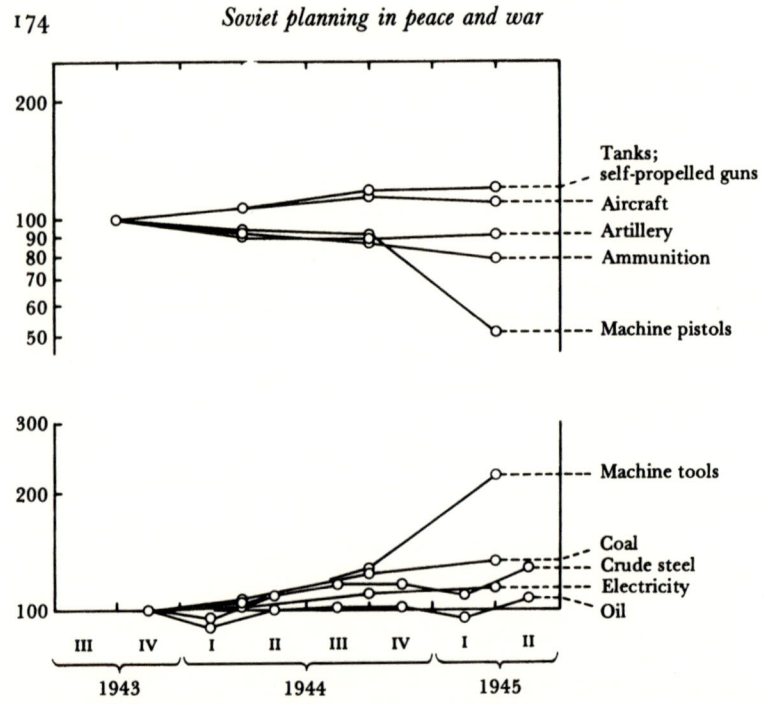

Figure 8. Changes in Soviet arms and heavy industrial production from the latter part of 1943 to early 1945 (indices of half-yearly or quarterly output; for military goods 1943 (second half) = 100, and for industrial goods 1943 (fourth quarter) = 100)
(*Source:* Appendices 1 and 2)

cumulative disruption of the underlying metals–energy–transport balance (an independent factor in tank supplies in early 1943 was German air raids on the Gor'ky tank factory). But on the demand side, too, just at this time army equipment loss rates moderated for a time, and in the case of armament showed a sustained fall.[44] Thus the slackening of arms manufacture in early 1943 could be explained as easily by the achievement of a higher level of satisfaction of military needs as by the difficulty of sustaining a high rate of supply.

The indications are that after the winter of 1942 there was marked a qualitative improvement in the metals–energy–transport balance. From 1943 onwards the structure of the whole complex of defence and heavy industries stabilised. The degree of imbalance did not improve in all sectors at the same rate, and of course the absolute level of shortage of basic goods remained far greater than in peacetime.

Nonetheless the commitment of new supplies of steel, fuel and power to the manufacture of weapons had reached its peak. The vicious circle of decline had been arrested, and from now on the balance would improve.

The reader may confirm these assertions in the following simple way. Figure 2 above illustrated the gap which opened up between arms expansion and heavy industrial decline in the first period of the war and into the spring of 1942. Figure 7 showed that in 1942 and 1943 the divergence widened further, but that by 1943 the elements of common movement among the various series had become more and more pronounced. These two figures may be compared visually with Figure 8, which shows the orderly progress of the last two years of warfare, from the latter part of 1943. By this stage further divergences between the military and civilian economies had been virtually eliminated (more precisely, any divergence was now to the benefit of the civilian economy, if we take into account some declines in arms output and the first steps of reconversion in the engineering industry). Barring seasonal fluctuations, which once more became noticeable, the economy marched in step.

PLANNING AND THE REGIME OF EMERGENCY MEASURES

Solution of the country's economic problems in 1942 rested on an extension of the 'regime of emergency measures' which had dominated economic life since 22 June 1941. To stabilise the metals–energy–transport balance the highest executive bodies issued a stream of directives of the highest priority to bolster, modify or override existing plans. The most important of these measures were as follows.

The first wave of special measures for the fuel and energy sector began in the dark days of December 1941. Coal was so scarce that restoration work began in the Moscow coalfield in mid-December, a fortnight before the Sovnarkom issued orders to start work and allocate supplies on 29 December.[45] And in fact in 1942 the Mosbass would yield over 8.5 million tons of coal, not far below its 1940 peak of 10 million tons.[46] Then attention switched away to other areas. The State Defence Committee did not become involved in the problems of the fuel and energy sector until the lagging output of the Kuzbass and Karaganda fields, together with the steady deterioration of the oil balance, forced their way to the head of the agenda in September

1942. On the 22nd the GKO ordered a crash programme of exploratory drilling and exploitation in the oil regions of the interior. This was followed on the 24th by a pair of stinging rebukes, one each for the party organisations of the Kuzbass and the Karaganda coalfields for inadequate leadership of workforce and management.[47] Tens of thousands of workers were drafted into the mines,[48] machinery was earmarked to help utilisation of spare capacity, and new smaller, shallower pits were opened.[49] Output from the Kuzbass responded only sluggishly, but from October 1942 a definite upswing was marked in Karaganda,[50] where 1943 output would be 37 per cent in excess of 1942.[51] More or less every organisational problem noted in 1942 would be still in evidence in 1943 and 1944,[52] but at least output was now rising on a nationwide scale.

In the autumn of 1942 attention therefore began to shift to the problem of allocating fuels correctly in the coming winter. Anxious to avoid the crises of the previous year, on 2 October 1942 the Sovnarkom ordered the formation of fuel teams under local government across the country.[53] But during the winter the fuel balance grew steadily tighter, and the coal shortage once again forced its way onto the GKO agenda. This time the distribution side was the object of special measures. On 1 February 1943 the transport commissariat was ordered to rank coal directly after military goods in its list of wartime priorities, and after coal itself empty trucks going to pick up coal. On 2 March the GKO ordered a cutback in passenger rail traffic to let coal through, and on 7 March again issued instructions to speed up the turnaround of coal trains and return of empty trucks to the pithead.[54]

The production side was not ignored, and as we have seen criticism of coal industry management continued to surface in 1943 and 1944. But by this stage the fuel shortage had clearly eased; railway depots, power stations and other important enterprises were able to end 1943 with adequate winter fuel reserves.[55] Basically it was coal and, where possible, timber which filled the fuel gap. The troubles of 1942 dogged the oil industry right through the war, and in the early months of 1944 emergency action was twice decreed by the GKO.[56]

In the power industry in 1942 and 1943 output fell further and further below capacity. At first this was due to supply breakdowns and especially the fuel shortage, but as fuel supplies eased the utilisation of capacity fell further. In the Ural region, where excess demand was at a peak, capacity utilisation was 11 per cent down in

1942,[57] compared to 8 per cent for the country as a whole; nationwide capacity utilisation fell by another 5 per cent in 1943.[58] Part of the problem stemmed from the growth of new construction in the industry in late 1942,[59] which resulted in a shortage of equipment and on 9 January 1943[60] prompted a GKO resolution on the need for spare parts. But this remedy alone was insufficient. Other aspects of the problem, exposed in April 1943, included the inexperience of the massively altered workforce, neglect and incompetent misuse of equipment and poor management of fuel stocks.[61] Special training measures and a management shake-out were set in motion.

Two waves of emergency measures hit the iron and steel industry. In early 1942 the problem of deficient capacity was the subject of a special commission headed by Voznesensky with the iron and steel commissar, I. F. Tevosyan.[62] The result was a crash programme of capacity construction approved by the GKO on 13 April 1942. Experience of the following year showed the focus of difficulty in the industry shifting to the area of material–technical supply; the crisis of the winter of 1942 which led to a shutdown of much of the country's iron and steel plant provoked a GKO resolution of 7 February placing personal responsibility on the appropriate commissars for the industry's supply of fuels, energy and raw materials.[63] After 1942 the situation eased; fuel costs per ton of steel fell from 1943 onwards, and capacity utilisation in existing plant improved, although the nationwide picture was complicated by the slow process of restoring plant in recaptured territory.[64]

Evolution of the wartime regime in transport was exceptionally complicated. This was reflected in the frequent turnover of transport commissars in wartime. L. M. Kaganovich, USSR People's Commissar for Transport since 1932, was replaced on 25 March 1942 by Red Army Quartermaster General A. V. Khrulev. Then in February 1943 Kaganovich was reappointed. He was replaced once more in December 1944 by his deputy, Lieutenant-General I. V. Kovalev.[65] Estimates of Kaganovich's role vary widely. Post-Stalin Soviet historiography, no doubt influenced by Kaganovich's participation in the 'anti-party' group of Stalinist reactionaries in 1957, portrayed him in unflattering terms as a leader who covered up his lack of expertise and competence with force of will and dictatorial methods.[66] He was blamed personally for the disorganisation of the railways in 1941, and his replacement by Shvernik as head of the Evacuation Council after only three weeks was attributed to official recognition of his incompetence.[67] On the other hand this cannot have been the reason for his replacement by Khrulev as transport commissar in March 1942, for he clearly retained Stalin's confidence, having been appointed to the GKO only five weeks previously; his later reappointment as transport commissar also does not square with the picture of Kaganovich's managerial failure. At least some of those who had to work with him – for example General Kovalev, who later succeeded him as transport commissar – held his technical competence in high esteem.[68] Doubtless Kaganovich was really a complicated mixture, like the rest of his colleagues.

As far as railway management is concerned, the rapid circulation of leading personnel was not necessarily the result of a cycle of individual failures. More likely there was a succession of deep-seated transport crises, while individual leaders were pushed into transport management, then pulled out and replaced according to changing perceptions at the war cabinet level of coordination priorities and available first-rank personnel. Thus the replacement of Kaganovich by Khrulev as transport commissar in March 1942 was certainly prepared by failure of the railways to measure up to the demands arising from the supply of the front, the evacuation and the mobilisation of industry in the rear. But the solution to these problems involved more than just replacing one commissar by another. In reality Khrulev was already operating as a de facto transport boss. From September 1941 he was in control of a network of personal plenipotentiary agents with wide executive powers in every organ of the transport commissariat. Where conventional mechanised transport failed him, he was responsible for finding stopgap solutions – for example the reintroduction of horse battalions in December 1941.[69] As transport capacity visibly decayed, he became an obvious choice for vesting combined military and civil authority in one set of capable hands.

On 14 February 1942 a Transport Committee was set up under the GKO; the committee was headed by Stalin personally, and included both Kaganovich and Khrulev in its membership.[70] The committee's job was to investigate and take charge of the work of the transport commissariat. The results were Khrulev's appointment (he retained his military post as chief of the Red Army's logistic organs) and a GKO resolution, also dated 25 March, which clearly set out the need for a more effective, centralised authority. The railways had disintegrated into a 'federation' of semi-autonomous administrations each with its own rules and priorities.[71] It became Khrulev's job to set them straight.

Under Khrulev's leadership the transport bottleneck was widened and capacity utilisation improved. In the summer of 1942, however, the German offensive in the south made his position more and more difficult. He organised certain essential tasks, for example emergency construction of new railway lines on the oil route from Orenburg to Krasnovodsk on the Caspian.[72] But in the disastrous situation which formed during the autumn and winter higher authorities stepped in once more. Central Committee secretary A. A. Andreev was despatched to the Urals to try to untangle the mess, and a decree of the Sovnarkom and Central Committee on the rationalisation of freight schedules in the Urals resulted on 20 January 1943.[73]

In February 1943 Khrulev was relieved of his post and Kaganovich was reappointed. But the situation failed to improve, and the emphasis now shifted away from high-level intervention and leadership changes to more radical measures. On 15 April 1943 a decree of the Supreme Soviet imposed martial law on the railways, and the decree was followed within ten days by a new code of military discipline for railway workers.[74] An article in *Pravda* explained railway militarisation by the undisciplined, irresponsible behaviour of a minority of workers,[75] but behind this must have stood a larger problem of discipline and morale. On 31 May the political departments of railway establishments were abolished in the name of strengthening individual managerial authority and responsibility.[76] Meanwhile, at the beginning of May, martial law had been extended to river and sea transport.[77]

A sustained improvement now set in. It lasted until the end of 1944. In the winter months, and with victory in sight, the longer lines of communication, new priorities of reverse evacuation and rehabilitation of recaptured territories, and the revival of transport-intensive industrial processes, all combined to upset the transport balance again.[78] Factory stocks ran down and coal shortages reappeared.[79] Kaganovich was sacked a second time, and his place was taken by Kovalev. But the war was now almost over.

As a system of economy-wide coordination the regime of emergency measures persisted through 1942, but by the spring of 1943 it was beginning to give way to something else. The most obvious sign of transition was that the flow of high-level, top-priority directives aimed at pumping new resources into one after another sector of basic industry in order to 'put out the fires' dried up. In the priority sectors of the economy the fires had been suppressed, and emergency mobilisation ceased to be the principal method of directing inputs into them. The reader should understand, however, that early 1943 marked the end of the regime of emergency measures only in so far as it had made up a temporary system for coordinating the economy as a whole; in the management of the economy at the industrial branch and sub-branch level emergency measures continued to feature throughout the war.

The persistence of an emergency atmosphere in industrial branch management after 1942 took different forms in different sectors. In priority branches like the energy and transport sectors it was always now combined with attempts to rationalise (on the railways, to militarise) the management system and thus give the results of emergency action a permanent form. An unbridled emergency form of management, on the other hand, was retained in agriculture.

The case of agriculture was differentiated from that of the basic industries by its low priority in the queue for new resources, and by the predominant emphasis on extracting resources from the sector rather than on pumping them in. The institutional basis for arbitrary extraction of resources had been laid down before the war in the Soviet collective farm and its servicing network of nationalised machine tractor stations. Of special importance in wartime were two rules laid down in April and August 1940. According to the first the basis for calculating compulsory deliveries of collective farm products to the state was changed from effectively realised farm capacity (area sown, dairy herd etc.) to an official assessment of potential farm capacity. According to the second the basis for calculating collective farm payments in kind to machine tractor stations in return for services rendered was changed from barn yields of harvested crops to an official estimate of the biological yield of crops still in the field.[80] These rules provided a 'legal' basis for arbitrary and excessive levies of foodstuffs from the rural population in wartime.

In the autumn of 1942 and during 1943 the emergency atmosphere in agriculture was intensified, rather than relaxed. Compilation of any information about crop levels other than biological yield evaluations was prohibited. In the Altai region the practice of compiling grain–forage balances within the collective farm, based on true barn (not biological) yields, was condemned as a ploy to weaken the procurement campaign, and police methods accompanied the campaign at all levels of government.[81] In 1943, however, farm output declined further and in the autumn the urban food ration was cut again. In November the Sovnarkom and Central Committee ordered 'measures to intensify the grain procurements';[82] Andreev, Voznesensky, Kosygin, Mikoyan, Shvernik and others were sent out to force the pace in the regions.[83] And in 1944, with the first signs of agricultural recovery, the procurement campaign was waged once more in a battlefront atmosphere. For a substantial increase in deliveries to the state, the campaign leaders were rewarded with military medals as though for heroism displayed under enemy fire.[84]

We may now come to an interim conclusion on the essential features of wartime economic coordination through the emergency regime. These features were threefold. First was that emergency power was unrestrained by rules. It recognised no other authority, and required its orders to be executed without reference to external constraints. Directly related to this was the personal responsibility of top-level leaders for drawing up and executing directives, their dictatorial authority to do everything necessary for their implementation, and the common resort to individual plenipotentiary agents of high-level bodies rather than to low-level functionaries to stimulate the required response from below.

The second feature of the regime of emergency measures was the centralisation of decision making in priority areas at the highest level and down to the smallest detail. At the moment when millions of tons of metal were being weighed in the military–economic balance, one decree of the USSR Sovnarkom dated 10 March 1942 disposed of 300 tons of iron castings, 340 tons of steel scrap, 8 tons of ferrosilicates and 10 tons of ferromanganese from government reserves for ammunition production.[85] Not all of the emergency economic mobilisation directives were in such fine detail, but for the key areas of the economy each major decree was specific and sharp-focused.

Each of these first two features could be observed in Soviet emergency administration at all levels and in all branches. Only when combined with the third feature did they become a system for temporary coordination of the economy in the period of restoration of economic balance in 1942. The third feature was the adaptive mechanism of 'postponement, putting out the fire'. This involved the sequential identification and recognition of intolerable crisis in one sector after another, bearing in mind that what might or might not be tolerated was defined not in technical terms but from a broad military, political and social point of view. As crisis broke in one sector and new resources were pumped in to 'put out the fire', another sector would be denied necessary inputs and would burst into flame, setting off the next round of urgent action. The result was very rapid, essentially unplanned changes in operational priority at the highest level, in the course of which everyone would be taken by surprise at each turn; but at each turn someone knew what had to be done and would eventually force it through. This rapid circulation in the ranking of most urgent needs was well reflected in (among other places) the experience of United States Lend–Lease officials, who recorded the sudden, unpredictable shifts in Soviet economic requirements from military goods to foodstuffs, then suddenly to chemicals and industrial equipment, from there to oil piping and refining equipment and aluminium for aviation before another sudden switch to urgent requests for hydroelectric equipment (all this was between the autumn of 1942 and the summer of 1943).[86]

How did the role of the economic planning system evolve during 1942? In the last six months of 1941 the plans and the planning institutions themselves had been displaced by the emergency regime. As long as the rule was no more complicated than 'putting out the fire' in arms manufacture (the mobilisation and evacuation of arms capacity) combined with 'postponement' everywhere else, the planners were not really needed. In 1942 the emergency regime persisted, but the character of the emergency became far more complicated, and the planners returned to the centre of economic life. They became essential to the emergency administration because without them no one would know which fire to tackle first, and with what to tackle it. Thus it was inherent in the success of the regime of emergency measures that the planners eventually be drawn back into operational decision making at the highest level.

The immediate way back lay through USSR Gosplan's responsibility for the progress of relocation of evacuated industrial capacity. Oversight of this process became a main preoccupation of Gosplan's central staff and plenipotentiary network in 1942.[87] In the context of the wartime economic plan for the interior regions for the last quarter of 1941 and for 1942 adopted on 16 August 1941, and of the schedule for industrial relocation agreed on 9 November 1941, this rapidly became an overall responsibility for development of the war economy as a whole in the interior. By the second half of 1942 Gosplan was compiling quarterly and monthly plans covering arms production, engineering and the basic industries.[88] However, the emergency context as yet robbed these plans of much operational force.

In 1942, apart from enemy action itself, there were two main sources of plan disruption stemming from the context of emergency. The first was that the informational basis of plan compilation had not yet been fully restored. The statistical apparatus was preoccupied with the backlog of special wartime tasks which had accumulated in the first period of the war. Consequently the information underlying economic plans in 1942 was often either out of date or hypothetical. For example, in calculating the supply side of balances for industrial goods, relocated enterprises were counted as having been providing output from the planned moment of restoration of production, whether or not production was actually restored on the planned date. Equipment losses or transport problems might delay the recommissioning of capacity, unknown to the planners.[89] Failure to restore engineering or basic industrial capacity would cause other enterprises to lose planned output in their turn. By the end of 1942, however, this problem had been largely overcome.[90]

The second source of plan disruption in 1942 was the constant overriding of plans by top-priority directives and military orders responding to unplanned emergencies and unexpected needs. For example the Moscow city authorities found their plans for arms production by local industries continually disrupted by the flow of urgent supplementary orders for immediate supplies direct from the GKO and USSR and RSFSR Sovnarkoms. In the first six months of 1942 they had to cope with a multiplicity of such orders for winter uniforms, pontoon bridges, camouflage material, airstrip landing lights, gas masks, antitank rifle limbers, buckets and funnels, signalling lamps and many other items.[91] Only with 1943 were such needs consistently met from the planned output of the enterprises under Moscow city jurisdiction, allowing input–output balances to regain operational significance.[92] In the second half of 1942 another kind of plan disruption associated with the emergency atmosphere had to be resisted – an attempt to initiate a new purge of industry from the USSR People's Commissariat of State Control under Stalin's former protégé General L. Z. Mekhlis. The tireless promotion of investigations of economic misconduct from within the state control apparatus (by November 1942 one rubber factory had suffered more than twenty investigations in a few months) met with a direct challenge from Voznesensky as deputy Sovnarkom chairman and USSR

Gosplan chairman Saburov. The matter was resolved within the USSR Sovnarkom by means of a more strict definition of the prerogatives of state control – a slap on the wrist for Mekhlis.[93]

At the end of 1942 the institutional balance between emergency mobilisation and the equilibrium functions of planning was altered, and one may speculate that this was a decisive shift. On 8 December the GKO set up a new, directly subordinate Operations Bureau to take on and execute its economic functions. Two different accounts are available of the context of this innovation, but the two are not necessarily alternatives. According to the authoritative official history the GKO Operations Bureau was formed amid the critical conditions of the winter of 1942 – the renewed economic disproportions following on the loss of additional territories in the south and the growing needs of the counteroffensive.[94] Another source, hardly less authoritative, places its formation in the longer-term context of exhaustion of the reserves of the civilian economy, completion of mobilisation and conversion to a war footing, and the unavoidable need to satisfy wartime needs and rebuild reserves from current production.[95] The aim of the Operations Bureau was to carry out 'operational supervision of fulfilment of military contracts' by means of further centralisation of industry and transport. Within its sphere of oversight were placed all the defence industry commissariats, transport, metallurgy, the fuel and power industries, chemicals and 'everything necessary' for compilation and fulfilment of their plans.[96]

The real significance of the Operations Bureau, its place in the administrative system and even its membership remain shadowy. Its main effect on the central system of decision making must have been to eliminate, or at least modify, the system of individual responsibility of GKO members for key branches of the national economy in the early phases of the war.[97] This is because for the first time there was an administrative apparatus to channel information from industry, to consult with Gosplan, and to draft proposals to and implement decisions of the GKO. The impression of a trend towards tightening up and formalising the central administrative system is bolstered by a significant appointment. Since March 1941 Voznesensky had exercised a general responsibility for economic plans and performance through his position as deputy Sovnarkom chairman. His authority in wartime had been greatly strengthened by his appointment to the GKO on 3 February 1942. Now on 8 December 1942, the same day as formation of the GKO Operations Bureau, he was reappointed chairman of USSR Gosplan.[98] He retained this post for the remainder of the war and until 1949, when his career was overtaken by a chain of events to be discussed in a later chapter.

To conclude, three considerations point to the winter of 1942 and early 1943 as a moment of transition for the central planning and management process. There was a movement away from the 'regime of emergency measures' towards an enhanced role for the planning institutions and the balance functions which they administered in the economy. The first consideration is that emergency mobilisation was at an end; the economic crisis induced by the German invasion had been resolved and a workable balance restored in the industrial economy. Secondly, USSR Gosplan was of necessity playing a more and more important role in administering an increasingly complicated priority system; personal rule by fiat was no longer competent to identify imbalances, direct resources and relax constraints. Thirdly, it may be argued that these trends were institutionalised at the highest level through changes in the way in which the GKO administered its economic responsibilities, directly affecting the relationship among its individual members, USSR Gosplan and the leadership of industry, and especially the personal position of Voznesensky. This argument is hypothetical and does not find direct confirmation. However, it is greatly strengthened when we widen our enquiry to include the concurrent changes in wartime controls over labour, which were comparatively well defined.

THE CENTRALISATION OF MANPOWER CONTROLS

Restoration of a workable economic balance in wartime could not have been achieved without some means for allocating labour among the competing military and industrial priorities. In wartime the prewar trend to tightening direct controls over the workforce was carried much further. Associated with this was a far-reaching centralisation of top-level 'manpower' policy which had implications, in turn, for economic planning.

In principle every major economy of World War II moved at least some distance along this road. Afterwards success would be judged in part by the distance travelled. Of the capitalist economies at war, Britain travelled furthest and the United States and Germany less far. In the North American case this was because the need to travel further did not arise. In the German case it was the result of both calculation and miscalculation: for most of the war her manpower deficit was met by drafting in the plundered assets and slave labour of conquered nations, and by the time the need for a thorough mobilisation of the German workforce was recognised it was too late. In Britain the path to be followed had been mapped out in advance by the experience of World War I.

This experience formed the subject of a report in 1922 by the Manpower Sub-Committee of the Committee of Imperial Defence, which set out three essential preconditions for successful mobilisation of the working population. These were universal liability to military service, a standard schedule of war-related occupations which would protect essential workers from conscription and reserve them from military service, and a powerful ministry of national service capable of arbitrating between the manpower claims of the armed forces and the war economy.[99] Although the application of these principles was almost endlessly extended and refined, they would provide the basis of British success in economic mobilisation in 1939 to 1945. The same three principles had been established in Soviet labour administration by the end of 1942, but they were established empirically, not according to a preconceived scheme.

Soviet manpower plans before the war had been based on demographic projections of supply, including estimates of numbers of youth workers available for training and further education, and potential entry into the workforce from the rural and female labour reserves; and demand estimates based on output plans and bargains with lower levels over implied labour requirements.[100] This work was apparently done in USSR Gosplan's labour department, which included sectors responsible for planning labour and wages, training and personnel allocation, and migration.[101] The ability of the government to realise at least the supply side of its allocation plans by means of direct controls had been somewhat strengthened according to new laws passed in the years of economic difficulty from 1938 to 1940.

These laws were partly an attempt to find a disciplinarian solution to the problems of low morale and commitment of the industrial workforce; this was reflected in establishment of a powerful combination of economic and legal disincentives to absenteeism and voluntary departure from work. The normal working day and working week were also lengthened. The disciplinarian trend was associated with a trend to limit freedom of contract of both new entrants into the labour market and of existing workers, especially those with special skills. Another part of the picture was a desire to enhance the skills of the workforce as a whole; this was seen to be a function both of 'learning by doing' (which required a clampdown on job turnover to increase average length of service) and of formal vocational training. So at the same time the network of industrial schools was centralised and expanded. Entry into vocational training, although not compulsory, became the subject of vigorous campaigning; the young trainee, once committed, could not freely change course, and would ultimately be directed into industrial work. Finally, increased attention to the process of internal renewal and turnover of the industrial workforce marked a turn away from the unsatisfactory institutions of 'organised recruitment', which had consistently failed to supply enough new workers from the countryside to industry in the years before the war.[102]

By the outbreak of war, therefore, there existed a great many controls over the movement of industrial labour. There were universal male liability to military service, of course, and a high degree of control over staff and manual workers already holding positions (or in vocational training) in industry or government service. It had become comparatively difficult to choose one's route of entry into the workforce or, once in it, to change one's job at will. There was not, as yet, any institutional method for ranking jobs according to priority and directing workers from lower to higher ones (except for limited categories of technical specialists). Nor was there an effective method for compelling those outside the system into the industrial workforce, except for the rickety and failing system of 'organised recruitment'.

Conversion of labour administration to a war footing passed through several stages, but the main process was complete by November 1942. In the first days of the war a variety of pressures on policy emerged both from above and from below. Nearest the factory floor, trade union committees met and discussed the situation. The range of responses can be judged in part (for doubtless there were other responses, not considered worthy of record) from resolutions adopted by the leaders of the Novosibirsk district of the ammunition workers' union, the factory committee of the Kuznetsk metallurgical combine and the factory committee of the Pervoural'sk steel tubes plant between 23 and 26 June 1941. All of them called, of course, for increased worker output through more work of higher quality. In Novosibirsk they told the local trade union branch chairmen to consider themselves mobilised at their posts, and reiterated the prohibition on unauthorised departures from work. Here the emphasis lay on protecting the existing workforce against encroachment of other agencies or desertion. In Kuznetsk stress was laid on expanding labour supplies by opening up the shop floor and the skilled trades to women. In Pervoural'sk it was taken for granted that young males would be withdrawn from the workforce for military service, and there was a call for recruitment of replacement workers from the families of conscripts to fill the gap.[103]

In the first days of the war important steps were taken towards a policy of direction of labour from above. On 23 June 1941 a Sovnarkom statute gave to Republican Sovnarkoms and regional party executives the right to transfer manpower between employers (away from home, if necessary) on the basis of the relative priority of wartime tasks.[104] This extension of direct controls was restricted to middle levels of the apparatus and did not in itself provide a basis for centralised coordination. The latter was created within a few days, on 30 June, with establishment of a Manpower Committee with nation-wide executive authority to act within the framework of policy dictated by the GKO, the USSR Sovnarkom and the Supreme Soviet.[105] Head of the Manpower Committee was P. G. Moskatov, formerly boss of the chief administration of labour reserves (the national vocational training network established in October 1940); other members represented the USSR Sovnarkom, Gosplan and the NKVD.[106]

These two measures laid a foundation for centralising processes, but at first it was local circumstances, local decisions and individual action which formed policy in operation. Circumstances altered too rapidly for any detailed, central manpower plan to be effective. This applied above all to the manpower losses suffered by the armed forces, the rapid retreat of the front line into the Russian interior, and the resulting unevenness of mobilisation needs across the country. It was impossible for anyone in Moscow to add up the labour supplies and requirements of industry in Zaporozh'e and Magnitogorsk when the workers of Zaporozh'e would be dismantling their factories today, fighting in the streets tomorrow and under enemy occupation the day after.

In practice manpower policy in 1941 was determined pragmatically at various levels of the government and party apparatus within rapidly changing parameters. One stream of decisions flowed from local government departments faced with resettling and reemploying evacuees in the interior.[107] Before 1942 such decisions were not worked out on the basis of either national or local manpower plans, and in fact local 'manpower committees' responsible to local government were set up in most places only 'during 1942'.[108] Another stream of decisions flowed from party leaders in industrial branch and enterprise management, who were responsible for exempting categories of workers from conscription or refusing them voluntary enlistment in the forces.[109] There is no real indication of a national scheme of reservation by occupation, industry, rank or other criterion in operation in 1941 – nor, perhaps, would one have been viable in the frontal regions where the bulk of defence and heavy industry had been located. As for new recruitment into the industrial workforce, the main source in 1941 was the flow of 800,000–900,000 volunteer students and youth workers, housewives and retired workers recruited by employers directly from the population, with the local commissions for 'organised recruitment' playing, apparently, no more than a permissive role.[110] In 1941 the Manpower Committee recruited about 120,000 workers into the defence and heavy industries, but this number was dwarfed by the three-quarters of a million drafted into industrial work directly by the defence commissariat.[111]

By now a pattern of high-level decision making was setting in, in which postponement was followed by harsh measures weakly followed through. Only in the winter of 1941 and spring of the next year were more far-reaching controls introduced by two major decrees of the Supreme Soviet. The first one came on 26 December, when defence industry workers were mobilised at their posts, with unauthorised departure from work to be treated as desertion.[112] By comparison construction work had been militarised by the GKO on 8 July 1941,[113] but the resulting barrack regime proved so bad for worker morale that 'normal' conditions of work were restored in March and April 1942.[114] In the transport industry, on the other hand, work would be militarised only in April and May 1943.

This first decree was followed by a second on 13 February 1942 which rendered the entire adult able-bodied population of the towns liable to compulsory mobilisation into war work if they were not already in employment or vocational training or solely responsible for the care of young children.[115] It was this law which belatedly prompted formation of regional and city 'manpower committees' at local level during 1942.[116] Local implementation of this nationwide decree must have relied at first on local criteria, since a full six months passed before the USSR Sovnarkom fulfilled its obligation under the decree to draw up a statute on the order of mobilisation of different categories of the population into different categories of work (the statute was not enacted until 10 August 1942).[117]

During 1942 the weaknesses of the system became fully apparent. The main problem was that new institutions had been simply superimposed on existing ones, which had continued to operate in competition with each other and with the new bodies in the labour market. The defence commissariat recruited soldiers and also drafted recruits not fit for active service into the defence industries and construction. The Manpower Committee was dealing mainly with mobilisation of the urban population into war work. There were separate government departments at all levels for mobilising the urban population into agricultural work at peak periods, and 'organised recruitment' commissions in the regions for recruitment of the agricultural labour reserve for work in industry. Lastly there were special departments for reemploying evacuees. In November 1942 a major rationalisation was pushed through by a Sovnarkom statute which resolved the competition in favour of the Manpower Committee. To the Manpower Committee were now allotted the tasks of registering the non-working population in both town and country and of coordinating labour mobilisation on an economy-wide scale. The committee acquired a new chairman, the trade union chief and leader of the evacuation N. M. Shvernik. The State Labour Reserves, once more led by Moskatov, continued with the task of ensuring the supply of skilled workers for industry. Lastly USSR Gosplan came into a closer, more formal relationship with manpower planning and acquired a new set of internal departments responsible for labour registration, planning, allocation and cadre training.[118]

The only element missing from this picture is the NKVD, which, under commissar L. P. Beriya, deployed large numbers of forced labourers through its chief administration of labour camps (GULag) and secured additions to their number by arrest.[119] According to Victor Kravchenko, who worked at the RSFSR Sovnarkom from May 1942 to April 1943, they played a significant role in wartime industry. Kravchenko associates this with Beriya's other wartime responsibility as GKO member in charge of armament and ammunition production, implying that GULag provided Beriya with a personal labour reserve. But this implication is to some extent contradicted by Kravchenko's detailed account of the allocative mechanism. Major plants and commissariats would encounter labour shortages in the course of trying to implement output plans. They would register these shortages through the Sovnarkom apparatus and request additional workers from NKVD GULag reserves. These requests would be forwarded (in Kravchenko's case, from RSFSR Sovnarkom chairman K. D. Pamfilov) through Voznesensky, Molotov or Beriya to the GKO, which would determine allocations. Orders would return from the GKO to the head of GULag over the signature of Molotov, Stalin or Beriya. Demand for forced labourers, however, exceeded supply.[120]

To what extent did the hidden role of the NKVD qualify the trend towards centralised manpower planning in wartime? On all the most important governmental bodies (the GKO and Sovnarkom, the evacuation commissions and committees, the Manpower Committee) NKVD representatives had to meet with others and agree on priorities and resource balances. Kravchenko's evidence suggests that GULag was not Beriya's independent empire and that the NKVD submitted its manpower resources to wartime manpower budgets. In this respect, therefore, there was no parallel with the three-way competition in the German war economy from 1942 onwards among the Armaments Ministry and Central Planning under Albert Speer, the Reichs Labour Offices (which controlled German labour and imported foreign slave labour) under Fritz Sauckel, and the 'state within a state' of the SS which ran the economy of the concentration camps.[121] The NKVD was not a state within a state. However, the terms on which it participated in wartime plans are not known.

In conclusion, by 1943 the three principles of successful wartime labour mobilisation had been implemented. Universal liability of the adult population to serve as either soldiers or workers had been established by law. A system of protected occupations had been evolved in some branches of the economy by means of wholesale militarisation, in others by means of perhaps local and pragmatic criteria of job reservation.[122] Lastly, from 1943 onwards the GKO limited military recruitment in favour of the economy while the Manpower Committee controlled the allocation of labour. Thus by 1943 the administration of labour had passed beyond the phase of emergency mobilisation and had been rationalised and centralised to a high degree. This centralisation was maintained until the second half of 1944, when signs of voluntary turnover of labour began to reappear in industry.[123]

PART TWO: GOSPLAN UNDER VOZNESENSKY AGAIN

RECONSTRUCTION AND RECONVERSION

The recapture of Soviet territory proceeded in three main phases. The territory of the Moscow coal basin was recovered in the winter months of 1941 and early 1942. There followed more months of retreat in the south. Then between the end of 1942 and the late summer of 1943 the North Caucasus, the Donbass and the Russian black-soil centre were all recaptured. During the following year, from the autumn of 1943 to the next autumn, almost all the remaining occupied territory was restored to Soviet control.[124]

The recaptured territories represented new resources and new demands. Each region was populated by human beings and assets which had once formed an organic part of the economy. They were not just incremental working hands and tons of materials or roubles of equipment, but were missing links formerly essential to the economic system's coherence. Thus each restored farm, factory or railway depot offered the possibility of greater harmony and balance among the parts of the system as a whole. But in the meantime everything was in ruins. Most enterprises were damaged or dismantled. Even the fields were contaminated by the debris of battle. The population itself was displaced and decimated, its most productive members stripped away. Thus the promise of restored output, of renewed coherence in the economy and indeed of collective life in general could not be realised without the commitment of new resources.

Therefore the first result of the recapture of territory was to set up a new competition for resources between the war economy in the regions of the interior and the newly liberated regions. The claim of the latter to a share of new resources was rendered still more problematic, since it was clear that under the prevailing conditions there was no question of mechanically copying the prewar economic structure.[125]

Until 1943 policy for economic reconstruction was made spontaneously. Restoration of the Moscow coalfield was begun in December 1941 for no other reason than the critical shortage of coal. Apart from that, where territory was recovered during 1942 and up to early 1943, recaptured plant was just as likely to be dismantled and cannibalised for the needs of industry in the interior as restored to

The search for economic balance in wartime   193

working order.[126] But recapture of the Donbass in February 1943 was an economic prize of a larger order than any before that date – it was a coal and steel region of formerly outstanding significance – and from this moment the competition for new resources between the interior and the extending zone of liberation took on a new complexity.[127]

The first recorded move to impose order on the situation came within USSR Gosplan on 29 January 1943 with a decision to draft a plan for economic reconstruction in the regions liberated so far, together with plans for industrial reconstruction of the Donbass and of besieged Leningrad.[128] The reconstruction plan for the territories already liberated was to focus on heavy industry and to be completed by 15 February;[129] the short compilation period suggests that a rough schedule with broad targets and deadlines was involved, not a detailed supply plan. In February a new Gosplan administration for economic reconstruction in the liberated territories was set up with A. Korobov at its head;[130] the new plan department corresponded to an equivalent subcommittee of the USSR Sovnarkom set up at the same time,[131] headed by Voznesensky himself.[132] As the zone of liberation widened, teams were despatched by Gosplan on 17 March from the centre to the Stalingrad and Khar'kov districts, the Donbass and the North Caucasus to assess damage and needs.[133]

Thus reconstruction planning was initiated as a specialised activity with its own institutions and goals. During 1943 and 1944, however, it tended to blend into planning for the economy as a whole. This was a two-way process, for, just as reconstruction planning had grown out of the economy-wide planning institutions, so its needs and experience would also influence the developments of plan methodology to be reviewed in the next section. The economy-wide context of reconstruction planning was formed by three relationships. These were first of all the current goals and priorities of reconstruction in the context of the war economy, secondly the impetus which it gave to economy-wide perspective planning for postwar reconstruction, and thirdly its close relationship to reconversion of the whole economy to production for peacetime needs.

On paper the current priorities of government for the liberated zones were narrowly defined. The most important goal was their rapid reintegration into the war economy, which meant first and foremost redevelopment of heavy industry.[134] In reality, however, reconstruction involved political and social aspects which necessarily modified narrowly economic goals. Thus right from the start housing and food supplies took equal precedence with coal and steel. The first Sovnarkom and Central Committee directive of 1943 on reconstruction, dated 23 January, ordered reequipment of farms with machinery and renewal of their ranks of farm mechanics. It was followed up on 21 August by approval of a supply programme for farming in the liberated areas, broken down by branch and region, with outline sourcing of inputs.[135] In the same way a GKO resolution of 22 February 1943 set out general objectives for restoration of the Donbass coalfield and required compilation of plans to meet these goals; several months later, a follow-up decree of 26 October made detailed provision.[136] Meanwhile Gosplan plenipotentiaries had been ordered to start five-day reports to the centre on the condition of the housing stock and needs of the newly recovered population.[137] Rehabilitation was in motion on a broad front. From now on the problems of the liberated areas arose constantly on Gosplan agendas.[138]

In 1943 resources devoted to reconstruction were comparatively slight – 16 per cent of nationwide investment,[139] which itself stood at only half the prewar level. The major success was restoration of the coal industry, where recaptured pits supplied a fifth of Soviet coal in that year.[140] In 1944 reconstruction claimed a far greater share of resources – 42 per cent of all investment, 45 per cent of industrial investment and 60–70 per cent of investment in the basic industries. In the iron and steel industry 1.5 billion roubles were spent from centrally allocated investment funds on reconstruction of plant in the liberated regions. But this was compared with only 80 million roubles for the textile industry, of which only 1 per cent was earmarked for rebuilding work from central funds.[141]

Thus most central government measures for reconstruction were focused on heavy industry. Most of these had been initiated, to judge from timing, within USSR Gosplan. For example the reconstruction of Leningrad's industry was raised again within Gosplan in February 1944[142] and became the subject of a detailed GKO directive on 29 March.[143] In January 1944, and then again in August and September, discussions were held in Gosplan on the rebuilding of the metallurgical, mining and electric power industries of the south, ending in recommendation of a two-year plan for 1945 and 1946 for redevelopment of the basic industries.[144] These also surfaced in GKO directives between September and November.[145] But housing needs were also raised in May 1944 by a GKO resolution on developing a mass house-building industry and a Sovnarkom decree on house-building in the recaptured territories.[146] These measures were reviewed within Gosplan only in the following month.[147]

Planning for reconstruction unavoidably raised issues about the balance and development of the postwar economy. Consequently it proved a powerful stimulus to crystallisation of perspective plans, both for particular industrial branches and regions and for the economy as a whole. During 1943, therefore, Gosplan entered into a number of commitments to formulate five-year plans for 1943–7 covering economic reconstruction in the zone of liberation,[148] the Ural region (especially its iron, steel and energy resources), agriculture and dairy farming, and light industry and the textile industry.[149] Apart from the first of these, the work of plan formulation drew heavily on the regional perspectives written into the prewar General Plan for 1943–57.[150]

In addition to these five-year plans of partial scope, Gosplan staff began work in 1943 on an economy-wide five-year plan for reconstruction and development up to 1947. They were encouraged in this by approval of the five-year Urals plan on 24 August.[151] However, the economy-wide perspective plan proved abortive. It was still being discussed and amended in July 1944. Interestingly the main directions of these last-minute amendments were to make greater use of reconverted arms industries for civilian output and to raise the estimate of potential capacity and labour productivity in the liberated areas.[152] This suggests that the initial version was criticised for being too modest in its goals for the civilian economy and for placing too much emphasis upon continued expansion of the war economy of the interior, but there is no indication of the source of criticism. Amendment of the draft five-year plan coincided with the moment of disappearance of reconstruction planning as a distinct, autonomous activity, since in July 1944 Gosplan's administration for economic reconstruction in the liberated regions was merged with the regional planning administration.[153]

The final version of the economy-wide plan for 1943–7, agreed within Gosplan in August 1944 with only three years and four months still to run, was a highly ambitious plan. Its targets implied not just very rapid industrial recovery but higher rates of growth of agricultural output and national income than those envisaged in either the Third Five Year Plan for 1938–42 or the Fourth (official) Five

Year Plan for 1946–50. It also turned out to be over-ambitious when its projections for 1945 and subsequent years could be compared with achieved levels of production.[154] However, the plan was apparently rejected by the government. It was replaced by a series of two- and three-year partial plans. These included the plan for redevelopment of the basic industries in 1945 and 1946, ordered by the GKO on 1 October 1944,[155] and two- to three-year plans for heavy engineering and textiles, discussed within Gosplan in November and December 1944.[156] Only in July 1945 was a new economy-wide plan agreed within Gosplan for reconstruction and development for 1945–7; in August it was resolved to extend the terminal year to 1950, so that this became a step on the way to the Fourth Five Year Plan.[157]

To what extent was revival of perspective planning for peacetime economic development associated with operational plans and measures for reconversion of industry to civilian output? The connection was slight, and rested mainly upon special needs of reconstruction in the liberated areas. In 1943 and 1944 reconversion was handled in a purely pragmatic way. The main branches singled out for limited reconversion were the mortar armament and aircraft industries. On 18 March 1943 the Sovnarkom ordered reconversion of some mortar manufacturing capacity to making farm machinery.[158] Of still less importance was an order slipped in among the measures of 21 August 1943 for reequipping agriculture in the liberated areas for poultry incubators to be met by the aircraft industry.[159] Some time later, in the second half of 1944, the aircraft industry began to undertake output of consumer goods more systematically, and to return part of its empire to civilian industry.[160]

Civilian needs are said to have been increasingly reflected in wartime economic plans compiled well before the final expulsion of the enemy from Soviet territory at the end of 1944.[161] But available accounts of operational priorities expressed in annual and quarterly plans for 1944 and right up to the moment of victory over Germany suggest no change in the high ranking of the arms and heavy industries,[162] although in practice the output of light industry was also allowed to expand. The paucity of examples of practical reconversion work may also be significant. Open discussion of a strategy for reconversion surfaced only in March 1945, and stressed the need to claim reconverted capacity to supply the input needs of heavy industry, vehicle building and construction.[163] Only on 26 May did the GKO set in motion widespread reconversion by striking a long list of factories from the category of defence plant. The commissariats responsible were to make proposals for their transfer to alternative uses, and to consult with Gosplan for revision of the current quarterly plan.[164] At the same time practical reconversion was being complicated and slowed down by Soviet entry into the war with Japan and the resulting strains on the economy of the Far East.[165] Through the summer and autumn defence output fell precipitously, but civilian output rose only sluggishly.[166] Given the lack of preparation and uncertainty it was easier just to stop building tanks and guns than to think of something socially useful and make it.

In summary, the detailed work on planning for economic reconstruction and postwar development carried on by Gosplan in wartime seems to have been markedly ineffective. The horizon for perspective plans was unstable. According to the record, far more plans were mooted and talked about than were ever approved. The plans with the best chance of success formed a jumble of regional and industrial branch programmes. In spite of reconversion planning, the transition to a peacetime economy in 1945 was still bumpy and uneven.

On the other hand, considered as an activity in itself, reconstruction planning was very important. It provided an institutional framework within which certain values could be asserted in a practical way. These were primarily values of social and economic balance. For example the needs of the war economy in the interior could not be granted exclusive priority, but had to be balanced against the need to secure the minimum necessities of life and work for the civilian population of the liberated territories. The reconstruction of economic life could not wait passively for military victory, and military needs now had to be balanced against broader social and economic goals. Short-term needs were no longer to be considered absolutely preeminent, and the long-term programme of completing the building of socialism would again be seen as a practical task. From this point of view Soviet reconstruction planning also performed some functions similar to wartime projects for a better postwar world in other countries. At the same time, in relation to the previously existing social and economic order of the thirties, Soviet reconstruction planning was far less radical than the programmes associated with Butler and Beveridge in wartime Britain. Unlike the latter it did not offer a comprehensive programme of reform. It was perhaps a vehicle for moderation and no more.

FURTHER CHANGES IN PLAN METHODOLOGY

The increased prominence of USSR Gosplan in economic management from 1943 onwards and the increased significance of planning in economic life are attested by a number of sources. 'From 1943 economy-wide planning became still more operational,' write the official historians.[167] Gosplan formulated wartime plans, supervised their implementation and reported on it monthly to the executive, evaluated the performance of lower-level agencies and made proposals to reinforce or correct plans for adoption by the Sovnarkom.[168] Increased centralisation of economic authority in Gosplan was reflected along several dimensions. The number of centrally planned products and plan indicators was substantially increased.[169] Central plans for high-priority industrial goods became more comprehensive.[170] Closer links between Gosplan and large-scale industrial enterprises were established through central compilation of their quarterly plans for material–technical supply.[171] Gosplan representatives participated extensively in executive decisions across a range of economic agencies,[172] including the highest-level users (such as the GKO Operations Bureau) and suppliers (such as the Manpower Committee).

The centralisation of authority did not in itself provide any guarantee of the effectiveness of authority. There was nothing in this to ensure that increasing the detail of economic plans would render the plans themselves more stable, more realistic or more accurately fulfilled. In fact, as the planning agencies took on new tasks they had to offload some old ones, so that part of the economy became less subject to central plans. As a result, side by side with the dominant centralisation process ran a secondary process of decentralisation; this process forms the subject of Part Three of this chapter. Even taking into account the shedding of some former responsibilities, however, the new demands on the planning organs drove them to renew the search for improvements in plan methodology. How could the quality of the plan process be improved to match up to the increased complexity of securing balance in the wartime economy and the increased volume of central decision making? Renewal of the search for coherence and consistency in planning coincided with Voznesensky's return to the leadership of Gosplan at the end of 1942. Doubtless there was no simple cause and effect at work; had Saburov continued in his post, with Voznesensky never far away, some similar

The search for economic balance in wartime 199

process would have been set in motion anyway. We can only speculate as to the motives behind Voznesensky's reappointment and the precise results which followed. Nonetheless we find in 1943 and 1944 a reemergence of the rationalising themes which we have already come to associate with Voznesensky.

Some of these themes have already been introduced. For example regional planning and perspective planning were both given new life by the tasks of reconstruction. Regional planning meant new roles for the network of Gosplan plenipotentiary agents together with an expansion in their number and territorial coverage.[173] Perspective planning meant more detailed work at the centre on the investment balance – the rate of reproduction of fixed assets, the role of gestation lags in the completion of projects, and the commissioning of new capacity compared with additions to the stock of unfinished investment.[174]

Other rationalisations were also introduced. As in the prewar years after 1937, the main drive was disciplinarian in the sense of seeking to make central authority more law-governed, more rooted in reality and thereby more effective. Associated with this was an attempt to refine the centre's understanding of the implications of central priorities and decisions for the autonomous market behaviour of the economy's basic units – its enterprises and households.

The first area of rationalisation was the practice of material balance compilation. Material balances were seen as the most important instrument of wartime planning – the essential method for allocating scarce inputs, pressurising suppliers and enforcing priorities on consumers.[175] The most important wartime balances covered investment goods (equipment and building materials), intermediate goods (metals, fuels and electricity, chemicals and raw materials) and consumer goods involved in army subsistence and retail trade – presumably rationed goods, anyway.[176] At the beginning of the war, under conditions of emergency mobilisation, balance accounts were set to one side.[177] But by 1943 balance compilation had been restored to its primary place in operational planning.[178]

In mid-1943 a reform of supply statistics was carried through. Before this date USSR Gosplan's administration for accounting and allocation of materials relied on information received direct from commissariats on the basis of enterprise and warehouse data, but this information was not supplied to Gosplan according to a consistent methodology of classification, nor was it comprehensive in scope. At this time TsSU formed a new department of material supply statistics in order to service the compilation of material balances within Gosplan. The role of the new TsSU department was to build accounts for past utilisation of metals and fuels, and to check on current realisation of planned material balances in industry. Improvements in the flow of information were recorded, but the goal of consistent, comprehensive coverage remained elusive.[179]

The enforcement of planned material balances on enterprises remained an area of unresolved difficulties. These difficulties arose both on the supply side (ensuring a steady flow of materials and equipment from suppliers) and on the demand side (cutting users' allocations to the efficient minimum and reducing utilisation norms by means of efficient substitutions and resource-saving innovations). Concern on the supply side was reflected mainly in the struggle to smooth out production levels through the month and year.[180] In wartime, apparently, seasonality of industrial output was exceptionally severe;[181] this impression may be confirmed by examination of Figures 7 and 8 above and the accompanying discussion of winter difficulties in 1942 and 1943. The tendency for lower-level bodies to make a 'winter deduction' from high-level plans could only be resisted by high-level winter campaigning to enforce plan targets.[182]

Monthly cycles of industrial output were also noted and condemned in 1943 and 1944.[183] The tendency of enterprises to respond to monthly output targets by slackening the pace in the first twenty days of the month, relying on a surge of effort ('storming') in the last ten days to produce the bulk of the month's required output and gain the bonus, increased the risk of plan failure and threatened the supply plans of other enterprises. The main method chosen to resist 'storming' was continuous shortening of the accounting period and increasing the frequency of fulfilment checks to ten or five days or even daily for key enterprises. In short, planners seeking to lessen seasonal and monthly output fluctuations resorted to unimaginatively authoritarian methods. Their effectiveness is hard to gauge. There is evidence of reduced monthly 'storming' in major arms plants in wartime compared with the prewar years, but this was ascribed to the introduction of serial production techniques, not tighter plan disciplines.[184]

Enforcement of economy upon users of scarce centrally rationed materials prompted a more imaginative but still authoritarian approach. A major step was the reintroduction of an annual 'techno-

The search for economic balance in wartime

logical plan' in 1944 and 1945. Drawing up the technological plan was the responsibility of USSR Gosplan's Council of Scientific and Technical Expertise formed under Voznesensky in April 1939. Technological planning had a double rationale. Some of it was directed towards design of rehabilitation projects for industry and agriculture in the liberated areas. For the rest it created a framework for selecting and imposing new materials and resource-saving technologies in industry.[185] This aspect of it was mainly concerned with process innovation, not innovation of new final products. The technological plan therefore helped to provide a framework for imposing reduced material input coefficients on enterprises from above, given the lack of an autonomous stream of progressive innovations from below.

Attempts to refine and intensify central controls over enterprise inputs and outputs did not exhaust wartime changes in plan methodology. Important work was carried on to try to improve the planners' concept of the macroeconomy as an equilibrium system through the 'balance of the national economy' (see Chapter 1, pp. 23–5). This defined the task of planning as securing an appropriate balance in the economy between industry and agriculture, between final consumption and production for accumulation and intermediate demand, and between the centrally administered economy and the market sphere. Study of the latter involved recognising the effects of centrally planned outputs and incomes upon the market for consumer goods, and especially on farm outputs and incomes, which lay largely outside central plans. Thus in the 'balance of the national economy' the market sphere appeared as one element contributing to the overall equilibrium. At the same time, of course, the appropriate balance among the various elements was defined according to permanent objectives of national defence and socialist transformation.

Work on the 'balance of the national economy', interrupted by the German invasion, was resumed as early as April 1942. The Gosplan department for consolidated accounts calculated changes in the national income and in gross industrial production divided between groups 'A' and 'B' and defence products.[186] Shares of the global social product claimed by defence output, investment, intermediate demand and final consumption were also calculated in 1942–3.[187] This work was continued in each following year up to the second half of 1945, when for the first time Gosplan produced preliminary disaggregated estimates for a planned 'balance of the national economy' during the period of the Fourth Five Year Plan.[188] It is true that starting in 1943 Gosplan had put out a document showing 'basic indicators of the balance of the national economy' up to 1948 – presumably in connection with the abortive economy-wide five-year plan for 1943–7 – but it is claimed that this was only an unstructured list of time-series projections of output, investment, employment and monetary circulation which did not attempt to derive the macro-economic equilibrium relationship among them.[189] So while the war lasted national income concepts were used mainly for accounting and analytical purposes, not directly for planning.

From the point of view of plan methodology the most important aspect of wartime work on the 'balance of the national economy' concerned financial balances. Here Gosplan economists tried to lay bare the flows of goods, services and money among the centrally administered economy, enterprises and households. To assist this work Gosplan went over to using current prices in current output and financial planning from the fourth quarter of 1942, although constant 1926/7 prices continued to be used for measuring the physical volume of production.[190] A quarterly balance of money income and spending of the population was introduced, with separate accounts for the farm and non-farm population; later a distinction between workers and staff employees was also introduced.[191] Special attention was devoted to estimates of farm output in kind, its valuation and the money incomes derived from it, based on surveys of kolkhoz market prices and turnover.[192]

The rationalisation of plan methodology in 1943 and 1944 was designed to improve the planners' authority over the economy's basic units and to raise their awareness of developments outside their sphere of direct control. Through them Gosplan built upon the successful resolution of economic crisis in 1942 and the emergence of a full-blown war economy in 1943 to expand its influence upon the central allocation of resources. Lower-level agencies had to compete in expressing demands to Gosplan for access to scarce material supplies. Plan rationalisation sharpened Gosplan's ability to define options, detect shortfalls and enforce priorities.

Gosplan's enhanced position did not make the plans themselves more internally coherent or accurately implemented. Evidence is altogether lacking on the overall fulfilment of annual and quarterly economy-wide plans in 1943 and 1944. With fighting still in progress on Soviet territory, it would not be surprising if the strategic environment prevented the detailed realisation of economic plans drawn up in advance of knowledge of the military outcomes. On the other hand the annual plan targets for a number of basic industrial goods for 1945 have been published. The plan was adopted by a decree of the GKO dated 25 March 1945, two weeks before victory in Europe. These targets failed to be achieved without exception, in some cases by a very wide margin.[193] While the output of engineering products and finished goods was certainly disrupted by the reconversion process, shortfalls of coal, steel and electric power are much harder to explain by such exceptional circumstances. At the same time, the authority and effectiveness of the planning institutions did not stand or fall by the accuracy of fulfilment of their plans.

While the position of Gosplan was enhanced, Voznesensky himself played a central role in Soviet government. A list of his most important wartime posts and duties would include the following:
(1) Stalin's first deputy as Sovnarkom chairman since 10 March 1941,
(2) head of the GKO commission appointed on 4 July 1941 to compile the wartime economic plan for the fourth quarter of 1941 and for 1942,
(3) head of the government in Kuibyshev from 25 October to the end of November 1941 with personal responsibility for arms production and for the war economy of the interior,
(4) member of the GKO from 3 February 1942,
(5) head of the GKO commission on the metals deficit in early 1942,
(6) head of USSR Gosplan from 8 December 1942,
(7) head of the Sovnarkom committee for economic reconstruction in the liberated areas from early 1943.[194]

In addition to these responsibilities of state, Voznesensky had been a candidate Politburo member since February 1941.

After 1941 Voznesensky's personal authority became sufficient to enable him not only to compete with such junior figures as Kosygin, Malenkov, Mekhlis and Mikoyan but to stand his ground in the Politburo. This is how he was remembered in wartime by Marshal A. I. Vasilevsky:

Naturally, in the Politburo different opinions would emerge about the possibilities of production to supply the requirements of the General Staff. Different proposals would be moved. Most authoritative was the word of

GKO member and USSR Gosplan chairman N. A. Voznesensky. He not infrequently disagreed with Stalin's view and that of other Politburo members, and would indicate precisely the quantity of material and technical means which industry could yield for the operation under review. His opinion would be decisive.[195]

Voznesensky may convincingly be portrayed as a figure who stood for moderation in wartime economic policy. He understood well that economic mobilisation for war could not proceed without limit, that even in wartime economic life retained its law-governed character and that the restoration of economic balance remained a necessary condition for a sustained economic mobilisation. Nonetheless it cannot be assumed that he stood for moderation in all things. As a GKO member he shared collective responsibility for a number of wartime acts of repression, and more than one crime against humanity, for example the mass deportation of Volga Germans, Crimean Tatars and other small nationalities from their national territories.[196]

PART THREE: WARTIME PLANNING AND ECONOMIC SELF-REGULATION

PLANNING AND SELF-REGULATION OF THE ENTERPRISE

Important areas of Soviet economic life are regulated from below. Wherever the needs of the economy's basic units – enterprises, households and local communities – are left unfilled by centrally planned supplies, alternative allocative mechanisms attempt to meet them. These mechanisms are either internal to the unit and result in a trend to self-sufficiency – the local community, household or firm tries to substitute its own resources directly for those denied by the central authorities; or the unit tries to acquire others' resources by offering its own in exchange through a legal, semi-legal or black market. Self-sufficiency of the basic unit and market exchanges between basic units are two alternative forms of self-regulation within the centrally administered economy.

The different kinds of self-regulation are so deeply entrenched in Soviet economic life that all efforts to eliminate them, recurring periodically over many years, have spent their energy without result. In the wartime period there was no attempt to eliminate the self-regulated sphere altogether, in spite of greatly increased centralisation of the economy. Some aspects of self-regulation were more strictly limited, while others were positively encouraged. For example, from the point of view of the enterprise, central agencies increasingly preempted outputs and rationed fixed capacity (capital goods and labour power). But in securing variable inputs and combining them with labour and fixed assets the enterprise was called upon to show greater initiative than before. The reason for this was the widespread breakdown of inter-plant, interregional exchange of industrial goods. Since the central plan was no longer capable of guaranteeing the enterprise's access to necessary inputs in required amounts, part of the organisation of supply slipped from the sphere of central administration to the self-regulated sphere.

For low-priority sectors of the economy this trend was already in evidence before the war. For example by early 1941 the pressures of several years' lost economic expansion followed by renewed mobilisation of resources into rearmament and heavy industry had created mounting problems in consumer supply. One response was a decree of the Sovnarkom and Central Committee dated 7 January 1941 which provided additional incentives for local government to increase output of consumer goods from 'local resources'.[197] Such a policy was a logical response to direct effects of the planning system. Economy-wide plans adopted at the centre tended to be inconsistent and infeasible, and were not coordinated with emergency sectoral programmes adopted from time to time. Consequently in trying to carry them out the planners caused actual disproportions in the economy and shortfalls of material supply. Diversion of scarce inputs to priority sectors left branches of lower priority such as the food and light industries without supplies. Those deprived in this way

are eventually advised to try to supply themselves from 'local resources' – that is, outside the system of the central plan ... the lack of coherence of the administrative plan and the resulting system of priorities restrict the scope of the central plan and enlarge ... that collection of activities in which the plans of enterprises and economic units are not covered by an over-all plan.[198]

Even before the war, however, the trend to self-regulation was not confined to low-priority branches. Severe problems of coordinating the supply of key sectors confronted the central planners. The reason for this was not only the lagging supply of basic industrial goods but also the rapid spread of subcontracting of defence and engineering orders from prime contractors to parts suppliers, which proceeded with little regard to the associated inter-plant, interregional transport costs. A widely quoted example was the Stalingrad tractor factory which in 1939 bought in parts from 287 suppliers, of which (by value) only 3.5 per cent originated in the factory's immediate hinterland of the Volga region.[199] For the Gor'ky motor factory the equivalent figure was 4.2 per cent.[200] Commentators of the time were well aware of the resulting strain on both transport capacity and central coordinating capabilities, and of the potential for wartime disruption. A favoured solution was the creation of semi-autonomous regional production complexes; this coincided with the desire to remove imbalances of regional industrial development stemming from the pre-revolutionary epoch.[201] But such a policy proved extremely difficult to implement in a few years. Therefore in some remarks on capital construction in his major speech of 18 February 1941 Voznesensky warned those in charge of new projects not to count on obtaining supplies such as metals or semimanufactures for future plants 'from outside', and especially not from other economic areas. It was the task of the industrial commissars (and by implication not of Gosplan) to plan for supply of future plant, and to do so on the basis of local resources.[202]

When war broke out the central authorities urged lower-level agencies to supply their needs from 'local resources' to reduce the strains of emergency mobilisation.[203] Trade commissar A. V. Lyubimov summed up this policy as: 'Give the state a little more, ask of it a little less ... one just has to show initiative and organising ability.'[204] The real scope for exercising such ingenuity, however, had become even narrower than in peacetime. The output of local industries was being preempted for direct supply of defence needs,[205] although the rate of conversion of local industries varied inversely with distance from the front.[206] At the same time the volume of local industrial capacity was sharply reduced. In the regions subject to enemy occupation the fixed assets of local industries had been largely abandoned;[207] in the interior the local industry workforce was stripped away by the armed forces.[208] Thus by 1942 the real output of RSFSR local industry had fallen by 45 per cent compared to 1940, and that of artisan cooperative industry by 59 per cent.[209] The real possibilities, therefore, for major plants to switch from central to local sources of essential supplies were absolutely minimal. For tank plants, for example, in the autumn and winter of 1941 relying on local resources included illegally breaking into warehouses and robbing trains in the search for needed materials and parts.[220]

The search for economic balance in wartime

In 1942 and 1943 as the war economy took shape new regional industrial complexes were forced into existence. The most clearly defined zones of self-reliance were either close to the front or in the interior regions of relocation of evacuated industry. The most extreme case of a locally closed industrial economy was in Leningrad during the city's long siege. The defence and metallurgical plant of the Urals exemplified a new industrial complex of the interior.[211] Side by side with changes in regional definition and breakdown of interregional transfers, the sheer difficulty of establishing new patterns of local sourcing for supplies led many enterprises to seek plant self-sufficiency by expanding operations to include manufacturing their own basic inputs.

The trend towards plant self-sufficiency was widespread and took many varied forms. Engineering plants worked to increase their internal sourcing of instruments and tools.[212] For example before the war armament factories had produced three-quarters of their instrumentation needs, but by 1943 they had raised their share to 96 per cent.[213] Even in the most complex processes like aircraft assembly, where subcontracted supplies had been used most widely before the war, significant advances were recorded.[214] At many industrial plants the share of externally sourced semimanufactures fell by 20 to 30 per cent.[215] The same processes affected the supply of tools for industry. External sources of machine tools disappeared because the factories which had produced them before the war were being converted to weapons manufacture, but at the same time arms factories established their own toolmaking facilities, especially in the armament and ammunition branches.[216] The enterprise toolroom became 'an indicator of the technical maturity and high skill level of the workers and staff'.[217]

Despecialisation and plant self-sufficiency even extended to supplies of basic industrial goods. Metalworking enterprises in the armament industry developed their own metallurgical bases for steel forgings, castings and special alloys.[218] Steelmaking capacity in heavy engineering also multiplied several times in the first eighteen months of the war.[219] The railway industry, too, added 320,000 tons of annual blast furnace capacity to the nationwide total during this period.[220] Metallurgical plants themselves manufactured their own basic and electrical equipment and created their own fuel bases.[221] Meanwhile all the key wartime industries set up their own construction teams (which in turn developed their own auxiliary units for supplying building materials and artisan products) and ran them independently of the construction commissariat.[222]

Last, but certainly not least, government decrees encouraged enterprises to attain self-sufficiency in foodstuffs for worker consumption by setting aside land for enterprise allotments,[223] and by setting targets for them.[224]

The main purpose of plant despecialisation and self-reliance was to provide the means for fulfilling central plans, but a price was paid in terms of lost economies of scale and increased production costs. Some Soviet accounts regard this price as having been excessive.[225] On the other hand it is hard to see how it could have been avoided, given three essential factors. First was the weakness of financial disciplines over enterprises. Enterprise budgets could be regarded as 'soft', i.e. any excess of costs over revenues tended to receive an automatic subsidy from the state budget, so that the penalties of inefficient management would be borne by the nation as a whole, not by the economic unit responsible.[226] Secondly, while penalties for obtaining inputs and producing outputs at excessive cost were negligible for the enterprise, the penalties for failing to obtain inputs at all and for the resulting zero outputs were severe. Thirdly, given the importance to the enterprise of obtaining inputs at any cost, plant managers would in many cases establish internal sourcing of inputs under their own control more easily than look to higher authority to enforce contracts for inputs upon distant, external suppliers. Each of these factors operated permanently in the Soviet economic system, whether at peace or at war, but the conditions of emergency mobilisation in 1941 and 1942 gave them decisive weight. The trend to increased plant self-sufficiency in wartime was a necessary result.

This shows that within the process of wartime centralisation the Soviet enterprise developed its own sphere of autonomous self-regulation, the means being increased input self-reliance. Thus there was indeed a sense, as Soviet accounts have maintained, in which the central authority of the plan was reconciled with the autonomy of the enterprise.[227] But the reconciliation arose pragmatically, without a clear design for a hierarchical division of authority appropriate to the knowledge and resources deployed at each level of administration. It was dominated by the overriding output drive of the central authorities. As a result plant managers did not necessarily use their autonomy efficiently from the point of view of the long term. For example enterprises sought to reduce their short-run uncertainty over external sources of supply, but the extent to which they did so was not necessarily conducive to emergence of an 'efficient and rapidly expanding war economy'. Criticism of the impact of short-run maximisation of output at any cost was soon voiced. Economists began to argue for the need to 'harden' enterprise budgets, restore cost accounting and increase penalties for cost overruns. There was even a deliberate evocation of the turn to cost accounting in 1931 in reaction against the early excesses of forced industrialisation at any price.[228]

For only a cost-conscious, financially independent enterprise would either fulfil plans efficiently or feel the incentive to resist unrealistic plans for maximum output regardless of cost.

PLANNING AND THE MARKET ECONOMY

Earlier I stated that self-regulation appeared in Soviet economic life where the needs of the economy's basic units were left unfilled by centrally planned supplies. However, not all such needs could be met by developing the economic units' self-reliance. The alternative to self-reliance was resort to the market, in which the economic unit seeks to acquire others' resources by offering its own in exchange. Thus markets exist in a planned economy because of the imperfect interaction between people's wants as producers and as consumers and society's ability to meet them through the central plan. This explanation of markets could be contrasted with the one provided by the voluntaristic philosophy of dictatorial planning; according to the latter, markets arise only because of imperfections of the people themselves, who cling to individualistic, petty bourgeois ambitions and conceptions of their own wants.

Various markets, characterised by varying degrees of spontaneity and legality, have always existed within the Soviet economic system. The central cash nexus, however, has always been the receipt by households of a cash labour income from enterprises and the expenditure of household cash balances on consumer goods. Consumer expenditure can be divided into two parallel flows – one yields revenue to state enterprises supplying the retail market, and the other yields a cash income to collective farmers. Collective farmers themselves acquire money balances from this part of their labour income, mainly for work done on their own account on the side; in turn they offer cash to state enterprises for consumer goods. As a rule prices and wages are fixed in all markets by the state, but there are two exceptions. In the internal market of the collective farm, labour incomes are determined as a residual after the state has taken its share, divided among the workers on the basis of accumulated labour points. And in the external 'kolkhoz market' worker households and collective farmers' households determine prices for the latter's products competitively.

Two main factors dominated the evolution of the market economy in wartime. First was the extension of rationing of both labour and goods. In wartime employment freedom of contract, choice of occupation and choice between labour and leisure largely disappeared. Self-regulation was recognised only through wider wage differentiation to enhance incentives for some categories of skilled war workers. In the same way as in state industry, the state intervened in the collective farm's internal labour market to widen material incentives, and also to raise the annual minimum of points to be accumulated by each member through labour.[229] On the side of consumer spending the volume of goods entering retail trade fell by 66 per cent between 1940 and 1942 and fell again in 1943.[230] At the same time a large part of the retail market was brought under centralised control by means of the rationing of foodstuffs for the armed forces and urban population.[231] Thus self-regulated market exhanges were almost eliminated from the labour market and, in the consumer goods market, restricted to a small proportion of a drastically reduced volume of trade.

The second factor dominating evolution of the market economy in wartime was the overfinancing of enterprises and households. Enterprises were provided with ambitious plans for increased output and, given the priority attached to output at any cost, their budgets were correspondingly 'soft'. Generous enterprise budgets were translated into generous worker incentives, but corresponding supplies of consumer goods were not realised; on the contrary worker purchasing power grew rapidly out of proportion to the dwindling quantity of goods actually on the market. All this corresponded to big public sector deficits between 1941 and 1943 which were not financed by borrowing;[232] between 1940 and 1944 the Soviet money stock expanded by 280 per cent.[233] But until 1944 retail prices in state outlets changed little; the increases were concentrated on alcohol and tobacco. Some of the supply shortfall was met by an increase in the share of non-centralised retail supplies from local industries; in the RSFSR central region their share rose from 13 per cent of state trade in 1941 to 24 per cent in 1942.[234] The main result, however, was to switch worker households' purchasing power into the kolkhoz market, where by 1943 prices for cereals and meat had risen by twelve or thirteen times compared with 1940.[235] In 1944 pressure on the kolkhoz market began to relax as additional supplies of consumer goods were made available by the state at so-called 'commercial' prices, which were inflated towards kolkhoz market levels. By 1945, however, kolkhoz market prices still exceeded the 1940 level by five or six times.[236]

The relative volumes of household consumption satisfied through state retail outlets and by means of exchanges with other households did not alter very much – both fell sharply and in similar proportion. But their relative shares in the family budget, valued at current prices, altered dramatically. In 1940 household purchases from other households made up 11 per cent of their expenditure, and 9 per cent of the Soviet money stock was tied up in such transactions. Even in 1944, when state trade had already begun to revive, no less than 55 per cent of household spending was being directed to other households, utilising 28 per cent of the money stock.[237] And in 1945 no less than 46 per cent of retail trade still passed through the kolkhoz market, compared with 14 per cent in 1940; for trade in foodstuffs the kolkhoz market share had risen from 20 to 51 per cent. Even so the real volume of kolkhoz trade was still 16 per cent below the prewar level.[238]

The main 'beneficiaries' of this process were the rural inhabitants. Inflation of collective farmers' cash balances proceeded more rapidly than wage inflation, a pattern which distinguished the wartime period from the previous period of rapid monetary expansion in 1928–32.[239] However, increased financial wealth did not mean increased welfare. Compulsory state procurements claimed a higher share of cereals and meat production than before the war,[240] so that rural availability fell even more sharply than output. State procurement prices per head of livestock actually fell as the quality of stock offered for sale by the kolkhoz deteriorated. True, kolkhoz market inflation was so rapid that collective farms were earning more roubles from free-market livestock sales in 1943 than they had in 1940, and the latter were contributing a bigger share of kolkhoz income.[241] But increased money income could not be translated into increased effective purchases, because there were no goods available to be bought.

Thus the market economy worked to balance the needs and

resources of worker households. But the price paid for this was accumulation by collective farm households of unspent monetary claims on the economy, representing the risk of a future inflationary imbalance.

In summary, the equilibrium of the Soviet wartime economy was secured through several different allocative mechanisms which operated simultaneously and interacted with each other. The planning system together with the system of administrative priorities provided the economy with its main drive, allocating and rationing key producer and consumer goods. But this alone could not complete the equilibrium and result in a stable solution for all the elements of the economic system in combination. For this, two further self-regulating mechanisms were required – the self-reliance of the economic unit and the market economy.[242] In wartime the central planning and management process claimed many additional powers, but even so many existing problems and some new ones were devolved upon the self-regulated sphere for resolution. Thus the coexistence of central planning and self-regulation received de facto recognition by the central authorities, along with the fact that the self-regulated sphere was actively contributing to the overall macroeconomic balance.

However, the role of the market economy, like that of management within the enterprise, was recognised in practice in a tentative and pragmatic way. Those responsible for compiling economy-wide plans were not in a position to weigh up in advance, fully and comprehensively, the plurality of economic forces which would influence the plans' success or failure. It is true that, as we have seen, in the course of 1943 and 1944 Gosplan staff advanced their understanding of the relationship between plan and market through analysis of the 'balance of the national economy'. But ultimately the relationship between plan and market was a political problem, not an analytical one. The political problem was that the plan methodology sought to define the principal resources and needs of the whole economy in a single way, through a central administrative plan, and to impose the implied outcomes on the economy's units, but the latter units perceived their resources and needs differently, in ways for which a single administrative plan did not and could not account. Thus the resulting economic equilibrium was rarely that foreseen in detail by the plan. War did not resolve this problem, but translated it into a new context where at some moments economic units might be drawn to identify their private interests more closely with the national struggle, yet at other times tension between the plans of the basic units and the central plan might break out with additional force.

CONCLUSIONS

In the first phase of wartime economic development, which lasted until the end of 1942, the economy as a whole was managed through emergency mobilisation. In the second half of 1941 the emergency regime focused on the mobilisation of arms capacity. With the downward slide of the supporting metals, energy and transport branches, in 1942 the emergency regime broadened its scope and adopted a 'firefighting' model for identifying crisis points and mobilising resources into them in an iterative sequence. This style of managing and adapting priorities by means of overriding, higher-level decrees was not without precedent in Soviet economic experience. It could be found in previous episodes of emergency mobilisation from the civil war to farm collectivisation and rapid industrialisation in peacetime. All the same, many of the detailed circumstances, demands and methods employed were quite novel.

By 1943 the crises induced by invasion and by initial Soviet responses had been overcome. The needs of economic balance, at first suppressed, had been reasserted. In the process the planning institutions recaptured the authority lost in the second half of 1941. As the economy moved towards full mobilisation, only an agency with economy-wide competence could maintain balance and defend priorities. Thus in 1943 and 1944 economy-wide planning resumed both a pattern recognisable from the prewar years and the associated preoccupation with plan rationalisation. The added tasks of reconstruction contributed to the process by adding new objectives to wartime economic priorities and by stretching the authorities' time horizon into a future postwar society.

Eugène Zaleski has argued that 'wartime economic plans did not replace traditional planning, but were simply superimposed on it'. Traditional plans either were not compiled at all or dealt only with secondary priorities.[243] In his view economy-wide planning was abandoned, strictly speaking, until 1945. It was replaced by more restricted 'wartime economic plans' and by partial plans confined to top-priority sectors; the rest of the economy was regulated by the budget, by rationing and by the market.[244]

This picture helps to highlight the contrast between prewar and wartime Soviet economic planning, but it requires two qualifications in order to retain conviction. First, even in peacetime Soviet economy-wide plans lacked coherence and comprehensive coverage; this meant that they were permanently liable to supplementation and modification by overriding emergency programmes from above or by forces from below in the self-regulated sphere. Secondly, therefore, the emergency mobilisation of 1941 and 1942 differed in degree from previous phases of peacetime economic mobilisation, but not in kind; moreover the return to recognisable norms of economy-wide coordination through the planning system began slowly in 1943 and not suddenly in 1945.

Of course in 1943 the Soviet economy was still a war economy at the height of its mobilisation. But the economy as a whole was no longer being managed by emergency measures, and maintaining economic balance was once again the responsibility of the planning institutions. With 1943 there arose new issues – reconstruction and long-term planning, technological planning, more comprehensive material balances, coordination of the central plan with autonomous behaviour of enterprises and households. These new issues would help form a bridge from wartime to the postwar world.

NOTES

1 Clausewitz, 1968, pp. 164–5.
2 Kornai, 1980, vol. A, pp. 226–33.
3 Ibid., p. 232.
4 Except in the case of ammunition, where expanding capacity remained a problem throughout 1942: Yakovlev, 1981, pp. 84, 117, 130.
5 In the first period of the war the prewar excess of engineering capacity over iron and steel supplies actually widened because engineering establishments lost their auxiliary metallurgical plant in the course of evacuation, and at the same time specialised metallurgical capacity suffered disproportionate losses: Chadaev, 1965, pp. 203, 254–5.
6 ISE, v. 5, 1978, p. 235.
7 See Chapter 2, p. 64 above.
8 Reported by A. S. Shcherbakov to the State Defence Committee. Cited by Prikhod'ko, 1973, p. 29.
9 Morekhina, 1974, p. 104.
10 The Kuzbass field produced 25.1 million tons (17 per cent of the all-Union total) in 1941, and only 21.1 million tons (28 per cent) in 1942; see Sov. ekon., 1970, p. 91. According to Zabolotskaya, 1977, pp. 210–11 Kuzbass output in the first eight months of 1942 fell short of target by 19.2 per cent, or 5.2 million tons, implying an eight-month target of 17.8 million tons, or 26.7 million tons at an annual rate. From the same source

The search for economic balance in wartime 215

this was associated with a 40 per cent drop in the number of underground workers, comparing the first half of 1942 with the 'prewar' level.
11 See Appendix 2.
12 ISE, v. 5, 1978, p. 292. Coal's share fell from 59 per cent in 1940 to 47 per cent in 1942 (in terms of Soviet conventional fuel).
13 Panov, 1944, p. 18.
14 IVMV, v. 4, 1975, pp. 142–3.
15 Mkrtchyan, 1945, pp. 57–60.
16 See Chapter 2, p. 64 above.
17 Calculated from output and capacity figures in ISE, v. 5, 1978, p. 275.
18 Based on a Gosplan memorandum attached to the 1942 second-quarter plan, cited in Po ed. plan., 1971, p. 92.
19 Kumanev, 1976, p. 141.
20 Obraztsov, 1944, p. 62.
21 Kumanev, 1976, p. 140. At the same time requests from below for material–technical supply should not be interpreted as simply reflecting 'absolute' needs, given the permanent incentives to acquire excess capacity.
22 Kumanev, 1976, p. 205.
23 Po ed. plan., 1971, p. 92.
24 Comparing the first half of 1942 with the same period in 1941, output losses exceeded decommissioned capacity in each main branch of the industry. For data see Appendix 2.
25 Clark, 1956, p. 114.
26 See Appendix 2.
27 Trevor Roper, ed., 1966, p. 178.
28 See Chapter 2, pp. 79–81.
29 G. S. Kravchenko, 1970, pp. 138–9.
30 IVOVSS, v. 6, 1965, p. 60.
31 See Appendix 2.
32 IVOVSS, v. 6, 1965, p. 60.
33 G. S. Kravchenko, 1970, p. 138.
34 Ibid., pp. 134–5.
35 Abakumov, 1943, pp. 20–1.
36 IVOVSS, v. 6, 1965, p. 71.
37 Yakovlev, 1981, p. 101. One ammunition train took three months to travel this route; another clocked up over 7,000 kilometres from the Urals to the Caucasus.
38 Kumanev, 1976, p. 264.
39 Morekhina, 1974, p. 104.
40 This included fifteen of the twenty-nine hearths and mills of Magnitogorsk, five of the seventeen blast furnaces at Chelyabinsk and all of the furnaces at Zlatoust. See Morekhina, 1974, pp. 176–7.
41 Kumanev, 1976, p. 218.
42 Po ed. plan., 1971, p. 92.
43 Kumanev, 1960, pp. 48–9.
44 According to Vannikov, 1962, p. 86 the capacity of the armament industry was adequate from 1942 onwards; growth of output up to 1943 took

place within existing limits, and during 1943 excess capacity appeared. But according to Yakovlev, 1981, p. 130, supply shortages and interruptions dogged the ammunition industry right up to 1944. According to IVOVSS, v. 6, 1965, p. 53, 'by the end of 1943 the ammunition problem had ... been solved.'

45 Prikhod'ko, 1970, p. 10.
46 Sov. ekon., 1970, p. 91.
47 Resheniya, v. 3, 1968, pp. 72–80.
48 Zelkin, 1974, pp. 57–8; Zabolotskaya, 1977, p. 212.
49 Panov, 1944, pp. 18–19.
50 IVMV, v. 6, 1976, p. 345.
51 Sov. ekon., 1970, p. 91.
52 Abakumov, 1943, pp. 20–2; Panov, 1944, pp. 26–7.
53 Kupert, 1977, p. 87. But the speed of local response was another matter; for example a full month passed before a fuel team of four was set up under the Omsk city soviet on 1 November.
54 IVMV, v. 6, 1976, p. 350. According to Kolotov, 1976, p. 279 this and other GKO decrees mentioned below were drafted by Voznesensky personally.
55 Kosyachenko, 1944, p. 11; IVOVSS, v. 6, 1965, p. 61.
56 IVMV, v. 8, 1977, p. 353.
57 In 1942 capacity in the Urals grew by two-thirds, but output was only 50 per cent up on 1940; see D'yakov, 1978, p. 43.
58 Calculated from ISE, v. 5, 1978, p. 275.
59 D'yakov, 1978, p. 43.
60 IVMV, v. 6, 1976, p. 345.
61 Venedeev, 1943, pp. 32–4.
62 IVMV, v. 5, 1975, p. 37.
63 Resheniya, v. 3, 1968, pp. 94–5.
64 Clark, 1956, pp. 114, 256–7.
65 See Appendix 4.
66 According to IVOVSS, v. 6, 1965, p. 70, 'all his activity in this high post was imbued with the unrestrained rule-by-fiat so characteristic of the Stalinist style of leadership'.
67 Kumanev, 1966, p. 117.
68 Sats, n.d., p. 8; see also the favourable estimate of this side of Kaganovich's work in Medvedev, 1983, p. 130.
69 Khrulev, 1961, pp. 75–6; see also Tyl SVS, 1977, p. 88.
70 Kumanev, 1976, p. 156. Other members were Central Committee secretary A. A. Andreev (deputy chair), foreign trade commissar A. I. Mikoyan, commissars for the maritime and river fleets P. P. Shirshov and Z. A. Shashkov, Lt-Gen. and deputy transport commissar I. V. Kovalev, G. B. Kovalev and A. G. Karponosov.
71 Ibid., pp. 158–9.
72 Khrulev, 1961, pp. 82–3.
73 Kumanev, 1976, pp. 218–20.
74 Ibid., pp. 222–3.
75 Sbornik dokumentov, 1981, p. 221. The article was dated 17 April.

The search for economic balance in wartime

76 Kumanev, 1976, p. 225.
77 IVMV, v. 7, 1976, p. 52.
78 Galitsky, 1945, p. 21.
79 Kumanev, 1976, pp. 293–4.
80 Arutyunyan, 1970, pp. 196–7.
81 Ibid., pp. 200–2.
82 IVOVSS, v. 3, 1961, pp. 187–90.
83 Ibid., p. 190; IVMV, v. 7, 1976, p. 51.
84 IVOVSS, v. 4, 1962, pp. 602–3.
85 Arsen'ev, 1972, p. 21.
86 FRUS 1943, v. III, 1963, pp. 742–5, 759, 763–4.
87 Arsen'ev, 1972, p. 23; Zalkind and Miroshnichenko, 1980, p. 209.
88 Zalkind and Miroshnichenko, 1980, pp. 211–12.
89 Arsen'ev, 1972, p. 19.
90 Starovsky and Ezhov, 1975, p. 6.
91 Aleschchenko, 1980, p. 123.
92 Ibid., p. 130.
93 Arsen'ev, 1972, pp. 28–9. Mekhlis's star had already begun to fall after the military disaster of May 1942 in the Crimea, for which he bore major responsibility. See Erickson, 1975, p. 349.
94 IVMV, v. 6, 1976, p. 344.
95 Belikov, 1974, p. 77.
96 Ibid.; see also IVMV, v. 6, 1976, p. 344. Later in the war (in the spring and summer of 1944) the responsibilities and apparatus of the Operations Bureau were expanded and the GKO Transport Committee dissolved into it.
97 See Chapter 2, pp. 94–6 above.
98 See Appendix 4.
99 Hancock and Gowing, 1949, pp. 56–7.
100 For a scheme of the manpower balance which formed part of the 'balance of the national economy' compiled in USSR Gosplan from 1939 onwards see Zalkind and Miroshnichenko, 1980, p. 170.
101 Zaleski, 1980, p. 712.
102 For the most important legislation see Resheniya, v. 2, 1967, pp. 662–4, 665–72, 757–8, 774–5. Useful evaluations can be found in Barber, 1979, pp. 12–13 and Filtzer, 1980, pp. 14–15. I have also drawn upon a recent account of the operation of the State Labour Reserves in Matthews, 1983, pp. 241–3. A further development associated with these measures was extension of the influence of USSR Gosplan and of plan offices at lower levels in the planning of 'organised recruitment'; see Chapter 1, pp. 22–3 above.
103 Belonosov, 1970, pp. 14–15.
104 Tel'pukhovsky, 1958, p. 31.
105 Its full title was the Committee for Registration and Allocation of Manpower.
106 Mitrofanova, 1971, p. 187.
107 Kaimoldin, 1966, p. 52.
108 Kupert, 1977, p. 87.

109 V. Kravchenko, 1947, pp. 360, 362. The results must sometimes have been accidental. For example at one large but unnamed artillery works several thousand workers, technicians and engineers were saved from immediate conscription only by the manager's personal appeal to the regional party secretary and to Marshal Voroshilov. See Olevsky, 1983, p. 19.
110 Mitrofanova, 1971, pp. 186, 433.
111 Ibid., pp. 187–8.
112 Ibid., p. 188.
113 D'yakov, 1978, p. 35.
114 Ibid., p. 60.
115 Resheniya, v. 3, 1968, p. 64.
116 Mitrofanova, 1971, p. 189.
117 Ibid., p. 191.
118 Ibid., pp. 191, 426; IVMV, v. 5, 1975, p. 50. Among the staff of the new Gosplan departments were B. P. Miroshnichenko, M. Ya. Sonin and others.
119 For discussion of possible numbers see Chapter 3, p. 141 above.
120 V. Kravchenko, 1947, pp. 403–6.
121 Milward, 1965, pp. 96–9, 159–60.
122 In contrast to the helpful detail supplied by historical accounts of the development of job reservation in wartime Britain, in Soviet history the subject is a virtual blank. For some rare hints see Mitrofanova, 1971, pp. 434–5.
123 Ibid., pp. 428–34.
124 Prikhod'ko, 1968, pp. 10–15.
125 Volodarsky, 1971, p. 64.
126 Prikhod'ko, 1973, p. 56.
127 Ibid., pp. 84–5.
128 Po ed. plan., 1971, p. 93.
129 Prikhod'ko, 1968, p. 13.
130 Prikhod'ko, 1973, p. 75.
131 IVMV, v. 7, 1976, p. 44.
132 BSE, 3rd edn, v. 5, 1971, p. 268.
133 Kolotov, 1976, pp. 288–9.
134 Sukharevsky, 1944, p. 19.
135 Resheniya, v. 3, 1968, pp. 90–4, 131–69.
136 Ibid., pp. 95–6, 169–82.
137 Kolotov, 1976, pp. 289–90.
138 Po ed. plan., 1971, p. 93.
139 Prikhod'ko, 1968, p. 16.
140 See Table 23 in Chapter 3, p. 132 above.
141 Prikhod'ko, 1968, pp. 16–18.
142 Po ed. plan., 1971, p. 93.
143 Resheniya, v. 3, 1968, pp. 195–200.
144 Po ed. plan., 1971, pp. 93–4.
145 Resheniya, v. 3, 1968, pp. 213–22.
146 Ibid., pp. 200–7.

The search for economic balance in wartime

147 Po ed. plan., 1971, p. 93.
148 Prikhod'ko, 1968, p. 15.
149 Zalkind and Miroshnichenko, 1973, p. 52.
150 See Chapter 1, pp. 25–6 above.
151 Sorokin, 1968, p. 123; for the exact date of endorsement of the Urals plan see Sorokin, 1971, p. 56.
152 Zalkind and Miroshnichenko, 1980, p. 220.
153 Prikhod'ko, 1973, p. 75.
154 Zaleski, 1980, pp. 297–8.
155 Resheniya, v. 3, 1968, p. 220.
156 Po ed. plan., 1971, p. 93.
157 Sorokin, 1971, p. 57.
158 Resheniya, v. 3, 1968, pp. 115–17.
159 Ibid., p. 141.
160 Shakhurin, 1974, p. 104.
161 Zalkind and Miroshnichenko, 1980, p. 217.
162 Ibid., pp. 218–19, 223–4.
163 Sukharevsky, 1945a, p. 17.
164 Resheniya, v. 3, 1968, pp. 231–2.
165 IVMV, v. 12, 1982, p. 173.
166 Comparing the first and fourth quarters of 1945, industry's defence output had fallen by 68 per cent; civilian output had risen by only 21 per cent. See IVMV, v. 11, 1980, p. 348.
167 Ibid., v. 6, 1976, p. 352.
168 Sorokin, 1971, p. 55; Arsen'ev, 1972, p. 18.
169 Zalkind and Miroshnichenko, 1980, pp. 202–3; see also Chapter 2, pp. 98–9 above.
170 For example the centrally planned energy balance was increased in coverage from six to seventeen electricity networks; see Kosyachenko, 1944, p. 11.
171 Chadaev, 1971, p. 55; see also Chapter 2, p. 98 above.
172 Zelenovsky, 1975, p. 63.
173 Volodarsky, 1971, p. 64.
174 Chadaev, 1965, p. 92.
175 Ibid., p. 89.
176 Kursky, 1944, p. 35.
177 Morozova, Moskvin and Eidel'man, 1969, pp. 461–2.
178 Zalkind and Miroshnichenko, 1980, p. 214.
179 Eidel'man, 1969, pp. 283–5.
180 Voznesensky, 1948, pp. 122–3.
181 Hutchings, 1971, pp. 88–9, 219.
182 Ibid., pp. 251–2.
183 Panov, 1944, p. 26.
184 Turetsky, 1948, pp. 111–12.
185 Baikov, 1944, p. 71; 1945, p. 53; Zalkind and Miroshnichenko, 1980, pp. 222, 225.
186 Zalkind and Miroshnichenko, 1980, p. 212.
187 Kursky, 1975, p. 13.

220 Soviet planning in peace and war

188 Braginsky, 1971, p. 71.
189 Morozova, Moskvin and Eidel'man, 1969, pp. 462–3.
190 Sorokin, 1971, p. 57.
191 Morozova, Moskvin and Eidel'man, 1969, p. 464; Starovsky and Ezhov, 1975, p. 10.
192 Morozova, Moskvin and Eidel'man, 1969, p. 465.
193 Planned and actual output growth in 1945, expressed with 1944 as the base for comparison, can be expressed as follows:

1945 as percentage of 1944	Target	Result
Pig iron	134	121
Crude steel	120	113
Rolled steel	123	116
Aluminium	114	104
Coal	126	123
Oil	109	106
Electricity	117	110

Plan figures for 1945 are taken from Resheniya, v. 3, 1968, p. 230 and IVMV, v. 10, 1979, p. 399. Realised growth in 1945 over 1944 is calculated from Appendix 2. According to the decree, industrial labour productivity was supposed to rise by 5 per cent, but the official index based on 1940 = 100 (see Table 28 above, p. 142) fell from 142 to 114. On the other hand retail trade was planned to rise by 20 per cent, and the official index rose by slightly more than this (from 37 to 45 with 1940 = 100).

194 To these posts, all of which have been mentioned previously, may be added membership with A. I. Mikoyan and A. V. Lyubimov of a GKO Operations Bureau special commission for supply of the Red Army and arms industry workforce with consumer goods, set up on 22 August 1944. See Belikov, 1974, p. 78.
195 Kolotov, 1976, p. 286.
196 Medvedev, 1983, p. 44.
197 Resheniya, v. 3, 1968, pp. 5–14; Lyubimov, 1968, pp. 10–11.
198 Zaleski, 1980, p. 491. Zaleski refers to 'that collection of activities in which the plans of enterprises and economic units are not covered by an over-all plan' as 'the regulated market economy (économie dirigée)', but neither the French nor the English term seems particularly apt.
199 Berri, 1940, p. 148.
200 Berri, 1944, p. 60.
201 Belov, 1939, p. 60–1; 1940b, p. 88.
202 Voznesensky, 1941, pp. 29–30.
203 Plan. khoz., 1941b, p. 16; Sen'ko, 1941, pp. 85–7.
204 Lyubimov, 1941, p. 26.
205 Zarutskaya, 1974, p. 293.
206 Kaimoldin, 1966, pp. 66–7.

207 Zarutskaya, 1974, p. 294.
208 Kaimoldin, 1966, p. 68.
209 Zarutskaya, 1974, p. 294.
210 Chalmaev, 1981, p. 206; see also Chapter 2, p. 92 above.
211 Chadaev, 1965, pp. 271–3; on Leningrad see also Gouré, 1964, pp. 176–8, 233–4.
212 Kursky, 1944, p. 30.
213 Berri, 1944, p. 64.
214 Ibid., pp. 58–9, 64.
215 Turetsky, 1948, p. 110.
216 Berri, 1944, p. 64; Efremov, 1944, p. 35.
217 Kuz'minov, 1943, p. 45.
218 Ustinov, 1944, p. 21.
219 Zinich, 1971, p. 97.
220 Kumanev, 1976, p. 262.
221 Chadaev, 1965, p. 82.
222 V. Sokolov, 1946, pp. 24–5, 41–2.
223 Resheniya, v. 3, 1968, p. 65 (decree of 7 April 1942).
224 Ibid., pp. 80–5 (decree of 18 October 1942).
225 IVOVSS, v. 6, 1965, p. 85; Sorokin, 1968, p. 170.
226 On 'hard' and 'soft' budgets see Kornai, 1980, v. A, pp. 28–9.
227 Tamarchenko, 1967, p. 25; Kokurkin, 1980, p. 25.
228 Atlas, 1942, pp. 18–22.
229 This was in April 1942; see IVMV, v. 5, 1975, p. 51.
230 IVOVSS, v. 6, 1965, p. 45.
231 The proportion of cereals and flour supplies withheld from the market was 27 per cent in 1942 compared with 14 per cent in 1940; 77 per cent of meat products (up from 57 per cent), 73 per cent of leather footwear supplies (up from 21 per cent) and 91 per cent of cotton textiles (up from 54 per cent) were also withheld. See Voznesensky, 1948, p. 101.
232 See Chapter 3, Table 30, p. 149 above.
233 Po ed. plan., 1971, p. 95. However, it appears from Table 30 above that in 1944 government borrowings exceeded the budget deficit, so that a slight monetary contraction began.
234 Voznesensky, 1948, p. 101.
235 Ibid., pp. 102–3.
236 Ibid., p. 103; P. V. Sokolov, 1968, p. 232.
237 Po ed. plan., 1971, p. 95.
238 ISE, v. 5, 1978, p. 478.
239 Davies, 1958, p. 315.
240 These can be calculated from data in IVOVSS, v. 2, 1961, pp. 521, 523; v. 6, 1965, pp. 67, 69; and IVMV, v. 3, 1974, p. 378.
241 Arutyunyan, 1970, pp. 210–12.
242 This approach was suggested to me by some remarks of Eugène Zaleski in Birmingham in 1982. See also Zaleski, 1980, pp. 491–2.
243 Zaleski, 1980, p. 290
244 Ibid., p. 491.

5
Soviet lessons from World War II

The present war has forcefully confirmed Lenin's well-known statement that war is an all-round test of a nation's material and spiritual forces. The history of wars teaches that only those states stood this test which proved stronger than their adversaries as regards the development and organization of their economy, as regards the experience, skill, and fighting spirit of their troops, and as regards the fortitude and unity of their people throughout the war.

Ours is just such a state. The Soviet state was never so stable and solid as now in the third year of the Patriotic War. The lessons of the war show that the Soviet system proved not only the best form of organizing the economic and cultural development of the country in the years of peaceful construction, but also the best form of mobilizing all the forces of the people for resistance to the enemy in time of war.

(I. V. Stalin, speaking on 6 November 1943)[1]

INTRODUCTION

The Soviet Union is an historically conscious society which returns systematically to its own past for lessons to help it understand present-day tasks. The lessons of history are drawn at many levels. Some of the learning takes place through reproduction of common sense and popular legends, in the same way as British political leaders might refer public opinion to the 'lessons' of appeasement, the 'spirit of Dunkirk' or the contribution of the labour movement to victory over Hitler. The learning process also operates through politically directed enquiry into the past, the expert analysis of records and so on.

In Soviet life there is a constant evocation of the lessons of World War II for both ideological and practical reasons. The practical lessons help to form attitudes to modern warfare, taking into account the changed strategic environment; the practical lessons include both questions of how war may be avoided and, once war has broken out, how it may be waged to a victorious conclusion. The ideological lessons are just as important, and stem from the war seen as a unifying national experience. Seweryn Bialer has argued that by the 1960s and 1970s the war had become a more important reference point than the events of October 1917, which were already largely lost to living memory:

> The revolution, remote in time, cannot elicit the same emotional response as the war which scarred every family alive in the Soviet Union. The revolution, moreover, divided the Russian people, while World War II united them. Indeed, two major elements regarded by Soviet leaders as essential to legitimacy may be illustrated by the war experience – the strength of the Soviet system of government and the invincibility of the nation unified, the theme of nationalism. Still further, the war experience serves to heal the breach in generations, for the patriotic self-denial of the fathers, creators of victory, warrants the respect and emulation of their sons.[2]

At the same time it should be said that no historical event gives rise automatically to objective, timeless lessons valid in each successive historical period. The drawing and redrawing of lessons is an independent, political and historical process. Once identified, the lessons are accepted or rejected on political grounds, and the grounds change with each successive generation and state of the world. All of these qualifications apply to the drawing of lessons from war.

For example Soviet Russia had been previously at war between 1918 and 1921. During and after this war a brief but intensive learning process took place. On one side were those who looked back to it as a period of inspired leadership and heroic mobilisations which had transformed society in the direction of socialism. But in the face of the tasks of postwar reconstruction, amid the ruin and debris another view quickly took shape: during the war evil necessities had been glorified and imposed on society to excess, resulting in unbearable stresses and the danger of counter-revolution even when military victory was already secure. The alternative lessons to be learnt from the experience of 'war communism' became an important factor in the struggle between left and right over how to resolve the strains of rapid industrialisation at the end of the 1920s.[3] The 'heroic' lessons of war came to prevail in association with the victory of Stalin, the resort to an intensified mobilisation drive and the incorporation of elements of army-like organisation into the Soviet economic system.

The formative impact of the civil war and war of intervention from 1918 to 1921 upon Soviet society has been well documented. What of the impact of the war of 1941 to 1945? In this concluding chapter we shall pursue two main lines of enquiry. Part One considers the changes in economic ideas during the war and in its aftermath; within this topic fall the role of Stalin and the fate of Voznesensky. Part Two proceeds to the lessons of the war and their part in the post-Stalin reform of Soviet institutions. The chapter concludes with a review of our findings.

PART ONE: THE POLITICAL ECONOMY OF SOCIALISM

THE LAW OF VALUE 1941-7

In 1929 and 1930 many Soviet economists formed exaggerated expectations of the early abolition of money, prices and trade. During the 1930s these expectations were disappointed. After Stalin's speech to the Seventeenth Party Congress in January 1934, money and trade at regulated prices were accepted as integral parts of the Soviet economic system. This did not mean, however, that market categories were accepted as playing an active role in regulating socialist economic development. The law-governed character of the Soviet economic system was recognised, but the 'law of value' was not included among its laws. On the contrary it was held (as Voznesensky wrote in January 1940) that 'The law of value has been abolished in the USSR, although the quantity and quality of labour are the measure of production, consumption and exchange ... In the Soviet economic system the plan as a directive of economic policy has obtained the force of a law.'[4]

However, this theory of antagonism between the law of value and the plan as an economic law was about to be revised. The occasion was the drafting of a new textbook on political economy to replace the previous text by I. Lapidus and K. Ostrovityanov, which had not been revised since 1928. Apparently a new draft was reviewed by the Central Committee in January 1941. The result was a decision to instal the law of value in Soviet economic thought as a law of the socialist economic system alongside the law of planning. It was held that not only the phenomena of money, price, wage, profit and rent but also the underlying law of value itself 'under socialism express objective economic relations, but have another social nature and fulfil another role than under capitalism'.[5] At the same time this did not mean approval of market socialism, because there was no retreat from the parallel concept of the plan as an economic law. However, our source does not reveal how the relationship between plan and value was regarded at this time – in particular, which was to be primary and which subordinate or whether each carried equal weight.

When war broke out the draft textbook and the accompanying discussion were set aside. Two years later, however, the subject was reopened in the July–August issue of the theoretical journal *Under the Banner of Marxism* for 1943. This was a much more public forum than hitherto, and it rapidly claimed international attention.[6] The opening foray was a lengthy editorial entitled 'Some Questions of Teaching Political Economy'. The occasion for renewed discussion seems to have been the resumption of advanced economic studies in the 1942/3 academic year and the associated need to clarify application of the decisions of the January 1941 Central Committee on the draft textbook. One may speculate that it also coincided in a rough way with the completion of wartime economic mobilisation and the revival of practical economic issues demanding a postwar perspective for coherent solution.

The article began by recalling recent Central Committee resolutions on the subject – presumably those of January 1941, although this was not made explicit.[7] It went on to define a number of 'errors' in previous teaching practice. The main emphasis was placed on reinstating the law of value in the political economy of socialism. First of all any crude equation of capitalism with commodity production and of socialism with a non-monetary economy was rejected. It was demonstrated that commodity production had existed long before capitalist society and, by implication, would outlast it too. Further, the idealisation of non-monetary systems such as the 'primitive communism' of antiquity, and the equation of socialism with primitive communism on the grounds that both were non-monetary systems, were also rejected. In this way the ground was laid for the concept of socialism as a mode of commodity production based on monetary exchange.[8]

The authors' next step was to attack the view that, because capitalism had been abolished in the Soviet Union, all the laws operating within the capitalist economic system had been abolished too, and that no laws would constrain the development of the socialist economy. In existing economics courses, for example,

after the sections on the law of value there were 'excursuses' which showed that under Soviet conditions this law does not apply. Since such 'excursuses' invariably followed the demonstration of *every* law of capitalism, then the student could only be left with the conviction that under socialism there is generally no opportunity for any kind of economic law to function.

As for the practical result,

to deny the existence of economic laws under socialism is to slip into the most vulgar voluntarism which may be summarized as follows: in place of an orderly process of development there is arbitrariness, accident, chaos. Naturally, with such an approach every standard of judgement of one doctrine or another or one practice or another is lost...[9]

What kind of economic laws operated within a socialist economy? Five were listed as objective necessities for the development of socialism in the USSR. These were the industrialisation of the country, the collectivisation of agriculture, the planned administration of the national economy, distribution of rewards according to labour contributed by society's members, and the law of value. The basis of the latter was given as the need for a common standard of measurement of qualitatively different kinds of labour – mental and manual, skilled and unskilled, mechanised and hand, labour performed within different social forms (nationalised industry, the kolkhoz household). Only monetary measurement and reward would allow society to stimulate the expenditure of labour power, control labour costs and distribute the products of labour.[10]

The law of value was thus accorded a central role in socialist political economy. At the same time it was argued that under socialism economic laws in general operate in a new way. The objective necessity on which they are based was one 'known to, and working through the consciousness and will of men, as represented by the builders of a socialist society, by the guide and leading force of the society – the Soviet state and the Communist Party, which guides all the activity of the toiling masses'. Thus the economic laws of socialism 'are not realized spontaneously, nor of their own accord, but operate as recognized laws consciously applied and utilized by the Soviet state in the practice of socialist construction'.[11] This applied not only to the laws of industrialisation, collectivisation, planning and distribution but also to the law of value, which

> functions under socialism but ... *in a transformed manner*. Under capitalism the law of value acts as an elemental law of the market, inevitably linked with the destruction of productive forces, with crises, with anarchy in production. Under socialism it acts as a law consciously applied by the Soviet state under the conditions of the development of an economy free from crises. The transformation in the function of the law of value in a planned, socialist economy is revealed, first of all, in this: that ... the distribution of money and labor power among the different branches of production is realized in a planned manner... Further ... the Soviet state can control production for the most fundamental interests of socialism and does not have to bow to the law which [under capitalism] makes impossible the development of a branch of production which at first must run at a loss...[12]

In summary the law of value had been 'transformed' in such a way as to reconcile it with the need of the authoritarian, centralised planning and management process for coherence and rationality. Planners could ignore the law of value in allocating land and especially capital goods to the central priorities of economic development and national defence, since land and capital goods had ceased to be commodities.[13] But in setting the balance between production and reproduction, consumption and labour the law of value must be taken into account and applied through economic plans.

One result of this doctrine, not to be neglected, was a change in the official view of conflict within the Soviet economy. The political economy of the far left had traditionally located the main conflict between plan and market. However, under the 'transformed' law of value there was no conflict between economic plans and monetary exchanges either directly accounted for within the plan or programmed to take place within planned parameters (such as retail sales of consumer goods at fixed prices). Conflict arose within the sphere ruled by the law of value only between 'the organized market, which is in the hands of the Soviet state' on the one hand, and on the other 'the elemental forces of the unregulated market'. Here was conceded the existence of a part of economic life not fully amenable to central economic plans for as long as the state itself remained unable to meet society's needs in full.[14]

The 'transformation' of the law of value into a tool of economic planning became the new orthodoxy for several years. A sign of its doctrinal legitimacy is that Stalin himself was frequently credited with its inspiration. The main elaboration of these ideas was carried out in 1944 and 1945 in the party's theoretical journal *Bol'shevik*. Each participant stressed the objectively law-governed character of the socialist economy, the conscious realisation and utilisation of these laws by the state and the role in economic planning of the 'transformed' law of value.[15] Kursky's contribution stressed mainly the subordination of monetary accounting and exchange to plan directives, although he was careful to include the role of both physical and financial balances in plan compilation and realisation.[16] His main message was carried in his chosen title: 'Socialist Planning is a Law of the Soviet Economic System'. A more even-handed approach was followed by the veteran Ostrovityanov. He used the occasion to reinforce the attack on those who had wanted to force the pace of industrialisation and collectivisation, to abolish trade and money forthwith, and arbitrarily to create new economic laws not based in objective necessities.[17] On the other hand he stressed that the law of value was no longer a law of the first rank, but had been 'transformed' from a basic law under capitalism to a subordinate one, 'constrained and limited by the basic laws of the socialist mode of production, above all the law of plan guidance'. In the plan process the law of value was only an 'auxiliary tool for planned distribution of labour and means of production'.[18] Ostrovityanov summed up by arguing that all the laws of socialist economics were just as important in wartime as in peacetime – it was just as vital as before to plan mobilisation, centralise distribution, account for costs of production and save resources, reward workers and so on.[19]

Ostrovityanov's concluding remarks were echoed in the opening of the last contribution, which was by Atlas. 'The war', the latter wrote,

has evoked serious economic and financial difficulties. In these circumstances a danger has been represented by undervaluation of the role of money in a socialist economy and the false view according to which questions of production cost, saving money and financial discipline have lost their significance in wartime, as though one must fulfil the needs of the front at any cost.[20]

Money and markets, Atlas argued, were indispensable to the articulation of socialist economic relations – not only among the varied socialist and pre-socialist forms of production making up the Soviet economy, but also among the basic units within the socially owned sector itself.[21] He stressed the importance of the operational autonomy of the socialist enterprise to respond to market signals such as

Soviet lessons from World War II 229

prices and costs, and attacked excessive centralisation of decision making from above in the following terms:

> ... the disposition of people and machinery within workplaces and factories, subcontracting among enterprises, and the circulation of raw materials, semimanufactures and finished products between enterprises, cannot be foreseen in detail in a single central organ ... Chief administrations, syndicates and enterprises must possess operational autonomy within the limits of the general national economic plan; their productive, technical and economic relations cannot be fully regulated from above. In accord with plans and directives these relations must be established directly by enterprises, syndicates and chief administrations on contractual principles; by the same token enterprises must operate to a certain degree as self-regulating (*samostoyatel'ny*) economic units.[22]

Of course for Atlas, like the others, the plan was still the most important thing. But the question was what style of planning and how best to stimulate plan fulfilment. Thus 'the transformed exchange of values (the planning of exchange by the state)' would help fulfilment of output plans while enabling enterprises to control expenditures on labour and material outputs.[23] By exercising legal opportunities for discretion within overall output targets defined from above, the autonomous socialist enterprise could influence the pattern of inputs and outputs towards those yielding the highest profit for the state.[24]

Thus by 1945 the basis existed for a thorough rationalisation of Soviet economic doctrine incorporating the 'transformed' law of value. This rationalisation would primarily have brought official political economy into closer touch with reality, and did not presage any major institutional reforms. There was however an associated concern to make existing economic institutions work more efficiently. For example in his speech to the USSR Supreme Soviet on 15 March 1946 about the Fourth Five Year Plan Voznesensky referred to the utilisation of the law of value in economic planning in order further to develop socialist production, and called for a more powerful role for 'economic levers in the organisation of production and distribution such as price, money, credit, profit, incentive'.[25] In line with this commitment a number of measures were undertaken in the postwar years to counteract inflationary pressures and restore financial disciplines. The most important were the currency reform of December 1947 and the wholesale-price reform of January 1949.[26]

The currency reform was aimed primarily at removing surplus cash balances held by households, especially peasant hoards, and raising retail prices (foodstuffs were derationed at the same time) in order to restore equilibrium in the consumer goods market and restore consumer incentives. The reform of wholesale prices was aimed at reducing state subsidies to industry through sharp increases in the prices paid to enterprises for industrial goods, in order to increase the financial autonomy of enterprises. These measures were necessary conditions for improving the match between the planned and the self-regulated spheres within existing institutions. But no major upheaval of the relationship between planning and self-regulation was intended or occurred.

Voznesensky's own views were set out in his 1947 history of the war economy (it was Voznesensky's book in the sense that he drafted it and it appeared under his name, although it was based of course on Gosplan papers, and it appeared in print only after annotation and 'correction' by Stalin personally).[27] In this book Voznesensky endorsed the doctrines of the state plan as a 'law' of Soviet economic development, and of the law of value 'transformed' under Soviet conditions into a tool for planning the cost, composition and allocation of output.[28] Given the continued absence of the long overdue political economy textbook, this amounted to a definitive statement of official doctrine, and Voznesensky's book became for a time the most important authority on the regularities of contemporary Soviet economic experience.

Thus from the point of view of economic doctrine it does not seem to be at all the case that the war had fostered crude voluntarism or a more thoroughly dictatorial approach to economic problems.[29] Within its broad commitment to the centralised system of authoritarian planning, Soviet economic thought possessed a more refined and flexible approach to the political economy of socialism in 1945 than it had achieved in 1940; central to this political economy was the concept of a law-governed economic system.

VOZNESENSKY, STALIN AND AFTERWARDS

In 1946 and 1947 Voznesensky appeared to become still more powerful. In October 1946 his name was added to the membership of the Politburo commission on foreign affairs.[30] And in 1947 he became a full Politburo member. The publication of his book in December 1947 also added greatly to his stature. But in 1949 Voznesensky became the victim of a political intrigue. His vulnerability emerged suddenly on several fronts. His popularity as a political intellectual and leader of moderation provoked Stalin's jealousy, for Voznesensky had begun to look too much like a rival. Stalin was ill and nearing his seventieth birthday. Voznesensky was still only forty-five. The very success of his book 'aroused Stalin's displeasure, since the latter regarded himself as the law-maker in the field of theory'.[31] At the same time Voznesensky incurred the enmity of two other Politburo members, NKVD chief L. P. Beriya and Central Committee secretary G. M. Malenkov, the latter also being an expert in the mechanics of terror.

Voznesensky and Malenkov had apparently clashed in 1945–6. Malenkov had been placed in charge of a committee responsible for organising war reparations from the Soviet occupation zone in Germany, which meant dismantling German industry and shipping the assets back to the Soviet Union. Voznesensky had objected to this short-sighted policy. A commission set up under Mikoyan to examine the disagreement had put a stop to Malenkov's activities by proposing the establishment of joint Soviet–German companies and the payment of reparations in finished industrial goods.[32] Soon afterwards, although not as a direct result, Malenkov fell from Stalin's favour and was temporarily posted to faraway Tashkent.

Voznesensky provoked Beriya's hostility by trying to distance himself from the new round of peacetime purges and executions. As a member of the Stalin leadership since 1941 he had necessarily shared collective responsibility for many repressive acts. Now he attempted to wash his hands of such involvements. For example, as a Politburo member he refused to sign death warrants which began to cross his desk in the routine course of administration.[33]

In 1948 and 1949 Malenkov restored his position by allying himself with Beriya in prosecution of the 'Leningrad affair'. This was the name given to a far-reaching purge of officials and others with past or present involvement in the political and cultural life of Leningrad. It began with the sudden dismissal of the former Leningrad party boss, Politburo member and most prominent of the Central Committee secretaries A. A. Zhdanov. The latter died soon afterwards (this was in August 1948) in obscure circumstances. The repression of those formerly associated with him or with Leningrad connections now sprang to life. Malenkov organised the purge in Leningrad, Beriya in Moscow. Voznesensky was only the most prominent of their many victims.

Voznesensky was removed from his positions in March 1949 as a result of a fabricated charge concerning the 'loss' of secret papers from Gosplan. The charge was aimed at Voznesensky personally from the start, but at first the authorities only arraigned his subordinates (not including Saburov, who eventually replaced Voznesensky as Gosplan chief). The intention was to use their 'evidence' to implicate their leader. Voznesensky himself testified at their trial, however, refuting the charges as a concocted provocation. Beriya ordered the case to be wound up, and the defendants received comparatively short prison terms.[34] Meanwhile Voznesensky, unable to work at his post, worked at home on a book about the political economy of communism. Eventually he was arrested all the same and in September 1950 was simply shot without trial.[35]

The disgrace and death of Voznesensky were followed by suppression of some of the ideas with which he had become most closely associated. Prominent among these was the 'transformed' law of value. In November 1951 a conference of Soviet economists once more discussed the draft textbook on political economy. Results of the discussion were now transmitted to Stalin for his personal judgement. Nearly a year later, in a tract dated September 1952, Stalin issued his verdicts.

He began by rejecting the idea of a 'transformed' scientific law. Such laws, according to Stalin, reflected 'processes which take place independently of the will of man' and could not be modified or transformed by deliberate human intervention, still less abolished, although the results of their operation could of course be influenced.[36] Thus if the law of value operated under Soviet conditions it must be the same, unreconstructed law of value inherited from pre-socialist times. Stalin found the basis of the law of value under Soviet conditions in the persistence of commodity production; the latter stemmed not from the essential structure of the socialised part of the economy but from the need for monetary exchanges between the latter and the kolkhoz peasantry. Thus the operation of the law of value reflected the fact that parts of the economy were not yet fully socialised. Once all the means of production, including collective farm property, had been 'seized' by society (here Stalin expounded some remarks of Engels's), commodity production would disappear.[37] In the meantime the law of value served the needs of Soviet society by articulating necessary exchanges with the peasantry, and would necessarily influence – but not directly regulate – plans and outputs of the socialised sector.[38] But in the long run both kolkhoz property and commodity exchange would prove an obstacle to the extension of central planning and state-regulated barter, and would have to be eliminated in the name of a greater law – the law of conformity between the productive forces and productive relations under socialism.[39]

In these comments it may be seen that Stalin moved one step forward, one step back.[40] On the one hand he stressed more strongly than before the objectively law-governed character of the socialist economic system, by ruling out the ambiguous category of 'transformed' laws realised either consciously through the state or otherwise, perhaps, not at all. He now dissociated himself from the voluntaristic ideology of Stalinism in its formative years which held 'that Soviet government can "do anything", that "nothing is beyond it", that it can abolish scientific laws and form new ones'.[41] Political will could only operate subject to objective constraints. But on the other hand, among these constraints the law of value was no longer featured prominently, since the planned, socialised sector had to recognise it only in exchanges with the kolkhoz peasantry. Thus at the same time as the law-governed character of the socialist economy was reaffirmed, it was deprived of its major content. In this way rule by decree was reinstated in the small print of Stalinist economic ideas.

Stalin's revision of economic theory was a major event in the build-up to the Nineteenth Party Congress in October 1952. It was left until after the congress, however, for the world to learn that Voznesensky and his adherents were indeed Stalin's main target. In December Central Committee secretary and Presidium (the renamed Politburo) member M. A. Suslov issued a sharply worded statement condemning the past dissemination of Voznesensky's 'idealistic viewpoint and subjectivism on the character of the economic laws of socialism'. According to Suslov it was Voznesensky's ideas which had bred voluntarism in economic policy, and in particular his famous history of the wartime economy. The latter, now downgraded to the status of a 'booklet',

confused the analysis of problems of the political economy of socialism, and showed itself to be a mishmash of voluntaristic views on the role of the plan and the state in Soviet society, and a fetishisation of the law of value, as though the latter was a regulator of the allocation of labour among the branches of the USSR's national economy.

Now Suslov revealed that the suppression of Voznesensky's ideas had been authorised as far back as July 1949.[42] The censure was reproduced elsewhere and extended to other figures in philosophy and the social sciences, for example A. Leont'ev, who as editor of *Under the Banner of Marxism* had helped to originate the doctrine of the plan as an economic law and the law of value 'transformed' into a tool of economic planning under socialism in 1943.[43]

A result of this process was that some of the most important lessons of wartime economic experience – the nature of the laws governing the socialist economic system, the important role of the self-regulated sphere in securing a macroeconomic equilibrium and the limits to emergency rule by dictatorial methods – were temporarily suppressed. Stalin's victory was represented after his death in the final publication in 1954, after a decade and a half of preparation, of the official political economy textbook. Two years later, however, these questions were thrown open again at the Twentieth CPSU Congress. Among Soviet economists Stalin's theses rapidly lost influence and the concept of the socialist economy as a system of commodity production gained wide acceptance. Orthodoxy after 1956 permitted far greater differentiation of views within the profession than before, and the relationship between central plans and autonomous enterprises and households became the object of a pluralistic debate which continues to the present day.[44]

One element in this debate has been the wartime economic experience and the legacy of Voznesensky. After the Twentieth CPSU Congress Voznesensky's name was quietly restored to the roll of honour. A more public rehabilitation, and opportunity for reconsidering his place in Soviet history, awaited the revelations of the Twenty-Second CPSU Congress in 1961 concerning the circumstances of his death, and the sixtieth anniversary of his birth which followed shortly, in 1963. His role as an innovator not only in the field of plan methodology but also in the use of economic stimuli to guide the development of the self-regulated sphere, and also in the field of political economy, formed the keynote struck in that year.[45] Of course most of the viewpoints expressed in Soviet economic debates since 1956 have been much more radical and even reform-minded than the formulae adopted by Voznesensky in 1946 and 1947. Some of the ideas which he endorsed, such as the plan as a 'law' of Soviet economic development, no longer fall within the limits of orthodox discussion. Nonetheless it seems to be the case that, across a broad spectrum, Soviet economists look back to Voznesensky and honour his memory as a pioneer who, from within the Stalinist epoch, indicated to future generations the directions they must follow in order to leave its most dreary wastelands behind them.

Voznesensky was part and parcel of the Stalin regime. He rose through it to high office, and his promotion was a consequence of lawless repressions. The policies which he pursued in the reorganisation of economic planning were designed to rationalise and enhance central authority, not to democratise it. At times he seemed to be leading the economic system on a contemporary 'treadmill of "reforms"',[46] in which the complexity of the planning process expanded towards the degree of complexity of the economic system, and the most important problem in plan methodology became the impossible burden upon the planners.

At the same time Voznesensky's search for coherence in economic planning had another side, which placed him in opposition to the most dictatorial aspects of Stalin's regime. This was his belief in the law-governed character of the socialist economic system and of the planning process. He understood that authority, to be effective, must accept constraints and that a lawless authority must ultimately fail. His commitment to a balance between planning and self-regulation in the economy and his acceptance of limits on the authority of the plan led him to accumulate legitimate authority rather than dictatorial power. He became associated with moderation of the Stalinist style of leadership, in response to the nation's need for coherence under the stress of rearmament, war and postwar reconstruction.

For these reasons Voznesensky's life became an important source of 'invented tradition' for the movement for reform of Stalinism after Stalin's death. However, Voznesensky did not personally bring this movement about, nor did he foresee or approve in advance the use of his memory to invalidate the Stalin cult. One can only speculate on where Voznesensky would have stood had he survived.

PART TWO: THE LESSONS OF WAR AND THE SYSTEM OF GOVERNMENT

THE REFORM OF STALINIST INSTITUTIONS

The debate on the law-governed character of a socialist economy, and the repression and rehabilitation of Voznesensky, formed one small aspect of a much broader process of learning from World War II. For

Soviet society between the immediate postwar years and the present day this process passed through three main phases. Its first phase had taken shape by 1948 or 1949 and lasted until 1956. These were the years in which the 'lessons' of experience were adapted to serve the Stalin cult. The second phase, the anti-Stalinist reaction, began in 1956 and lasted until about 1967. There then began a third phase in which the lessons were revised once more, and some 'permanent' lessons emerged.

In the first, Stalinist, phase the evil experiences of war were suppressed and the achievement of victory was portrayed in voluntaristic terms. Setbacks and objective difficulties were minimised and errors concealed. Soviet opinion learnt that the Soviet system had proved unconquerable from the outset, that its leaders had calculated everything correctly and with due foresight, and that in wartime everything went according to Stalin's plan.[47] These 'lessons' of war did not crystallise all at once. Some had been laid down in advance in Stalin's wartime speeches and other commentaries. Others were thrown up in the course of the postwar political intrigues. As far as the history of the war economy is concerned, Voznesensky's account of 1947 bore a number of traces of the voluntaristic reinterpretation, such as its stress on the smoothly planned character of mobilisation and conversion at the beginning of the war, and on the continuity of expanded reproduction processes (even in agriculture) throughout the war years. On balance, though, it tended towards realism. By 1949, however, Voznesensky's book had been suppressed and the publication of historical research on the wartime economy had ceased, not to recommence until 1957.

Apart from the brief appearance of Voznesensky's book, there was no official history of the war during this period. Or rather a distinguishing feature of the first phase of learning from World War II was that 'Stalin's wartime writings and speeches collected in *The Great Patriotic War of the Soviet Union* ... constituted for all practical purposes the only official history of the war during his lifetime.'[48] The dismal consequences were characterised by Khrushchev in the closed session of the Twentieth CPSU Congress in 1956 in the following terms:

When we look at many of our novels, films and historical 'scientific studies', the role of Stalin in the Patriotic War appears to be entirely improbable. Stalin had foreseen everything. The Soviet Army, on the basis of a strategic plan prepared by Stalin long before, used the tactics of so-called 'active defence', i.e. tactics which, as we know, allowed the Germans to come up to Moscow and Stalingrad. Using such tactics, the Soviet Army, supposedly thanks to Stalin's genius, turned to the offensive and subdued the enemy. The epic victory gained through the armed might of the land of the Soviets, through our heroic people, is ascribed in this type of novel, film and 'scientific study' as being completely due to the strategic genius of Stalin.[49]

As well as serving the Stalin cult, a number of the lessons drawn in this first phase served the continued militarisation of economic life. Here too postwar ideologies were constructed on the basis of wartime developments. Militarist ideas gained circulation in two complementary senses – the justification of the socialist economic system by reference to its adaptability to military goals, and the idealisation of wartime expedients as permanent features of a socialist economic system.

The clearest justification of the socialist economic system in terms of military goals was provided by Stalin himself in his speech of 6 November 1943: 'war is an all-round test', he declared, 'of a nation's material and spiritual forces'. In this phrase was focused and compressed the whole of classical European military thought on war and the nation.[50] The Soviet state, he continued, had not only passed this test with distinction, but had proved the Soviet system best at both peaceful and warlike tasks.[51] Stalin's formula quickly became a new dogma, with a significant amendment – in subsequent versions war became defined not just as one 'test' among many, but as 'the greatest' of them.[52]

A feature complementary to this idea was the suppression of the real difficulties encountered by the Soviet people at war, and an idealisation of the temporary expedients employed to overcome them. These expedients were portrayed not as necessary evils suffered in the cause of military survival, but as permanent features of a socialist economic system. Before the Stalinist revision of wartime history was firmly established, most accounts maintained some degree of ambiguity over this issue, attributing the army-like qualities of extreme economic centralisation and authoritarian discipline from above sometimes to the needs of socialist economic development, sometimes to the needs of war. Thus in Voznesensky's 1947 history, for example, the subordination of the whole of economic life to 'a single aim ... the definite goal set by the socialist state' was described as a permanent feature of the Soviet system whether in peacetime or at war;[53] but at the same time Voznesensky was fully prepared to acknowledge that, in the course of the military struggle, crude expedients had been imposed which had in practice ridden roughshod over the norms of economic life appropriate to peacetime.[54]

Even so, the basis had been laid for a more far-reaching idealisation of wartime evils. This was especially the case with the emergency labour laws of 1940-2, which were maintained in force until the early 1950s. Already during the war these laws were being justified not as temporary impositions but as permanent features essential to 'the planned distribution of labour power in a socialist national economy'.[55] Once the Stalinist revision had got under way all qualifications were forgotten, and the army-like model of the socialist economy was resolutely endorsed.

Stalin's death in March 1953 was followed by the rapid unravelling of the cult surrounding his person and an upsurge of new forces in Soviet politics and culture. The first phase of learning from World War II was brought decisively to a close by official condemnation of the 'cult of the individual' and of Stalin's role at the Twentieth CPSU Congress in 1956. Serious historical research on the wartime experience was set in motion, along with the rethinking and criticism of many Stalinist formulae. Work began on a six-volume *History of the Great Patriotic War of the Soviet Union* which would provide the first authoritative scholarly account. Soviet historians moved into a second phase of activity in which, for the first time, wartime difficulties and sacrifices, the real costs incurred by the Soviet people at war, would be honestly portrayed by and large.

A most striking feature of this second phase was the highlighting of the personal contributions of Soviet wartime leaders to disaster and resurgence. An entire generation of wartime leaders received honourable mention for the first time, where previously it had seemed that Stalin was solely responsible for organising the brilliant successes of the front and rear. Casualties of postwar Stalinism such as Voznesensky were rehabilitated. On the other hand Stalin himself, Kaganovich and others immediately associated with him were censured for acts of omission and commission leading to unnecessary losses for the Soviet people.[56] At the same time, some of the results of this phase proved highly controversial – for example the stress laid on Stalin's personal failure to heed the diplomatic and intelligence warnings of German plans for surprise attack in 1941, and his dogmatic enforcement of inappropriate operational concepts and orders before and after the invasion materialised.

Another revision of the second phase struck at the Stalinist concept of the army-like economy administered from the centre on the basis of rule by decree. Soviet economists returned to the discussion of plan and value, and reasserted the objective character of the laws constraining administrative plans in a socialist economy. In this they could benefit from the work of their colleagues in Eastern Europe, who in some respects were still more adventurous. For example the Polish economist Oskar Lange launched a famous attack on the idealisation of wartime expedients in a lecture in 1957. He declared that 'concentration of all resources towards one basic objective ... centralisation of disposal of resources in order to prevent leakages of resources to everything that was considered non-essential ... Allocation of resources by administrative decisions according to administratively established priorities and large-scale use of political incentives to maintain the productivity and discipline of labour through patriotic appeals' – all these were features not of a socialist economy specifically, but of a war economy independently of its social system. There was nothing inherently socialist about extreme centralisation and the replacement of economic levers by administrative ones. It was only the coincidental needs of national security and of rapid economic development starting from a backward, agrarian base which had led the existing socialist economies all to adopt such measures. 'The difficulty starts', he commented, 'when these methods are identified with the substance of socialism and are treated as being essential to it.'[57]

As far as Soviet economic life under Khrushchev was concerned, these considerations were of limited practical importance. The most important measure of relaxation of administrative rule over the economy was the repeal of wartime labour laws and the return to comparatively unrestricted urban labour mobility. But the legitimacy of the traditional, centralised system of authoritarian planning proved far more difficult to shake. Hindsight enables us to judge that the movement for basic institutional reform in the economy was largely destined for disappointment.

Thus the main results of this second phase proved to be in line with the attitude towards the Stalin cult struck at the outset by the Twentieth CPSU Congress: the basic institutions of Soviet society laid down under Stalin were satisfactory. Their triumphal progress had been obstructed not by systemic defects but by the failings of individual leaders – their personal ambitions, their aggrandisement of power and their leanings towards voluntarism and personal despotism. The impersonally law-governed character of economic life in general, and of economic planning in particular, was endorsed. The appropriate lesson drawn from wartime experience was therefore the need for collective, law-governed administrative authority to assert itself within existing Soviet institutions against personal ambition and unrestrained personal rule.

Politically this lesson was of the first importance because in 1956–7 it had lent validity to Khrushchev's struggle against the old-time Stalinists – in particular Voroshilov, Molotov, Malenkov and Kaganovich.[58] Time passed, however, and Khrushchev's own regime was in turn undermined by the lesson which he himself had helped to draw, as his administration acquired more and more of the flavour of personal rule. Past condemnation of the 'cult of the individual' was an important factor in Khrushchev's dismissal in 1964 and his replacement by a new team, led by Brezhnev and Kosygin and pledged to 'collective leadership'.

The second phase of learning from World War II thus outlasted Khrushchev – but only by a few years. Shortly after publication in 1965 of the sixth and last volume of the official war history begun under Khrushchev, its authors came under critical fire from within the establishment. The charges were that, while making an indispensable and many-sided contribution to historical science, they had exaggerated the role of leading individuals; they had idealised some figures and blamed others too much – for example Stalin. They had underestimated the role of impersonal institutions and of collective leadership – the Supreme Command, the party, the people and its representatives.[59] Thus in about 1967 a new, third, phase of research and revision was initiated. Historical activity took on even broader dimensions than in the second phase. Work began on a new official twelve-volume *History of the Second World War*, which would take over a decade to complete.

In this third phase all but the most sensitive wartime difficulties and setbacks remained open to discussion, but their objective nature was reasserted. For example the degree of peacetime preparation of the Soviet economy for war on the eve of the German invasion was rated much more highly than before; greater stress was laid on the creation of a long-run military–economic potential through industrialisation, large-scale collective agriculture and vocational training of the workforce. Identifiable defects and mistakes in military–economic preparations were belittled on the grounds that they had been identified only with the help of hindsight.[60] The catastrophe of June 1941 was no longer blamed on Stalin's personal failure to foresee or respond to war, but on the predatory nature of Nazi imperialism, the breakdown of international anti-fascist unity, and the lack of time to complete defensive preparations in the light of Hitler's treachery.[61] Expunging the individual errors from the record went hand in hand with a reassertion of the role of collective leadership (which included Stalin, of course) and of basic Soviet institutions in organising victory. The actions of individuals, their deeds or misdeeds, were eradicated or else ascribed to impersonal offices, committees and agencies. Only their names were retained, listed largely without comment.[62]

As for the lessons drawn from the war by Stalin himself, the process of open criticism of Stalinist formulae came to an end. Those which had already been discarded were quietly buried – in the main, those directly connected with the Stalin cult and with Stalin's postwar revisions of Soviet philosophy and political economy. Others were retained and elaborated through scholarly research, but their association with Stalin was no longer advertised.

It may seem paradoxical, therefore, to state that during the Brezhnev era the political lessons of World War II did not fundamentally change. But in fact this was the case. The lessons of war continued to stress the legitimacy of the basic Soviet institutions laid down under Stalin and the importance of collective, law-governed administrative authority in their management. What changed was the 'history' from which these lessons were derived. Under Khrushchev they had been justified by reference to the damage ascribed to Stalin's lawless dictatorship in the years of terror and war. Under Brezhnev this negative example was written out of history, and the same lessons were related to more positive examples of Soviet institutional response to difficulties and setbacks imposed by objective factors in the external environment.

Thus Stalin's name was mentioned once more, and positive values were attributed to his leadership. But there was no attempt to justify or excuse his mistakes and crimes, concerning which silence reigned.

Symbolic of this phase was the reappearance of one of the first, Stalinist, political lessons of war in a new form. This was the doctrine that the Soviet system had proved best at both peaceful and warlike tasks. In its new form it was held that the Soviet system had successfully adapted to wartime needs of conversion and mobilisation without major change in the institutions laid down in peacetime under Stalin.[63] The system of government had been ready for war when it came, and had proved equally suited to rapid economic development and wartime military mobilisation. The conservative connotations of this lesson gave it added force under the Brezhnev regime. Associated with it was the disappearance of a wide range of topics for fundamental research – the dynamically evolving character of basic Soviet institutions and the government system, their disruption by war and the shifting balance between law-governed administration and emergency rule by decree, the lack of coherence and conditions for stabilisation of economic authority.

During the postwar decades, therefore, important lessons drawn from World War II evolved in response to the findings of research and the needs of competing political currents. Not all was subject to change, however. Through the process of periodic revision a number of 'permanent' lessons became evident, and these lessons were passed on without amendment from one period to the next.

PERMANENT LESSONS FROM WORLD WAR II

The first and most important permanent lesson from World War II was the importance of peace. The conditions surrounding the formation of the Soviet state had led it to form a dual outlook on war. On the one hand war was regarded as the wasteful, inhuman product of imperialism – of the national rivalries generated by the expansion drive of monopoly capital. War in this sense was alien to socialism. On the other hand the Soviet Union constituted a national state among other nations. Under the conditions of 'socialism in a single country', its leaders could not dispense with the use of force as an instrument of national policy if the imperialist states would not renounce it too. Thus on the one hand the Soviet security outlook aimed at avoiding war through peaceful coexistence of states based on different social systems, restricting competition to the political, economic and cultural spheres; but on the other hand the warmaking tendencies of imperialism could only be held in check by maintenance of a high level of Soviet armament and preparedness for war.

Once the militarist excesses of postwar Stalinism had been rejected, this outlook was continuously reinforced. Today the Soviet history of the war lays exceptional stress on the costliness of modern warfare and war preparations, and on the importance of peace for solution of the 'economic, social and ecological problems of the globe'. At the same time imperialism is seen to be a permanent threat to world peace. As before, therefore, war avoidance continues to depend on preparedness for war – 'the all-round consolidation of the economic and defensive might of the Soviet Union and of other countries of the socialist community', in whose political make-up 'are fused the love of peace and readiness to give a fitting rebuff to aggression'.[64]

Within this context war is still seen as a 'test' of different societies' viability and cohesiveness.[65] Thus side by side with practical lessons concerning economic preparations and wartime economic conversion,[66] the war continues to provide the Soviet Union's socialist economic system with comparative legitimacy. Here the permanent lessons of World War II include several complementary propositions, which may be summed up in the following terms. First of all, the war revealed the correctness of prewar Stalinist policies for rapid industrialisation and collectivisation.[67] Secondly, the war revealed the exploitative character of imperialism, especially through the privilege and profit received by the imperialist classes and the unequal sacrifice borne by working people, who could be motivated to fight only by means of 'demagogy, deception, bribery and force';[68] in contrast the war proved the unity and stability of Soviet society through the equal contribution and equal sacrifice borne by all its component classes and strata.[69] Thirdly, the Soviet economic system was shown to be free of the class and competitive antagonisms which weakened the ability of the imperialist states to pass the test of war.[70] Fourthly and in conclusion, these properties of socialism made the Soviet economy capable of greater centralisation and concentration of resources, greater mobilisation and manoeuvrability than its imperialist rivals.[71] In these permanent lessons of the war are found a direct echo of Stalin's formula about the superiority of the Soviet system at both peaceful and warlike tasks.[72]

CONCLUSIONS

The Stalinist economic system formed in the 1930s was driven by the conflicting needs of economic mobilisation versus balance. In the course of mobilisation the economy's fixed assets expanded rapidly, but at the same time the economy tended to lose its inner harmony. If the mobilisation persisted, growing shortages would eventually disrupt the supply of consumption, the recruitment and motivation of labour and the commissioning of new industrial capacities. The restoration of balance would become a precondition for resumed mobilisation.

Associated with phases of mobilisation were stress on a military style of leadership, individual rule by decree and an army-like model of coercive organisation. In managing economic expansion the compilation and implementation of detailed economy-wide plans would prove less important than overriding administrative priorities and emergency measures. Such crude and brutal disciplines proved effective in galvanising the short-term expansion of output and investment. But they proved inflexible and inept at taking account of the repercussions of policy upon the economy as a whole, in the context of a continuously changing environment. Moreover, if ignored for long enough, these repercussions and changes could put at risk the permanent objectives of the Stalin leadership.

Essential aspects of the restoration of economic balance therefore included the moderation of dictatorial rule and the rationalisation and promotion of administrative systems for information, analysis and control of the economy's basic units. These required some recognition of the limits of authority in the face of the fundamental regularities of economic life, rooted in society and not amenable to alteration by government decrees.

In wartime the cycle of alternating phases did not come to a halt, but continued to operate under new conditions. The permanent objectives of economic development and national defence remained, but the imperatives of defence became incomparably more urgent, while the economy was threatened by deadly entrapments. At first the Stalin leadership's exertion of will, the imposition of its absolute authority combined with the learnt responses of the people, was sufficient to slow the enemy's advance and frustrate Hitler's blitzkrieg. But by itself this was insufficient to sustain protracted warfare and long-term economic effort.

The outstanding mobilisation of the Soviet economy achieved by 1943 rested on more than the exercise of naked will. Beneath it lay a slow return to economy-wide coordination for the restoration of economic balance. Effective centralisation of controls through the planning system was associated with resumed rationalisation of plan methodology and limitation of dictatorial rule. The return to detailed economic coordination through the planning system was fostered by the receding threat to survival and growing awareness of the needs of economic reconstruction and reconversion; the latter would eventually stretch the horizons of wartime policy into the postwar world.

The experience of war carried profound implications for Soviet government and economic life – for plan methodology and the economic system, for their relations of command and interaction, and for the models of socialism underlying them. These implications were expressed not in a single set of unified values and lessons but in a multiplicity of conflicting postwar themes. War did not only stimulate Stalinist absolutism and dictatorial rule. Through the blood and toil of war, Soviet people learnt the limits of naked authority and mobilisation by decree. Side by side with the conservative and militarist lessons of war, which helped to shore up Stalin's regime once the war was over, other lessons were stored up which inspired reform of the most oppressive and violent aspects of Stalinism after Stalin's death.

Of course this conclusion does not mean that the war was a necessary or desirable condition for postwar reform. There were surely less costly ways of learning such lessons than through a struggle which deprived 55 million people of their lives. For the Soviet Union, attached to her own 20 million dead was an additional price – the harmful reinforcement of a backward-looking, nationalist outlook, the idealisation of the authoritarian state, the exceptional stress on military and coercive aspects of national security. Thus the conservative and militarist lessons of the war became entangled with the peaceable and reformist ones, and proved to be equally long-lived.

NOTES

1 Stalin, 1945, p. 100.
2 Bialer, ed., 1970, p. 19.
3 See Szamuely, 1974, pp. 99–109; Cohen, 1975, pp. 129–40; Lewin, 1975, pp. 73–84.
4 Voznesensky, 1949, p. 85.
5 Pashkov, 1972, pp. 25–6. According to Lewin, 1975, p. 110 Stalin personally was to be credited with this sudden 'admission'; but in fact the admission may not have been unprepared, and direct evidence on Stalin's role is lacking.
6 The article appeared in translation in the *American Economic Review* for September 1944. Between June 1944 and September 1945 a number of comments were also published. The contributors included Paul Baran, Oscar Lange and the translator Raya Dunaevskaya.

7 PZM, 1943, pp. 56–8.
8 Ibid., pp. 58–62. The force of these comments on the monetary and non-monetary systems of the ancient world was lost on the international audience of the time. They were either ignored or considered to be 'of little concern to non-Marxians'; see Landauer, 1944, p. 340.
9 PZM, 1943, p. 65. Dunaevskaya's translation is used.
10 Ibid., pp. 68–70. See also the related views on the role of money under socialism expressed by Voznesensky in 1935 (Chapter 1, p. 16 above).
11 PZM, 1943, p. 66.
12 Ibid., p. 75. Emphasis added.
13 Ibid., p. 76.
14 Ibid., p. 73.
15 Kursky, 1944, p. 26; Ostrovityanov, 1944, p. 47–58; Atlas, 1945, pp. 43–4.
16 Kursky, 1944, pp. 28–35.
17 Ostrovityanov, 1944, p. 47.
18 Ibid., p. 58. McCagg, 1978, pp. 139–40 attempts to draw a line between the 'voluntarist' arguments of Ostrovityanov in 1944 and the spirit of 'pragmatism' displayed by the editors of *Under the Banner of Marxism* in 1943. It must be said that there is absolutely no foundation for this distinction. Virtually all the innovations ascribed by McCagg to Ostrovityanov can be found in *Under the Banner of Marxism*, including, most importantly, the 'transformed' law of value. In each statement both plan and value are portrayed as laws of socialism, while Ostrovityanov defines more sharply the subordination of value to plan. Both statements reveal the same balance between 'voluntarism' and acceptance of constraints, and the affinity between them is fundamental, not just 'technical'.
19 Ostrovityanov, 1944, p. 59.
20 Atlas, 1945, p. 37.
21 Ibid., pp. 41–2. This is the same Atlas who advocated increased enterprise financial autonomy and responsibility in 1942; see Chapter 4, p. 209 above.
22 Atlas, 1945, p. 42. Emphasis omitted.
23 Ibid., p. 43.
24 Ibid., pp. 44–6.
25 Voznesensky, 1979, p. 465.
26 Zaleski, 1980, pp. 428–9, 469–70.
27 Kolotov, 1976, pp. 316–17.
28 Voznesensky, 1948, pp. 115–20. According to McCagg, 1978, pp. 138–41, in the postwar period Voznesensky identified himself with economic voluntarism in both theory and practice. McCagg begins by linking Voznesensky with the 'voluntarism' of Ostrovityanov's 1944 lecture on the 'transformed' law of value in opposition to the 'pragmatism' of the editors of *Under the Banner of Marxism*. (This interpretation of Ostrovityanov's views is rejected in n. 18 above.) McCagg draws further 'evidence' about Voznesensky's personal position from an account of the Fourth Five Year Plan. 'If it were true', McCagg writes, 'that the state planners could, as Ostrovityanov and Voznesensky argued, manipulate the law of value to achieve economic miracles – if a balance between income and output was,

Soviet lessons from World War II

in fact, irrelevant to the planning of Soviet investments – then a choice between heavy industry and consumer goods need not be made: if the planners in peacetime, as during the war, were capable of miracles, then the Soviet state could push both heavy industry and consumer goods ... As Western observers, to their considerable bewilderment, immediately recognised, Voznesensky's Five Year Plan was drawn up with regard almost exclusively to needs, as opposed to capacities.' Ironically neither in this nor in other regards was the Fourth Five Year Plan an outstandingly 'voluntarist' document (whether or not it should be described as 'Voznesensky's'). For example ambitious plans for consumption had many prewar precedents. Moreover a number of the most important output targets for 1950 were surpassed in reality. From the point of view of internal balances for income and output the plan showed a comparatively high degree of coherence. An overall verdict on the plan (not to mention exploration of Voznesensky's part in it) requires far more qualification than that offered by McCagg. See for example Zaleski, 1980, pp. 347–54. McCagg's main argument, that Ostrovityanov and Voznesensky believed in a miracle-working state and helped to form a voluntarist tendency in postwar Soviet economic policy, is unsupported and implausible.

29 Contrary to the view for example of Lewin, 1975, p. 110.
30 Khrushchev, 1976, p. 77.
31 Kolotov, 1963a, p. 97; also Kolotov and Petrovichev, 1963, p. 39.
32 Medvedev, 1983, pp. 146–7.
33 V. V. Kolotov, 'Ustremlennyi v budushchee' (unpublished), cited by Medvedev, 1972, p. 481.
34 Kolotov, 1963b, p. 2.
35 Kolotov and Petrovichev, 1963, p. 47.
36 Stalin, 1973, pp. 445–50. Reference is made to Stalin's *Economic Problems of Socialism in the USSR*.
37 Ibid., pp. 451–3.
38 Ibid., pp. 459–62.
39 Ibid., p. 498.
40 Nove, 1965, pp. 284–5.
41 Stalin, 1973, p. 451.
42 Suslov, 1952.
43 Kommunist, 1953.
44 See Nove, 1965, pp. 286–91; 1977, pp. 334–43.
45 Sorokin, 1963, pp. 150–3.
46 Schroeder, 1979, p. 312 uses this phrase to describe the fifteen years of 'economic reform' initiated by prime minister Kosygin in 1965.
47 Gallagher, 1963, pp. 39–60 summarises this phase. Gallagher's account contains chapters on the military, the professional historians and the writers but not, unfortunately, the economists.
48 Ibid., p. 38.
49 Khrushchev, 1976, p. 48.
50 Stalin echoed also Lenin, who had described war as 'a test of all the economic and organisational forces of each nation', and even Marx, who had written in 1855: 'Such is the redeeming feature of war; it puts a nation

248 *Soviet planning in peace and war*

to the test. As exposure to the atmosphere reduces all mummies to instant dissolution, so war passes supreme judgement upon social organisations that have outlived their vitality.' The latter passage is cited in Marxism–Leninism, 1972, p. 21.

51 Stalin, 1945, p. 100; for the full passage see the quotation which heads this chapter.
52 See for example Kosyachenko, 1944, p. 4: 'Modern war is the greatest test for the national economy and its social structure.'
53 Voznesensky, 1948, p. 115.
54 Ibid., pp. 120–1.
55 Kursky, 1943, p. 71.
56 IVOVSS, v. 6, 1965, p. 85.
57 Lange, 1962, p. 18.
58 Saburov, Voznesensky's old deputy and successor as Gosplan chief, also turned out to be a leader of this group. See Medvedev, 1982, p. 117.
59 Mutovkin and Selyanichev, 1967, pp. 192–4.
60 Sorokin, 1975, p. 4.
61 IVMV, v. 12, 1982, pp. 13–15, 38.
62 Ibid., p. 39. The one unmentionable name remained that of Stalin's NKVD chief, L. P. Beriya.
63 This view is discussed and qualified in Chapter 2, pp. 93–4 above.
64 IVMV, v. 12, 1982, pp. 456–60.
65 This formula remained current in the sixties, and, if less popular today, its sense is still fully preserved. See for example IVOVSS, v. 1, 1961, p. 407 and v. 6, 1965, p. 41; P. V. Sokolov, 1968, p. 19.
66 See for example P. V. Sokolov, 1968, p. 211; ISE, v. 5, 1978, pp. 95–103.
67 Granovsky, 1943, pp. 7–18; Voznesensky, 1948, pp. 22–6; Belov, 1951, pp. 173, 179–82; Gladkov, 1970, p. 408; Ist. KPSS, v. 5(i), 1970, p. 58; Seregin, 1971, p. 308; Zhukov, 1971, p. 192; Kosyachenko, 1975, p. 53; Pedosov, 1976, pp. 80–2; IVMV, v. 12, 1982, pp. 153–7.
68 These words are cited from IVMV, v. 12, 1982, p. 38. See also IVOVSS, v. 6, 1965, pp. 80–1; Sorokin, 1968, pp. 160–3.
69 IVMV, v. 12, 1982, pp. 41–5, 149.
70 Kuz'minov, 1942, pp. 52–3; Voznesensky, 1948, pp. 135–7; Belov, 1951, pp. 71–4; IVOVSS, v. 6, 1965, p. 82; P. V. Sokolov, 1968, pp. 200, 205; Gladkov, 1970, pp. 23–4; Ist. KPSS, v. 5(i), 1970, p. 274; G. S. Kravchenko, 1970, p. 363; Sorokin, 1971, p. 52; 1975, p. 6; Narochnitsky, 1976, p. 342; Pedosov, 1976, p. 84; ISE, v. 5, 1978, p. 174; IVMV, v. 12, 1982, pp. 38, 146.
71 Belov, 1951, pp. 170–4, 187–91; Gladkov, 1970, pp. 25–6; Ist. KPSS, v. 5(i), 1970, pp. 274–5; G. S. Kravchenko, 1970, p. 363; 1974, p. 47; Baibakov, 1976, p. 61; Gatovsky, 1976, pp. 358–9; Narochnitsky, 1976, pp. 343–4; ISE, v. 5, 1978, pp. 175, 178, 185; IVMV, v. 12, 1982, pp. 161, 166, 170.
72 Tamarchenko, 1967, p. 3; G. S. Kravchenko, 1970, p. 209; Sov. ekon., 1970, p. 27; ISE, v. 5, 1978, p. 178; IVMV, v. 12, 1982, p. 153.

Appendix 1 Soviet arms production 1930–45

Appendices 1 and 2 contain time series for Soviet production of military and basic industrial goods listed under a number of headings. Each appendix falls into two main parts – a table of annual data covering the years from around 1928 or 1930 to 1945, and a table of quarterly data covering the wartime period only. In each appendix, these tables are designed to be read together – each table supplements the other, and does not merely repeat the information in the other table in more or less detail. This feature arises from the very large number of gaps in the Soviet statistical record. Inadequacies of published information mean that annual statistics must sometimes be pieced together from more detailed series, and quarterly figures must often be deduced or approximated from data for surrounding periods. Where no estimate is possible, the appropriate cell in the table is left blank. The reader who seeks a figure in the annual series and finds it missing may nonetheless be helped by finding incomplete quarterly data provided for the year concerned. Similarly, where the quarterly series is incomplete, an annual figure may nonetheless be provided.

Annual rates

	1930	1931	1932	1933	1934	1935	1936	1937	1938	1939	1940	1941	1942	1943	1944
1. Aircraft	899	860	1,734	2,952	3,109	2,529[a]	3,770	4,435	5,467	10,382	10,565	15,735	25,436	34,845	40,246
2. Trainers	—	—	—	—	—	—	—	—	—	—	549	267	457	1,260	1,528
3. Transport	—	—	—	—	—	—	—	—	—	—	1,691	3,091	3,298	3,744	5,508
4. Combat aircraft	—	220	146	627	962	835	—	—	—	6,995	8,325	12,377	21,681	29,841	33,210
5. Bombers	—	100	72	291	392	59	—	—	—	—	3,571	3,748	3,537	4,074	4,186
6. Fighters	—	120	74	336	570	776	—	—	—	—	4,574	7,086	9,924	14,590	17,913
7. Assault	—	—	—	—	—	—	—	—	—	—	0	1,543	8,219	11,177	11,110
8. Tanks and self-propelled guns	—	—	—	—	—	—	—	—	—	—	—	—	—	24,089	28,963
9. Medium; heavy	—	—	—	—	—	—	—	—	—	—	—	—	—	—	21,896
10. Tanks	170	740	3,038	3,509	3,565	3,055	4,800	1,559	2,271	2,950	2,794	6,590	24,446	—	—
11. Medium; heavy	—	—	—	—	—	—	—	—	—	—	—	—	—	—	—
12. KV	—	—	—	—	—	—	—	—	—	—	243	1,326	—	—	—
13. IS	—	—	—	—	—	—	—	—	—	—	—	—	—	—	2,210
14. T-34	—	—	—	—	—	—	—	—	—	—	115	2,996	12,531	—	—
15. Artillery pieces[b]	952	1,966	2,574	4,698	4,123	4,383	4,324	5,473	12,340	17,348	15,300	42,300	127,000	130,300	122,400
16. Medium and large calibre[c]	608	926	1,602	1,754	1,602	988	952	1,705	5,214	8,863	—	49,100[g]	48,400	56,100	—
17. Mortars	—	—	—	—	—	—	0	1,600	1,200	4,100	38,500	52,500	229,900	69,500	7,100
18. Medium and large calibre[d]	—	—	—	—	—	—	—	—	—	—	—	—	125,570	—	—
19. Machine guns	9,700	41,000	45,000	32,700	29,200	29,600	32,000	42,000	77,000	114,000	—	356,100	458,500	439,100	—
20. Machine pistols, thou.	—	—	—	—	—	—	0	1	1	22	81	99	1,506	2,024	1,971
21. Rifles; carbines, thou.	126	174	224	241	303	222	403	578	1,175	1,503	1,461	—	4,049	3,437	2,450
22. Ammunition, thou.[f]	—	—	—	—	—	—	—	—	—	—	—	67,097	127,387	207,737	229,374
23. Shells[f] mines	—	—	—	—	—	—	1,577	4,889	12,435	11,242	14,000	—	73,487	132,037	218,900
24. Shells	—	—	—	—	—	—	482	1,798	5,209	6,034	—	—	—	—	—
25. Medium and large calibre[c]	—	—	—	—	—	—	11,900	15,600	25,900	34,100	—	—	—	—	—
26. Gunpowder, tons	—	—	—	—	—	—	—	—	—	—	—	—	—	—	—
27. Ships, basic classes	—	—	—	—	—	—	—	—	—	—	—	41	15	14	4

[a] 1,612 delivered to the Defence Commissariat.
[b] Excludes naval artillery.
[c] In excess of 76 mm.
[d] 82 mm and over.
[e] Shells; mines; bombs.
[f] Excludes aircraft shells.
[g] This figure is not consistent with available quarterly data.
For sources see 'Quarterly rates' table below.

Quarterly rates[h]

	1940	1941 I	II	III	IV	1942 I	II	III	IV	1943 I	II	III	IV	1944 I	II	III	IV	1945 I	II
1. Aircraft	2,641	2,979	→	6,600	3,740	3,177	6,004	7,388	8,304	7,614	8,931	9,150	→	9,800	→	10,323	→	10,051	→
2. Trainers	—	—	—	—	—	—	—	—	—	—	—	—	—	—	—	—	—	—	—
3. Transport	—	—	—	—	—	—	—	—	—	—	—	—	—	—	—	—	—	—	—
4. Combat aircraft	2,081	2,088½	→	4,100	3,301	4,967	6,219	7,194	6,372	7,369	8,050	→	8,150	→	8,455	→	8,209	→
5. Bombers	—	—	—	—	—	—	—	—	—	—	—	—	—	—	—	—	—	—	—
6. Fighters	—	—	—	—	—	—	—	—	—	—	—	—	—	—	—	—	—	—	—
7. Assault	—	—	—	—	—	—	—	—	—	—	—	—	—	—	—	—	—	—	—
8. Tanks and self-propelled guns	—	—	—	—	—	—	—	—	5,660	5,539	6,450	→	6,900	—	7,581½	→	7,709½	→
9. Medium; heavy	699	895	→	2,400	4,861	6,317	6,490	6,778	—	—	5,100	5,100	5,100	—	5,818	→	5,926½	→
10. Tanks	—	—	—	—	—	—	—	—	—	—	4,450	4,050	—	—	—	—	—	—
11. Medium; heavy	61	196¼	→	492	44¼	—	4,208	4,788	—	—	—	—	—	—	—	—	—	—
12. KV	—	—	—	—	—	—	—	—	—	—	—	—	—	—	—	—	—	—
13. IS	—	—	—	—	—	—	—	—	—	—	—	102	250	525	717½	→	—	—
14. T-34	29	555	→	1,121	765	1,606	2,654	3,946	4,335	—	—	—	—	—	—	—	—	—
15. Artillery pieces[e]	3,845	6,050	→	15,100	→	26,800	→	37,300	36,100	31,900	30,000	34,200	30,800	→	30,400	→	31,000	→
16. Medium and large calibre[c]	—	—	—	—	6,872	8,503	9,411	8,325	—	—	12,300	13,550	—	14,500	→	14,300	→
17. Mortars	9,625	5,100	→	21,150	→	61,400	57,900	49,200	35,400	20,900	6,600	1,850	—	1,700	→	1,300	→
18. Medium and large calibre[d]	—	—	—	9,550	21,831	33,611	37,656	32,472	23,800	15,000	—	—	—	—	—	—	—
19. Machine guns	—	—	—	53,100	67,050	111,000	→	—	114,500	121,500	111,250	115,250	→	104,300	→	58,750	→
20. Machine pistols, thou.	20	4½	→	45	268	→	485	→	463	496	532¼	502	→	483½	→	275½	→
21. Rifles; carbines, thou.	365	530	→	800	1,000	→	—	→	938	946	776	629	—	596	—	287	→
22. Ammunition, thou.[e]	—	—	—	31,450	32,900	→	—	→	—	—	64,008	59,737	—	54,950	483½	50,400	→
23. Shells[f]/mines	—	16,774	→	→	17,139	27,875	39,732	42,641	49,266	38,371	60,050	55,950	—	53,500	—	—	—
24. Shells	—	—	—	—	—	—	—	—	—	—	—	—	—	—	—	—	—	—
25. Medium and large calibre[c]	—	—	—	—	—	—	—	—	—	—	→	—	—	—	→	—	—
26. Gunpowder, tons	—	—	—	→	—	—	6	7	3¼	→	→	—	—	—	—	—	—
27. Ships, basic classes	—	11¼	→	→	—	—	—	—	—	—	—	—	—	—	—	—	—	—

For notes *b–f* see 'Annual rates' table above.

[h] 'Quarterly' rates for 1940 are annual rates divided by four. Some 'quarterly' rates for subsequent years are really half-yearly and in two cases yearly rates divided by the appropriate number. In these cases the average 'quarterly' figure calculated in this way is entered under the first quarter of the period involved and is followed by an arrow across subsequent columns to show the half-year or year which has been treated in this way. Take row 1 as an example. The average rate of production in the first half of 1941 was 2,979 aircraft per quarter. In the third quarter 6,600 aircraft were produced, in the fourth quarter 3,177 and so on. Figures not followed by arrows are actual quarterly output data.

Sources

1. 1930–5: IVMV, v. 1, 1973, p. 214. 1936–40; Cooper, 1976, Table II. 1941.I–1945.II: IVMV, v. 4, 1975, pp. 150–1, 158; v. 5, 1975, p. 48; v. 6, 1976, p. 353; v. 8, 1977, p. 357; v. 9, 1978, p. 394; v. 10, 1979, p. 415.
2. 1940–5: calculated from rows 1 and 4 and G. S. Kravchenko, 1970, pp. 179, 297.
3. 1940–5: as row 2.
4. 1931–5, 1940: sums of rows 5–7. 1939: Nikitin, 1960, p. 21. 1941.I–1945.II: IVMV, v. 4, 1975, p. 158; v. 5, 1975, p. 48; v. 6, 1976, p. 353; v. 8, 1977, p. 357; v. 9, 1978, p. 394; v. 10, 1979, p. 415.
5. 1931–5: IVMV, v. 1, 1973, p. 214. 1940–4: calculated from rows 1 and 4 and G. S. Kravchenko, 1970, pp. 179, 297.
6. 1931–5, 1940–4: as row 5.
7. 1940–4: as row 5.
8. 1943.I–1945.II: IVMV, v. 6, 1976, p. 353; v. 8, 1977, p. 357; v. 9, 1978, p. 394; v. 10, 1979, p. 415.
9. 1943.III–1945.II: IVMV, v. 8, 1977, p. 357; v. 9, 1978, p. 394; v. 10, 1979, p. 415.
10. 1930–5: IVMV, v. 1, 1973, p. 214. 1936–40: Cooper, 1976, Table III. 1941.I–1942.IV: IVMV, v. 4, 1975, p. 158; v. 5, 1975, p. 48.
11. 1942.III–IV: IVMV, v. 6, 1976, p. 343. 1943.III–1944.II: IVMV, v. 8, 1977, p. 357.
12. 1940–1.IV: IVOVSS, v. 1, 1961, p. 415; IVMV, v. 4, 1975, p. 149.
13. 1943.IV–1944.IV: IVMV, v. 8, 1977, p. 356.
14. 1940–1.IV: IVOVSS, v. 1, 1961, p. 415; IVMV, v. 4, 1975, p. 149. 1942.I–II interpolated from G. S. Kravchenko, 1970, p. 175. 1942.III–IV: IVMV, v. 5, 1975, p. 47.
15. 1930–5: IVMV, v. 1, 1973, p. 214. 1936–40: Cooper, 1976, Table V. 1941.I–1945.II: IVMV, v. 4, 1975, p. 158; v. 6, 1976, pp. 343. 353; v. 8, 1977, p. 357; v. 9, 1978, p. 394; v. 10, 1979, p. 415.
16. 1930–5; calculated from row 15 and IVMV, v. 1, 1973, p. 214. 1936–9: IVMV, v. 2, 1974, p. 191. 1942–3: IVMV, v. 7, 1976, p. 57. 1942.I–II: IVMV, v. 5, 1975, p. 48 (not consistent with figure for 1942 in v. 7). 1943.III–1945.II: IVMV, v. 8, 1977, p. 357; v. 9, 1978, p. 394; v. 10, 1979, p. 415.
17. 1936–9: IVMV, v. 2, 1974, p. 191. 1940: Cooper, 1976, Table V. 1941.I–1945.II: IVMV, v. 4, 1975, pp. 150–1, 158; v. 6, 1976, pp. 343. 353; v. 8, 1977, p. 357; v. 9, 1978, p. 394; v. 10, 1979, p. 415.
18. 1941.III–1943.III: IVMV, v. 4, 1975, p. 158; v. 5, 1975, p. 48; v. 6, 1976, p. 353.
19. 1930–5: IVMV, v. 1, 1973, p. 214. 1936–9: IVMV, v. 2, 1974, p. 191. 1940: Cooper, 1976, Table IV. 1941.III–1942.IV: IVMV, v. 4, 1975, p. 158; v. 12, 1982, p. 168.
20. 1943.I–1945.II: IVMV, v. 1, 1973, p. 214. 1936–9: IVMV, v. 6, 1976, p. 353; v. 8, 1977, p. 357; v. 9, 1978, p. 394; v. 10, 1979, p. 415.
21. 1936–9: IVMV, v. 2, 1974, p. 191. 1940–1: Bolotin, 1983, p. 87. 1941.III–1945.II: IVMV, v. 4, 1975, p. 158; v. 6, 1976, p. 353; v. 7, 1976, p. 57; v. 8, 1977, p. 357; v. 9, 1978, p. 394; v. 10, 1979, p. 415.
21. 1930–40, 1941.III–1942.II, 1943.I–1945.II: as row 19. 1941.I–II: estimated by Tupper, 1981, Table 1.
22. 1941.III–1942.II: IVMV, v. 4, 1975, p. 158. 1943.III–1945.II: IVMV, v. 8, 1977, p. 357; v. 10, 1979, p. 415.
23. 1941.I–1944.IV: IVMV, v. 5, 1975, p. 48; v. 6, 1976, p. 353; v. 8, 1977, p. 357; v. 9, 1978, p. 394.
24. 1936–9: IVMV, v. 2, 1974, p. 191. 1940: Yakovlev, 1981, p. 83. 1942–3: IVMV, v. 7, 1976, p. 57.
25. 1936–9: as row 24.
26. 1936–9: as row 24.
27. 1941–5.II: IVMV, v. 5, 1975, p. 48; v. 7, 1976, p. 57; v. 12, 1982, p. 168.

Appendix 2 Soviet heavy industry output 1928–45

Annual rates

	1928	1929	1930	1931	1932	1933	1934	1935	1936	1937	1938	1939	1940	1941	1942	1943	1944	1945
1. Iron ore, mn tons	6.1	8.0	10.7	10.6	12.1	14.5	21.5	26.8	27.8	27.8	26.6	26.9	29.9	24.7	9.7	9.3	11.7	15.9
2. Pig iron, mn tons	3.3	4.0	5.0	4.9	6.2	7.1	10.4	12.5	14.4	14.5	14.7	14.5	14.9	13.8	4.8	5.6	7.3	8.8
3. Crude steel, mn tons	4.3	4.9	5.8	5.6	5.9	6.9	9.7	12.6	16.4	17.7	18.1	17.6	18.3	17.9	8.1	8.5	10.9	12.3
4. Rolled steel, mn tons	3.4	3.9	4.6	4.3	4.4	5.1	7.0	9.4	12.5	13.0	13.3	12.7	13.1	12.6	5.4	5.7	7.3	8.5
5. High-grade	—	—	—	0.4	0.7	0.9	1.2	1.6	2.1	2.4	2.6	—	3.2	4.7	3.4	4.2	—	4.1
6. Ordinary	—	—	—	3.9	3.7	4.2	5.8	7.8	10.4	10.6	10.7	—	9.9	7.9	2.0	1.5	—	4.4
7. Steel tubes, thou. tons	171	189	233	284	310	348	470	639	859	923	909	917	966	—	—	—	—	571
8. Copper, thou. tons	—	—	—	—	—	—	—	—	—	—	—	—	—	—	—	—	—	135
9. Aluminium, thou. tons	—	—	—	—	—	—	—	—	—	37.0	—	—	—	—	118	105	82.7	86.3
10. Coal, mn tons	35.5	40.1	47.8	56.8	64.4	76.3	94.2	109.6	126.8	128.0	133.3	146.2	165.9	151.4	51.7	62.3	121.5	149.3
11. Oil, mn tons	11.6	13.7	18.5	22.4	21.4	21.5	24.2	25.2	27.4	28.5	30.2	30.3	31.1	33.0	75.5	93.1	18.2	19.4
12. Electricity, bn kWh	5.0	6.2	8.4	10.7	13.5	16.4	21.0	26.3	32.8	36.2	39.4	43.2	48.3	46.6	22.0	18.0	39.2	43.3
13. Machine tools, thou.[a]	2.0	4.3	8.0	18.2	19.7	21.0	25.4	33.9	44.4	48.5	55.3	55.0	58.4	44.5	29.1	32.3	39.2	38.4
14. Tractors, thou.	1.3	3.3	9.1	37.9	48.9	73.7	94.0	112.9	136.5	51.0	49.2	48.1	31.6	—	22.9	23.3	34.0	7.7
15. Motor vehicles, thou.	0.8	1.7	4.2	4.0	23.9	49.7	72.4	96.7	131.5	199.9	211.1	201.7	145.4	—	3.5	1.1	3.2	74.7
16. Heavy vehicles	0.7	1.5	4.0	3.9	23.7	39.1	54.6	76.9	—	180.3	182.4	178.8	136.0	—	30.9	45.5	52.6	68.5
17. Light vehicles	0.1	0.2	0.2	0.0	0.0	10.3	17.1	19.0	3.7	18.2	27.0	19.6	5.5	—	—	—	—	5.0

[a] Metal-cutting machine tools only.
For sources see 'Quarterly rates' table below.

Quarterly rates[b]

	1940	1941 I	II	III	IV	1942 I	II	III	IV	1943 I	II	III	IV	1944 I	II	III	IV	1945 I	II	III	IV
1. Iron ore, mn tons	7.5	8.3	↑	4.05	↑	2.3	↑	2.8	2.4	2.0	2.4	2.5	2.4	2.6	1.8	3.25	↑	3.75	↑	4.2	↑
2. Pig iron, mn tons	3.7	4.5	↑	2.4	↑	1.15	↑	1.3	1.2	1.1	1.4	1.5	1.6	1.5	↑	2.0	2.0	1.9	2.3	2.3	2.3
3. Crude steel, mn tons	4.6	5.7	↑	3.25	↑	1.95	↑	2.2	1.9	1.7	2.1	2.2	2.5	2.4	2.7	2.9	2.9	2.7	3.2	3.3	3.0
4. Rolled steel, mn tons	3.3	4.1	↑	2.2	↑	1.3	↑	1.5	1.3	1.2	1.4	1.5	1.6	1.6	1.8	2.0	1.9	1.9	2.2	2.2	2.2
5. High-grade	—	—	—	—	—	—	—	—	—	—	—	—	—	—	—	—	—	—	—	—	—
6. Ordinary	—	—	—	—	—	—	—	—	—	—	—	—	—	—	—	—	—	—	—	—	—
7. Steel tubes, thou. tons	—	—	—	46.6	↑	30.0	↑	33.0	25.0	27.5	↑	25.0	↑	—	—	—	—	33.75	↑	↑	—
8. Copper, thou. tons	—	—	—	14.25	↑	12.1	↑	12.7	14.8	12.55	↑	18.6	↑	—	↑	21.2	↑	—	—	—	—
9. Aluminium, thou. tons	—	—	—	29.75	↑	17.85	↑	18.5	21.3	20.8	22.1	23.9	26.3	20.15	↑	32.5	↑	35.3	↑	39.35	↑
10. Coal, mn tons	41.5	45.95	↑	7.85	↑	5.85	↑	5.6	4.7	4.3	4.5	4.6	4.6	28.25	4.6	4.7	4.7	4.4	4.9	5.0	5.1
11. Oil, mn tons	7.8	8.65	↑	7.85	↑	7.05	↑	7.3	7.6	7.2	7.7	8.1	9.3	4.3	2.7	10.2	2.9	10.6	3.2	11.1	↑
12. Electricity, bn kWh	12.1	13.7	↑	9.65	↑	4.0	↑	7.5	7.4	4.4	5.6	5.6	7.7	9.4	↑	9.1	↑	9.45	↑	9.75	↑
13. Machine tools, thou.[a]	14.6	14.05	↑	8.2	↑	0.9	↑	↑	↑	0.15	↑	0.4	↑	7.9	↑	1.05	↑	1.7	↑	2.15	↑
14. Tractors, thou.	7.9	—	—	—	—	—	—	—	—	—	—	—	0.55	—	—	15.55	↑	16.7	↑	20.65	↑
15. Motor vehicles, thou.	36.4	—	—	—	—	—	—	—	—	—	—	—	↑	—	—	↑	↑	↑	↑	↑	↑
16. Heavy vehicles	34.0	—	—	—	—	7.7	↑	↑	↑	10.1	11.6	10.2	13.6	13.15	↑	↑	↑	17.1	↑	↑	↑
17. Light vehicles	—	—	—	—	—	—	—	—	—	—	—	—	—	—	—	—	—	—	—	—	—

[a] Metal-cutting machine tools only.
[b] Quarterly rates defined in the same sense as in the notes to Appendix 1. An arrow indicates that the preceding figure is the quarterly average calculated from a half-yearly or yearly rate.

254

Sources

1–4 and 10–13.

1928–40, 1945: Prom. SSSR, 1957, pp. 106, 115, 140, 153, 171, 207, 223, 226. 1941.I–1945.IV: IVMV, v. 3, 1974, p. 376; v. 4, 1975, p. 157; v. 6, 1976, pp. 341, 344; v. 7, 1976, p. 49; v. 8, 1977, p. 355; v. 9, 1978, p. 390; v. 10, 1979, p. 403; v. 11, 1980, p. 340.

1–4.1941.I–1945.IV: additionally, Sov. ekon., 1970, p. 81; G. S. Kravchenko, 1970, p. 235.

5. 1931–8, 1940, 1943, 1945: Clark, 1956, p. 20. 1941–2 calculated from row 4 and from shares given by Clark.
6. 1931–8, 1940–3, 1945: row 4 minus row 5.
7. 1928–40, 1945: Prom. SSSR, 1957, p. 106.
8. 1941.III–1943.II: IVMV, v. 4, 1975, p. 157; v. 6, 1976, pp. 341, 344. 1943.III–IV, 1945: Zaleski, 1980, p. 603.
9. 1937: Kas'yanenko, 1972, p. 213. 1941.III–1945: G. S. Kravchenko, 1970, p. 282; IVMV, v. 4, 1975, p. 157; v. 6, 1976, pp. 341, 344; v. 8, 1977, p. 355; v. 9, 1978, p. 390.
11. 1941.I–1945.IV: additionally, G. S. Kravchenko, 1970, p. 246.
14. 1928–40, 1945: Prom. SSSR, 1957, p. 226. 1942–5.IV: IVOVSS, v. 5, 1963, p. 382; IVMV, v. 7, 1976, p. 49; v. 11, 1980, p. 340; Zaleski, 1980, p. 604.
15. 1928–40, 1945: Prom. SSSR, 1957, p. 223. 1944.III–1945.IV: IVMV, v. 10, 1979, p. 403; v. 11, 1980, p. 340.
16. 1928–40, 1945: Prom. SSSR, 1957, p. 223. 1942–4: IVMV, v. 7, 1976, p. 49; Zaleski, 1980, p. 604.
17. 1928–40, 1945: Prom. SSSR, 1957, p. 223.

Appendix 3 Soviet arms balances 1941–5

The purpose of an 'arms balance' is to reveal, in each period, the relationship between the initial stock of weapons, the additional supplies from domestic and external sources, the deployment and loss of available supplies, and the stock remaining at the end of the period. For Soviet arms in each successive phase of the war, fully reliable balances cannot be compiled, because essential data are lacking. As far as the changing stock of weapons is concerned, we are told of first-line force levels at various moments (see Chapter 3, Table 11), but we have no comparable information about second and third echelons and reserves. Appendix 1 provides us with information about additional supplies from Soviet sources in considerable detail, but comparable time-series for external supplies can only be estimated on the basis of a series of questionable assumptions. Evidence on the deployment of new supplies between the front and the rear, and on the rate of losses arising from different causes, is completely lacking. Of the consecutive assumptions required for us to proceed, some give rise to offsetting errors, some to multiplicative ones. The results must be considered in this light.

Official Soviet data on first-line force levels in Chapter 3, Table 11 provide the foundation for everything which follows; that is, this table defines the three weapons categories used (artillery and mortars, tanks and self-propelled guns, combat aircraft) and the periodisation (seven periods of variable length, but averaging six months each); in addition the data in the table are considered to be definitive except that, in accordance with notes to the table, the first-line deployment of tanks and combat aircraft on 22 June 1941 is revised upwards substantially in order to take into account the Soviet deployment of 'obsolete' types at the outbreak of war.

New supplies of weapons from Soviet sources within the same periods as those used in Table 11 can be calculated from Appendix 1. Here we find half-yearly and often quarterly data for domestic production of combat aircraft, tanks and self-propelled guns, and artillery and mortars. From these, average monthly output levels can be calculated, reweighted and recombined to fit the periodisation used in Table 11. The resulting data are assumed to reflect potential supplies immediately available for first-line deployment, without any time-lag (casual inspection suggests that the introduction of any time-lag of one month or less would not significantly affect the results). Results can be inspected in Table 3.9 below.

Nine-tenths of the work of compiling these balances arises from trying to take due account of the role of external arms shipments to the Soviet Union. This controversial subject has provided ample employment for postwar historians,[1] but from the point of view of the quantitative economist the results can only be described as meagre. For this reason the significance of external arms shipments, the nature of available data and the manipulations carried out to fit them to the present task are all described below in some detail.

US aid accounted for the vast bulk of wartime Allied assistance to the Soviet Union. Goods supplied to the USSR under American Lend–Lease are partly listed in Table 3.1. A wide range of military and economic aid was involved. Compared with Soviet production cumulated over the same period, US aid shipments were significant in some categories. The United States helped to feed and clothe the Red Army and gave it much of its motorised transport. Aid filled some critical equipment gaps like telephone wire and aviation fuel. Aided provision of motor vehicles and tractors exceeded contemporary Soviet output several times. Supplies of aircraft and tanks amounted to a significant but far smaller proportion of the Soviet productive effort. US provision of artillery and ammunition was significant in proportion to US aid as a whole, but insignificant in comparison with the huge volume of Soviet domestic supply. Aid in industrial goods eased particular bottlenecks and was significant for particular categories such as alloy steel.[2] Bergson estimates that at its 1944 peak aid to the Soviet Union from all sources (nearly 90 per cent from the USA) came to 10 to 12 per cent of Soviet 1944 GNP, when both were valued in 1937 Soviet roubles.[3]

The dynamic and composition of Lend–Lease shipments in dollar values is shown in Tables 3.2 and 3.3. Table 3.2 shows the steady

Table 3.1. *Partial list of goods shipped from the United States to the USSR under the Lend–Lease programme*

	Unit[a]	Quantity
Aircraft		14,795
Tanks		7,056
Anti-aircraft guns		8,218
Submachine guns		131,633
Explosives	Short tons	345,735
Cargo vessels		90
Submarine chasers		105
Torpedo boats		197
Marine engines		7,784
Locomotives		1,981
Freight cars		11,155
Jeeps		51,503
Trucks		375,883
Motorcycles		35,170
Tractors		8,071
Tyres	Thousand	3,786
Machinery and equipment	$ million	1,079
Construction machinery	$ thou.	10,900
Steel	Thou. short tons	2,800
Non-ferrous metals	Thou. short tons	802
Petrochemicals	Thou. short tons	2,670
Chemicals	Thou. short tons	842
Cotton cloth	Thou. yards	106,900
Wool cloth	Thou. yards	62,500
Leather	Short tons	49,860
Army boots	Thou. pairs	15,417
Buttons	$ thou.	1,650
Foodstuffs	Mn short tons	4,478

[a] One short ton equals 0.9 metric tons approximately.
Source: US President, No. 21, 1945, p. 25.

growth of shipments up to 1944 (remember too that in 1942 no less than 27 per cent of the tonnage shipped was lost to enemy action, but in 1943 only 1 per cent). At first the most important component was military goods. Aircraft and motor vehicles together never amounted to less than 30 per cent of the total value of US shipments in any year.

Table 3.2. *Value and composition of Lend–Lease to the USSR 1941–5*

	1941	1942	1943	1944	1945[a]
Total value shipped, $ billion	[b]	1.35	2.89	3.43	1.37
Per cent shares in total value					
Military goods	20	63.2	49.9	43.8	40.7
Ordnance and ammunition		15.8	12.8	5.6	2.6
Aircraft and parts	–	22.4	17.4	16.3	12.7
Tanks and parts		13.1	2.6	4.9	4.0
Motor vehicles		11.0	14.1	14.7	19.3
Water-craft and parts		0.8	3.2	2.5	2.1
Industrial goods	80	23.1	29.6	39.3	39.5
Agricultural goods	—	13.7	20.5	16.9	19.8
Total value shipped	100	100.0	100.0	100.0	100.0

[a] First six months only.
[b] Approximately $500,000.
Sources: 1941–3: US President, No. 14, 1944, p. 31; 1944–5: US President, No. 19, 1945, p. 15 and No. 21, 1945, p. 21.

Early shipments of fighter planes were found to be inferior to their Soviet equivalents, and not until the advent of the P-39 Airacobra late in 1943 was US aid in this category fully appreciated. Road vehicles were another matter, and Jeeps and Studebaker trucks became the backbone of Red Army mobility. Mainly light and medium tanks were supplied, and these were never very well adapted to conditions on the Eastern front.[4] Shipment of tanks and armament (the latter mainly consisted of anti-aircraft and infantry hand weapons) were important at first but rapidly declined. As the war proceeded economic aid in the form of machinery, industrial materials and foodstuffs became more and more important; according to Stalin about two-thirds of all major Soviet industrial plant was eventually rebuilt with some input of US equipment or technical assistance.[5]

From now on we shall be interested only in shipments of aircraft and tanks. In narrowing the focus, we should retain three considerations in view. First, shipments of aircraft and tanks were a very important part of the total US contribution to Soviet arms and material balances in general. Secondly, on the other hand the US contribution to the Soviet artillery and mortar armament balance was

Table 3.3. *Value of monthly Lend–Lease shipments to the USSR 1941–5 ($ million)*

	1941	1942	1943	1944	1945
January	—	15	174	313	212
February	—	55	193	232	229
March	—	97	217	260	223
April	—	164	217	254	241
May	—	70	178	315	336
June	—	110	141	286	130
July	—	103	234	335	—
August	—	150	316	305	—
September	—	102	308	305	—
October	—	128	263	258	—
November	—	191	345	299	—
December	1	167	380	268	—

Sources: 1941–2: US President, No. 14, 1944, p. 58; 1943–5: US President, No. 20, 1945, p. 49. For 1943 these two sources give discrepant data, and I have preferred the later version of the two.

Table 3.4. *Lend–Lease shipments of selected products 1941–5*

	1941	1942	1943	1944[a]	1945[b]	1941–5[c]
Aircraft	150	2,500	5,150	4,200	2,450	14,450
Combat aircraft	—	—	—	—	—	13,500
Tanks	180	3,000	920	1,900	1,000	7,000
Self-propelled guns		1,800[d]			—	1,800
Trucks		173,000[e]		190,000[f]		363,000
Jeeps		33,000[e]		13,000	6,000	52,000

[a] Eleven months ending 30 November 1944.
[b] Seven months 1 December 1944 to 30 June 1945.
[c] Period ending 30 June 1945.
[d] 1941 to 30 November 1944.
[e] 1941–3.
[f] 1944 to 30 June 1945.

Sources: Aircraft, tanks, trucks and jeeps 1941–3: US President, No. 14, 1944, pp. 31–2. All series 1944 and self-propelled guns 1941–4: US President, No. 18, 1945, pp. 19–20. All series 1945, trucks 1944–5 and all series totals to June 1945: US President, No. 20, 1945, p. 22.

Soviet arms balances 1941–5

Table 3.5. *Estimated arriving shipments to USSR of Lend–Lease combat aircraft, tanks and self-propelled guns 1941–5*

	1941	1942	1943	1944[a]	1945[b]	1941–5[c]
Combat aircraft	140	1,705	4,811	3,924	2,289	12,869
Tanks and self-propelled guns	234	2,847	1,196	2,470	1,000	7,747

[a] Eleven months ending 30 November 1944.
[b] Seven months 1 December 1944 to 30 June 1945.
[c] Period ending 30 June 1945.
Source: Calculated from Table 3.3 (for methods see text).

negligible. Thirdly, if we were able to compile a 'mobility balance' for the Red Army the role played by Lend–Lease would be more significant than will appear from the arms balances alone.

As far as aircraft and tanks are concerned, from the Lend–Lease documents we can pick out the data in Table 3.4 showing annual shipments (motor vehicles are included in the table for comparative purposes). As yet neither the arms categories nor the periods of measurement are comparable with those of Table 11, nor does Table 3.4 take account of the heavy shipping losses in 1942. To make these data usable we must adjust them in four ways, three of which are shown in Table 3.5. First, we convert aircraft units to combat aircraft only. Up to the end of June 1945 the proportion of combat types to all aircraft supplied through Lend–Lease during the war stood at 93.4 per cent, and we apply this proportion to aircraft supply data in each period shown in Table 3.4. Secondly, we assume that the 1,800 self-propelled guns supplied up to December 1944 arrived at the same rate, in proportion, as tank shipments, so that we can generate a combined series for tanks and self-propelled guns together. Thirdly, we assume that the 27 per cent of shipments lost in 1942 was spread evenly across all supply categories. The results are shown in Table 3.5.

The fourth adjustment is to convert the periodisation of the data in Table 3.5 onto the same basis as in Table 11. Here we use the monthly shipment values given in Table 3.3 to estimate the proportion of annual shipments of aircraft and tanks which must have arrived in each month. Resulting monthly data are then recombined on the required basis to show totals arriving in each period. The final estimates are shown in Table 3.8.

Appendix 3

Table 3.6. *Anglo-Canadian aircraft and tank supplies to the USSR 1941–5*

	Arrivals reported 1941 to 30 April 1944 (i)	Estimated arrivals in 1944 (ii)	Estimated arrivals 1941–3 (iii)
Aircraft[a]	6,988	1,275	6,594
Tanks[a]	4,292	589	4,110
	UK shipments reported 1941–2[b] (iv)	Estimated Canadian shipments 1941–2[b] (v)	Estimated total arrivals 1943 (vi)
Aircraft[a]	2,974	631	2,989
Tanks[a]	3,080	0	1,030

[a] The sources do not mention any Anglo-Canadian provision of noncombat aircraft or of self-propelled guns, so that the headings 'aircraft' and 'tanks' are treated as equivalent to what we are looking for.

[b] No estimate has been made of shipments which failed to arrive in 1942 because of enemy action.

Sources: Col. (i) is from a USSR People's Commissariat of Foreign Trade statement reported by Werth, 1964, pp. 625–6. Col. (ii) results from subtracting the estimate of US shipments in 1944 given in Table 3.5 (plus an allowance for December 1944 based on Table 3.3) from the totals of tanks and aircraft received by the Soviets in 1944 from all sources (5,877 aircraft, 3,223 tanks and self-propelled guns: IVMV, v. 9, 1978, p. 395). From Table 3.3 we can estimate the proportion of 1944 shipments shown in col. (ii) which should have arrived by the end of April; applying this proportion to col. (ii) and subtracting the results from col. (i) gives us shipments for 1941–3 in col. (iii). Col. (iv) gives British shipments for 1941–2 reported in BIS, 1943, pp. 14–15. From the source of col. (i) we know the proportions of Canadian to British shipments of aircraft and tanks for most of the war (to the end of April 1944), and we apply these proportions to col. (iv) to estimate Canadian shipments over 1941–2 in col. (v). Summing cols. (iv) and (v) and subtracting from col. (iii) yields col. (vi).

In addition to US shipments we must include supplies arriving from the UK and Canada. Anglo-Canadian shipments were concentrated in 1942 and 1943, and among them military supplies predominated. After mid-1943 British shipments were negligible apart from Spitfires and some specialised industrial materials. The total value of British aid through the war was given in 1946 as £318 million, hardly significant compared with the $9 billion involved in Lend–Lease.[6]

Soviet arms balances 1941–5

Table 3.7. *Estimated Anglo-Canadian aircraft and tank supplies to the USSR 1941–4*

	1941–2	1943	1944
Aircraft	3,605	2,989	1,275
Tanks	3,080	1,030	589

Sources: See Table 3.6.

Table 3.8. *Estimated Allied shipments of combat aircraft and of tanks and self-propelled guns arriving in the USSR in selected periods 1941–5*

Period beginning on first day of	1941 June	1941 Dec.	1942 May	1942 Nov.	1943 July	1944 Jan.	1944 June	1945 Jan.[a]
Duration, months	5.3	5	6	8	6	5	7	6
Combat aircraft, estimated arrivals								
US Lend–Lease	0	558	835	2,270	2,992	1,707	2,592	1,914
UK and Canada	0	883	1,766	2,085	1,859	511	764	0
Tanks and self-propelled guns, estimated arrivals								
US Lend–Lease	0	932	1,395	1,207	744	1,074	1,560	836
UK and Canada	0	746	1,509	1,206	641	236	353	0

[a] First six months.
Sources: Tables 3.3, 3.5 and 3.7 (for methods see text).

The process of estimating the Anglo-Canadian contribution to Soviet arms balances is similar to the case of Lend–Lease in principle, but more messy in practice. The lamentably sparse available data for aircraft and tank shipments, and the process of breaking them down into an annual time series, are shown in Table 3.6. The results are summarised in Table 3.7. The annual estimates are again converted into a monthly series with the help of the US shipping data in Table 3.3, which are used as before to provide an indicator of the pattern of arrivals through each year. Monthly arrivals are recombined on the basis of the required periodisation and shown, together with estimated arriving US shipments, in Table 3.8.

We now have consistent data for first-line force levels at the beginning and end of each period, and for newly available supplies in each period from both domestic and internal sources. These are combined in Table 3.9. In each period the initial first-line force level,

Table 3.9. *Arms balances for selected categories 1941–5*

Period beginning on first day of	1941 June[a]	1941 Dec.	1942 May	1942 Nov.	1943 July	1944 Jan.	1944 June	1945 Jan.[b]
Duration, months	5.3	5	6	8	6	5	7	6
Combat aircraft								
Initial force	8,105[c]	2,495	3,160	3,088	8,290	8,500	11,800	14,500
Domestic supply	7,042	6,323	11,928	18,537	16,100	13,583	19,627	16,418
External supply	0	1,441	2,601	4,355	4,851	3,103	3,356	1,914
Estimated loss	12,652	7,099	14,601	17,690	20,741	13,386	20,283	—
Tanks and self-propelled guns								
Initial force	7,000[c]	1,730	4,065	6,014	9,580	4,900	8,000	11,000
Domestic supply	4,090	7,767	12,960	15,708	12,900	11,500	17,463	15,419
External supply	0	1,678	2,904	2,413	1,385	1,310	1,913	836
Estimated loss	9,360	7,110	13,915	12,142	18,965	9,710	16,376	—
Artillery and mortars								
Initial force	34,965	22,000	43,640	72,500	98,790	88,900	83,200	91,400
Domestic supply	61,532	129,683	182,433	175,067	81,600	54,417	75,083	64,600
Estimated loss	74,497	108,043	153,753	148,777	91,490	60,117	66,883	—

[a] Period beginning 22 June 1941.
[b] Period ending 30 June 1945.
[c] These figures are revised upward from official data in Table 11 in accordance with information given in the notes to the table, in order to take into account Soviet deployment of 'obsolete' types of equipment on the front line at the outbreak of war.

Sources: Table 11, Appendix 1 and Table 3.8.

Table 3.10. *Arms balances for selected categories 1941–4*

Period beginning on first day of	1941 June[a]	1941 Dec.	1942 May	1942 Nov.	1943 July	1944 Jan.	1944 June
Duration, months	5.3	5	6	8	6	5	7
Combat aircraft, monthly average							
Force level	5,300	2,828	3,124	5,689	8,395	10,150	13,150
As per cent of force level:							
Domestic supply	16.4	44.7	63.6	40.7	32.0	26.8	21.3
External supply	—	10.2	13.9	9.6	9.6	6.1	3.6
Estimated loss	45.0	50.2	77.9	38.9	41.2	26.4	22.0
Tanks and self-propelled guns, monthly average							
Force level	4,365	2,898	5,040	7,797	7,240	6,450	9,500
As per cent of force level:							
Domestic supply	17.7	56.6	42.9	25.2	29.7	35.7	26.3
External supply	—	11.6	9.6	3.9	3.2	4.1	2.9
Estimated loss	40.5	49.1	46.0	19.5	43.7	30.1	24.6
Artillery and mortars, monthly average							
Force level	24,843	32,820	58,070	85,645	93,845	86,050	87,300
As per cent of force level:							
Domestic supply	46.7	79.0	52.4	25.6	14.5	12.6	12.3
Estimated loss	56.6	65.8	44.1	21.7	16.2	14.0	10.9

[a] Period beginning 22 June 1941.
Source: Calculated from Table 3.9 (for methods see text).

plus domestic and external supply, minus the final force level, equals the estimated loss attributable to all causes: combat losses and wear and tear, withdrawals for rear formations and reserves, and so on. Further interpretation and qualification of the results are contained above in notes to Chapter 3, Figure 3 (pp. 114–15).

For the purposes of Chapter 3, Figures 3 and 4, estimates of domestic and external supplies and losses must be expressed in proportion to the average first-line force level maintained over each period. In Table 3.10 initial and final force levels are averaged for each period, and supplies and losses are converted to monthly averages. Average supplies and average losses are finally divided by average force levels to yield percentage monthly rates of supply and loss. This completes the provision of data for Figures 3 and 4.

Appendix 3

NOTES

1. From recent years see Jones, 1969; Herring, 1973; Martel, 1979.
2. Thus 2.8 million short tons (about 2.5 million metric) of mainly alloy steel imports shown in Table 3.1 can be compared with Soviet output of about 4 million metric tons of high-grade rolled steel products annually during the war years.
3. Bergson, 1961, pp. 99–100.
4. Herring, 1973, pp. 75–6, 117.
5. Ibid., p. 116.
6. McNeill, 1953, pp. 445, 782.

Appendix 4 Composition of the USSR Sovnarkom 1938–45

Defining the evolution of the ministerial structure and of appointments to ministerial posts in Soviet government proved to be an unexpectedly substantial research task in its own right. There did not appear to be any one definitive listing of posts and their occupants, and the findings shown in this appendix were culled from a variety of official, biographical and scholarly sources. The results can be consulted in conjunction with the indispensable and much more comprehensive work of S. G. Wheatcroft and R. W. Davies on prominent officials in the Soviet Union before 1941.

Below are listed all USSR People's Commissariats and other posts bringing membership of the USSR Council of People's Commissars (the Sovnarkom) on 19 January 1938, and all additional commissariats and posts created between this date and the close of the Great Patriotic War. The starting date of this list relates to information given at the first session of the first USSR Supreme Soviet to be elected under the 1936 'Stalin' Constitution (the term of this first Supreme Soviet was extended after the outbreak of war in 1941, and new elections were not held until 1946).

During this period there were many changes in the structure of government and in official appointments. Posts were created, abolished or renamed. Often the subdivision or merger of big bureaucracies was involved. Also associated with this was a rapid turnover of leading personnel. These organisational processes operated right through the period from 1938 to 1945, but we shall see that their pace altered when war broke out.

With each post are given details of substantial changes in its status which were enacted during the period. The most complex changes involved the subdivision of industrial commissariats and the creation of new ones, and these are afterwards summarised in a set of charts. Under each post are listed those known to have held the portfolio concerned, with the date of their appointment (occasionally the date on which their appointment was confirmed). The last named official usually held the given post until the war ended or the post was abolished, whichever came first.

Defence industry (abolished 11.01.39)
19.01.38   M. M. Kaganovich[1]

Aircraft industry (created 11.01.39)[2]
11.01.39   M. M. Kaganovich[3]
10.01.40   A. I. Shakhurin[4]

Armament (created 11.01.39)[5]
11.01.39   B. L. Vannikov[6]
09.06.41   D. F. Ustinov[7]
Vannikov was a former deputy of the defence commissar.[8] His removal from armament in June 1941 was occasioned by his arrest; when war broke out he was released and became one of Ustinov's deputies.[9]

Ammunition (created 11.01.39)[10]
11.01.39   I. P. Sergeev[11]
03.03.40   P. N. Goremykin[12]
16.02.42   B. L. Vannikov[13]
Goremykin had been Sergeev's deputy since 28 January 1939.[14] When Vannikov was shifted from the armament commissariat to ammunition and promoted to commissar status in February 1942, Goremykin became a deputy commissar again.[15]

Shipbuilding (created 11.01.39)[16]
11.01.39   I. F. Tevosyan[17]
17.05.40   I. I. Nosenko[18]
In May 1940 Tevosyan was shifted over to ferrous metallurgy. Nosenko had been his first deputy since 21 October 1939.[19]

Engineering (abolished 05.02.39)
19.01.38   A. D. Bruskin[20]
16.07.38   V. K. L'vov[21]
Bruskin's removal was effected by the organs of state security.[22]

Heavy engineering (created 05.02.39)[23]
05.02.39   V. A. Malyshev[24]
Mid-1940   A. I. Efremov[25]
05.06.41   N. S. Kazakov[26]
Efremov had been Malyshev's deputy since 16 February 1939.[27] From heavy engineering he was transferred to machine tool making.

Machine tool making (created 05.06.41; dissolved 11.09.41; reformed February 1942)
05.06.41   A. I. Efremov[28]
Feb. 1942   A. I. Efremov[29]

Medium engineering (created 05.02.39)[30]
05.02.39   I. I. Likhachev[31]
02.10.40   V. A. Malyshev[32]
11.09.41   S. A. Akopov[33]
Akopov had been a deputy commissar at the heavy engineering commissariat since 16 February 1939,[34] and first deputy commissar since 3 May 1940.[35]

Tank industry (created 11.09.41)
11.09.41   V. A. Malyshev[36]
14.07.42   I. M. Zal'tsman[37]
28.06.43   V. A. Malyshev[38]

General engineering (created 05.02.39),[39] *later known as:*
Mortar armament (renamed 26.11.41)[40]
05.02.39   P. I. Parshin[41]

Heavy industry (abolished 24.01.39)
19.01.38   L. M. Kaganovich[42]

Ferrous metallurgy (created 24.01.39)[43]
24.01.39   F. A. Merkulov[44]
17.05.40   I. F. Tevosyan[45]
Tevosyan was brought over from shipbuilding. On 3 July 1940 Merkulov was appointed one of his deputies.[46]

Nonferrous metallurgy (created 24.01.39)[47]
24.01.39   A. I. Samokhvalov[48]
09.07.40   P. F. Lomako[49]
Lomako had been appointed one of Samokhvalov's deputies on 13

270   *Appendix 4*

September 1939,[50] and was apparently promoted to first deputy only on 7 June 1940.[51]

Construction materials (created 24.01.39)[52]
24.01.39   L. A. Sosnin[53]
End 1944   L. M. Kaganovich[54]
This was a Union–Republic commissariat.[55] Sosnin had been one of the deputy commissars for heavy industry since 20 April 1938.[56]

Electricity generation and electrical industry (created 24.01.39;[57] *abolished 17.04.40)*
24.01.39   M. G. Pervukhin[58]
Since 29 June 1938 Pervukhin had been Kaganovich's first deputy in the heavy industry commissariat.[59]

Electricity generation (created 17.04.40)[60]
17.04.40   A. I. Letkov[61]
End 1942   D. G. Zhimerin[62]
Letkov had previously been one of Pervukhin's deputies in the old electricity generation and electrical industry commissariat (he was appointed to this position on 20 April 1939).[63] Zhimerin, in turn, had been Letkov's first deputy since 26 April 1940.[64]

Electrical industry (created 17.04.40)[65]
17.04.40   V. V. Bogatyrev[66]
Aug. 1941   I. G. Kabanov[67]
Like Letkov, Bogatyrev had been one of Pervukhin's deputies in the parent commissariat, having been appointed to this position also on 20 April 1939.[68] And Kabanov had been Bogatyrev's first deputy since 30 June 1941.[69]

Fuel industry (created 24.01.39; abolished 12.10.39)[70]
24.01.39   L. M. Kaganovich[71]
This was just a piece of Kaganovich's former heavy industry empire, and it was about to be subdivided again.

Coal industry (created 12.10.39)
12.10.39   V. V. Vakhrushev[72]

Composition of the USSR Sovnarkom 1938-45   271

Oil industry (created 12.10.39)[73]

12.10.39   L. M. Kaganovich[74]
03.07.40   I. K. Sedin[75]
30.11.44   N. K. Baibakov[76]

Sedin was appointed Kaganovich's first deputy on the same day as Kaganovich's appointment.[77] Baibakov, who had been appointed one of Kaganovich's deputies on 9 February 1940,[78] was made Sedin's first deputy on 6 July 1940.[79]

Chemical industry (created 24.01.39)[80]

24.01.39   M. F. Denisov[81]
26.02.42   M. G. Pervukhin[82]

Rubber industry (created 28.03.41)[83]

28.03.41   T. B. Mitrokhin[84]

Timber industry

19.01.38   M. I. Ryzhov[85]
31.05.39   N. M. Antselovich[86]
27.04.40   F. V. Sergeev[87]
19.08.42   M. I. Saltykov[88]

This was a Union–Republic commissariat.[89] Sergeev had been a deputy commissar since 9 December 1938.[90] On the day of his promotion to commissar, Saltykov was made his first deputy.[91]

Cellulose and paper industry (created 27.04.40)[92]

27.04.40   N. N. Chebotarev[93]
24.05.44   B. M. Orlov[94]

Chebotarev had previously been Antselovich's first deputy in the timber industry commissariat, having been appointed to this post on 15 September 1939.[95]

Food industry[96]

19.01.38   A. L. Gilinsky[97]
07.08.38   I. G. Kabanov[98]
19.01.39   V. P. Zotov[99]

This was a Union–Republic commissariat.[100] Zotov had been Gilinsky's and then Kabanov's deputy since 11 May 1938.[101]

Meat and milk industry (created 19.01.39)[102]
19.01.39   P. V. Smirnov[103]
This was a Union–Republic commissariat.[104]

Fish industry (created 19.01.39)[105]
19.01.39   P. S. Zhemchuzhina[106]
03.07.40   A. A. Ishkov[107]
This was a Union–Republic commissariat.[108] Ishkov had been one of Zhemchuzhina's deputies since 20 January 1939.[109]

Light industry
19.01.38   V. I. Shestakov[110]
02.01.39   S. G. Lukin[111]
This was a Union–Republic commissariat.[112]

Textile industry (created 02.01.39)[113]
02.01.39   A. N. Kosygin[114]
17.04.40   I. N. Akimov[115]
This was a Union–Republic commissariat.[116] Akimov had been a deputy of the commissar for light industry since 11 December 1938[117] and a deputy of Kosygin since 10 January 1939.[118]

Transport
19.01.38   A. V. Bakulin[119]
(09.04.38)   L. M. Kaganovich[120]
25.03.42   A. V. Khrulev[121]
Feb. 1943   L. M. Kaganovich[122]
Dec. 1944   I. V. Kovalev[123]
The date given for the start of Kaganovich's first term in this office is the date of confirmation, not of appointment. At the same time he remained commissar for heavy industry (later the fuel industry; by 1939 just the oil industry). Kovalev had been a deputy to successive transport commissars since 21 May 1941.[124]

Water transport (abolished 09.04.39)
19.01.38   N. I. Pakhomov[125]
08.04.38   N. I. Ezhov[126]
Pakhomov was purged.[127] The curious appointment of Ezhov as his successor marked a stage in the latter's own downfall.[128] Meanwhile Ezhov remained in charge of internal affairs, but not for long.

Composition of the USSR Sovnarkom 1938–45 273

Maritime fleet (created 09.04.39)[129]
09.04.39   S. S. Dukel'sky[130]
08.02.42   P. P. Shirshov[131]

River fleet (created 09.04.39)[132]
09.04.39   Z. A. Shashkov[133]
Shashkov had been a deputy commissar of water transport since 20 February 1938.[134]

Construction (created 29.05.39)[135]
29.05.39   S. Z. Ginzburg[136]
Since 17 March 1938 Ginzburg had been chairman of the Sovnarkom committee on construction affairs.[137]

Agriculture
19.01.38   R. I. Eikhe[138]
(23.06.39)   I. A. Benediktov[139]
11.12.43   A. A. Andreev[140]
This was a Union–Republic commissariat.[141] Eikhe's appointment was a stage in the downfall of a high party official; he was subsequently arrested, and was shot on 4 February 1940.[142] The date is given for confirmation of Benediktov's appointment; the appointment itself may have taken place earlier. Benediktov had been Eikhe's first deputy since 21 April 1938.[143] When Andreev was appointed he became the latter's first deputy again.[144]

State farms
19.01.38   T. A. Yurkin[145]
Dec. 1938   P. P. Lobanov[146]
This was a Union–Republic commissariat.[147]

Procurements
19.01.38   M. V. Popov[148]
05.05.38   S. E. Skrynnikov[149]
28.03.40   V. A. Donskoi[150]
05.07.41   K. P. Subbotin[151]
(02.09.44)   V. A. Dvinsky[152]
Popov was apparently purged.[153] His successor, Skrynnikov, had previously been first deputy to the food industry commissar.[154] Subbotin had been a deputy commissar for procurements since 4

274   *Appendix 4*

August 1939[155] and Donskoi's first deputy since 9 April 1940.[156] On replacement by Dvinsky he became deputy commissar once more.[157]

Finance
19.01.38   A. G. Zverev[158]
This was a Union–Republic commissariat.[159]

Trade
19.01.38   M. P. Smirnov[160]
(15.02.39) A. V. Lyubimov[161]
This was a Union–Republic commissariat.[162] Lyubimov's appointment was confirmed on the date given.

Foreign trade
19.01.38   E. D. Chvyalev[163]
Early '39   A. I. Mikoyan[164]

Communications
19.01.38   M. D. Berman[165]
(16.06.39) I. T. Peresypkin[166]
20.07.44   K. Ya. Sergeichuk[167]
Peresypkin's appointment was confirmed on the date given and may have been enacted earlier. On 23 July 1941 Peresypkin was also appointed a deputy defence commissar.[168] Sergeichuk had been a deputy communications commissar since 15 August 1939.[169]

Justice
19.01.38   N. M. Rychkov[170]
This was a Union–Republic commissariat.[171]

Health
19.01.38   M. F. Boldyrev[172]
08.09.39   G. A. Miterev[173]
This was a Union–Republic commissariat.[174]

Internal affairs
19.01.38   N. I. Ezhov[175]
08.12.38   L. P. Beriya[176]
This also was a Union–Republic commissariat.[177] Ezhov was purged

Composition of the USSR Sovnarkom 1938–45   275

and subsequently shot.[178] Beriya was previously party leader in the Transcaucasus.[179]

State security (created 03.02.41; dissolved 26.07.41)[180]
03.02.41   V. N. Merkulov[181]
Like its parent, the commissariat of internal affairs, state security was a Union–Republic commissariat.[182] Merkulov had been Beriya's first deputy since 16 December 1938.[183]

Foreign affairs
19.01.38   M. M. Litvinov[184]
03.05.39   V. M. Molotov[185]
Foreign affairs was reclassified a Union–Republic commissariat in February 1944.[186]

Defence
19.01.38   K. E. Voroshilov[187]
07.05.40   S. K. Timoshenko[188]
19.07.41   I. V. Stalin[189]
This also was reclassified a Union–Republic commissariat in February 1944.[190]

Navy
19.01.38   P. A. Smirnov[191]
28.04.39   N. G. Kuznetsov[192]

State control (created 06.09.40)[193]
06.09.40   L. Z. Mekhlis[194]
This was a Union–Republic commissariat.

Chairman of the USSR State Planning Commission
19.01.38   N. A. Voznesensky[195]
Mar. 1941   M. Z. Saburov[196]
08.12.42   N. A. Voznesensky[197]
Saburov had been appointed one of Voznesensky's deputies on 28 March 1938[198] and his first deputy on 9 December 1940.[199]

Chairman of the Board of the USSR State Bank
19.01.38   A. P. Grichmanov[200]
Early '39   N. A. Bulganin[201]

17.04.40   N. K. Sokolov[202]
Early '41   N. A. Bulganin[203]

Chairman of the Committee for the USSR school of higher education
19.01.38   A. I. Nazarov[204]
?   S. V. Kaftanov[205]

Deputies of the Chairman of the USSR Sovnarkom
19.01.38   V. Ya. Chubar'[206] (until 1939)[207]
19.01.38   S. V. Kosior[208] (until 1939)[209]
19.01.38   A. I. Mikoyan[210] (throughout)[211]
(21.08.38) L. M. Kaganovich[212]
31.05.39   N. A. Bulganin[213] (until 1941)[214]
31.05.39   N. A. Voznesensky[215] (until 10.03.41)
31.05.39   R. S. Zemlyachka[216] (until 1943)[217]
31.05.39   A. Ya. Vyshinsky[218] (until 1944)[219]
(16.04.40) V. A. Malyshev[220] (until 1944)[221]
(16.04.40) M. G. Pervukhin[222]
(16.04.40) A. N. Kosygin[223] (throughout)[224]
07.05.40   K. E. Voroshilov[225] (throughout)[226]
06.09.40   L. Z. Mekhlis[227]
03.02.41   L. P. Beriya[228]
10.03.41   N. A. Voznesensky (first deputy)[229]
06.05.41   V. M. Molotov[230]
1944   L. M. Kaganovich[231]

Dates given in brackets are dates of confirmation, not appointment. Chubar' and Kosior were purged and were both shot on the same date, 26 February 1939.[232] Kaganovich's first appointment must have lapsed before 1944, when he was reappointed. Molotov was appointed a deputy chairman on the same day that Stalin replaced him as chairman.

Chairman of the USSR Sovnarkom
19.01.38   V. M. Molotov[233]
06.05.41   I. V. Stalin[234]

Before concluding this list of appointments, it is necessary to mention a few bodies connected with the Sovnarkom which were too important for economic administration to be ignored here. In peacetime a significant role was filled by the Sovnarkom Economic Council, created at the end of 1937.[235] It was chaired first by Mikoyan and then by Molotov, who replaced him in early 1940. Voznesensky followed Molotov on 10 March 1941, the same date as his appointment as first deputy of the USSR Sovnarkom chairman.[236] Supporting the work of the Economic Council were a number of industrial branch councils formed in March 1940.[237] The following appointments were made on 16 April 1940 as chairmen of the respective branch councils: Bulganin (metallurgy and chemicals), Voznesensky (the defence industries), Malyshev (engineering), Pervukhin (fuel and electricity), Kosygin (mass consumption goods).[238] A sixth council was supposed to be formed to deal with agriculture and procurements,[239] but no chairman was announced.

In wartime the most important political, military and economic decisions were taken by the State Defence Committee formed on 30 June 1941. Its initial membership was Stalin (chairman), Molotov (deputy chairman), Beriya, Malenkov and Voroshilov.[240] On 3 February 1942 Voznesensky and Mikoyan were added, and on 20 February Kaganovich. During the rest of the war there was only one change, when Bulganin replaced Voroshilov on 22 November 1944.[241] Apart from Stalin, who was fully occupied as Supreme Commander-in-Chief of the armed forces, each member had an area of responsibility for industry, for example Voznesensky (armament and ammunition), Molotov (tankbuilding), Malenkov (aircraft and aeroengines), Mikoyan (consumer goods), Kaganovich (railway transport).[242] Sometimes this was formalised, as with the State Defence Committee's Transport Committee created on 14 February 1942.[243] As a result the old Sovnarkom Economic Council and industrial branch councils tended to lose their rationale and fall into disuse.[244] A stage in the crystallisation of these new arrangements was marked on 8 December 1942 by the creation of a State Defence Committee Operations Bureau, into which such other bodies as the Transport Committee were collapsed. Particularly associated with the work of the Operations Bureau were Mikoyan, Voznesensky and Lyubimov.[245] The date of its creation, incidentally, was also the date of Voznesensky's reappointment as chief of USSR Gosplan.

The information contained in the foregoing lists can be rearranged to show two aspects of general interest. One is the process of subdivision of industrial commissariats and the creation of new ones between 1938 and 1942, and the other is the related movements in the careers of leading officials.

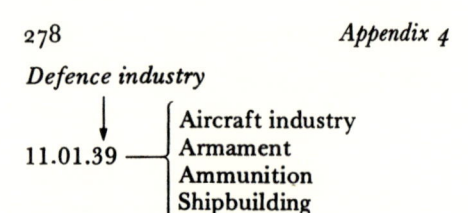

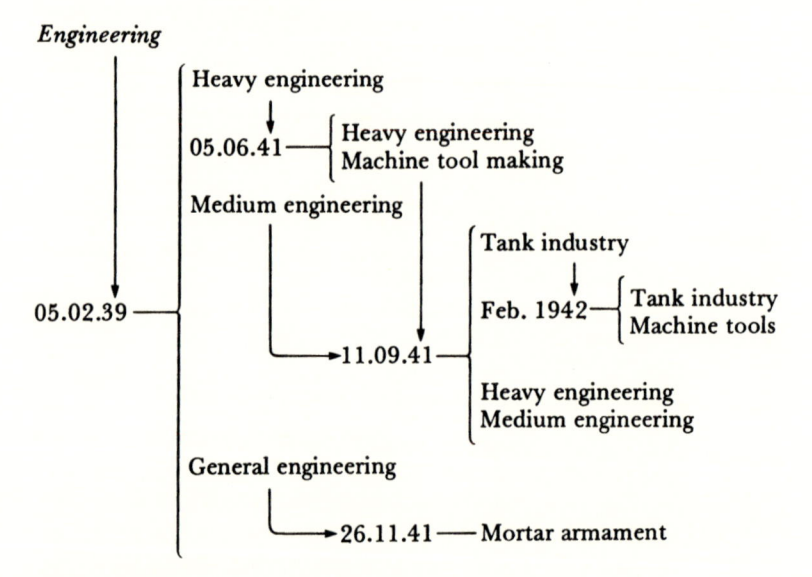

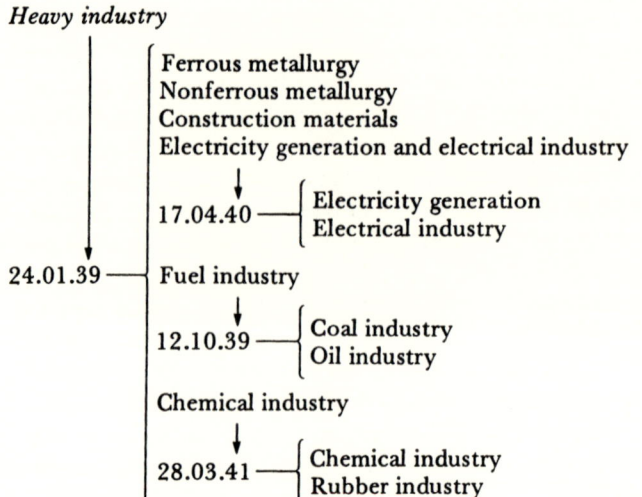

Appendix 4

Defence industry

11.01.39 ⟶ { Aircraft industry / Armament / Ammunition / Shipbuilding }

Engineering

05.02.39 ⟶ {
　Heavy engineering
　　05.06.41 ⟶ { Heavy engineering / Machine tool making }
　Medium engineering
　　⟶ 11.09.41 ⟶ {
　　　Tank industry
　　　　Feb. 1942 ⟶ { Tank industry / Machine tools }
　　　Heavy engineering
　　　Medium engineering
　　}
　General engineering
　　⟶ 26.11.41 ⟶ Mortar armament
}

Heavy industry

24.01.39 ⟶ {
　Ferrous metallurgy
　Nonferrous metallurgy
　Construction materials
　Electricity generation and electrical industry
　　17.04.40 ⟶ { Electricity generation / Electrical industry }
　Fuel industry
　　12.10.39 ⟶ { Coal industry / Oil industry }
　Chemical industry
　　28.03.41 ⟶ { Chemical industry / Rubber industry }
}

Timber industry
27.04.40 ⟶ { Timber industry
Cellulose and paper industry

Food industry
19.01.39 ⟶ { Food industry
Meat and milk industry
Fish industry

Light industry
02.01.39 ⟶ { Light industry
Textile industry

Water transport
09.04.39 ⟶ { Maritime fleet
River fleet

The subdivision of industrial commissariats and the creation of new ones is outlined in the charts above.

Finally the changing portfolios of industrial and political leaders can also be illustrated. Let us restrict our attention to People's Commissars alone (i.e. excluding chairmen of boards and committees, deputies to the Sovnarkom chairman and the chairman himself). Of the twenty-one People's Commissars listed on 19 January 1938 only two still held their initial offices at the outbreak of war – one of them, A. G. Zverev, would retain it until 1960. One had been transferred to another post of commissar status. No fewer than eighteen had been shifted off the Sovnarkom altogether; for most this meant demotion, and for not a few imprisonment or worse.

In contrast let us examine the period from 22 June 1941 to the end of April 1945. At the beginning of the war there were forty-three People's Commissars, but this time twenty-seven of them kept their posts throughout the wartime period. Two were transferred to other posts of the same status. Only fourteen were removed from the Sovnarkom altogether. Thus the wartime picture is one of much greater stability.

NOTES

1. SSSR ... Sessiya 1-ya, 1938, pp. 155–7.
2. SSSR ... Sessiya 3-ya, 1939, pp. 450–1.
3. Ibid., pp. 455–7.
4. SSSR ... Sessiya 6-ya, 1940, pp. 297–8. Shakhurin remained in this position throughout the war; see BSE, 3rd edn, v. 29, 1978, p. 310.
5. SSSR ... Sessiya 3-ya, 1939, pp. 450–1.
6. Ibid., pp. 455–7.
7. *Izvestiya*, 10.06.41, cited by Wheatcroft and Davies, forthcoming. Ustinov held this position throughout the war; see BSE, 3rd edn, v. 27, 1977, p. 129.
8. BSE, 3rd edn, v. 4, 1971, p. 291.
9. Vannikov, 1962, p. 85.
10. SSSR ... Sessiya 3-ya, 1939, pp. 450–1.
11. Ibid., pp. 455–7.
12. Goremykin, 1974, pp. 116–19. Exact dates of his appointment and replacement: personal communication.
13. BSE, 3rd edn, v. 4, 1971, p. 291.
14. SPRP, 1939, No. 8, art. 56. According to Goremykin, 1974, p. 119 he was first deputy commissar for armament, not ammunition, at this time – perhaps a slip of the pen?
15. Goremykin, 1974, pp. 116–19.
16. SSSR ... Sessiya 3-ya, 1939, pp. 450–1.
17. Ibid., pp. 455–7.
18. *Izvestiya*, 18.05.40, cited by Wheatcroft and Davies, forthcoming.
19. SPRP, 1939, No. 56, art. 558.
20. SSSR ... Sessiya 1-ya, 1938, pp. 155–7.
21. SSSR ... Sessiya 2-ya, 1938, pp. 773–4.
22. Medvedev, 1972, p. 197.
23. SSSR ... Sessiya 3-ya, 1939, pp. 450–1.
24. Ibid., pp. 455–7.
25. SSSR ... Sessiya 7-ya, 1940, pp. 159–60.
26. Zinich, 1971, p. 93. For confirmation see IVMV, v. 7, 1976, p. 45.
27. SPRP, 1939, No. 12, art. 77.
28. BSE, 3rd edn, v. 9, 1972, p. 109; Strizhkov, 1980, p. 24.
29. BSE, 3rd edn, v. 9, 1972, p. 109.
30. SSSR ... Sessiya 3-ya, 1939, pp. 450–1.
31. Ibid., pp. 455–7.
32. SSSR ... Sessiya 8-ya, 1941, pp. 306–7. Exact date: personal communication.
33. Strizkhov, 1980, p. 24. See also BSE, 2nd edn, v. 1, 1949, p. 607.
34. SPRP, 1939, No. 12, art. 77.
35. SPRP, 1940, No. 12, art. 299.
36. Strizhkov, 1980, p. 24.
37. Personal communication. According to BSE, 3rd edn, v. 15, 1974, p. 295, however, Malyshev was tank industry commissar throughout the war without a break.

38 Personal communication. The appointment was (re)affirmed on 10.07.43; see SPRP, 1943, No. 10, art. 175.
39 SSSR ... Sessiya 3-ya, 1939, pp. 450–1.
40 Strizhkov, 1980, p. 24.
41 SSSR ... Sessiya 3-ya, 1939, pp. 445–7; Strizhkov, 1980, p. 24.
42 SSSR ... Sessiya 1-ya, 1938, pp. 155–7.
43 SSSR ... Sessiya 3-ya, 1939, pp. 450–1.
44 Ibid., pp. 455–7.
45 *Izvestiya*, 18.05.40, cited by Wheatcroft and Davies, forthcoming.
46 SPRP, 1940, No. 16, art. 402.
47 SSSR ... Sessiya 3-ya, 1939, pp. 450–1.
48 Ibid., pp. 445–7.
49 SSSR ... Sessiya 7-ya, 1940, pp. 159–60. Exact date: personal communication.
50 SPRP, 1939, No. 52, art. 454.
51 SPRP, 1940, No. 17, art. 414.
52 SSSR ... Sessiya 3-ya, 1939, pp. 450–1.
53 Ibid., pp. 455–7. Sosnin was still listed in this position at the beginning of 1944; see SSSR ... Sessiya 10-ya, 1944, pp. 332–4.
54 BSE, 2nd edn, v. 19, 1953, p. 283.
55 SSSR ... Sessiya 3-ya, 1939, pp. 453–4.
56 SPRP, 1938, No. 19, art. 120.
57 SSSR ... Sessiya 3-ya, 1939, pp. 450–1.
58 Ibid., pp. 455–7.
59 SPRP, 1938, No. 32, art. 194.
60 SSSR ... Sessiya 7-ya, 1940, p. 158.
61 Ibid., pp. 159–60.
62 BSE, 3rd edn, v. 9, 1972, p. 219.
63 SPRP, 1939, No. 27, art. 176.
64 SPRP, 1940, No. 14, art. 336.
65 SSSR ... Sessiya 7-ya, 1940, p. 158.
66 Ibid., pp. 159–60.
67 Strizhkov, 1980, p. 24.
68 SPRP, 1939, No. 27, art. 175.
69 SPRP, 1941, No. 16, art. 309.
70 SSSR ... Sessiya 3-ya, 1939, pp. 450–1. Exact date of dissolution: personal communication.
71 Ibid., pp. 455–7.
72 SSSR ... Sessiya 6-ya, 1940, pp. 297–8. The appointment was confirmed on the same day; see SPRP, 1939, No. 55, art. 536.
73 SSSR ... Sessiya 6-ya, 1940, pp. 297–8.
74 BSE, 2nd edn, v. 19, 1953, p. 283; for confirmation see SPRP, 1939, No. 55, art. 534.
75 SSSR ... Sessiya 7-ya, 1940, pp. 159–60. Exact date: personal communication.
76 BSE, 3rd edn, v. 2, 1970, p. 529. Exact date: personal communication.
77 SPRP, 1939, No. 55, art. 533.
78 SPRP, 1940, No. 4, art. 136.

79 SPRP, 1940, No. 19, art. 478.
80 SSSR ... Sessiya 3-ya, 1939, pp. 450-1.
81 Ibid., pp. 455-7.
82 BSE, 2nd edn, v. 32, 1955, p. 369. Exact date: personal communication.
83 Rubin, 1969, pp. 126-7.
84 *Izvestiya*, 29.03.41, cited by Wheatcroft and Davies, forthcoming.
85 SSSR ... Sessiya 1-ya, 1938, pp. 155-7.
86 *Izvestiya*, 03.06.39, cited by Wheatcroft and Davies, forthcoming.
87 SSSR ... Sessiya 7-ya, 1940, pp. 159-60. Exact date: personal communication. The appointment was confirmed on 22.05.40; see SPRP, 1940, No. 15, art. 378.
88 The name can be found for early 1944 in SSSR ... Sessiya 10-ya, 1944, pp. 323-4. Exact date: personal communication.
89 SSSR ... Sessiya 3-ya, 1939, pp. 453-4.
90 SPRP, 1938, No. 57, art. 323.
91 SPRP, 1940, No. 12, art. 301.
92 SSSR ... Sessiya 7-ya, 1940, p. 158.
93 Ibid., pp. 159-60.
94 Personal communication.
95 SPRP, 1939, No. 53, art. 469.
96 SSSR ... Sessiya 3-ya, 1939, pp. 453-4.
97 SSSR ... Sessiya 1-ya, 1938, pp. 155-7.
98 SSSR ... Sessiya 2-ya, 1938, pp. 773-4.
99 Wheatcroft and Davies, forthcoming.
100 SSSR ... Sessiya 3-ya, 1939, pp. 453-4.
101 SPRP, 1938, No. 25, art. 164.
102 SSSR ... Sessiya 3-ya, 1939, pp. 450-1.
103 Wheatcroft and Davies, forthcoming.
104 SSSR ... Sessiya 3-ya, 1939, pp. 453-4.
105 Ibid., pp. 450-1.
106 Ibid., pp. 455-7.
107 SSSR ... Sessiya 7-ya, 1940, pp. 159-60. Exact date: personal communication. Ishkov still held this post in early 1944; see SSSR ... Sessiya 10-ya, 1944, pp. 332-4.
108 SSSR ... Sessiya 3-ya, 1939, pp. 453-4.
109 SPRP, 1939, No. 8, art. 54.
110 SSSR ... Sessiya 1-ya, 1938, pp. 155-7.
111 SSSR ... Sessiya 3-ya, 1939, pp. 455-7. Exact date: personal communication. The appointment was confirmed on 17.01.39; see SPRP, 1939, No. 12, art. 84. Lukin still held this post at the end of the war; see SSSR ... Sessiya 11-ya, 1945, pp. 230-2.
112 SSSR ... Sessiya 3-ya, 1939, pp. 453-4.
113 Ibid., pp. 450-1.
114 Ibid., pp. 455-7.
115 SSSR ... Sessiya 7-ya, 1940, pp. 159-60. Exact date: personal communication. Akimov was still in this post in early 1944; see SSSR ... Sessiya 10-ya, 1944, pp. 332-4.
116 SSSR ... Sessiya 3-ya, 1939, pp. 453-4.

117 SPRP, 1938, No. 57, art. 326.
118 SPRP, 1939, No. 5, art. 23.
119 SSSR ... Sessiya 1-ya, 1938, pp. 155-7.
120 SPRP, 1938, No. 16, art. 104.
121 Kumanev, 1976, p. 159.
122 Ibid., p. 220. Kumanev's documentation seems convincing. However, Tyl SVS, 1977, p. 101 suggests May 1943 as the date of handover.
123 Kumanev, 1976, p. 294.
124 SPRP, 1941, No. 14, art. 264.
125 SSSR ... Sessiya 1-ya, 1938, pp. 155-7.
126 SSSR ... Sessiya 2-ya, 1938, pp. 773-4.
127 Medvedev, 1972, p. 197.
128 Ibid., p. 308.
129 SSSR ... Sessiya 3-ya, 1939, pp. 450-1.
130 Ibid., pp. 455-7.
131 BSE, 3rd edn, v. 29, 1978, p. 417. Exact date: personal communication.
132 SSSR ... Sessiya 3-ya, 1939, pp. 450-1.
133 Ibid., pp. 455-7.
134 SPRP, 1938, No. 6, art. 31.
135 SPRP, 1939, No. 46, art. 359; see also Ginzburg, 1974, p. 137.
136 Ginzburg, 1974, p. 137; SSSR ... Sessiya 6-ya, 1940, pp. 297-8.
137 SPRP, 1938, No. 12, art. 76.
138 SSSR ... Sessiya 1-ya, 1938, pp. 155-7.
139 SPRP, 1939, No. 40, art. 308.
140 BSE, 3rd edn, v. 2, 1970, p. 16. Exact date: personal communication.
141 SSSR ... Sessiya 3-ya, 1939, pp. 453-4.
142 Medvedev, 1972, pp. 192-3, 302.
143 SPRP, 1938, No. 19, art. 119.
144 SPRP, 1944, No. 1, art. 11.
145 SSSR ... Sessiya 1-ya, 1938, pp. 155-7.
146 SSSR ... Sessiya 3-ya, 1939, pp. 455-7. Month of appointment: personal communication.
147 Ibid., pp. 453-4.
148 SSSR ... Sessiya 1-ya, 1938, pp. 155-7.
149 SSSR ... Sessiya 2-ya, 1938, pp. 773-4.
150 SSSR ... Sessiya 6-ya, 1940, pp. 297-8. Exact date: personal communication. The appointment was confirmed on 09.04.40; see SPRP, 1940, No. 11, art. 278.
151 Strizhkov, 1980, p. 24.
152 Personal communication.
153 Medvedev, 1972, p. 197 refers to 'N. [*sic*] Popov, Commissar of Agricultural Procurements, one of the youngest members of the Soviet government, not yet thirty-five'.
154 SPRP, 1938, No. 25, art. 171.
155 SPRP, 1939, No. 48, art. 385.
156 SPRP, 1940, No. 11, art. 277.
157 SPRP, 1944, No. 13, art. 181.
158 SSSR ... Sessiya 1-ya, 1938, pp. 155-7.

159 SSSR ... Sessiya 3-ya, 1939, pp. 453–4.
160 SSSR ... Sessiya 1-ya, 1938, pp. 155–7.
161 SPRP, 1939, No. 16, art. 111.
162 SSSR ... Sessiya 3-ya, 1939, pp. 453–4.
163 SSSR ... Sessiya 1-ya, 1938, pp. 155–7.
164 SSSR ... Sessiya 3-ya, 1939, pp. 455–7. Mikoyan kept this post throughout the war; see BSE, 3rd edn, v. 16, 1974, p. 222.
165 SSSR ... Sessiya 1-ya, 1938, pp. 155–7.
166 SPRP, 1939, No. 40, art. 307.
167 Personal communication.
168 SPRP, 1941, No. 17, art. 333.
169 SPRP, 1939, No. 48, art. 386.
170 SSSR ... Sessiya 1-ya, 1938, pp. 155–7. Rychkov appears to have been the only incumbent of this post during our period.
171 SSSR ... Sessiya 3-ya, 1939, pp. 453–4.
172 SSSR ... Sessiya 1-ya, 1938, pp. 155–7.
173 *Izvestiya*, 09.09.39, cited by Wheatcroft and Davies, forthcoming. Miterev still held this post at the end of the war; see SSSR ... Sessiya 11-ya, 1945, pp. 230–2.
174 SSSR ... Sessiya 3-ya, 1939, pp. 453–4.
175 SSSR ... Sessiya 1-ya, 1938, pp. 155–7.
176 Conquest, 1971, p. 622; see also SSSR ... Sessiya 3-ya, 1939, pp. 455–7.
177 SSSR ... Sessiya 3-ya, 1939, pp. 453–4.
178 Medvedev, 1972, p. 240.
179 Ibid., p. 243.
180 Strizhkov, 1980, p. 24.
181 SSSR ... Sessiya 8-ya, 1941, pp. 306–7.
182 Ibid., p. 300.
183 SPRP, 1938, No. 57, art. 319.
184 SSSR ... Sessiya 1-ya, 1938, pp. 155–7.
185 SSSR ... Sessiya 3-ya, 1939, pp. 455–7; see also BSE, 3rd edn, v. 16, 1974, p. 484.
186 SSSR ... Sessiya 10-ya, 1944, pp. 326–8.
187 SSSR ... Sessiya 1-ya, 1938, pp. 155–7.
188 SSSR ... Sessiya 7-ya, 1940, pp. 159–60. Exact date: personal communication.
189 Strizhkov, 1980, p. 24; see also BSE, 2nd edn, v. 40, 1957, p. 421.
190 SSSR ... Sessiya 10-ya, 1944, pp. 326–8.
191 SSSR ... Sessiya 1-ya, 1938, pp. 155–7.
192 *Izvestiya*, 29.04.39, cited by Wheatcroft and Davies, forthcoming. See also BSE, 3rd edn, v. 13, 1973, p. 562.
193 SSSR ... Sessiya 8-ya, 1941, p. 300.
194 Ibid., pp. 306–7.
195 SSSR ... Sessiya 1-ya, 1938, pp. 155–7.
196 Strizhkov, 1980, p. 27.
197 Personal communication. The break in Voznesensky's leadership of USSR Gosplan is not mentioned in a number of authoritative Soviet sources, for example his brief biographies in BSE, 3rd edn, v. 5, 1971,

Composition of the USSR Sovnarkom 1938–45

p. 268 and Voznesensky, 1979, p. 4. Strizhkov, 1980, p. 27 refers to Voznesensky's transfer and Saburov's promotion to fill the gap, but states that Voznesensky led Gosplan once more 'with the beginning of the war'. Confirmation that Voznesensky returned to Gosplan only at the end of 1942 can be found in a document cited by Arsenev, 1972, p. 28; dated 10 November 1942, the document is signed by Voznesensky as a deputy of the Sovnarkom chairman and Saburov as chairman of USSR Gosplan.

198 SPRP, 1938, No. 11, art. 65.
199 SPRP, 1940, No. 31, art. 800.
200 SSSR... Sessiya 1-ya, 1938, pp. 155–7.
201 SSSR... Sessiya 3-ya, 1939, pp. 455–7.
202 *Izvestiya*, 18.04.40, cited by Wheatcroft and Davies, forthcoming.
203 SSSR... Sessiya 8-ya, 1941, pp. 306–7.
204 SSSR... Sessiya 1-ya, 1938, pp. 155–7.
205 Kaftanov is listed in this position in 1944 and 1945; see SSSR... Sessiya 10-ya, 1944, pp. 326–8 and Sessiya 11-ya, 1945, pp. 230–2.
206 SSSR... Sessiya 1-ya, 1938, pp. 155–7.
207 BSE, 3rd edn, v. 29, 1978, p. 239.
208 SSSR... Sessiya 1-ya, 1938, pp. 155–7.
209 BSE, 3rd edn, v. 13, 1973, p. 232.
210 SSSR... Sessiya 1-ya, 1938, pp. 155–7.
211 BSE, 3rd edn, v. 16, 1974, p. 222.
212 *Izvestiya*, 24.08.38, cited by Wheatcroft and Davies, forthcoming.
213 Ibid., 03.06.39, cited by Wheatcroft and Davies, forthcoming.
214 BSE, 3rd edn, v. 4, 1971, p. 105.
215 *Izvestiya*, 03.06.39, cited by Wheatcroft and Davies, forthcoming.
216 Ibid.
217 BSE, 3rd edn, v. 9, 1972, p. 499.
218 *Izvestiya*, 03.06.39, cited by Wheatcroft and Davies, forthcoming.
219 BSE, 3rd edn, v. 5, 1971, p. 574.
220 SPRP, 1940, No. 10, art. 259.
221 BSE, 3rd edn, v. 15, 1974, p. 295.
222 SPRP, 1940, No. 10, art. 260.
223 Ibid.
224 BSE, 3rd edn, v. 13, 1973, p. 282.
225 *Izvestiya*, 08.05.40, cited by Wheatcroft and Davies, forthcoming.
226 BSE, 3rd edn, v. 5, 1971, pp. 371–2.
227 *Izvestiya*, 07.09.40, cited by Wheatcroft and Davies, forthcoming.
228 Ibid., 04.02.41, cited by Wheatcroft and Davies, forthcoming.
229 Strizhkov, 1980, p. 27.
230 *Izvestiya*, 07.05.41, cited by Wheatcroft and Davies, forthcoming.
231 BSE, 2nd edn, v. 19, 1953, p. 283.
232 Medvedev, 1972, p. 192.
233 SSSR... Sessiya 1-ya, 1938, pp. 155–7.
234 BSE, 2nd edn, v. 40, 1957, p. 421.
235 Ist. KPSS, v. 5(i), 1970, p. 36.
236 Strizhkov, 1980, p. 27.

237 Ist. KPSS, v. 5(i), 1970, p. 33.
238 SPRP, 1940, No. 10, arts. 257–61.
239 *Izvestiya*, 18.04.40.
240 *Izvestiya*, 01.07.41, cited by Wheatcroft and Davies, forthcoming.
241 Fainsod, 1963, pp. 391–2.
242 IVMV, v. 4, 1975, pp. 52, 133.
243 Kumanev, 1976, p. 156.
244 Strizhkov, 1980, p. 22.
245 Belikov, 1974, pp. 77–8.

Appendix 5 Abbreviations and technical terms

'A' AND 'B' GROUP INDUSTRIES

Industries of group 'A' produce the means of production or industrial goods, and industries of group 'B' produce the means of consumption. This is a classification of industry by product utilisation, as distinct from the division of industries into heavy and light industry (q.v.), which is based on the production technology of the industrial branch. For example private cars are produced in the engineering industry (a heavy industry) but are classified as means of consumption (group 'B').[1]

ARMS INDUSTRIES

Before the war the Soviet arms industries were organised under commissariats (q.v.) for aircraft, armament, ammunition and shipbuilding. These industries also produced some civilian goods, and some military goods (e.g. armoured vehicles, aircraft components) were produced in the nominally civilian engineering industry. During the war new commissariats were created to cover the tank industry and also mortar armament. The arms industries are normally included under group 'A' industry (q.v.), but some Soviet economists believe that they should be classified separately as industries producing the means of destruction.[2]

BALANCE

In Soviet usage the word balance carries many different meanings, but they all have a common core. Among the English equivalents are words like equilibrium, proportion (as in 'well-proportioned') and harmony. The main alternative uses are as follows. First, a material balance (e.g. the oil balance or the balance of machine tools) refers to the equilibrium or lack of it between supply and demand for a particular good; this is a microeconomic balance. It may be used to denote the actual state of supply and demand, or the document which shows this as it is (the accounting balance), or the document which shows this as it should be (the planned balance). A state of imbalance may be referred to as a disequilibrium or disproportion. Secondly, the balance of the national economy refers to the proportions among macroeconomic processes: the rates of production, consumption and accumulation, the balance between production and the flow of funds, the balance between production and the factors of production. At a conceptual level it is similar to the modern social accounting matrix. A state of imbalance in the national economy might be brought about by excessive accumulation or overfinancing of enterprises and households, and would also be referred to as a disequilibrium or disproportion.

Corresponding to these economic uses is a third, social, usage: the plurality of forces and interests constituting a society may be harmoniously balanced, or alternatively imbalanced and antagonistic. Achieving a state of balance in society may be among the goals of socialist planning, or it may be viewed as a means to other objectives of social and economic transformation, or it may be viewed as positively harmful to the achievement of these other objectives.

Lastly, in the study of both political and military conflicts the term balance of forces may be used to denote the quantity of forces of all kinds arrayed against each other on the opposing sides, with a lack of parity or presence of one-sided advantage defined as an imbalance.

BASIC INDUSTRIES

I use this term to refer to metallurgy (the mining and production of metals and alloys), the energy sector (the extraction of fuels and electricity generation) and transport services. These three sectors form a close mutual interdependence and make up a tightly interlocking complex which plays a special role in Chapters 3 and 4 above.

COMMISSARS

People's Commissars were government ministers responsible for all the branches of administration, including the nationalised industries, transport and agriculture. Their ministries were called commissariats. People's Commissars were appointed mainly at the USSR and Republican or SSR (q.v.) government level. Those referred to in the text are always USSR People's Commissars unless otherwise specified. The government of the USSR was made up of a Council of People's Commissars or Sovnarkom (q.v.), the structure of which in our period is examined in Appendix 4. The same arrangement existed in the USSR's constituent Republics. People's Commissars should not be confused with the political commissars of the armed forces, who play no part in this book. In 1946 the title of People's Commissar was replaced by the more conventional title of Minister.

CPSU

The governing Communist Party of the Soviet Union, known from 1925 to 1952 as the All-Union Communist Party (Bolsheviks).

EASTERN USSR

The USSR falls partly in Europe, partly in Asia, with the traditional boundary between the continents marked by the Ural Mountains. The Eastern USSR comprises the Ural region and everything to the east of it: Western and Eastern Siberia, Kazakhstan and Central Asia, the Far East. It does not include the Volga region or the Caucasus. Note that the Soviet Union's largest constituent Republic, the RSFSR (q.v.), falls partly in the Eastern, partly in the Western USSR.

GKO

The State Defence Committee (Gosudarstvennyi Komitet Oborony): Stalin's war cabinet and the supreme wartime authority in both military and civil affairs.

GOSPLAN

The State Planning Commission (Gosudarstvennaya Planovaya komissiya): the economic planning office of the Sovnarkom (q.v.) at the USSR and Republican levels. In the text reference is always to the USSR Gosplan unless otherwise specified.

HEAVY AND LIGHT INDUSTRIES

This industrial classification is often used as though it coincided with the distinction between 'A' and 'B' group industries (q.v.). Actually it is a much cruder distinction, but the advantage is that it is easier to apply. It is a simple classification of industries partly by product and partly by technology. The heavy industries include the basic industries (q.v.), engineering and consumer durables. The light industries comprise mainly food processing, other household non-durables and clothing. The finer points of product utilisation (for example whether electricity is used by industry or by consumers) are ignored.

KOLKHOZ

Collective farm (*kollektivnoe khozyaistvo*). Legally the kolkhoz is a cooperative enterprise. Its land is granted to it in perpetuity by the state. Its reproducible assets are the collective property of the member households. Its management is elected. Management choices open to the membership are governed partly by the leading role claimed by the CPSU (q.v.), partly by external controls over the provision of inputs and the allocation of outputs. The income of the members is received as a dividend of the residual income of the kolkhoz after prior claims of the state and of various kolkhoz internal funds have been met. The residual is divided among the members on the basis of work points accumulated by them during the year.

KOLKHOZ MARKET

The kolkhoz (q.v.) comprises two coexisting spheres of operation. One is the collective sector. The other is the household sector. Each household has the right to farm a small plot of land and to carry on small-scale livestock and poultry operations. The produce may be sold for household gain at unregulated prices at designated places called kolkhoz markets. The kolkhoz market is therefore the place where non-kolkhoz agricultural produce is traded. The kolkhoz may also dispose of residual surpluses in the kolkhoz market (hence its name).

MTS

Machine and tractor station (*mashinno-traktornaya stantsiya*). The MTS was a nationalised enterprise operating agricultural machinery. Each MTS would serve several kolkhozy (q.v.) falling within its area. In return for the capital services provided the kolkhoz would be required by the MTS to make payment in kind out of the crops harvested each autumn, and these payments would form part of the food supplies disposed of by the state.

NKVD

People's Commissariat of Internal Affairs (Narodnyi komissariat vnutrennykh del): the Soviet equivalent of the Home Office. Among the NKVD's responsibilities were internal and frontier security and the administration of labour camps.

NMP

Net material product: the Soviet measure of national income, net of double counting and of depreciation of fixed assets. It differs from Western net national income measures by excluding the output of the 'nonproductive' (i.e. final services) sector. On the other hand it is measured at market prices and so includes the indirect taxation which finances the bulk of nonproductive sector output.[3]

POLITBURO

The Political Bureau or decisive core of the Central Committee of the CPSU (q.v.).

RSFSR

The Russian Soviet Federative Socialist Republic, the largest of the Soviet Union's fifteen constituent Republics, stretching from the Gulf of Finland to the Bering Strait – some 15,000 kilometres.

SOVIET

The basic organ of representative government in the Soviet Union. Literally the word means 'council'. Candidates, nominated by the

Communist Party on the basis of one per vacancy, are elected periodically by universal franchise to serve on soviets in plebiscite-type polls. Soviets are elected at all levels from the local to the Republican and USSR Supreme Soviet. The latter body appoints a Presidium to direct its affairs, and a Council of Ministers with executive authority, formerly the Sovnarkom (q.v.). So do the Republican soviets.

SOVKHOZ

State farm (*sovetskoe khozyaistvo*). Legally the sovkhoz is a nationalised enterprise, the property of the state. Management is appointed by the state and the workers receive a wage.

SOVNARKOM

The Council of People's Commissars (Sovet Narodnykh Komissarov). This was the government of the Soviet Union. Each of the Union's constituent Republics had a Sovnarkom too. In the text reference is always to the USSR Sovnarkom unless otherwise specified. The USSR Sovnarkom was composed of commissars (q.v.) and heads of agencies and commissions such as Gosplan (q.v.). The structure and membership of the USSR Sovnarkom is further described in Appendix 4. The chairman of the USSR Sovnarkom was effectively the Soviet prime minister and is sometimes so described in the text. In 1946 the Sovnarkom was renamed the Council of Ministers.

SSR

Soviet Socialist Republic: the title of fourteen of the USSR's constituent Republics, the fifteenth being the RSFSR (q.v.). The others were the Estonian, Latvian, Lithuanian, Belorussian, Ukrainian, Moldavian, Georgian, Armenian and Azerbaidzhan SSRs and, in the Eastern USSR (q.v.), the Kazakh, Turkmen, Uzbek, Tadzhik and Kirgiz SSRs.

TsSU

The Central Statistical Administration (Tsentral'noe Statisticheskoe upravlenie). This was the title of the government statistical office from the Bolshevik revolution to January 1930, and from March 1941 to the present day. From January 1930 to December 1931 there was no

Abbreviations and technical terms 293

separate statistical office, and from December 1931 to March 1941 it went by the title TsUNKhU (q.v.).

TsUNKhU

Central Administration of National Economic Accounts (Tsentral'-noe upravlenie Narodno-khozyaistvennogo Ucheta). This was the title of the government statistical office, formerly TsSU (q.v.), from December 1931 to March 1941.

USSR

Union of Soviet Socialist Republics. The Union was constituted in 1922 by the RSFSR (q.v.) and a number of SSRs (q.v.), of which by 1940 there were eleven. They were joined in 1940 by the annexation of Estonia, Latvia and Lithuania, making the present-day total of fifteen.

VALUE

In Marxian economics a commodity must have a use-value (utility), an exchange-value (market price) and a labour-value (the average quantity of socially necessary labour time required to produce it, including both living labour time spent and the labour time embodied in non-labour inputs into it). The law of value states that commodities exchange against each other at prices which tend to be either directly proportional to their labour-values or else related to their labour-values in some calculable way. Soviet controversy over whether or not the law of value operates in the Soviet economy is featured in Chapter 5.

VSNKh

Supreme Council of the National Economy (Vysshyi Sovet Narodnogo Khozyaistva). This was the body responsible for administering large-scale nationalised industries until 1930, when its main functions were transferred to the People's Commissariat for Heavy Industry. This term is sometimes rendered as it is spoken: Vesenkha.

NOTES

1 Nove, 1977, p. 331.
2 G. S. Kravchenko, 1970, p. 6.
3 Nove, 1977, p. 327.

Bibliography

Abakumov, E., 1943. 'Nepreryvno uvelichivat' dobychu uglya', *Bol'shevik* no. 5

Aleshchenko, N. M., 1980. *Moskovskii sovet v 1941-1945 gg.*, Moscow

Arsen'ev, V. I., 1972. *O nekotorykh izmeneniyakh v organizatsii upravleniya voennoi ekonomiki v pervyi period Velikoi Otechestvennoi voiny*, Moscow

Arutyunyan, Yu. V., 1970. *Sovetskoe krest'yanstvo v gody Velikoi Otechestvennoi voiny*, 2nd edn, Moscow

Atlas, Z., 1942. 'Printsip khozyaistvennogo rascheta v usloviyakh sovremennoi voennoi ekonomiki SSSR', *Pod znamenem marksizma* no. 7

1945. 'Den'gi i obmen v sovetskoi sisteme khozyaistva', *Bol'shevik* no. 6

Avramchuk, F., 1975. 'Voennaya ekonomika SSSR i ee rol' v dostizhenii pobedy', *Ekonomicheskie nauki* no. 4

Baibakov, N. K., 1976. 'Voennaya ekonomika v gody Velikoi Otechestvennoi voiny', in Velikaya pobeda, 1976 (q.v.)

Baikov, A., 1944. 'Tekhnicheskii plan 1944 goda', *Planovoe khozyaistvo* no. 1

1945. 'Tekhnicheskii plan 1945 goda', *Planovoe khozyaistvo* no. 2

Barber, John, 1979. 'The Organised Recruitment of Soviet Labour in the 1930s', University of Birmingham (unpublished)

Bardin, I., 1943. 'Chernaya metallurgiya vo vremya voiny', *Bol'shevik* nos. 11-12

1944. 'Nekotorye voprosy vosstanovleniya yuzhnoi chernoi metallurgii', *Planovoe khozyaistvo* no. 3

Barsov, A. A., 1969. *Balans stoimostnykh obmenov mezhdu gorodom i derevnei*, Moscow

Belikov, A. M., 1961. 'Transfert de l'industrie soviétique vers l'est', *Revue de la deuxième guerre mondiale* no. 41

1966. 'Tyazheluyu promyshlennost'' - v glubokii tyl', in Eshelony, 1966 (q.v.)

1974. 'Gosudarstvennyi Komitet Oborony i problemy sozdaniya slazhennoi voennoi ekonomiki', in Sovetskii tyl, v. 1, 1974 (q.v.)

Belikov, A. M., Kumanev, G. A. and Mitrofanova, A. V., 1976. 'Voennaya

Bibliography

ekonomika SSSR na sluzhbe frontu', in *SSSR v bor'be protiv fashistskoi agressii. 1933-1945 gg.*, Moscow

Belonosov, I. I., 1966. 'Evakuatsiya naseleniya iz prifrontovoi polosy v 1941-1942 gg.', in Eshelony, 1966 (q.v.)

    1970. *Sovetskie profsoyuzy v gody voiny*, 2nd edn, Moscow

Belov, P. A., 1939. 'Sotsialisticheskoe razmeshchenie proizvoditel'nykh sil v SSSR', *Problemy ekonomiki* no. 1

    1940a. 'O voennoi i ekonomicheskoi moshchi sotsialisticheskogo gosudarstva', *Bol'shevik* no. 4

    1940b. 'Osnovnaya ekonomicheskaya zadacha SSSR i sotsialisticheskoe razmeshchenie proizvoditel'nykh sil', *Problemy ekonomiki* nos. 5-6

    1951. *Voprosy ekonomiki v sovremennoi voine*, Moscow

Bergson, Abram, 1961. *The Real National Income of Soviet Russia since 1928*, Cambridge, Mass.

Berri, L., 1940. 'K voprosu o spetsializatsii i kooperirovanii v mashinostroenii', *Problemy ekonomiki* nos. 11-12

    1944. 'Spetsializatsiya i kooperirovanie v usloviyakh voiny', *Planovoe khozyaistvo* no. 3

Bialer, Seweryn, 1980. *Stalin's Successors: Leadership, Stability and Change in the Soviet Union*, Cambridge

Bialer, Seweryn, ed., 1970. *Stalin and His Generals: Soviet Military Memoirs of World War II*, London

Birman, A., 1941. 'Nekotorye voprosy ukrepleniya khozyaistvennogo rascheta v promyshlennosti', *Problemy ekonomiki* no. 1

BIS, 1943. *British Aid to Russia*, British Information Services, New York

Bolotin, D. M., 1983. *Sovetskoe strelkovoe oruzhie*, Moscow

Bol'shevik, 1943. 'Nashi boevye zadachi v tylu', *Bol'shevik* nos. 23-4

Braginsky, B., 1971. 'Planovaya sistema v pervoi poslevoennoi pyatiletke (1946-1950 gody)', *Planovoe khozyaistvo* no. 1

BSE, - ed., v. -, 19-. *Bol'shaya sovetskaya entsiklopediya*, Moscow

Carr. E. H., 1976. *Foundations of a Planned Economy 1926-1929*, v. 2, Harmondsworth

Carr, E. H. and Davies, R. W., 1974. *Ibid.*, v. 1, Harmondsworth

Chadaev, Ya. E., 1965. *Ekonomika SSSR v period Velikoi Otechestvennoi voiny*, Moscow

    1971. 'Sovetskaya ekonomika i sotsialisticheskoe planirovanie v gody Velikoi Otechestvennoi voiny (1941-1945 gg.)', *Planovoe khozyaistvo* no. 6

Chalmaev, V., 1981. *Malyshev*, 2nd edn, Moscow

Chuyanov, A. S., 1966. 'V trudnye dni', in Eshelony, 1966 (q.v.)

Clark, M. Gardner, 1956. *The Economics of Soviet Steel*, Cambridge, Mass.

Clausewitz, Carl von, 1968. *On War*, Harmondsworth

Cohen, Stephen F., 1975. *Bukharin and the Bolshevik Revolution*, New York

Conquest, Robert, 1971. *The Great Terror*, revised edn, Harmondsworth

Conquest, Robert, ed., 1967. *Industrial Workers in the USSR*, London

Cooper, J. M., 1976. *Defence Production and the Soviet Economy, 1929-1941*, Soviet Industrialisation Project Series no. 3, Centre for Russian and East European Studies, University of Birmingham

Davies, R. W., 1958. *The Development of the Soviet Budgetary System*, Cambridge
    1977. *The Emergence of the Soviet Economic System, 1927–1934*, Soviet Industrialisation Project Series no.9, Centre for Russian and East European Studies, University of Birmingham
    1982. *Capital Investment and Capital Stock in the USSR, 1928–1940: Soviet and Western Estimates*, Soviet Industrialisation Project Series no. 22, Centre for Russian and East European Studies, University of Birmingham
Dobrov, M., 1941. 'Ispol'zovanie novoi tekhniki', *Planovoe khozyaistvo* nos. 6–7
Dubronin, N. F., 1966. 'Eshelon za eshelonom...', in Eshelony, 1966 (q.v.)
Dunmore, Timothy, 1980. *The Stalinist Command Economy: The Soviet State Apparatus and Economic Policy 1945–1953*, London and Basingstoke
D'yakov, Yu. L., 1978. 'Promyshlennoe i transportnoe stroitel'stvo v tylu v gody Velikoi Otechestvennoi voiny', *Istoricheskie zapiski* no. 101, Moscow
Efremov, A., 1944. 'Sovetskoe stankostroenie i voennoe khozyaistvo SSSR', *Planovoe khozyaistvo* no. 2
Eidel'man, M. R., 1969. 'Statistika material'no–tekhnicheskogo snabzheniya', in ISGS, 1969 (q.v.)
Ellman, Michael, 1978. 'The Fundamental Problem of Socialist Planning', *Oxford Economic Papers*, July
Erickson, John, 1975. *Stalin's War with Germany*, v. 1, *The Road to Stalingrad*, London
Eshelony, 1966. *Eshelony idut na Vostok. Iz istorii perebazirovaniya proizvoditel'nykh sil SSSR v 1941–1942 gg.*, Moscow
Fainsod, Merle, 1963. *How Russia is Ruled*, revised edn, Cambridge, Mass.
Filtzer, D., 1980. 'The Response of Workers, Managers and the Legal Apparatus to the Draconian Labour Laws of December 1938 and June 1940', University of Birmingham (unpublished)
FRUS 19–, v. –, 19–. *Foreign Relations of the United States*. Washington, D.C.
Galitsky, A., 1945. 'Zheleznedorozhnyi transport v 1945 godu', *Planovoe khozyaistvo* no. 1
Gallagher, Matthew P., 1963. *The Soviet History of World War II: Myths, Memories and Realities*, New York and London
Gatovsky, L. M., 1976. 'Ekonomicheskaya pobeda SSSR v Velikoi Otechestvennoi voine', in Velikaya pobeda, 1976 (q.v.)
Ginzburg, S. Z., 1974. 'Narkomstroi v gody voiny', in Sovetskii tyl, v. 2, 1974 (q.v.)
Gladkov, I. A., 1970. *Ekonomicheskaya pobeda SSSR v Velikoi Otechestvennoi voine*, Moscow
Gladkov, I. A. and Zalkind, A., 1940. 'Za glubokuyu razrabotku problem sotsialisticheskogo planirovaniya', *Bol'shevik* no. 10
Gorbunov, V., 1981. 'Foresight', *Soviet Military Review* no. 5
Goremykin, P. N., 1974. 'O proizvodstve vooruzheniya i boepripasov', in Sovetskii tyl, v. 2, 1974 (q.v.)
Gos. plan, 1941. *Gosudarstvennyi plan razvitiya narodnogo khozyaistva SSSR za 1941 god*, printed not for publication in Moscow, reproduced in the United States in 1948 by the American Council of Learned Societies
Gouré, Leon, 1964. *The Siege of Leningrad*, New York, Toronto and London

Granovsky, E., 1943. 'Material'no–tekhnicheskaya baza sotsializma i oboronnaya moshch' SSSR', *Pod znamenem marksizma* nos. 9–10

Hancock, W. K. and Gowing, M. M., 1949. *The British War Economy*, London

Harrison, Mark, 1983. *N. A. Voznesensky (1 December 1903–30 September 1950): A Soviet Commander of the Economic Front*, Warwick Economic Research Papers no. 242

Herring, George C., 1973. *Aid to Russia 1941–1946: Strategy, Diplomacy, the Origins of the Cold War*, New York

Holloway, David, 1980. 'War, Militarism and the Soviet State', in E. P. Thompson and Dan Smith, eds., *Protest and Survive*, Harmondsworth

Hutchings, Raymond, 1971, *Seasonal Influences in Soviet Industry*, London, New York and Toronto

ISE, v. 5, 1978. *Istoriya sotsialisticheskoi ekonomiki SSSR*, v. 5, *Sovetskaya ekonomika nakanune i v period Velikoi Otechestvennoi voiny*, Moscow

ISGS, 1969. *Istoriya sovetskoi gosudarstvennoi statistiki*, 2nd edn, Moscow

Ist KPSS, v. 5(i). *Istoriya Kommunisticheskoi partii Sovetskogo Soyuza*, v. 5, *Kommunisticheskaya partiya nakanune i v gody Velikoi Otechestvennoi voiny, v period uprocheniya i razvitiya sotsialisticheskogo obschestva, 1938–1958 gg.*, book (i), *(1938–1945 gg.)*, Moscow

Ivanov, G. A. and Pribluda, A. Sh., 1967. *Planovye organy v SSSR*, Moscow

IVMV, v. –, 19–. *Istoriya vtoroi mirovoi voiny 1939–1945* (in 12 volumes, 1973–82), Moscow

IVOVSS, v. –, 19–. *Istoriya Velikoi Otechestvennoi voiny Sovetskogo Soyuza 1941–1945* (in 6 volumes, 1961–5), Moscow

Jones, Robert H., 1969. *The Roads to Russia: United States Lend–Lease to the Soviet Union*, Norman, Okla.

Kaimoldin, S., 1966. 'Khozyaistvenno-organizatorskaya rabota mestnykh sovetov v gody Velikoi Otechestvennoi voiny', in *Iz istorii deyatel'nosti Sovetov*, Moscow

Kaldor, Nicholas, 1945/6. 'The German War Economy', *Review of Economic Studies* no. xiii

Kap. str., 1961. *Kapital'noe stroitel'stvo SSSR*, Moscow

Kas'yanenko, V. I., 1972. *Zavoevanie ekonomicheskoi nezavisimosti SSSR, 1917–1941 gg.*, Moscow

Kats, A., 1940. 'Ispol'zovanie rezervov v promyshlennosti SSSR', *Problemy ekonomiki* nos. 5–6

Khrulev, A. V., 1961. 'Stanovlenie strategicheskogo tyla v Velikoi Otechestvennoi voine', *Voenno-istoricheskii zhurnal* no. 6

Khrushchev, N. S., 1976. *The Secret Speech*, Nottingham

Kiparisov, N. A., 1940. 'K voprosu o edinoi sisteme narodno-khozyaistvennogo ucheta', *Planovoe khozyaistvo* no. 8

Kirstein, Tatjana, 1980. 'The Ural–Kuznetsk Combine: A Case-Study in Soviet Policy-Making', paper to Second World Congress for Soviet and East European Studies, Garmisch

Knickerbocker, H. R., 1931. *The Soviet Five-Year Plan and Its Effect on World Trade*, London

Kokurkin, P., 1980. 'O nekotorykh osobennostyakh razvitiya planovoi ekonomiki v gody voiny', *Planovoe khozyaistvo* no. 5

Kolotov, V. V., 1963a, 'Vidnyi partiinyi i gosudarstvennyi deyatel'', *Voprosy istorii KPSS* no. 6
    1963b. 'Predsedatel' Gosplana', *Literaturnaya gazeta*, 30 November
    1976. *Nikolai Alekseevich Voznesensky*, 2nd edn., Moscow
Kolotov, V. V. and Petrovichev, G., 1963. *N. A. Voznesensky (biograficheskii ocherk)*, Moscow
Komkov, G. D., 1968. 'K voprosu o korennom perelome v rabote sovetskogo tyla v gody Velikoi Otechestvennoi voiny', *Istoriya SSSR* no. 2
Kommunist, 1953. 'Za voinstvuyushchii materializm v obshchestvennoi nauke', *Kommunist* no. 2
Koopmans, T. C., 1957. *Three Essays on the State of Economic Science*, New York, Toronto and London
Kornai, János, 1980. *Economics of Shortage* (in 2 volumes), Amsterdam, New York and Oxford
Kosyachenko, G., 1939. 'Osnovnaya ekonomicheskaya zadacha SSSR i sotsialisticheskoe vosproizvodstvo', *Problemy ekonomiki* no. 3
    1944. 'Voennoe khozyaistvo SSSR', *Planovoe khozyaistvo* no. 1.
    1975. 'Sozdanie voennoi ekonomiki SSSR v 1941–1945 gg.', *Planovoe khozyaistvo* no. 5
Kosygin, A. N., 1980. 'V edinom stroyu zashchitnikov Otchizny', *Kommunist* no. 7
Kravchenko, G. S., 1970. *Ekonomika SSSR v gody Velikoi Otechestvennoi voiny*, 2nd edn, Moscow
    1974. 'Ekonomicheskaya pobeda sovetskogo naroda nad fashistskoi Germaniei', in Sovetskii tyl, v. 1, 1974 (q.v.)
Kravchenko, Victor, 1947. *I Chose Freedom: The Personal and Political Life of a Soviet Official*, London
Kromov, I., 1943. 'Otchestvennaya voina i stroitel'stvo', *Bol'shevik* no. 10
Kumanev, G. A., 1960. 'Sovetskie zhelezno-dorozhniki vo gody Velikoi Otechestvennoi voiny', *Voprosy istorii* no. 6
    1966. 'Podvig zheleznedorozhnikov', in Eshelony, 1966 (q.v.)
    1974. 'Zheleznedorozhnyi transport na sluzhbe tyla', in Sovetskii tyl, v. 2, 1974 (q.v.)
    1976. *Na sluzhbe fronta i tyla. Zheleznedorozhnyi transport SSSR nakanune i v gody Velikoi Otechestvennoi voiny. 1938–1945*, Moscow
Kupert, N. V., 1977. 'Perestroika na voennyi lad raboty gorodskikh Sovetov deputatov trudyashchikhsya Zapadnoi Sibiri', in *Sibir' v Velikoi Otechestvennoi voine*, Novosibirsk
Kursky, A., 1939. 'Promyshlennost' SSSR v tret'ei pyatiletke', *Problemy ekonomiki* no. 4
    1940. 'K voprosu o balanse narodnogo khozyaistvo', *Bol'shevik* no. 24
    1941a. 'Plan i balans narodnogo khozyaistvo', *Planovoe khozyaistvo* no. 2
    1941b. 'Narodno-khozyaistvennye rezervy – na sluzhbu oborony strany', *Planovoe khozyaistvo* nos. 6–7
    1943. 'O sotsialisticheskom vosproizvodstve v dni voiny', *Bol'shevik* nos. 19–20
    1944. 'Sotsialisticheskoe planirovanie – zakon razvitiya sovetskoi ekonomiki', *Bol'shevik* nos. 19–20

1974. *Nauchnye osnovy sovetskikh pyatiletok*, Moscow
1975. 'Planirovanie v gody Velikoi Otechestvennoi voiny', *Ekonomicheskie nauki* no. 4
Kuz'minov, I., 1942. 'Sotsialisticheskaya ekonomika v usloviyakh voiny' (part I), *Bol'shevik* nos. 23–4
1943. Ibid. (part II), *Bol'shevik* nos. 3–4
Landauer, Carl, 1944. 'From Marx to Menger: The Recent Development of Soviet Economics', *American Economic Review*, June
Lange, Oskar, 1962. 'Role of Planning in Socialist Economy', in Oskar Lange, ed., *Problems of Political Economy of Socialism*, New Delhi
Lersky, I. A., 1943. *Kapital'noe stroitel'stvo v usloviyakh Otechestvennoi voiny*, Moscow
1945. *Vosproizvodstvo osnovnykh fondov promyshlennosti SSSR v usloviyakh voiny*, Moscow
Lewin, Moshe, 1975. *Political Undercurrents in Soviet Economic Debates: From Bukharin to the Modern Reformers*, London
Lipatov, N. P., 1966. 'Stranitsy pobedy (kratkii obzor literatury o perebazirovanii promyshlennosti SSSR v 1941–1942 gg.)', in Eshelony, 1966 (q.v.)
Lokshin, E. Yu., 1938. 'Problemy kapital'nogo stroitel'stva v tyazheloi promyshlennosti', *Problemy ekonomiki* no. 2
1939. 'Organizatsionnye problemy promyshlennosti SSSR', *Problemy ekonomiki* no. 4
1940. 'Ocheredny zadachi chernoi metallurgii SSSR', *Bol'shevik* no. 23
1964. *Promyshlennost' SSSR. Ocherk istorii*, Moscow
Lyubimov, A. V., 1941. 'Vsemerno ispol'zovat' mestnye prodovol'stvennye resursy', *Bol'shevik* no. 16
1968. *Torgovlya i snabzhenie v gody Velikoi Otechestvennoi voiny*, Moscow
McCagg, William O., 1978. *Stalin Embattled, 1943–1948*, Detroit
McNeill, W. H., 1953. *America, Britain and Russia: Their Cooperation and Conflict 1941–1946*, London, New York and Toronto
Martel, Leon, 1979. *Lend-Lease Loans and the Coming of the Cold War: A Study of the Implementation of Foreign Policy*, Boulder, Colo.
Marxism–Leninism, 1972. *Marxism–Leninism on War and Army*, Moscow
Matthews, Mervyn, 1983. 'The "State Labour Reserves": An Episode in Soviet Social History', *Slavonic and East European Review*, April
Medvedev, Roy, 1972. *Let History Judge: The Origins and Consequences of Stalinism*, New York, Toronto and London
1982. *Khrushchev*, Oxford
1983. *All Stalin's Men*, Oxford
Millar, James R., 1980. 'Financing the Soviet Effort in World War II', *Soviet Studies*, January
Millar, James R. and Linz, Susan J., 1978. 'The Cost of World War II to the Soviet People: A Research Note', *Journal of Economic History*, December
Miller, Jack, 1964. 'Soviet Planners in 1936–37', in Jane Degras and Alec Nove, eds., *Soviet Planning: Essays in Honour of Naum Jasny*, Oxford
Milsom, John, 1971. *Russian Tanks 1900–1970*, Harrisburg, Pa.
Milward, Alan S., 1965. *The German Economy at War*, London
1977. *War, Economy and Society 1939–1945*, London

Mitrofanova, A. V., 1971. *Rabochii klass SSSR v gody Velikoi Otechestvennoi voiny*, Moscow
Mkrtchyan, M., 1945. 'Neftyanaya promyshlennost' SSSR v gody Otechestvennoi voiny', *Planovoe khozyaistvo* no. 2
Morekhina, G., 1974. *Velikaya bitva za metall*, Moscow
Morozova, I. A., Moskvin, P. M. and Eidel'man, M. R., 1969. 'Balans narodnogo khozyaistva SSSR', in ISGS, 1969 (q.v.)
Munchaev, Sh. M., 1975. 'Evakuatsiya naseleniya v gody Velikoi Otechestvennoi voiny', *Istoriya SSSR* no. 3
Mutovkin, N. S. and Selyanichev, A. K., 1967. 'Velikaya Otechestvennaya voina v sovetskoi istoriografii', in *Ocherki po istoriografii sovetskogo obshchestva*, Moscow
Nar. khoz., 1961. *Narodnoe khozyaistvo SSSR v 1960 godu*, Moscow
 1972. *Narodnoe khozyaistvo SSSR 1922–1972*, Moscow
 1982. *Narodnoe khozyaistvo SSSR 1922–1982*, Moscow
Narochnitsky, A. L., 1976. 'Sotsialisticheskii stroi – osnova voenno-ekonomicheskogo mogushchestva SSSR v gody voiny', in Velikaya pobeda, 1976 (q.v.)
Nikitin, A., 1960. 'Sostoyanie vazhneishikh otraslei promyshlennosti SSSR nakanune Velikoi Otechestvennoi voiny', *Voenno-istoricheskii zhurnal* no. 3
Nosov, V., 1941. 'Plan v sotsialisticheskom khozyaistve', *Pod znamenem marksizma* no. 4
Notkin, A., 1941. 'Economiya syr'ya i topliva', *Planovoe khozyaistvo* nos. 6–7
Nove, Alec, 1965. *The Soviet Economy*, 2nd edn, London
 1977. *The Soviet Economic System*, London
Obraztsov, V., 1944. 'Zheleznodorozhnyi transport – vazhneishee sredstvo svyazi fronta i tyla', *Planovoe khozyaistvo* no. 1
Ogorkiewicz, Richard M., 1970. *Armoured Forces: A History of Armoured Forces and Their Vehicles*, New York
Olevsky, M., 1983. 'Contribution of the Ordnance Makers to the Overall War Effort', *Soviet Military Review* no. 11
Ostrovityanov, K., 1944. 'Ob osnovnykh zakonomernostyakh razvitiya sotsialisticheskogo khozyaistva', *Bol'shevik* nos. 23–4
Panov, A., 1944. 'Ugol'naya promyshlennost' v gody Otechestvennoi voiny', *Planovoe khozyaistvo* no. 1
Pashkov, A., 1938. 'O balanse narodnogo khozyaistva SSSR', *Problemy ekonomiki* no. 1
 1972. 'Osnovnye etapy razvitiya politicheskoi ekonomii sotsializma', in *Problemy ekonomicheskoi nauki i praktiki*, Moscow
Pedosov, A. D., 1976. 'Istochniki pobedy Sovetskogo Soyuza v Velikoi Otechestvennoi voiny 1941–1945 gg.', in Velikaya pobeda, 1976 (q.v.)
Pervukhin, M. G., 1974. 'Perebazirovanie promyshlennosti', in Sovetskii tyl, v. 2, 1974 (q.v.)
Plan. khoz., 1941a. 'Za ravnomernoe vypolnenie plana', *Planovoe khozyaistvo* no. 5
 1941b. 'Vse sily naroda – na razgrom vraga', *Planovoe khozyaistvo* nos. 6–7
 1944. 'Novyi pod'em voennogo khozyaistva SSSR', *Planovoe khozyaistvo* no. 3
Po ed. plan., 1971. *Po edinomu planu*, Moscow

Bibliography

Pogrebnoi, L. I., 1966. 'O deyatel'nosti Soveta po evakuatsii', in *Eshelony, 1966* (q.v.)
Pollard, Sidney, 1969. *The Development of the British Economy 1914–1967*, 2nd edn, London
Prikhod'ko, Yu. A., 1968. 'Vosstanovlenie promyshlennosti v osvobozhdennykh ot nemetsko-fashistskoi okkupatsii raionakh SSSR (1942–1945 gg.)', *Istoriya SSSR* no. 6
    1973. *Vosstanovlenie industrii. 1942–1950*, Moscow
Prom. SSSR, 1957. *Promyshlennost' SSSR*, Moscow
PZM, 1943. 'Nekotorye voprosy prepodavaniya politicheskoi ekonomii', *Pod znamenem marksizma* nos. 7–8 (translated as 'Teaching of Economics in the Soviet Union' by Raya Dunaevskaya in *American Economic Review*, September 1944)
Resheniya, v. –, 19–. *Resheniya partii i pravitel'stva po khozyaistvennym voprosam*, Moscow
Rubin, A. M., 1969. *Organizatsiya upravleniya promyshlennost'yu v SSSR (1917–1967 gg.)*, Moscow
Rzheshevsky, O. A., 1971. 'O deistvitel'nom znachenii postavok po lend-lizu v SSSR', in *Vsemirno-istoricheskaya pobeda sovetskogo naroda. 1941–1945 gg.*, Moscow
Sats, I. A., n.d. 'Zametki na polyakh knigi R. Konkvesta "Velikii Terror"', samizdat
Sbornik dokumentov, 1981. *Sbornik dokumentov po istorii SSSR dlya seminarskikh i prakticheskikh zanyatii. Epokha sotsializma*, v. 4, *1941–1945 gg.*, Moscow
Schroeder, Gertrude E., 1979. 'The Soviet Economy on a Treadmill of "Reforms"', in United States Congress Joint Economic Committee, *Soviet Economy in a Time of Change*, v. 1, Washington, D.C.
Scott, John, 1973. *Behind the Urals: An American Worker in Russia's City of Steel* (first published 1942), Bloomington, Ind.
Sen'ko, A., 1941. 'Mobilizovat' resursy mestnoi promyshlennosti na oboronu strany', *Planovoe khozyaistvo* nos. 6–7
Seregin, V. P., 1971. 'Osobennosti sovetskoi ekonomiki v gody Velikoi Otechestvennoi voiny', in *Vsemirno-istoricheskaya pobeda sovetskogo naroda. 1941–1945 gg.*, Moscow
Shakhurin, A. I., 1974. 'Aviatsionnaya promyshlennost' nakanune i v gody Velikoi Otechestvennoi voiny', in *Sovetskii tyl*, v. 2, 1974 (q.v.)
    1975. 'Aviatsionnaya promyshlennost' v gody Velikoi Otechestvennoi voiny (Iz vospominanii narkoma)', *Voprosy istorii* no. 3
Shelekhov, N., 1941. 'Stakhanovskii trud v dni otechestvennoi voiny', *Planovoe khozyaistvo* nos. 6–7
Shvernik, N., 1940. 'O perekhode na vos'michasovoi rabochii den', na semidnevnuyu nedelyu i o zapreshchenii samovol'nogo ukhoda rabochikh i sluzhashchikh s predpriyatii i uchrezhdenii. Doklad na IX plenum VTsSPS 25 iyunya 1940 goda', *Bol'shevik* nos. 11–12
Sokolov, P. V., 1968. *Voenno-ekonomicheskie voprosy v kurse politekonomii*, Moscow
Sokolov, V., 1946. *Promyshlennoe stroitel'stvo v gody Otechestvennoi voiny*, Moscow
Sonin, M., 1941. 'Novye kvalifitsirovannye kadry promyshlennosti', *Planovoe khozyaistvo* nos. 6–7

Sorokin, G. M., 1963. 'Vydayushchiisya deyatel' kommunisticheskoi partii i ekonomicheskoi nauki (K 60-letiyu so dnya rozhdeniya N. A. Voznesenskogo)', *Voprosy ekonomiki* no. 12

1968. 'Ekonomika i planirovanie v pervye gody tretei pyatiletki i v gody Velikoi Otechestvennoi voiny (1938–1945 gg.)', in *Shagi pyatiletok. Razvitie ekonomiki SSSR*, Moscow

1971. 'Gosplan v gody Velikoi Otechestvennoi voiny', *Planovoe khozyaistvo* no. 1

1975. 'Velikaya ekonomicheskaya pobeda SSSR v voine s fashistskoi Germaniei', *Voprosy ekonomiki* no. 5

Sov. ekon., 1970. *Sovetskaya ekonomika v period Velikoi Otechestvennoi voiny 1941–1945 gg.*, Moscow

Sovetskii tyl, v. -, 1974. *Sovetskii tyl v Velikoi Otechestvennoi voine* (in two volumes), Moscow

SPRP, 19—, No. –. *Sobranie postanovlenii i rasporyazhenii Pravitel'stva SSSR*, Moscow

SSSR ... Sessiya -ya, 19-. *SSSR. Verkhovnyi sovet. Sozyv pervyi. Sessiya -ya. Stenograficheskii otchet*, Moscow

Stalin, I. V. (Joseph), 1940. *Leninism*, London

1945. *The Great Patriotic War of the Soviet Union*, New York

v. -, 19-. *Sochineniya* (in 13 volumes, 1946–51), Moscow

1973. *The Essential Stalin: Major Theoretical Writings 1905–1952*, London

Starovsky, V. N., 1969. 'Polveka Sovetskoi statisticheskoi nauki i praktiki', in ISGS, 1969 (q.v.)

Starovsky, V. N. and Ezhov, A., 1975. 'Sovetskaya gosudarstvennaya statistika v gody Velikoi Otechestvennoi voiny', *Vestnik statistiki* no. 5

Strizhkov, Yu. K., 1980. 'Sovet Narodnykh Komissarov SSSR v pervye mesyatsy Velikoi Otechestvennoi voiny', *Istoriya SSSR* no. 3

Sukharevsky, B., 1941. 'Zadachi promyshlennosti v usloviyakh otechestvennoi voiny', *Planovoe khozyaistvo* nos. 6–7

1944. 'Vosstanovlenie khozyaistva osvobozhdennykh raionov', *Planovoe khozyaistvo* no. 2

1945a. 'Pobeda v Otechestvennoi voine i sovetskaya ekonomika', *Planovoe khozyaistvo* no. 3

1945b. *Sovetskaya ekonomika v Velikoi Otechestvennoi voine*, Moscow

Suslov, M., 1952. 'Po povodu statei P. Fedoseeva', *Pravda*, 24 December

Szamuely, László, 1974. *First Models of the Socialist Economic Systems: Principles and Theories*, Budapest

Tamarchenko, M. L., 1967. *Sovetskie finansy v period Velikoi Otechestvennoi voiny*, Moscow

Tel'pukhovsky, V. B., 1958. 'Obespechenie promyshlennosti rabochimi kadrami v pervyi period Velikoi Otechestvennoi voiny', *Voprosy istorii* no. 11

1974. 'Nekotorye voprosy obespecheniya industrii kadrami', in *Sovetskii tyl*, v. 2, 1974 (q.v.)

Trevor Roper, H. R., ed., 1966. *Hitler's War Directives 1939–1945*, London

Tsikulin, V. A., 1966. *Istoriya gosudarstvennykh uchrezhdenii. 1936–1965 (Uchebnoe posobie)*, Moscow

Tupper, Stephen M., 1981. 'The Mobilisation of Soviet Industry for Defence Needs 1937–1941', paper to West European Conference on Soviet Industry and the Working Class in the Inter-War Years, Birmingham
  1982. 'The Red Army and Soviet Defence Industry 1934–1941', unpub. Ph.D. thesis, University of Birmingham
Turetsky, Sh. Ya., 1948. *Vnutripromyshlennoe nakoplenie v SSSR*, Moscow
Tyl SVS, 1977. *Tyl Sovetskikh Vooruzhennykh Sil v Velikoi Otechestvennoi voine 1941–1945 gg.*, Moscow
Upravlenie, 1968. *Upravlenie narodnym khozyaistvom SSSR 1917–1940 gg. Sbornik dokumentov*, Moscow
US President, no. –, 19–. *United States President's –th Report to Congress on Lend–Lease Operations. For the Period Ended – –, 19–*, Washington, D.C.
Ustinov, D., 1944. 'Promyshlennost' vooruzheniya v gody Otechestvennoi voiny', *Planovoe khozyaistvo* no. 3
Van Creveld, Martin, 1977. *Supplying War: Logistics from Wallenstein to Patton*, Cambridge
Vannikov, B. L., 1962. 'Iz zapisok narkoma vooruzheniya', *Voenno-istoricheskii zhurnal* no. 2
  1968. 'Oboronnaya promyshlennost' SSSR nakanune voiny (Iz zapisok narkoma)' (part I), *Voprosy istorii* no. 10
  1969. Ibid. (part II), *Voprosy istorii* no. 1
Velikaya pobeda, 1976. *Velikaya pobeda Sovetskogo naroda. 1941–1945*, Moscow
Venedeev, B., 1943. 'Za obraztsovuyu rabotu elektrostantsii', *Bol'shevik* nos. 7–8
VO voina, 1970. *Velikaya Otechestvennaya voina Sovetskogo Soyuza 1941–1945. Kratkaya istoriya*, 2nd edn, Moscow
Volodarsky, L., 1971. 'Upolnomochennye Gosplana', *Planovoe khozyaistvo* no. 1
Voznesensky, N. A., 1931a. 'Khozraschet i planirovanie na sovremennom etape', *Bol'shevik* no. 9
  1931b. 'K voprosu ob ekonomike sotsializma' (part I), *Bol'shevik* nos. 23–24
  1932. Ibid. (part II), *Bol'shevik* nos. 1–2
  1933a. 'O sotsialisticheskom rasshirennom proizvodstve v pervoi pyatiletke', *Bol'shevik* no. 4
  1933b. 'Diktatura proletariata i ekonomika sotsializma', *Bol'shevik* nos. 20–1
  1935. 'O sovetskikh den'gakh', *Bol'shevik* no. 2
  1936. 'Ob unichtozhenii protivopolozhnosti umstvennogo i fizicheskogo truda', *Bol'shevik* no. 4
  1938. 'K itogam sotsialisticheskogo vosproizvodstva vo vtoroi pyatiletke', *Bol'shevik* no. 2
  1940. 'Tri stalinskie pyatiletki stroitel'stva sotsializma', *Bol'shevik* no. 1
  1941. *Economic Results of the USSR in 1940 and the Plan of National Economic Development for 1941: Report Delivered to the 18th All-Union Conference of the CPSU(B), Feb. 18, 1941*, Moscow
  1948. *War Economy of the USSR in the Period of the Patriotic War*, Moscow (originally published as *Voennaya ekonomika SSSR v period Otechestvennoi voiny*, Moscow, 1947)

1979. *Izbrannye proizvedeniya 1931–1947*, Moscow
Werth, Alexander, 1964. *Russia at War*, London
Wheatcroft, Stephen G., 1981. 'On Assessing the Size of Forced Concentration Camp Labour in the Soviet Union, 1929–1956', *Soviet Studies*, April
Wheatcroft, Stephen G. and Davies, R. W., forthcoming. *Prominent Officials in the Soviet Union 1922–1941*, Birmingham
Wheatcroft, Stephen G. and Davies, R. W., eds., forthcoming. *Materials for a Balance of the Soviet National Economy 1928–1930*, Cambridge
Yakovlev, N. D., 1981. *Ob artillerii i nemnogo o sebe*, Moscow
Zabolotskaya, K. A., 1977. 'Bor'ba shakhterov Kuzbassa za uvelichenie dobychi uglya v voennye gody', in *Sibir' v Velikoi Otechestvennoi voine*, Novosibirsk
Zaleski, Eugène, 1971. *Planning for Economic Growth in the Soviet Union 1918–1932*, Chapel Hill, N.C.
    1980. *Stalinist Planning for Economic Growth 1933–1952*, London and Basingstoke
Zalkind, A. I. and Miroshnichenko, B.P., 1973. 'Iz opyta Gosplana SSSR po podgotovke dolgosrochnykh planov', *Planovoe khozyaistvo* no. 4
    1980. *Ocherki razvitiya narodno-khozyaistvennogo planirovaniya*, Moscow
Zarutskaya, E. V., 1974. 'Mestnaya promyshlennost' i promkooperatsiya RSFSR', in Sovetskii tyl, v. 2, 1974 (q.v.)
Zelenovsky, A., 1941. 'Ocherednye zadachi Gosplana', *Planovoe khozyaistvo* no. 2
    1975. 'Iz opyta raboty Gosplana SSSR v gody Velikoi Otechestvennoi voiny', *Planovoe khozyaistvo* no. 5
Zelkin, I. I., 1974. 'Razvitie ugol'noi promyshlennosti v 1941–1945 gg.', in Sovetskii tyl, v. 2, 1974 (q.v.)
Zhukov, G. K., 1971. *The Memoirs of Marshal Zhukov*, New York
Zinich, M. S., 1971. 'Iz istorii stankostroeniya i tyazhelogo mashinostroeniya v pervyi period Velikoi Otechestvennoi voiny', *Istoriya SSSR* no. 6
Zverev, A. G., 1943. 'Velikaya Otechestvennaya voina i rol' gosudarstvennykh zaimov', *Bol'shevik* no. 9
    1973. *Zapiski ministra*, Moscow

Index

accountancy, economic role of, 26-7
agriculture
  emergency measures in, 89, 180-1
  evacuation of, 68, 74, 80
  food procurements from, 89, 180-1
  kolkhoz sector of, 74, 83, 138, 141-2, 161n, 180, 211-12, 232
  and kolkhoz trade, 211-12; defined, 290
  livestock in, 64, 74, 80, 129, 131
  machinery in, 74, 80, 137, 194, 196
  and machine tractor stations, 77, 180, 291
  material supply of, 129, 136-7, 194
  production of, 6, 64, 73-4, 81, 130-1; defence share of production, 8, 152
  reconstruction of, 194-6
  recruitment of labour from, 146, 190
Agriculture, People's Commissariat of, 273
aircraft industry, 7-8, 30, 51, 57, 68-9, 73, 78, 81, 82, 85, 87-8, 91-2, 116-20, 128-30, 161nn, 173, 174, 196, 207, 250-2, 264-5; *see also* arms balances; arms industries
Aircraft Industry, People's Commissariat of, 268, 278
Akimov, I. N., 272, 282n
Akopov, S. A., 269
Allied aid to the USSR, 116-17, 130, 149-50, 153-4, 163n, 182, 256-66
Altai region, 180-1
aluminium, *see* nonferrous metallurgy
Ammunition, People's Commissariat of, 268, 278
ammunition industry, 55-7, 68, 82, 85, 86, 87-9, 94-5, 118-20, 126, 161n, 173, 181, 187-8, 214n, 250-2; *see also* arms industries

Andreev, A. A., 179, 181, 216n, 273
'anti-party' group, 177, 240
Antselovich, N. M., 271
Armament, People's Commissariat of, 268, 278
armament industry, 7-8, 30, 51, 54, 56-7, 68-9, 80, 81, 82, 85, 86, 88, 92, 94-5, 116-20, 126, 129-30, 161n, 173, 174, 207, 215-16n, 218n, 250-2, 264-5; *see also* arms balances; arms industries
Armed Forces of the USSR
  combat losses of, 87, 91-2, 110-15; anticipated, 60
  force levels of, 8, 111, 138, 146; quantity versus quality in, 60
  General Staff of, 53, 55, 96, 203
  material supply of, 91-2, 115-21, 122-3, 172, 215-16n, 256-66
  military plans of, 60-1
  Supreme Headquarters of, 91, 92
arms balances, 91-2, 115-21, 256-66
arms industries
  defined, 287
  evacuation of, 65, 68-9, 73, 77-8, 80-1
  material supply of, 8-10, 98, 121-30, 168, 172-4, 181-2, 206-7
  measures of production of, 7-8, 30, 81, 82, 115-21, 126, 127, 128-9, 173-4, 219n, 250-2
  production costs in, 120-1, 160-1n
  see also particular industries
artillery
  conventional, *see* armament industry; arms balances
  self-propelled, *see* arms balances; tank industry
Arutyunov, B. N., 104n, 106n

305

Atlas, Z., 228-9, 246n
Australia, economic mobilisation of, 163n
Azerbaidzhan, 171; *see also* Transcaucasus

Baibakov, N. K., 271
Baku, 171, 172
  'second Baku', 50
Bakulin, A. V., 272
balance, various meanings of, 287-8; *see also* planning, economic
balance of the national economy, 21, 23-5, 32, 201-2, 212, 217n, 288
Baltic republics, 40n, 69-70, 104n, 141
Baran, Paul, 245n
Bardin, Academician I. P., 38n
basic industries
  defined, 288
  wartime role of, 122-3, 168-85
  see also particular industries
Belikov, A. M., 77
Belorussia, 69
Benediktov, I. A., 273
Bergson, Abram, 9, 119, 121, 150, 257
Beriya, L. P., 92, 94-5, 98, 190-1, 231, 248n, 274-5, 276, 277
Berman, M. D., 274
Beveridge, Sir William, 197
Bialer, Seweryn, 223
blitzkrieg, 64, 109, 244
Bogatyrev, V. V., 270
Boldyrev, M. F., 274
Bol'shevik, 228-9
Brezhnev, L. I., 240, 241-2
Brezhnev generation, 18
Bruskin, A. D., 268
budgets, 'hard' and 'soft', 208-9, 210
Bukharin, N. I., x
Bulganin, General N. A., 108n, 275, 276, 277
Butler, R. A., 197

Canada
  aid to the USSR from, 262-3
  economic mobilisation of, 154, 163n
capital stock of the USSR
  measures of change in, 133-4, 158-60n
  war damage to, 160n
  see also investment
Caucasian republics, *see* Transcaucasus
Caucasus, 75, 169-70, 171, 172, 215n
  North, 192, 193

Cellulose and Paper Industry, People's Commissariat of, 271, 279
Central Asia, 71, 74, 78, 90, 135, 171-2; *see also* Eastern USSR
centralisation, economic, and decentralisation, *see* emergency measures; planning, economic; Soviet economic system
Chebotarev, N. N., 271
Chelyabinsk, 215n
chemical industry, 68, 145; *see also* heavy industries
Chemical Industry, People's Commissariat of, 271, 278
Chubar, V. Ya., 276
Chuyanov, A. S., 80
Chvyalev, E. D., 274
Clausewitz, Carl von, 48, 165
coal industry, 6, 30, 50, 64, 81, 82, 84, 122-6, 132-3, 136, 169, 172, 173, 175-6, 179, 192-3, 194, 203, 214-15n, 215n, 220n, 253-5; *see also* basic industries; heavy industries
Coal Industry, People's Commissariat of, 270, 278
Cohen, Stephen F., x
commissars
  defined, 288-9
  listed, 268-76
  see also individual names and commissariats
Communications, People's Commissariat of, 274
Communist Party of Belorussia, 69
Communist Party of the Soviet Union
  Central Committee of, 28, 53, 94, 224, 225; *for joint decisions of the Central Committee and USSR Sovnarkom, see under* Sovnarkom of the USSR
  Central Control Commission, 15
  Commission for Soviet Control, 15
  as 'officer corps', 47
  Politburo of, 52, 53, 65, 68; defined, 291
  production-branch departments of, 27
  role and various titles of, 289
  17th Congress of, 15, 16, 224
  18th Conference of, 33, 61
  18th Congress of, 33
  19th Congress of, 233
  20th Congress of, x, 234, 236-7, 238, 239
  22nd Congress of, 234
Construction, People's Commissariat of, 29, 208, 273

construction, residential, 136, 193–4
construction industry, 5–6, 7, 31, 134–5, 141–2, 189, 190, 207–8; *see also* basic industries
Construction Materials, People's Commissariat of, 29, 270, 278
consumption
civilian personal, 9, 83, 130–1, 151–3, 181, 210–12
of military personnel, 83, 151
see also food supplies
contingency planning for war, *see* planning, economic; plans, economic
control theory, 167
conversion of industry to defence needs, 9–10, 54–7, 85–6
copper, *see* nonferrous metallurgy
Crimea, military disaster in the, 217n
Crimean Tatars, 204
currency reform (December 1947), 229–30

Dagestan, 71; *see also* Central Asia
Davies, R. W., 267
Defence, People's Commissariat of, 55, 189, 190, 275
Defence Industry, People's Commissariat of, 268, 278; *see also* arms industries
Denisov, M. F., 271
Dnepr river, 68
Dneprstroi hydroelectric station, 73
Don region, 80, 171
Don river, 71, 79, 171
Donets basin (Donbass), 13, 69, 72, 75–6, 80, 88, 143, 161n, 169, 192–3
Donskoi, V. A., 273–4
Dubronin, N. M., 104n
Dukel'sky, S. S., 273
Dunaevskaya, Raya, 245
Dvinsky, V. A., 273–4

Eastern USSR, 22, 49–52, 83–5, 90
share in production of military and basic industrial goods, 83–5; in state employment, 138
Efremov, A. I., 269
Eikhe, R. I., 273
Electrical Industry, People's Commissariat of, 270, 278
electricity, 6, 22, 30, 64, 68, 73, 81, 82, 84, 122–6, 128, 132, 134–7, 170, 173, 174, 176–7, 194–5, 203, 216n, 219n, 220n, 253–5; *see also* basic industries; heavy industries
Electricity Generation, People's Commissariat of, 270, 278
Electricity Generation and Electrical Industry, People's Commissariat of, 270, 278
electrification, 25, 40n
Ellman, Michael, 34–5
emergency measures
of economic centralisation, 22, 35–7, 89, 95–6, 98–9
of economic decentralisation, 99
and economic plans, 89–90, 97–9, 182–3
regime of, 97–8, 101–2, 175–85
see also planning, economic; plans, economic
Engels, Friedrich, 232
engineering, 8, 31, 50, 54, 56, 68, 77, 122–3, 126, 135–6, 144, 145, 196, 203, 205, 207; *see also* heavy industries
Engineering, People's Commissariat of, 268, 278
Ermolin, P. A., 106n
Estonia, 69; *see also* Baltic republics
evacuation, 64–81
of industries, 65, 67–9, 72–7, 90, 101; lack of plans for, 61, 79; significance of, 77–8
of refugees, 63–5, 67, 69–72
Evacuation, Committee for, 67
Evacuation Commission, 79–80, 171
Evacuation Council, 65–6, 67–9, 74, 79, 177
Ezhov, N. I., 272, 274

Far East, 53, 74–5, 84, 135, 147, 197; *see also* Eastern USSR
ferrous metallurgy, 6–7, 8–9, 10, 29–31, 40n, 49–51, 57, 62, 64, 68–9, 72, 73, 75–6, 77, 78, 81, 82, 84, 122–6, 128–30, 134, 135–6, 144–5, 169, 170–1, 172–5, 177, 181, 187–8, 194, 203, 207, 214n, 215n, 220n, 253–5, 266n; *see also* basic industries; heavy industries
Ferrous Metallurgy, People's Commissariat of, 269, 278
finance, *see* budgets, 'hard' and 'soft'; currency reform; money supply of

the USSR; State Budget of the USSR
Finance, People's Commissariat of, 274
Finland, 'winter war' with, 31, 55
Fish Industry, People's Commissariat of, 272, 279
Food Industry, People's Commissariat of, 271, 279
food supplies, 130–1, 194, 208, 211, 221n
rationing of, 181, 210–11
Foreign Affairs, People's Commissariat of, 275
foreign trade, *see* Allied aid to the USSR; import self-sufficiency
Foreign Trade, People's Commissariat of, 274
France, 64
Freight Dispersal, Committee for, 67
friction, 44, 48, 59–60, 62, 165
Fuel Industry, People's Commissariat of, 270, 278

General Engineering, People's Commissariat of, 269, 278
Georgia, 171; *see also* Transcaucasus
Germany
 blitzkrieg of, 48, 64, 109, 244
 economic mobilisation of, 109, 128, 137, 185–6
 invasion of USSR by, 63, 70, 72–3, 79–80, 91
 postwar reparations to USSR from, 231
Gilinsky, A. L., 271
Ginzburg, S. Z., 273
GKO
 decisions of, 65, 73, 89, 105n, 108n, 146, 161–2n, 175–8, 183, 184, 188, 189, 194–7, 203
 defined, 289
 formation of, 94, 277
 and Gosplan of the USSR, 95–7, 184
 individual authority within, 94–6, 184, 190, 277
 Operations Bureau of, 184, 198, 220n, 277
 Transport Committee of, 178, 217n, 277
Goremykin, P. N., 268, 280n
Gor'ky, 174, 206
Gosplan of the USSR
 and accountancy, 27, 32
 and the balance of the national economy, 23–5, 32, 201–2, 212, 217n, 288
 centralisation of authority in, 22, 26–8, 32, 96–100, 182–5, 190–1, 198–203
 and contingency plans for war, 54, 58
 and coordination of basic industries, 172
 Council of Scientific–Technical Expertise of, 39n, 201
 defined, 289
 departments of, for arms industries, 98; for equipment balances, 23; for labour, 22–3, 186, 190, 218n; for material balances, 23, 199–200; for reconstruction of liberated territories, 193, 195; for regional planning, 22, 34, 195
 and evacuation of industries, 74, 76–7, 182
 and GKO, 95–7, 184
 Institute of Technical and Economic Information of, 39n
 and labour allocation, 22–3, 188, 190
 and local planning boards, 21–2
 and long-term economic planning, 25–6, 37
 and material supply planning, 23, 199–200
 minor role of, in initial wartime economic mobilisation, 96–7
 and plan fulfilment checks, 21–2, 23, 27–8, 32, 98–9, 198, 199–200
 plenipotentiary agents of, 21–2, 26, 27, 37, 199
 Prices Bureau of, 39n
 purges of, 12–13, 18, 20, 231–2
 and reconversion planning, 195–7
 and regional planning, 22–3, 199
 and Sovnarkom Economic Council, 28
 and statistics, 26–7, 31, 99, 199–200
 Statutes of, (2 February 1938) 19–20, 23, 27; (21 March 1941) 27, 34
 and technical planning, 32, 200–1
 see also planning, economic; plans, economic
Grichmanov, A. P., 275
GULag, *see* labour, forced; NKVD

Health, People's Commissariat of, 274
Heavy Engineering, People's Commissariat of, 104n, 269, 278
heavy industries
 defined, 290

evacuation of, 68–9, 72–3
material supply of, 121–3, 168–82, 205–8
measures of production of, 6, 30, 81–2, 83, 124–7, 173–4, 253–5
reconstruction of, 194–6
see also particular industries
Heavy Industry, People's Commissariat of, 104n, 269
fragmentation of (1936–41), 11–12, 278
war-mobilisation administration of, 54
Hitler, Adolf, 49, 79, 171, 222, 244

import self-sufficiency, degree of Soviet, 52
industrial production
defence share of, 8, 152
groups 'A' and 'B', defined, 287; index of, 127; measurement of, 24, 201
index of gross, 127
seasonality of, 175, 200
input–output analysis, 24, 58
Institute of Red Professors, 13, 15
Internal Affairs, People's Commissariat of, *see* NKVD
investment
completion rate of, 6, 7, 28–9, 37n, 134–5
defence share of, 9, 107n, 136–7
overinvestment, 4, 6, 7, 10
in 1st Five Year Plan, 6, 78
in 2nd Five Year Plan, 6, 134, 135
in 3rd Five Year Plan, 7, 9–10, 134, 135, 136
in wartime, 133–7, 194
iron and steel, *see* ferrous metallurgy
Ishkov, A. A., 272, 282n
Ivanovo, 76
Izmailov, F. T., 104n

Japan, 147, 197
Justice, People's Commissariat of, 274

Kabanov, I. G., 270, 271
Kaftanov, A. I., 276
Kaganovich, L. M., 65–6, 94, 177–9, 216n, 238, 240, 269, 270, 271, 272, 276, 277
Kaganovich, M. M., 268
Kaldor, Nicholas, 137
Karaganda, 50, 172, 175–6
Karponosov, A. G., 216n

Kazakhstan, 78, 90, 135; *see also* Eastern USSR
Kazakov, N. S., 269
Kazan, 70, 76
Khar'kov, 51, 69, 72–3, 77, 193
Khrulev, General A. V., 177–9, 272
Khrushchev, N. S., x, 236, 240
Kiev, 74, 143
Kirov, 70, 76
Kirov, S. M., 15
Kirpichnikov, A. I., 104n
kolkhoz, defined, 290; *see also* agriculture
Kolotov, V. V., 38n
Konev, Marshal I. S., 42
Kornai, János, 167
Korobov, A., 193
Kosior, S. V., 276
Kostroma, 76
Kosygin, A. N., 18, 66–7, 71, 80, 107n, 181, 203, 240, 247n, 272, 276, 277
identified incorrectly as 'Kasygin', 89–90
Kovalev, G. B., 216n
Kovalev, Lieutenant-General I. V., 177, 178, 179, 216n, 272
Krasnodar, 171
Krasnovodsk, 171, 172
Kravchenko, Colonel G. S., 128
Kravchenko, Victor, 140–1, 190–1
Kruglov, S. N., 104n
Kuibyshev, 70, 91
Kursk, 69
battle of, 172
Kursky, A., 228
Kuz'min, M. R., 104n
Kuznetsk, 187–8
basin (Kuzbass), 50, 169, 172, 175–6, 214–15n
Kuznetsov, Admiral N. G., 275

labour
defence share of, 8, 143–8
discipline, 10, 172, 176, 177, 179, 189
forced, 140–1, 190–1
of German prisoners of war, 138, 147
industrial training of, 139–40, 187
measures of mobilisation of, 142–8, 162–3n
mobilisation of (1938–40), 31, 186–7; (1941–2), 83–4, 96, 137–42, 144–6, 176, 179, 187–90; (1943–5), 138, 147, 191
productivity of, 7, 141–2, 160–1n, 220

labour (*cont.*)
  recruitment of, 7, 22–3, 138–41, 186–91
  relocation of, 70, 77, 144
  as an 'ultimate bottleneck', 137
Lange, Oskar (or Oscar), 239, 245n
Lapidus, I., 224
Lenin, V. I., 25, 247n
Leningrad
  arms industries of, 31, 51, 73, 143, 207
  city planning office, 15, 17–18, 21
  evacuation of, 69–70, 73, 80, 104n
  siege of, 63, 70
  reconstruction of, 193, 194
Leningrad affair, 231–2
Leont'ev, A., 234
Letkov, A. I., 270
light industries
  defined, 290
  evacuation of, 67, 68
  investment in, 126–7
  material supply of, 205
  measures of production of, 131–2
  reconstruction of, 194
  see also particular industries
Light Industry, People's Commissariat of, 272, 279
Likhachev, I. I., 269
Lithuania, 69; *see also* Baltic republics
Litvinov, M. M., 275
Lobanov, P. P., 273
local industries, 99, 144, 205–6
location
  of industries, 49–52, 83–5, 132–3, 206
  of investment, 135
  of strategic reserves, 52–3
Lomako, P. F., 269
Lugansk, 69
Lukin, S. G., 272, 282n
L'vov, V. K., 268
Lyubimov, A. V., 206, 220n, 274

McCagg, William O., 246–7nn
machine tools, 6, 31, 50, 81, 82, 93, 121, 122–3, 124, 128–30, 144, 173–4, 207, 253–5; *see also* heavy industries
Machine Tools, People's Commissariat of, 121, 144, 269, 278
Magnitogorsk, 50, 77, 188, 215n
Makhachkala, 71
Malenkov, G. M., 92, 94, 203, 231, 240, 277
Malyshev, V. A., 107n, 269, 276, 277, 280n

Manpower Committee, 94, 144–6, 188, 190–1, 198, 217n; *see also* labour
Maritime Fleet, People's Commissariat of, 273, 279
Mariupol', 72
Marx, Karl, 247–8n
Meat and Milk Industry, People's Commissariat of, 272, 279
Medium Engineering, People's Commissariat of, 269, 278
Mekhlis, General L. Z., 53, 183–4, 203, 217n, 275, 276
Merkulov, F. A., 269
Merkulov, V. N., 275
metals–energy–transport balance, 168–75; *see also* basic industries
Mezhlauk, V. I., 18, 19
Mikoyan, A. I., 29, 66, 67, 80, 94, 181, 203, 216n, 220n, 231, 274, 276, 277, 284n
militarism, 47, 239, 243
military–economic potential of the USSR, 45–53
Miller, Jack, 20
Minsk, 69
Miroshnichenko, B. P., 218n
Miterev, G. A., 274, 284n
Mitrokhin, T. B., 271
mobilisation, economic (prewar), 5–11, 28–34; (1941–2), 81–93, 155–7, 168–90; (1943–5), 157–8, 192–7
  crisis of excessive, 4, 6, 7, 101–2, 156–7
  measures of wartime, 128–9, 142–54, 163n
  phases of, 35–6, 154–8
  see also planning, economic
mobilisation of industry, experimental partial (September 1939), 55
Moldavia, 69
Molotiv, V. M., 33, 94, 191, 240. 275, 276, 277
money supply of the USSR
  held by households, 211, 229
  increase in, 149, 210, 234n
  used in retail transactions, 211
  see also currency reform
mortar armament, 81, 82, 93, 196, 250–2; *see also* arms industries
Mortar Armament, People's Commissariat of, 93, 269, 278
Moscow
  arms industries of, 55, 85–6, 144
  basin (Mosbass), 132, 169, 175, 192

battle of, 63, 67, 91, 172
city planning office, 98, 183
evacuation of, 69, 91
labour mobilisation in, 143, 144
Moskatov, General P. G., 40n, 188, 190
Murmansk, 69

national income of the USSR
accounts for, 201–2
changes in, 5, 83, 151
defence share of, 8, 83, 150–4
defined, 291
Navy, People's Commissariat of, 275
Nazarov, A. I., 276
New Zealand, economic mobilisation of, 163n
NKVD, 106n, 140, 188, 190–1, 274, 291
nonferrous metallurgy, 52, 64, 124, 145, 173, 181, 220n; *see also* heavy industries
Nonferrous Metallurgy, People's Commissariat of, 269, 278
Nosenko, I. I., 268
Novgorod, 70
Novosibirsk, 187
Novo-Tagil, 50

oil industry, 30, 61, 64, 79, 81, 82, 84, 102n, 123, 124–6, 169–70, 171–2, 173, 174, 176, 220n, 253–5; *see also* basic industries; heavy industries
Oil Industry, People's Commissariat of, 271, 278
Omsk, 71, 216n
Operations Bureau, *see* GKO
Ordzhonikidze, G. K., 11
Orel, 69
Orenburg, 171
Orlov, B. M., 271
Ostrovityanov, K., 224, 228, 246–7nn

Pakhomov, N. I., 272
Pamfilov, K. D., 71, 104n, 191
Penza, 70
Peresypkin, I. T., 274
Pervoural'sk, 187–8
Pervukhin, M. G., 66, 107n, 270, 271, 276, 277
Planned Economy (Planovoe khozyaistvo), 32
planners, economic, role of in political decisions, 3–4
planning, economic
as an adaptive process, 1, 9–10, 14, 17, 20, 34–7, 42, 47, 87–90, 100–1, 165–8, 202
administrative priorities in, 3, 9–10, 86–90, 93, 146, 181–5, 196–7, 213–14
degree of centralisation of, 26, 31–2, 96–100, 198–201, 219n
and emergency measures, 89–90, 97–8, 181–2
and evacuation of industries, 79, 182–3
and 'firefighting', 167–8, 181–2, 213
'genetic' versus 'teleological', 4, 23
of investment, 3, 10, 28–9, 35–6
as a law, 14, 16, 224, 226–8, 230, 234
as a law-governed process, 3, 24, 199, 235
mobilisation versus balance functions of, 3–5, 14, 25, 33, 34–7, 42–3, 93, 101–2, 181–2, 243–5
reorganisation of (1938–41), 5, 19–28, 32–4, 35–7; (1941–2), 93–100, 175–85; (1943–5), 198–204, 213–14; (1946–9), 229–30
voluntarism in, 4, 33, 209, 230, 233, 246–7nn
for war, 42–63
plans, economic
annual, prewar, 29–31
annual, wartime (for 4th qtr 1941 and for 1942), 65, 90–1, 182; (1944), 196; (1945) 203, 220n
for arms production, 55–6, 58, 88, 92
for construction, 7
for the contingency of war, 53–63, 85–6
Five Year, First (1928–32), 1, 5, 16, 17, 46; Second (1933–7), 5, 16, 134–5; Third (1938–42), 7, 28–30, 134–5; draft Fourth (1943–7), 195–6, 202; Fourth (1946–50), 195–6, 201–2, 229, 247n
fulfilment of, 7, 28–31, 87–90, 92, 170, 172, 203, 214n, 220n
for labour recruitment, 7
long-term (1943–57), 25–6, 195
quarterly and monthly (3rd qtr 1940), 31; (3rd qtr 1941), 58, 78, 86–7; (2nd qtr 1942), 215n; (1st qtr 1943), 172; (1944), 196
for reconstruction and reconversion, 192–7
regional, 193–5
for strategic reserves, 52–3
technical, 200–1
for transport, 172

plans, military, *see* Armed Forces of the USSR
Podol'sk, 51
Poland, 63, 64, 141
Poltava, 74
Popkov, P. S., 104n
Popov, M. V., 273
  identified incorrectly as N. Popov, 283n
population of the USSR, 64, 72, 130
  war casualties amongst, 72, 245
Pravda, 102n, 179
prices, Soviet
  accounting, 24, 202
  'commercial', 211
  free market, 202, 210–11
  retail, 210–11
  state-regulated, 16, 227
  wholesale transfer, 120, 158n; reform of (January 1949), 229–30; related to factor cost, 150–1
procurements, agricultural, *see* agriculture
Procurements, People's Commissariat of, 273
Protasov, A. M., 104n
Pskov, 70
purges, 10–11, 18, 231
  of Gosplan of the USSR, 13, 18, 20, 231–2
  of industry, 13, 183–4
  of statisticians, 24
  of the armed forces, 60

railways, *see* transport
rearmament
  of Germany, 48
  'in depth', 47, 49
  of the USSR, 7–10, 47–51
reconstruction of liberated territories, 132–3, 161n, 192–5
reconversion of industry to civilian needs, 195–7, 219n
reform
  of currency (December 1947), 229–30
  economic, x, 34–7, 234–5, 239, 245, 247n
  of wholesale prices (January 1949), 229–30
River Fleet, People's Commissariat of, 273, 279
Rostov on Don, 69
RSFSR, defined, 291

rubber industry, 52, 183; *see also* heavy industries
Rubber Industry, People's Commissariat of, 271, 278
Rychkov, N. M., 274, 284n
Ryzhov, M. I., 271

Saburov, M. Z., 33, 88, 104n, 106n, 107nn, 184, 232, 248n, 275, 285n
Saltykov, M. I., 271
Samokhvalov, A. I., 269
Sauckel, Fritz, 191
School of Higher Education of the USSR, Committee for, 276
Sedin, I. K., 271
Semichastnov, I. F., 104n
Sergeev, F. V., 271
Sergeev, I. P., 268
Sergeichuk, K. Ya., 274
Shakhurin, A. I., 62, 73, 268, 280n
Shaposhnikov, Marshal B. M., 104n
Shashkov, Z. A., 216n, 273
Shcherbakov, A. S., 214n
Shestakov, V. I., 272
shipbuilding, 54, 90, 250–2; *see also* arms industries
Shipbuilding, People's Commissariat of, 268, 278
Shirshov, P. P., 216n, 273
Shvernik, N. M., 66, 67, 80, 177, 181, 190
Siberia, 49, 65, 69, 74, 76, 78, 84, 90, 135; *see also* Eastern USSR
Skrynnikov, S. E., 273
Smirnov, G. I., 18, 19
Smirnov, M. P., 274
Smirnov, P. A., 275
Smirnov, P. V., 272
Sokolov, N. K., 276
Sonin, M. Ya., 218n
Sorokin, G. M., 22, 155
Sosnin, L. A., 270, 281n
Soviet economic system
  adaptation to war of, x–xi, 45–63
  cost accounting in, 14, 16, 208–9, 226, 228–9
  decentralised decisions in, 99–100, 204–13, 228–9
  degree of centralisation of, 21–2, 32, 98–9, 148–9, 181–4, 188–91, 204–13
  law of value in 224–30, 232–4, 293
  as a permanent 'war economy', x, 237–8, 239

planning as a law of, 14, 16, 224, 226–8, 230, 234
reform of, x, 34–7, 234–5, 239, 245, 247n
role of enterprise self-sufficiency in, 205–9
role of individual bosses in, 3, 238, 240
role of markets in, 16–17, 24, 201, 209–13, 225, 227
role of money in, 14–16, 224–30
role of regional self-sufficiency in, 206–7
seen as law-governed, 14–15, 16–17, 204, 224–35
tendency to institutional change in, 1–5
Soviet Socialist Republics, listed, 292
soviets, 291
sovkhoz, 292; *see also* agriculture
Sovnarkom of the RSFSR, 140, 183, 190
Sovnarkom of the USSR
decisions of, 7, 19, 22–3, 55, 58, 65, 66, 69, 76–7, 89, 146, 161n, 175, 179, 181, 183, 184, 188, 190, 193, 194, 196, 205
Defence Committee of, 54, 55
defined, 292
Economic Council of, 13, 23, 28, 96, 108n, 276–7
and the GKO, 96
and Gosplan of the USSR, 19, 23, 28
and the Manpower Committee, 188, 191
membership of, 268–76; turnover in, 11, 93, 279
Speer, Albert, 191
SS, 191
Stalin, I. V.
lessons of war drawn by, 103n, 155, 222, 236–7, 241–2, 243
positions of state, 275, 276, 277
posthumously condemned, 236–7, 238–40; then partially rehabilitated, 241
and preparations for war, 46–7, 53, 55–6, 61, 238–9, 241
role in decision making, 25–6, 53, 55–6, 65, 80, 91, 92–3, 94–5, 96, 191, 236–7, 241
views on economic planning, 1, 34
views on political economy, 16, 224, 232–4, 245n

and Voznesensky, 25–6, 92–3, 203–4, 230–5
Stalingrad
arms industries of, 80, 206
battle of, 78, 156, 171, 172
evacuation to, 71, 80; from, 80, 101
reconstruction of, 193
Stalinism
alternatives to, ix
characterised by administrative 'shapelessness', 12, 93, 94
reform of, x, 35–7, 234–5, 239, 245
State Bank of the USSR, 275–6
State Budget of the USSR, 148–50, 221n
State Control, People's Commissariat of, 183, 275
State Defence Committee, *see* GKO
State Farms, People's Commissariat of, 273
State Labour Reserves of the USSR, 140, 188, 190, 217n
State Planning Commission of the USSR, *see* Gosplan of the USSR
State Security, People's Commissariat of, 275; *see also* NKVD
statistics, economic role of, 26–7; *see also* Gosplan of the USSR; TsSU
steel, *see* ferrous metallurgy
strategic reserves, 52–3
strategy, military, 60–1, 109
Strumilin, S. G., 158n
Subbotin, K. P., 273
subcontracting of defence and engineering orders, 9, 22, 56–7, 205–6
Sukharevsky, B., 155–6
Supreme Soviet of the USSR, 229, 267
decisions of, 141, 179, 189–90
Suslov, M. A., 18, 233
Sverdlovsk, 70
Svirstroi hydroelectric station, 73

tank industry, 7–8, 30, 51, 54, 56, 57, 65, 68, 77, 80, 81, 82, 85, 90, 92, 93, 94, 95, 115–21, 128–9, 144, 161nn, 173–4, 206, 250–2, 264–5; *see also* arms balances; arms industries
Tank Industry, People's Commissariat of, 121, 269, 278
Tashkent, 231
territory of the USSR, effects of changes in
in 1940, 40n

territory of USSR (*cont.*)
  in 1941–2, 64, 125, 132–3, 192
  in 1943–5, 132–4, 135, 192–5
Tevosyan, I. F., 38n, 177, 268, 269
textile industry, 29, 130–1, 132, 194, 195; *see also* light industries
Textile Industry, People's Commissariat of, 272, 279
timber industry, 126, 169, 176; *see also* heavy industries
Timber Industry, People's Commissariat of, 271, 279
Timoshenko, Marshal S. K., 275
Tomsk, 76
trade
  domestic, in theory, 16, 224, 227, 232–3; in practice, 209–13
  foreign, *see* Allied aid to the USSR; import self-sufficiency
Trade, People's Commissariat of, 274
trade unions, 187–8
Transcaucasus, 79, 84, 135, 171
transport, 6, 19, 26, 123, 124, 168, 170–1, 172, 177–9, 189
  defence share of output, 8, 152
  efficiency of, 74–6, 141–2, 170–1
  for evacuation, 68–71, 74–6, 78, 80
  horse, 178
  inland water, 71, 80
  material supply needs of, 170–1, 207
  measures of output of, 124
  railway, 31, 64, 66, 67, 68, 70, 71, 73, 75–6, 78, 86, 87, 124, 170–1, 172, 176, 178–9, 207
  see also basic industries
Transport, People's Commissariat of, 68, 75, 106n, 178, 272
Transport Committee, *see* GKO
Trotsky, L. D., x
TsSU (or TsUNKhU), 21, 26, 76, 99, 183, 200, 292–3
TsUNKhU, *see* TsSU
Tula, 69
Turkmenia, 171; *see also* Central Asia
'turning point' in the war, radical or not, 154–8

Ukraine, 63, 68, 70, 74
Under the Banner of Marxism (Pod znamenem marksizma), 225–7, 234, 246–7nn
United Kingdom
  aid to the USSR from, 262–3
  economic mobilisation of, 128, 137, 147–8, 151–2, 154, 163n, 185–6
  'lessons' of wartime experience of, 222
  plans for postwar reconstruction in, 197
  wartime administration of labour in, 186
United States of America
  economic mobilisation of, 128, 137, 162n, 163n, 185
  Lend–Lease to the USSR from, 116–17, 130, 149–50, 153–4, 163n, 182, 256–66
Ural region, 49, 56, 65, 70, 75, 77, 78, 88, 90, 135, 170, 172, 176, 179, 195, 207, 215n; *see also* Eastern USSR
Ustinov, D. F., 18, 268, 280n

Vakhrushev, V. V., 270
value, law of, 224–30, 232–4, 293
Vannikov, B. L., 268
Vasilevsky, Marshal A. I., 203–4
Volga Germans, 204
Volga region, 65, 69, 75, 78, 80, 90, 171, 206
Volga river, 53, 71, 78, 80
Volodarsky, L., 22
Voronezh, 80
Voroshilov, Marshal K. E., 94, 108n, 218n, 275, 276, 277
Voroshilovgrad, 80
Voznesensky, N. A.
  early life of, 13
  economic writings of (1931–6), 14–16, 246n
  in Leningrad (1935–7), 15, 17–18
  as Gosplan chief (1938–41), 13, 18, 19–28, 32–4, 37, 38nn, 275
  political authority of (1941), 33–4
  and war preparations, 55–6, 61, 62
  as a wartime economic leader, 65, 88–9, 92, 94, 95–7, 107n, 177, 181, 183–5, 193, 203–4, 216n, 220n, 275, 277
  as Gosplan chief again (1942–9), 184–5, 198–204, 229–30, 275, 284–5n
  political authority of in wartime, 203–4
  and law of value (1941–7), 224, 230, 233
  and crimes against humanity, 204, 231
  famous book of (1947), ix, 156, 230, 233, 236, 237–8

political authority of (1946–9), 230–1
disgrace and death of, 231–2;
  posthumously attacked, 233–4;
  subsequently rehabilitated, 234–5
and reform of Stalinism, 235
mentioned, 87, 118, 120, 161n, 191, 206
VSNKh, 54, 293
Vyshinsky, A. Ya., 276

Water Transport, People's Commissariat of, 272, 279
war
  costs of, 160n, 243, 245
  formative Soviet experience of (1914–21), 46, 79, 223–4
  friction in, 44, 48, 59–60, 165
  lessons of, x–xi, 46–7, 222–4, 228–30, 235–45, 247–8nn
  strategy for avoidance of, 60–1, 242–3

Wheatcroft, S. G., 267
women, the chief element in 'manpower', 137, 139, 160n

Yurkin, T. A., 273

Zakharov, Major-General M. V., 104n
Zaleski, Eugène, ix, 29, 34, 213, 220n
Zal'tsman, I. M., 269
Zaporozh'e, 78, 188
Zemlyachka, R. S., 276
Zhdanov, A. A., 15, 33, 231
Zhemchuzhina, P. S., 272
Zhimerin, D. G., 270
Zhukov, Marshal G. K., 55, 91, 92–3
Zlatoust, 215n
Zotov, V. P., 271
Zverev, A. G., 274, 279

Printed in the United Kingdom by
Lightning Source UK Ltd., Milton Keynes
138440UK00001B/93/A